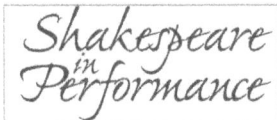

Founding editor: J. R. MULRYNE
General editors:
JAMES C. BULMAN, CAROL CHILLINGTON RUTTER

Titus Andronicus

Manchester University Press

Already published in the series

Geraldine Cousin *King John*
Anthony B. Dawson *Hamlet*
Mary Judith Dunbar *The Winter's Tale*
Jay L. Halio *A Midsummer Night's Dream* (2nd edn)
Stuart Hampton-Reeves and Carol Chillington Rutter The *Henry VI* plays
Bernice W. Kliman *Macbeth* (2nd edn)
Alexander Leggatt *King Lear* (2nd edn)
James Loehlin *Henry V*
Scott McMillin *Henry IV, Part One*
Lois Potter *Othello*
Hugh M. Richmond *King Henry VIII*
Margaret Shewring *King Richard II*
Virginia Mason Vaughan *The Tempest*

Titus Andronicus

Michael D. Friedman
with Alan Dessen

Second edition

Manchester University Press

Copyright © Michael D. Friedman with Alan Dessen 2013

The right of Michael D. Friedman and Alan Dessen to be identified as the authors of this work has been asserted by them in accordance with the Copyright, Designs and Patents Act 1988.

Published by Manchester University Press
Altrincham Street, Manchester M1 7JA, UK
www.manchesteruniversitypress.co.uk

British Library Cataloguing-in-Publication Data is available

ISBN 978 0 7190 8252 8 *hardback*
ISBN 978 1 5261 3943 6 *paperback*

First published by Manchester University Press in hardback 2013

This edition first published 2019

The publisher has no responsibility for the persistence or accuracy of URLs for any external or third-party internet websites referred to in this book, and does not guarantee that any content on such websites is, or will remain, accurate or appropriate.

Typeset by Action Publishing Technology Ltd, Gloucester

To Deborah,
Brian, Donald, Estelle,
and Sonia

CONTENTS

	List of illustrations	*page* ix
	Series editors' preface	xi
	Prefatory note	xiii
	Prefatory note to second edition	xv

PART ONE

	Introduction: The Problem	3
Chapter I	**From Edward Ravenscroft to Peter Brook**	7
Chapter II	**To stylise or not to stylise**	28
Chapter III	**Trusting the script: Deborah Warner at the Swan**	56
Chapter IV	**Problems then and now**	76
Chapter V	**The sense of an ending**	97
	Conclusion: What price *Titus*?	118

PART TWO

	Segue	125
Chapter I	**Jeannette Lambermont, Daniel Mesguich, and Michael Maggio**	131
Chapter II	**Peter Stein and Silviu Purcarete**	151
Chapter III	**Gregory Doran**	177

Chapter IV	**Julie Taymor: 1994 and 1999**	197
Chapter V	**Yukio Ninagawa, Bill Alexander, Gale Edwards, Richard Rose, and Lucy Bailey**	229

Epilogue: Looking toward the future 274
Appendix: Major actors and staff for
productions discussed in this volume 285
Bibliography 292
Index 303

LIST OF ILLUSTRATIONS

1 Tamora pleads for the life of Alarbus. The Peacham drawing, 1594 or 1595. (The Marquess of Bath, Longleat House). *page* 8
2 Kevin Miles as Chiron, Vivien Leigh as Lavinia, and Lee Montague as Demetrius in Peter Brook's Stratford-upon-Avon production (1955). Photo by Angus McBean. Courtesy of the Shakespeare Centre Library. 21
3 Michael Denison as Lucius, Vivien Leigh as Lavinia, Laurence Olivier as Titus, and Alan Webb as Marcus in Peter Brook's Stratford-upon-Avon production (1955). Photo by Angus McBean. Courtesy of the Shakespeare Centre Library. 23
4 Janet Suzman as Lavinia and Colin Blakely as Titus in Trevor Nunn's Royal Shakespeare Company production (1972). Photo by Joe Cocks Studio. 44
5 Bruce Young as Aaron, Stephen Jones and Brett Harvey as Goths in Mark Rucker's Santa Cruz production (1988). Photo by Ann Parker. 48
6 Donald Sumpter as Marcus and Sonia Ritter as Lavinia in Deborah Warner's Royal Shakespeare Company production at The Pit (1988). Photo by Richard Mildenhall. 65
7 Brian Cox as Titus in Deborah Warner's Royal Shakespeare Company production at The Pit (1988). Photo by Richard Mildenhall. 69
8 Brian Cox as Titus, Estelle Kohler as Tamora, Richard McCabe as Chiron, and Piers Ibbotson as Demetrius in Deborah Warner's Royal Shakespeare Company production (1987). Photo by Joe Cocks Studio. 86
9 Andrew Jackson as Chiron, Nicholas Pennell as Titus, Goldie Semple as Tamora, and Juan Chioran as Demetrius in Jeannette Lambermont's Stratford, Ontario production (1989). Photo by Michael Cooper. 133

10 Kate Mulgrew as Tamora and Keith David as Aaron in Michael Maggio's New York Shakespeare Festival production (1989). Photo by Martha Swope. © Billy Rose Theatre Division, The New York Public Library for the Performing Arts. 149

11 Raf Vallone as Marcus, Almerica Schiavo as Lavinia, Eros Pagni as Titus, and Laurence Ales as Young Lucius in Peter Stein's Teatro Ateneo production (1989). Photo by Marco Caselli Nirmal. 162

12 Ozana Oancea as Lavinia in Silviu Purcarete's National Theatre of Craiova, Romania production (1992–97). Photo by Alastair Muir. 170

13 Dorothy Ann Gould as Tamora in Gregory Doran's Market Theatre production (1995). Photo by Ruphin Coudyzer. 183

14 Publicity poster for Julie Taymor's Theatre for a New Audience production (1994). Photo by Ken Van Sickle. 222

15 Wolf heads on the handlebars of motorcycles and the hood of Saturninus's car in Julie Taymor's film *Titus* (1999). Produced by Julie Taymor and Conchita Airoldi. 223

16 Hitomi Manaka as Lavinia in Yukio Ninagawa's production for the Ninagawa Company (2006). Photo by Ellie Kurttz. ©Royal Shakespeare Company. 237

17 Eve Myles as Lavinia in Bill Alexander's Royal Shakespeare Company production (2003). Photo by John Haynes. © Royal Shakespeare Company. 246

18 Christopher Scheeren as Quintus, Danny Binstock as Mutius, Chris Genebach as Lucius, David Murgittroyd as Martius, and Sam Tsoutsouvas as Titus in the Shakespeare Theatre Company's 2007 production of Shakespeare's *Titus Andronicus*, directed by Gale Edwards. Photo by Carol Rosegg. 255

19 James Blendick as Titus and Xuan Fraser as Aaron in Richard Rose's Stratford, Ontario production (2000). Photo by Cylla von Tiedemann. 260

20 Tamora (Geraldine Alexander) as Revenge, accompanied by Chiron (Richard Riddell) and Demetrius (Sam Alexander) in Lucy Bailey's production at Shakespeare's Globe Theatre (2006). Photo by John Tramper. 271

SERIES EDITORS' PREFACE

Recently, the study of Shakespeare's plays as scripts for performance in the theatre has grown to rival the reading of Shakespeare as literature among university, college and secondary-school teachers and their students. The aim of the present series is to assist this study by describing how certain of Shakespeare's texts have been realised in production.

The series is not concerned to provide theatre history in the traditional sense. Rather, it employs the more contemporary discourses of performance criticism to explore how a multitude of factors work together to determine how a play achieves meaning for a particular audience. Each contributor to the series has selected a number of productions of a given play and analysed them comparatively. These productions – drawn from different periods, countries and media – were chosen not only because they are culturally significant in their own right but also because they represent something of the range and variety of the possible interpretations of the play in hand. They illustrate how the convergence of various material conditions helps to shape a performance: the medium for which the text is adapted; stage-design and theatrical tradition; the acting company itself; the body and abilities of the individual actor; and the historical, political and social contexts which condition audience reception of the play.

We hope that theatregoers, by reading these accounts of Shakespeare in performance, may enlarge their understanding of what a play-text is and begin, too, to appreciate the complex ways in which performance is a collaborative effort. Any study of a Shakespeare text will, of course, reveal only a small proportion of the play's potential meaning; but by engaging issues of how a text is translated in performance, our series encourages a kind of reading that is receptive to the contingencies that make theatre a living art.

J. R. Mulryne, Founding editor
James C. Bulman, Carol Chillington Rutter, General editors

PREFATORY NOTE

Research for this book was aided by a grant from the University of North Carolina Research Council. Various librarians and archivists were generous with their help: Marian Pringle of the Shakespeare Centre Library, Stratford-upon-Avon; Georgianna Ziegler of the Furness Shakespeare Library; Daniel Ladell of Stratford Festival Canada; and Serge Mogilat of the New York Shakespeare Festival. Of the many scholars and theatrical professionals who responded to my queries or otherwise provided material, I wish to single out Edward Rocklin, William Shaw, Tim Pigott-Smith, Patrick Godfrey, Patrick Stewart, Brian Cox, Estelle Kohler, Donald Sumpter, Sonia Ritter, Paul Barry, Barry Kraft, Pat Patton, Henry Woronicz, James Edmondson, Larry Paulsen, Bruce Young, Mark Rucker, J. Kenneth Campbell, Mary Kay Gamel, and Domini Blythe. For shrewd comments and advice I am indebted to my editor, J. C. Bulman, and to James Shapiro, Robert Miola, Homer Swander, and Audrey Stanley. My thanks also go to my graduate assistant, Michael Cornett, and to the many playgoers who shared with me their reactions at performances of *Titus*.

Unless otherwise noted, quotations from *Titus* are from Eugene Waith's 1984 Oxford edition.

ACD
1989

PREFATORY NOTE TO SECOND EDITION

Research for the second edition of this book was supported by the University of Scranton in the form of faculty development funds, annual released time, and a sabbatical leave. For providing me with access to theatrical materials, I owe a great deal to the staff members at various institutions, including the Shakespeare Centre Library, the National Theatre Archive, the Globe Education Centre, the Stratford, Ontario Shakespeare Festival Archive, and the Shakespeare Theatre of Washington, DC. I also appreciate the editorial assistance and prompt answers to questions that I invariably received from my contacts at Manchester University Press.

I offer thanks to general editors Jim Bulman and Carol Rutter for their invitation to take on this project, as well as for their constant encouragement of my efforts and their constructive criticism of my early drafts. Mariangela Tempera, one of my predecessors as a stage historian of *Titus Andronicus*, was also incredibly generous with her help. And, of course, I could not have completed this project without the love of my family: Cheryl, Rachael, and Casey. Finally, I am monumentally indebted to Alan Dessen, not only for nominating me to continue his work, but also for the tremendous support he has offered to me throughout my career as a Shakespearean.

MF
2012

PART ONE

INTRODUCTION

The Problem

To offer a book-length study of *Titus Andronicus* is to risk derision. For centuries, bardolaters have either ignored the play or denied 'their' Shakespeare could have written it. Even sympathetic critics begin their essays or chapters with apologies or with a sampling of the derisive and highly quotable comments of their predecessors. Those who do see merit and potential in this play must therefore start in a defensive posture so as to confront an initial disbelief in a significant part of their audience.

That this tragedy does have its devotees should come as no surprise, for many Shakespeare plays have had an uneven history of reception (e.g., *All's Well That Ends Well)* or have offended an earlier age *(Measure for Measure* in the nineteenth century) only to be prized today. Moreover, many items in the canon have had intermittent production histories or have been presented in some altered state (most notably, the Nahum Tate version of *King Lear).* Indeed, the proposition that *'King Lear* is unactable' was believed for many generations and was only put to rest by a series of highly successful productions after the Second World War.

Titus, in turn, had a landmark production in 1955 – directed by Peter Brook and starring Laurence Olivier – and has subsequently been produced with some regularity (at least compared to the previous 350 years). Similarly, since the 1960s sympathetic critics and editors have greatly enhanced our understanding of the play's characters, images, and themes. As both academics and theatrical professionals have pointed out, an age that takes for granted violence and brutality on television and in the cinema may finally be ready for this tragedy of blood.

Still, the 'Shakespeare in performance' approach that is well suited to most of the canon has its limitations when the play in question is *Titus Andronicus.* Admittedly, since that landmark production in 1955, directors and actors have been finding meaning and power in this script. Nonetheless, to make the play 'work' for audiences today, those directors (with a few notable exceptions – most significantly, Deborah Warner in her 1987–88 Royal Shakespeare Company rendition) have resorted to substantial cuts and other alterations. To look closely at the performance history of *Titus* between 1955 and 1988 is therefore to confront some provocative questions. My goal in this book is to raise and address those questions.

First and most obvious is: why has this particular play posed such severe problems for generations of readers, critics, editors, actors, directors, and playgoers? What immediately comes to mind are violent and potentially grotesque moments such as the rape and mutilation of Lavinia, the self-maiming of Titus, the bloody murders of Chiron and Demetrius, and the climactic banquet in which Tamora is served her two sons in a meat pie. Indeed, given the details of the final scene, jokes about 'bad taste' are inevitable.

Various other factors further complicate our response to this play. First, although exact dating of its composition and first performance is impossible (and is often linked to stated or unstated value judgements about the dramatist's 'achievement', or lack thereof), no one denies that *Titus* is early Shakespeare, probably among the first of the plays to be written. If *Titus* antedates *Romeo and Juliet* by a few years and *Julius Caesar* and *Hamlet* by about a decade, readers and playgoers should not be surprised to find that the verse, characterisation, and decorum we take for granted in 'Shakespearean tragedy' have here not yet been fully formed or come into being (although some critics and editors do find later practices or paradigms in embryo here – as in the iterated comparison between the opening scenes of *Titus* and *King Lear*). That reader or playgoer can easily forget that when the play was first written and performed the 'hot' plays were not the Shakespeare titles familiar today but rather Thomas Kyd's *The Spanish Tragedy* and Christopher Marlowe's *Tamburlaine, The Jew of Malta,* and *Doctor Faustus* (and the latter two may postdate *Titus*). In dealing with *Titus* we are therefore confronting one of the earliest versions of revenge and the revenge play, with many conventions later to be associated with that sub-genre still to be worked out. The pyramiding of horrors and grotesque moments in both Kyd and *Titus* preview what is to come in such plays as *The Tragedy of Hoffman* and *The Revenger's*

Tragedy, not to mention *3 Henry VI*, *Hamlet*, and *The Duchess of Malfi*.

As an early revenge play that may suffer in comparison to *Hamlet* and other masterpieces to follow, *Titus* has had to undergo various indignities. For example, the scholarly-editorial tradition, best represented by J. C. Maxwell's New Arden edition (first published in 1953), has often served as a roadblock rather than as an aid to understanding this tragedy (e.g. in the challenge to Shakespeare's authorship or the undervaluing of the play's theatrical effectiveness), even though most of these objections *have* been answered effectively by such scholars as H. T. Price and Eugene Waith. Various scholarly or editorial 'truths' die hard. On the theatrical front, despite several noteworthy productions, the play's suspect reputation and the consequent absence of a fruitful, continuing on-stage life has prevented many readers from seeing the strengths in this script bodied forth in production, an opportunity that has been available for most plays in the canon.

For those who have seen productions of the play or who attend to its stage history, what lessons are to be found? To answer such a question is to focus primarily upon what has been discovered or realised on the stage, with special emphasis on facets of the play not available to the reader. Attention to such discoveries are a major component of this book. But when investigating the performance record of *Titus*, a twin question emerges: what can be learned from the cuts, alterations, and reshaping that form a significant part of that record? Which moments in the script do modern theatrical professionals deem unplayable or flawed or ridiculous? *Why*? If a majority of actors, directors, and designers conclude that *Titus* must be cut or adapted to be playable today, does that assessment reveal flaws in the script that survives in the quarto or does it reveal something important about *our* sense of theatre or 'realism' or style? For the historicist, do such cuts or changes provide any revealing 'windows' into the early 1590s, especially when directors on different continents, unaware of each other's work, cut or change the same things?

As will be evident in the chapters that follow, I am not offering the 'play in performance' approach as a panacea, a wiping clean of the slate of several centuries of *Titus*-bashing, for, despite some well-acted and well-crafted renditions, modern productions of this script at times can be part of the problem, not a solution.

Rather, my approach is two-pronged. First, in keeping with the goals of this series, I build upon examples from the theatrical record so as to explore this script and present some of its strengths. At the same time, I take a hard look at the limits of such an approach to a play with such firm roots in the early 1590s. My emphasis therefore lies on both the value of attending to performance issues *and* the limitations or drawbacks of that method in the attempt to understand a tragedy that, in some respects, may be of an age and not for all time.

So, to return to my questions: What are the perceived strengths and limitations of this daunting script? Is it playable for us today or is it a museum piece only? Can a modern 'performance' approach geared to the 1950s or 1990s fit with a 'historical' approach geared to the 1590s? Attention to these varied questions seems to me the best way to do justice today to this pre-realistic, Ovidian–Spenserian, stageworthy revenge tragedy that, in a variety of ways, resists 'our' theatrical, critical, and editorial ways of thinking.

Behind my series of questions lies the assumption that *Titus* is the most 'Elizabethan' of Shakespeare's plays and, as a result, the most resistant to easy translation into our idiom. The changes made by directors today can therefore reveal much both about the script and about us. Brook and Olivier proved in 1955 that the play *can* work today – but at a price. My goal is to demonstrate what actors and directors have discovered but also to ask: what price *Titus*?

CHAPTER I

From Edward Ravenscroft to Peter Brook

Although the modern stage history of *Titus Andronicus* starts in 1955, a selective account of the fortunes of this play on stage between the 1590s and the 1950s can be revealing. According to the accepted chronology, the first performances of *Titus* took place in the early 1590s, perhaps the late 1580s. The play was first published in a 1594 quarto (that survives in a unique copy not discovered until 1904); subsequent quarto editions appeared in 1600 and 1611. The version printed in the First Folio of 1623 is based on the third quarto but also contains some new stage directions (mostly sound effects) and a new scene (3.2). The reprintings in 1600 and 1611 suggest some interest among readers at the time Shakespeare was writing *Hamlet* and *The Tempest*. Such continuing interest (or notoriety) is also suggested by the scornful words of Ben Jonson's Bookholder in the Induction to *Bartholomew Fair* (1614) 'that he that will swear *Jeronimo* or *Andronicus* are the best plays yet, shall pass unexcepted at here as a man whose judgment shows it is constant, and hath stood still these five and twenty, or thirty years'. As Eugene Waith points out, by thus linking *Titus* with *The Spanish Tragedy* 'Jonson is saying that it was one of the most popular plays of its time, and also that it is now, in 1614, very old-fashioned' ('Introduction' to Oxford edition, 1984, p. 1).

Little information has survived about the early stage life of *Titus* (for documentation, see Waith, pp. 2–4). Philip Henslowe records three performances of the play by the Earl of Sussex's Men in January–February 1594 and two further performances in June. A drawing, presumably by Henry Peacham, of Tamora pleading for the life of Alarbus (see Figure 1) is usually dated 1594 or 1595 and may reflect Peacham's memory of a performance. A letter from a Frenchman records a private performance by a London troupe at a country home in January 1596 (and reveals that the author found the spectacle – *le monstre* – to be the best part of the show). In 1598 Francis Meres lists *Titus* among Shakespeare's tragedies. Although these scattered bits of evidence tell us little, they amount to more than we have for most of Shakespeare's plays. As Waith notes, 'although we have records of only these six performances before the Restoration, the title pages of Q2 and Q3 suggest frequent revivals' (p. 45); Jonson's snide allusion, moreover, indicates the play's notoriety in 1614. Apparently, *Titus* was known, on the page and on the stage, during the years that span Shakespeare's career as a playwright.

The reasons for this early popularity or notoriety can only be inferred. Especially in the early 1590s, the very features that have proved problematic for subsequent editors, directors, actors, and readers (e.g., the mythological allusions, the long, rhetorical passages, the on-stage violence) may have appealed to playgoers still under the spell of *The Spanish Tragedy* and *Tamburlaine*. The Peacham drawing poses many problems (and, conceivably, could represent the reaction of a reader of the printed text, not a play-goer), but this rendition of a key moment from 1.1 is the only such contemporary illustration from a Shakespeare play. Despite the limitations of the drawing (e.g., the kneeling Tamora is the same height as the standing Titus), the fact that the artist singled out this particular moment points to the power in both the plea and Titus's reaction. That the artist, in defiance of the play as we know it, includes Aaron as a sword-wielding guard of two Goth

1 Tamora pleads for the life of Alarbus. The Peacham drawing, 1594 or 1595.

prisoners may attest to the ability of that villainous figure to catch the imagination of a reader or playgoer (so, in this 'reading' of the drawing, Aaron is present, regardless of the facts of the scene, because he is too important or memorable to be left out). That an observer of what was presumably a scaled-down performance at a country house praised the spectacle or 'show' may then suggest not a pleasure in enormous on-stage display (Titus's first entrance with his sons and prisoners calls for *'as many as can be'*, 1.1.69) but rather a sense of striking images or configurations (as in the Peacham drawing). For whatever reasons – theatrical, rhetorical, literary, imagistic – the play *did* appeal to playgoers and readers in the 1590s and early 1600s.

After the Restoration, *Titus* was one of a group of twenty-one plays cited by John Downes that were 'acted but now and then' but 'being well performed, were very satisfactory to the town' (*Roscius Anglicanus*, 1708, p. 9). Edward Ravenscroft then provided a version of the tragedy that superseded Shakespeare's script (which apparently did not reappear on the professional stage until 1923). This version was probably first acted in the fall of 1678, revived in the mid-1680s, and published in 1687. Performed intermittently in the early years of the eighteenth century, Ravenscroft's *Titus* in 1717 became a major vehicle for James Quin, the first of many actors (e.g., Ira Aldridge, George Hayes, Anthony Quayle, Moses Gunn, Hugh Quarshie, and Bruce Young) who found grand opportunities in the role of Aaron.

The first in a long series of adaptations of *Titus*, Ravenscroft's version is noteworthy in the many ways that it anticipates the subsequent three hundred years of scholarship and stage productions. First, in his preface 'To the Reader', Ravenscroft starts the tradition of ascribing some, much, or all of *Titus* to a hand other than Shakespeare's, for he notes that he has 'been told by some anciently conversant with the Stage, that it was not Originally his, but brought by a private Author to be Acted, and he only gave some Master-touches to one or two of the Principal Parts or Characters'. Since to Ravenscroft the play as he finds it 'seems rather a heap of Rubbish then a Structure', he announces that he is 'apt to believe' this story (rpt. by Cornmarket Press, 1969, A2r). Like subsequent adapters and directors, he therefore feels free to tinker with Shakespeare's version. Thus, Ravenscroft adds various moralisations (often in couplets), makes several substantive changes in the plot and motivation, adds some striking stage effects, eliminates much on-stage violence, buttresses the parts of Tamora and Aaron, and reconstitutes Shakespeare's Act V, particularly the last scene. An account of some of these changes can provide a useful preview of comparable albeit less visible choices by twentieth-century directors.

Gone completely from the 1687 *Titus* are: (1) 2.2 (the preparation for the hunt); (2) 3.2 (the fly-killing scene); (3) most of 4.3 (the on-stage arrow-shooting); and (4) the clown of 4.3 and 4.4. In addition, elements from various 1594 scenes are reconstituted. For example, Lavinia's writing the names of her attackers in the sand (here with an arrow, not a staff) is inserted into 3.1 (and the idea comes from Titus, not Marcus) so as to precede the return of the two heads. The capture of Aaron comes not in 5.1 but at the outset of the final scene (so Titus as well as Lucius confronts the villain), with Aaron's defiant speeches placed much later (after the murders). The supporters of Lucius, moreover, are not the Goths, his former enemies, but 'old legions' loyal to Titus and his family. Some of Titus's mad speeches in the arrow scene (4.3) are factored into 4.4 when Titus, much like Hieronimo in *The Spanish Tragedy*, accosts the Emperor and his court. After the exit of Saturninus, this scene then becomes a version of Shakespeare's 5.2, although Tamora and her sons do not disguise themselves as Revenge, Rapine, and Murder.

At several points, Ravenscroft changes the motivation for a figure's action or choice. Perhaps most revealing is a change at the outset. Thus, many academic and theatrical interpreters today follow the Peacham drawing in placing great emphasis upon Titus's initial choice to ignore Tamora's plea, listen to his sons, and allow Alarbus's limbs to be lopped in Roman rites, a decision that initiates much of the subsequent action. But in the 1687 version Titus and Lucius reveal that Tamora herself, when she had a son of Titus as captive, had been 'deaf like the Gods when Thunder fills the Air' and so 'unmov'd beheld him made a Sacrifice / T'appease your Angry Gods'. In a long speech, Titus recounts a vow he made to his remaining sons to do the same 'if any of the Cruel *Tamora's* Race / Should fall in *Roman* hands' and states categorically that Alarbus's death is 'not to revenge their Bloods we now bring home' (p. 4). What for many interpreters is a pivotal choice or error in Shakespeare's first scene is significantly altered by Ravenscroft so as to set forth a less culpable Titus and a less sympathetic Tamora.

Elsewhere, Martius and Quintus do not fall casually into a pit but are lured into a trap by a letter that promises them lovely young ladies, just as Chiron and Demetrius, in a parallel scene that is a distant version of Shakespeare's 5.2, are similarly lured into a trap, this time by a promise of gold. Tamora's role can be expanded in the final third of the play because in this version she is not delivering a baby off-stage between 2.3 and 4.2. Rather, a Goth woman reveals (pp. 38–9) that the baby had been born earlier and kept privately by a nurse (who has just died). As in Shakespeare's 4.2, Aaron kills this woman in order to preserve his secret, but her husband, with aid from other Goths, captures Aaron to revenge the wife and delivers father and baby to Lucius and Titus. In another change, Shakespeare's boy, young Lucius, is metamorphosed into Junius who, in Titus's plan, is the agent who lures Chiron and Demetrius to their destruction.

More revealing than such tinkering with plot and motivation are Ravenscroft's solutions for a series of problematic moments that continue to bedevil today's directors (and often can serve as litmus tests for productions of this tragedy). Most of these moments involve on-stage violence or images that can elicit unwanted audience laughter. For example, Ravenscroft substitutes a 'vault' for Shakespeare's 'pit' in 2.3 (Quintus *'Kneels and Looks down into the Vault'*, p. 24), so that Quintus and Martius *are* discovered in suspicious circumstances near the body of Bassianus but do not fall into a trap below (so do not engage in any potentially awkward reaching up and down of hands). The 47-line speech Shakespeare gives to Marcus in 2.4 when he confronts the maimed Lavinia (the most maligned passage in the original script) here is pared down to 34 lines, with only 26 addressed to Lavinia (p. 27). Rather than cutting off his hand onstage, this Titus exits with an executioner and re-enters *'with his hand off'*, giving Aaron the opportunity for a new 8-line soliloquy that, typically, climaxes with a couplet ('When once the mind is to destruction bent, / How easy 'tis new Mischiefs to invent', pp. 32–3). The moving lines Shakespeare gives Marcus ('Alas, poor heart, that kiss is comfortless / As frozen water to a starved snake', 2.1.249–50) do not refer to Lavinia kissing Titus but rather follow the stage direction: *'Lucius Kisses one head'* (p. 36). The problematic *exeunt* in 3.1, in which Titus and Marcus each carries a head and Lavinia is directed to carry the hand in her mouth, is avoided when the boy Junius, asked to 'share in this Ceremony', is ordered to 'bring thou that hand – and help thy handless Aunt' (p. 38). The bloodiest moment in Shakespeare's script, the on-stage murders of Chiron and Demetrius with Lavinia holding a basin to catch their blood, is not witnessed by the audience; rather, Titus appears afterward 'like an Executioner' with a bloody weapon in his hand and his 'gray-hairs sprinkl'd with blood' (p. 51). Titus, moreover, does not appear in 5.3 *'like a cook, placing the dishes'* as in Shakespeare, so that curious image is also gone.

The most telling changes come in Ravenscroft's last scene, with Aaron's role especially enhanced. The build-up to the death of Lavinia is basically the same, though here 'Titus *pulls off* Lavinia's *Veil*' (an action that echoes Marcus pulling off her veil when she first appeared to Titus after the rape) and has some new lines ('See there – no hands, no tongue is left, / Nothing that could explain her Injuries', p. 53). In response to the emperor's questions (and in defiance of Tamora's objections), Titus produces Aaron (*'The Moor discover'd on a Rack'*) to get a confession, but initially Aaron *'shakes his head in sign he will not'*. When Tamora asks 'where are my Sons', the stage direction reads: *'A Curtain drawn discovers the heads and hands of* Dem. *and* Chir. *hanging up against the wall. Their bodys in Chairs in bloody Linnen'* (p. 54). Here as elsewhere, the audience to this 1687 version witnesses the bloody effects of violence (as with the maimed Lavinia, Titus's severed hand, and the two heads) but not the deed itself. Titus then announces the constituents of the banquet dishes (including 'And all the Wine y'ave drunk mixt with their blood'), and the three stabbings follow, although both Tamora and Saturninus live on for further speeches.

In this version Aaron has not spoken since he rescued his baby from Chiron and Demetrius. Now, although Aaron 'laughs upon the Wheel and mocks our torments', Marcus gets him to speak when he *'holds the Child as if he wou'd Kill it'*. Ravenscroft here factors in material from Shakespeare's 5.5 though it is Marcus rather than Lucius who is the key interlocutor. After a pared-down version of Aaron's confession, the dying Tamora asks to have her only remaining child brought to her 'that I may leave with it my parting Kiss' and then stabs it ('Dye thou off-spring of that Blab-tongu'd Moor', p. 55). Even Aaron admits Tamora here has 'out-done me in Murder – Kill'd her own Child', and reacts with the most remarkable line in this play: 'Give it me – I'll eat it'. The assembled Romans choose Lucius as their new emperor, the

Andronici briefly mourn Titus, and Aaron, still on the rack, gets a memorable theatrical send-off when he delivers his final defiant lines (e.g., 'If one good deed in all my Life I did / I now repent it from my very heart') while *'the Fire flames about the Moor'* (p. 56). The refusal to talk though tormented on the rack, the last moment confession when faced with a threat to his son, the witnessing of Tamora's stabbing of the baby, and the death in flames accompanied by curses provide Aaron, in this version, with what Waith terms 'a final virtuoso turn' (p. 46) that had obvious appeal for a James Quin or any other bravura actor.

To the interested observer, Ravenscroft's adaptation can reveal much about new opportunities available in Restoration theatre (as with the spectacle of Aaron burning on the rack) or changes in literary or theatrical taste (so various violations of decorum have been eliminated) or even political issues of the period (as argued by Matthew Wikander in *Shakespeare Quarterly*, 37 (1986), 342–3). But, as can be seen in this and subsequent chapters, the moments in the original script that apparently troubled Ravenscroft's sense of character, plot logic, or decorum continue to trouble theatrical professionals today. Some of his solutions may appear extreme, but, in many interesting ways, the tortuous journey of *Titus Andronicus* as playscript after the age of Shakespeare starts here.

Except for the Ravenscroft adaptation, *Titus* was more of a curiosity than a theatrical playscript between the seventeenth and the twentieth centuries. Waith (p. 47) cites four performances of *Titus* in Philadelphia in 1839 with American actor-playwright N. H. Bannister in the title role. According to the playbill, 'every expression calculated to offend the ear, has been studiously avoided'. In his *History of the Philadelphia Stage* (1878, IV, 157), Charles Durang notes that Bannister 'ably preserved the beauties of its poetry, the intensity of its incidents' and 'excluded the horrors with infinite skill, yet preserved all the interest of the drama in the moral deductions that Shakespere ever draws in his drama'. Unfortunately, as Waith notes, 'we do not know exactly which horrors were excluded nor which offensive expressions were avoided', but this version, like Ravenscroft's, apparently anticipated many twentieth-century renditions that also eliminate what is deemed offensive or laughable.

A second major adaptation that, even more than Ravenscroft's, rewrote the script to suit Aaron, emerged in the mid-nineteenth century. Thus, a play by the same name as Shakespeare's became a vehicle in the 1850s for black American actor Ira Aldridge. Adapted by C. A. Somerset and Aldridge himself, this version 'was very much curtailed and altered from the original of Shakespeare' (J. J. Sheahan, *N & Q*, 17 August 1872), with at least one scene imported from another play (*Zaraffa, The Slave King*). As might be anticipated, behind the alteration lay the goal to make Aaron the hero. According to one reviewer (*The Era*, 26 April 1857), Aldridge omitted 'the deflowerment of Lavinia, cutting out her tongue, chopping off her hands, and the numerous decapitations and gross language which occur in the original' so as to provide 'a play not only presentable but actually attractive'. In the process, 'Aaron is elevated into a noble and lofty character, Tamora, the Queen of Scythia, is a chaste though decidedly strong-minded female, and her connection with the Moor appears to be of a legitimate description'. In addition, Chiron and Demetrius become 'dutiful children, obeying the behests of their mother'; Titus 'is a model of virtue'; only Saturninus 'retains the impurity of the original throughout'. Aldridge's Aaron, the centrepiece of this show, is described as 'gentle and impassioned by turns; now burning with jealousy as he doubts the honour of the Queen; anon, fierce with rage as he reflects upon the wrongs which have been done him ... and then all tenderness and emotion in the gentle passages with his infant' (quoted in Marshall and Stock, *Ira Aldridge*, 1958, pp. 171–2).

A less sanguine reviewer (*Brighton Herald*, 6 October 1859) pointed to the obvious limitations of this 'adaptation'. He notes that 'Mr. Aldridge has not attempted to grapple with the difficulties presented to the modern adapter; he has not wasted time in puzzling over the Gordian knot. He has cut it.' For this observer, 'beyond the title, a few incidents, and some scraps of language, his *Titus* has nothing in common with Shakespeare's'. Rather, the adapters have 'constructed a melodrama "of intense interest" of which Aaron is the hero' (Marshall and Stock, p. 251). As attested by the curtain calls, the Aaron that results was a strong and appealing character, but only with some strain can the Aldridge version be viewed as part of the stage history of Shakespeare's *Titus*. Rather, it represents the most extreme example of a long series of attempts (starting with Ravenscroft) to reshape this script so as make it palatable or meaningful to later audiences who are deemed unlikely to accept essential features of the original.

The stage history of *Titus* during the century after the Aldridge adaption is not a distinguished one. Before Brook-Olivier, the most notable production was the 1923 rendition at the Old Vic, directed by Robert Atkins as part of a mounting of all thirty-seven plays over a seven-year period. To Gordon Crosse, Wilfrid Walter's Titus was 'a grand performance': 'I can never forget his horrified glare at the vessel containing the heads of his sons when he realizes how he has been tricked' (*Fifty Years of Shakespearean Playgoing*, 1941, p. 79). Other critics, however, were less charitable (one repeated verdict on Walter's performance was 'monotonous'). In contrast (as so often happens), George Hayes got much praise as Aaron. Doris Westwood notes that 'the venom, the cruelty and wickedness he put into the part, his rendering of the horrible lines, his inhuman laughter and yet, at a certain moment, the sudden great tenderness he shewed for the safety of his infant son, made the whole performance one of exceptional brilliance' and gained for Hayes 'the honours of the evening' (*These Players*, 1926, p. 40). Crosse also praises this Aaron as 'splendidly done' with 'the mixture of savagery and sardonic humour in strong, broad strokes as befitted the play' and records a memorable moment at the end of 3.1 when the director, 'allowing himself for once a bit of embroidery, brought on Aaron to fill the vacant stage with peals of laughter' (p. 79). Noteworthy also is that the one actor singled out for special praise by Herbert Farjeon (*The Shakespearean Scene*, p. 115) was Hay Petrie as the clown (e.g., 'every word he speaks and every movement he makes is a living, thrilling thing').

Atkins provided pageantry whenever possible (as in the opening moments), but, as a disciple of William Poel, eschewed realistic scenery in favour of a neutral backdrop and rapidly moving action. He chose, moreover, not to cut heavily (Crosse refers to 'a nearly complete text') and not to gloss over the horrors. Thus, 'when Lavinia takes her father's chopped-off hand between her teeth', according to Farjeon, 'she delicately turns her back' (p. 115), but it was a 'real' hand. Farjeon, who 'abominates' the script, complains that Atkins did not go far enough. For example, this director in the final scene 'degenerates into italics and bathes his stage in purple and crimson mists', so as to emasculate rather than strengthen the effect; thus Tamora does not 'gobble up her sons with unction' but rather 'pecks at them daintily, leaving the coloured electric lights to do the rest' (p. 115). Still, Farjeon praises the director who 'launches into the horrors and lunges through them far more courageously than nine modern producers out of ten would launch and lunge'. Crosse reacts differently. For him, owing to the excellence of the production, 'the play proved thoroughly enjoyable in spite of the horrors', which the audience received 'very well until near the end when they refused to take them seriously any longer'. Thus, he notes 'a murmur of amusement when Titus overpowered Chiron and Demetrius with one arm'; then, 'at the end some of us fairly broke down and laughed when the deaths of Tamora, Titus, and Saturninus followed each other within about five seconds, as in a burlesque melodrama' (pp. 78–9).

Atkins's rendition is significant in that it represents the first reappearance since the 1660s of Shakespeare's script in a major professional production. The mixed reaction of those who saw it, however, took its toll, for theatrical professionals who remembered the audience laughter at the Old Vic, especially at the climactic murders, were reluctant to commit their time, energy, and resources to this tragedy. Thus, for the 1929 jubilee season in Stratford, *Titus* was proposed and even announced (as the only play that had not been done there in the fifty years since 1879), but box-office logic prevailed. Its place was taken by *Much Ado About Nothing*.

Throughout the first half of the century the play was performed by university drama societies (at Yale in 1924, at Cambridge in 1954 as part of a double bill with *Friar Bacon and Friar Bungay*) and by the occasional professional company (e.g., Denver's Bungalow Players in 1928, Nugent Monck's Norwich Players at the Maddermarket Theatre in 1931), but many of the productions before 1955 turn out to be novelties or adaptations (with selected scenes). For example, in the autumn of 1951 a 30-minute streamlined version entitled *Andronicus* (that omitted Aaron and Saturninus) was included as part of a Grand Guignol programme at the Irving and Embassy Theatres in London. Here and elsewhere, directors interested in The Theatre of Cruelty singled out for presentation just those elements in the original script that had been responsible for its absence from the standard repertoire for centuries. In 1956, a group of young actors (that included Colleen Dewhurst as Tamora) put on what was billed as the first New York production at the Shakespeare Theatre Workshop on East Sixth Street. The *New York Times* reviewer (3 December 1956) found this rendition 'for the most part a bloody bore', but, as opposed to the 'meaningless villainy' of the other characters, did praise Roscoe Browne's rendition of Aaron as a near burlesque fiend.

Given the stage fortunes of this daunting script from Ravenscroft to the 1950s, more than a few eyebrows were raised in 1955 when Peter Brook (already a star director though only in his late twenties) spurned the offer to direct *Macbeth* at Stratford and chose instead to stage *Titus*. As might be expected, many jokes were bandied about, along with some strange headlines (e.g., 'Red Meat at Stratford'). But Brook saw far more in this tragedy than did the wits and critics, so what was thought to be a parody or joke turned into a major event in theatre history. Indeed, according to J. C. Trewin (*Peter Brook*, 1971, p. 82), 'curtain-fall that August evening brought the longest, loudest cheer in Stratford memory'. Audiences only ten years removed from the horrors of the Second World War were apparently ready for Brook's *Titus Andronicus*. The second birthday for this script was 16 August 1955.

In his programme note, Brook described the play as 'an austere and grim Roman Tragedy, horrifying indeed, but with a real primitive strength, achieving at times a barbaric dignity'. Later in *The Empty Space* he observed that 'this obscure work of Shakespeare touched audiences directly because we had tapped in it a ritual of bloodshed which was recognized as true' (p. 47). According to Brook, the play 'begins to yield its secrets the moment one ceases to regard it as a string of gratuitous strokes of melodrama and begins to look for its completeness'. In these terms, 'everything in *Titus* is linked to a dark flowing current out of which surge the horrors, rhythmically and logically related – if one searches in this way one can find the expression of a powerful and eventually beautiful barbaric ritual' (p. 95). Similarly, when commenting on the success of the European tour of this production, Brook concluded that 'the real appeal' of the show 'was obviously for everyone in the audience about the most modern of emotions – about violence, hatred, cruelty, pain – in a form that, because *unrealistic*, transcended the anecdote and became for each audience *quite abstract and thus totally real*' ('Search for a Hunger', *Encore*, July–August 1961, pp. 16–17).

To gain this sense of barbaric ritual or total reality, Brook drew upon all the elements of theatre. As he noted some years later (in a 1979 interview with Sally Beauman), he was blessed with some marvellous leading actors ('I could not have done it without Olivier and Quayle and Vivien Leigh'), but, as opposed to his rendition of *A Midsummer Night's Dream* some fifteen years later, 'the rest of the company were not all strong, and so the production had to be: it could not have been born out of company work'. Rather, in *Titus* 'it was the totality – the sound, the visual interpretation, everything interlocking, that made it happen' (Beauman, *The Royal Shakespeare Company*, 1982, p. 224).

Consider first the set conceived and designed by Brook. To J. C. Trewin (p. 82), the basic design 'looked like a grove of organ pipes, ribbed and fluted'. The effect, according to Richard David (*Shakespeare Survey*, 10, 1957, 126), 'was powerfully simple: three great squared pillars, set angle-on to the audience, fluted, and bronzy-grey in colour'. Sally Beauman (p. 225) describes the set as 'sombre and huge, dwarfing the figures of the actors with its tall square-ribbed pillars, which later moved back to create an echoing empty space'. When the two sides were swung back, David notes, they revealed 'inner recesses that might be used as entrances or, in the central pillar, as a two-storeyed inner stage'. This inner stage could then serve as the tomb, 'sombre and shadowy against the vivid green of the priests' robes and mushroom-hats' or 'festooned with lianes it became the murder-pit and the forest floor above it' or 'blood red, it made a macabre eyrie of the upper chamber from which the Revenger peers out upon his victims, come in fantastic disguise to entrap him'. According to the *Punch* reviewer (26 August 1955), the overall effect was 'a brooding splendour'.

Brook achieved strong effects elsewhere as well. For example, Beauman describes the lighting as 'shadowy, smoky, flaring with the torches whose flames were contained within strange distorted cages'. Brook, she notes, 'worked with a limited palette of colours in both costumes, and set and lighting: bile green, blacks, reds and browns, and the liverish colour of dried blood'. The production began 'in an unearthly greenish darkness'; by the last scene 'the stage was bathed in an ominous blood-red light, the costumes were red, and it was as if the whole universe on the stage had been drenched with blood'.

Consider too the music, one of the most striking features of this production. Together with a young composer, William Blezard, Brook started with a baby grand piano and a tape recorder and then 'clashed experimentally with pots and warming pans, played with pencils on Venetian glass phials and turned wire baskets into harps'; for the call to the hunt he experimented with a plastic trumpet from Harrods (Francis Martin, *Edinburgh Evening Dispatch*, 27 August 1955). To get a gigantic effect for the opening funeral march, Brook put 'one microphone inside the piano and one underneath, stamping on the pedal in such a way as to make all the strings shudder, and then recording it slowly'. Add to that 'an off-beat cymbal; on top of that a recorder tune, simple, pentatonic, over-recorded, and slowed down' and the result was 'overtones of melancholy and tremendous blast-furnace breathiness' (Trewin, p. 87).

Elsewhere, to accompany the cutting-off of Titus's hand, Brook produced 'a throbbing effect' by playing 'two alternating chords quite slowly on the piano within which was a microphone'; he then 'over-recorded the result, and slowed it down to make it deeper'. To Trewin's ear, 'played back loudly, it resembled an alarming mixture of an immense organ and a gigantic doublebass in a primitive blood-lust rhythm'. When Tamora appears as Revenge to Titus in 5.2, 'Brook wanted to get the effect of time dragging – as it were, a chime slowed down' so he found 'the appropriate ringing note' by striking six carefully chosen wine glasses with a pencil. This little tune (very like 'Three Blind Mice'), combined with one chord and a piano string plucked rhythmically in the background, 'provided the most haunting of knells' (p. 88). At the climax, writes David (p. 127): 'A slow seesaw of two bass notes, a semitone apart, wrought the tension of the final scene to an unhearable pitch, and ceased abruptly, with breath-taking effect, as the first morsel of son-pie passed Tamora's lips.' Beauman (p. 225) sums up the reactions of most of the reviewers: 'The music created a sense of dislocation, threat, and unease.'

Brook's theatrical artistry produced some memorable scenes. For example, Ravenscroft had cut both the clown and the arrow-shooting, but Brook fashioned a spectacular moment by adding new elements and reshaping what he found in the script. This clown (Edward Atienza) did not merely enter with his pigeons; rather, he descended from the flies in a basket manipulated by an unseen gibbet-maker uncle who served as puppeteer. David (p. 127) observes that 'here Brook cheated' by adding this spectacular entrance 'and writing in a line about "fetching down his pigeons from the walls" to make this plausible', but concludes that 'it was certainly in keeping, and added a crowning touch of fantasy to a most fantastical invention'. Brook also moved the shooting of the second set of arrows to the end of the scene, so that the audience saw arrows shot into the wings and then immediately, at the beginning of 4.4, saw the arrows streak on-stage and strike the throne and the palace walls. 'Hidden in the scenery', Trewin notes (p. 88), 'they sprang out as needed, and whenever one arrived we heard a weird sound that Brook had made by striking single notes on the piano and immediately switching on his recording machine' (an effect that produces 'an extraordinary contortion of pitch') so that 'the entire sequence of "pings" formed a mad little tune'.

Equally impressive was Brook's presentation of the fate of Lavinia. For her entrance in 2.4 (see Figure 2), 'a small stylized tune was played on harp harmonics followed by piano: one microphone rested on the harp pedals, one on top of the harp' so as to produce 'an eloquent, not a horrific moment' (Trewin, p. 87). 'Harrowing' is David's term (p. 127) for 'the hurrying carillon of electronic bells that led up to the abduction of Lavinia and the slow plucking of harp-strings, like drops of blood falling into a pool, that accompanied her return to the stage'. He describes Vivien Leigh, 'right arm outstretched and head drooping away from it, left arm crooked with the wrist at her mouth', with her hair 'in disorder over face and shoulders', and 'scarlet streamers, symbols of her mutilation' trailing from her wrists and mouth. Chiron and Demetrius 'retreat from her, step by step, looking back at her, on either side of the stage' so that 'their taunts fall softly, lingeringly, as if they themselves were in a daze at the horror of their deed' while 'the air tingles and reverberates with the slow plucking of harp-strings'.

Much of the credit for the success of this production must go to Sir Laurence Olivier who single-handedly brought the part of Titus back into the classical repertoire. For Kenneth Tynan, 'this is a performance which ushers us into the presence of one who is, pound for pound, the greatest actor alive', an actor who 'raises one's hair with the risks he takes'. Tynan describes Olivier's first entrance

2 Kevin Miles as Chiron, Vivien Leigh as Lavinia, and Lee Montague as Demetrius in Peter Brook's Stratford-upon-Avon production (1955).

not as a beaming hero but as a battered veteran, stubborn and shambling, long past caring about the people's cheers. A hundred campaigns have tanned his heart to leather, and from the cracking of that heart there issues a terrible music, not untinged by madness. One hears great cries, which, like all of this actor's best effects, seem to have been dredged up from an ocean-bed of fatigue. One recognised, though one had never heard it before, the noise made in its last extremity by the cornered human soul. (*Curtains*, 1961, pp. 104–5)

To Trewin's ear, 'certain of the early lines are mere bathos', but not when spoken by Olivier.

> This Titus was a white-haired warrior, desperately tired. The lines of his body drooped; his eyes, among the seamed crowsfeet, were weary; though he greeted Rome because it was a thing of custom, his voice had neither spring nor light. The business must be endured; later on, no doubt, there might be surcease from these eternal wars, heroic rants, useless lengths of rhetoric. Immediately, Titus was real to us, and having established him as a man,

fixed him in our thoughts as he first appeared, Olivier was able to move into a wider air, to expand the part to something beyond life-size, to fill stage and theatre with a swell of heroic acting. (p. 83)

David (p. 127) describes this Titus as 'cantankerous, choleric, and at the same time compelling'. In the opening scene, Olivier provided a 'blazing rage, that with "Barr'st me my way in Rome?" sweeps his youngest son out of existence'. In 3.1, Olivier 'so grew and proliferated in the astonishing variety of his reactions to disaster (the enormous physical agony of the severed hand was almost unbearable) that with the crowning frenzy of "I am the sea" Olivier seemed to break through the illusion and become, not old Hieronimo run mad again, but madness itself'. This scene (see Figure 3) impressed many playgoers. In Olivier's delivery of 'when will this fearful slumber have an end?', Harold Hobson (*Sunday Times*, 21 August 1955) finds 'an effect of weary desperation comparable with some of the best things in his Macbeth: he misses nothing of the tragedy implicit in a great man's cry for mercy'. For Trewin (p. 84): 'As Olivier cried "I am the sea", its surge beat on the world's far shore.' According to Richard Findlater, when Titus received the news about heads and hand, 'he leans against a pillar, head tilted back, and his face is a tragic unforgettable mask of grinning whiteness' so in response to Marcus's, 'Now is a time to storm; why art thou still?' his answer was 'a gentle laugh' (*Tribune*, 26 August 1955); for Trewin, 'the slow answering laugh was like the menace of a tide upon the turn'. According to Trewin: 'The actor had thought himself into the hell of Titus; we forgot the inadequacy of the words in the splendour of their projection.'

Anthony Quayle's Aaron also received high praise (although, for once, the villain did not overwhelm the protagonist). Tynan (p. 104) described Quayle's 'superbly corrupt flamboyance'; Milton Shulman (*Evening Standard*, 17 August 1955) admired the 'eyeball rolling Moorish lover of Tamora' who revels 'exultantly in his lipsmacking evil'; the reviewer for *Sphere* (17 August 1955) cited 'the muffled organ-throb voice, the savagery, and the sudden tenderness'. Harold Hobson, who had many objections to Shakespeare's script, found Aaron 'far and away the most likeable character'. 'He murders, strangles, deceives, and betrays with the gayest and most vital devotion to his own interests, but when the game turns against him he takes his misfortunes with the same

3 Michael Denison as Lucius, Vivien Leigh as Lavinia, Laurence Olivier as Titus, and Alan Webb as Marcus in Peter Brook's Stratford-upon-Avon production (1955).

swinging high spirits. No whining, no complaining here: murder for him is the same airy trifle whether it is on his side or his enemies.' For another reviewer (L.A.M., *Oxford Mail*, 17 August 1955) Quayle's Aaron was 'a magnificent portrait of uncomplicated villainy which, in a superstitious age, would surely be regarded as evil incarnate'; for J. L. Johnston (*Birmingham Evening Dispatch*, 17 August 1955), he was 'a picture in brimstone of living evil that is yet endowed with a strange dignity'.

Various moments in particular were singled out. Desmond Pratt (*Yorkshire Post*, 15 August 1955) noted Aaron's 'hurling his last defiance with magnificence at his captors'; Rosemary Anne Sisson (*Stratford-on-Avon Herald*, 19 August 1955) found 'a moment of greatness' in 5.1 when Aaron told Lucius: 'Touch not the boy; he is of royal blood' (p. 49). A large number of reviewers were impressed by Aaron's defence of his child in 4.2. For example, J. L. Johnston notes that 'when the Moor first sees his infant son' he 'almost – but rightly not quite – arouses sympathy for this man'. Similarly, according to Alex Walker (*Birmingham Gazette*, 17 August 1955), Quayle's Aaron, 'although inhuman in his purposeless cruelty, pulls off the seemingly impossible feat of winning our compassion for him and the blackamoor child'. For the *Oxford Mail* reviewer, Aaron's defence of the child, especially his question 'is black so base a hue?', was 'worthy of Edmund' (as was his defiant death); for Sisson, at this point 'a flood of genuine emotions flowed into the play'.

As seen in these comments, what most surprised and impressed reviewers was how convincing, even appealing, Aaron could be. According to T. C. Worsley (*New Statesman*, 27 August 1955), 'if anyone could persuade us now into a belief in that incredible Renaissance conception, the figure of pure evil, Mr Quayle with his daemonic energy might have done it'; for *The Times* reviewer (16 August 1955), Aaron is 'a volcanic vitality which makes that monster of black-hearted wickedness alarmingly credible'. The reviewer for *Stage* (18 August 1955) found 'no jot of nobility here'; nonetheless, 'the sheer power of the man is so fully revealed that admiration, however grudgingly, is wrung from us'. Like Olivier, Quayle surprised many playgoers with the richness of his role.

In other major roles, Maxine Audley's Tamora was praised for a regal beauty ('glittering' according to Tynan) that set off her treachery. For Wilfred Clark (*Solihull and Warwick Country News*, 20 August 1955), this Tamora was 'a woman with terrific power of delivery, wild-cat action, a striking if petite figure in dress, cape and headgear of gold'; for Milton Shulman, in her spitting and hissing, Audley was 'lusciously horrific'.

Reactions to Vivien Leigh's Lavinia were mixed. Some reviewers admired her elegance and beauty; for example, Rosemary Anne Sisson was impressed by her 'beautiful, motionless, grief-stricken face' and by the 'contrast between the anguished movements of her first return and her still, suffering dignity later, when the violence was past, but the horror remained with her'. Others, however, felt some effects were too prettified. Wilfred Clark, for one, although finding Leigh's rendition 'extremely pathetic', nonetheless concluded that 'a little more blood seemed indeed to be called for'; he notes that for him 'it was difficult to accept the cutting out of Lavinia's tongue despite the fine expressive acting', because 'though her mouth was half open, pityingly expressive and voiceless, the chin was clean, impossibly clean'. Another reviewer (N. T., *Leamington Spa Courier*, 19 August 1955) found this Lavinia 'too cold, too remote to excite our pity' so that 'her final entrance at the banquet' had 'no effect whatsoever'. Trewin (p. 84) described her as 'piteous' but thought that 'a few more hairs might credibly have been misplaced after her morning in the wood'. Tynan (p. 104) commented wryly that this Lavinia 'receives the news that she is about to be ravished on her husband's corpse with little more than the mild annoyance of one who would have preferred foam rubber'.

To gain his distinctive effects and to sidestep potential pitfalls, Brook (like Ravenscroft) made several key decisions that, in turn, have had a large influence upon subsequent productions. In particular, he chose (1) to stylise or formalise many moments, and (2) to cut heavily from Shakespeare's script (about 650 lines). In Ivor Brown's terms: 'Brook's method was to drain off the rivers of gore, never to parade the knife-work, and, instead, to symbolise a wound with a scarlet ribbon' (*Shakespeare Memorial Theatre 1954–56*, 1956, p. 10). As Beauman notes, Brook chose 'to formalize the horrors, to confine them within a ritualistic framework so that the agonies were distanced, episodes in a black progress towards greater and greater atrocity'. As a result, 'Brook played on the nerve-endings of his audience, but he played subtly; in a play replete with murders there was no visible gore', so that 'the atrocities of the play were the more horrifying – certainly audiences did not laugh, though many among them fainted'. For Beauman, 'the latent absurdities of the play were skirted', so that 'for post-Buchenwald generations the play's profligate brutalities no longer seemed comfortably remote, or ridiculous' (p. 225).

The most often-cited choice was the beribboned appearance of Lavinia in 2.4, but other bloody or grotesque moments were similarly transformed. Like Ravenscroft, Brook had Chiron and Demetrius murdered off-stage, so this Lavinia did not hold a basin to catch their blood. The two heads were delivered in 3.2 concealed in black cloths and steel baskets; Titus's severed hand was not displayed and Lavinia did not carry it off in her mouth; the midwife in 4.2 was strangled rather than stabbed; in 4.1 Lavinia guided the staff with her hands rather than her mouth. All of Marcus's speech in 2.4 to the maimed Lavinia was gone.

Most reviewers and critics (many of them less than enthusiastic about the original script) praised the cuts and adjustments.

G. R. Proudfoot (*Themes in Drama*, 2, 1980, p. 163) notes that 'Brook cut the text severely, rearranging action to clarify the plot and removing any line or action which threatened [to] provoke bathetic laughter'. Daniel Scuro ('A Crimson-Flushed Stage!', p. 42) felt that the various 'grotesqueries' of the original 'were tastefully edited' (e.g., 3.2, 4.1); he notes that 'all references to Titus' amputated hand are gone and the tongueless Lavinia no longer chases the young Lucius around the stage, her stumps flailing helplessly about her'. To Scuro, Marcus is a 'nobler' figure because relieved of the fly-killing in 3.2 (assigned to the young Lucius); in his view, 'Brook wisely cut the extravagant poetry and melodrama of the original', whether the speeches of the two boys at the pit in 2.3 or Marcus to Lavinia in 2.4. Brook thereby 'squeezed every drop of inhumanity out of the drama while dropping very little gore on the stage of the Memorial Theatre' (p. 44) so is to be praised for his 'visual restraint'. Similarly, Edward Trostle Jones argues that Brook's 'stylized distancing effects' allowed the spectator to 'accept the horror of the play without experiencing total revulsion'; to reach 'the beauty beneath the barbarism of *Titus Andronicus* requires the repressive mode for presentation' (*Following Directions*, 1985, p. 98).

Most critics therefore praised Brook's response to the problems posed by the script, for 'whenever the text threatened to descend from barbaric dignity to bathos, he cut' (Beauman, p. 224). Trewin notes that Brook 'manipulated the uneven text so that his actors could let fly without dread of mocking laughter; whenever he spied a possible laugh, he either cut the offending phrase or unmasked his protective atmospherics' (p. 82). According to Tynan, 'much textual fiddling is required if we are to swallow the crudities, and in this respect Mr Brook is as swift with the styptic pencil as his author was with the knife'. Tynan, like others, approves of the elimination of 'all visible gore' and praises Brook for his tact in cutting 'the last four words of Titus' unspeakable line, "Why there they are both, baked in that pie", as he serves to Tamora his cannibalistic speciality – *tête de fils en pâté (pour deux personnes)*' (p. 104).

A few reviewers were less charitable. Evelyn Waugh, for one, felt that 'the only complaint that could be made against Mr Brook was of squeamishness'. Waugh approved of having Chiron and Demetrius murdered off-stage and the midwife strangled rather than stabbed, but missed the severed hand and visible heads. In particular, Waugh mocked the accumulated corpses at the climax ('very elegant, particularly the ladies') as 'lying gracefully disposed, all unlike the real debris of carnage' (*Spectator*, 2 September 1955). Richard David, who registered the most forceful minority opinion, described himself as 'spell-bound and yet quite unmoved'. For David, the original script is 'twaddle', but 'in striving to make it more than this Brook made it less than nothing'. Shakespeare's blood and other effects were 'turned to favours and to prettiness', for 'severed heads were not allowed to appear unless decently swathed in black velvet and enclosed in ornate funerary caskets'. The severed hand, 'swaddled and coffered, was decorously cradled in Lavinia's arms, not carried off between her teeth as the text directs'. David's account ends with a question: 'Has Shakespeare's *Titus* really any life left in it?' For David (unlike most of the other critics) 'the question is not yet answered', because 'Brook's romantic play of the same name was still-born' (p. 128).

Few critics, then or now, agree with David's negative conclusion. Rather, the praise for the achievements of Brook, Olivier, Quayle, and others was overwhelming. This production therefore has had an enormous impact on the stage life of this tragedy since 1955 and, in a variety of ways, has defined the options open to subsequent directors.

CHAPTER II

To stylise or not to stylise

The 1955 triumph of the Brook-Olivier *Titus* demonstrated that Shakespeare's script was, or could be, actable. Although the reputation of this tragedy continues to daunt theatrical professionals, Brook's solutions and Olivier's achievement have served as a touchstone or stimulus for subsequent actors, directors, and designers who have experimented with ways to deal with the problems posed by this script. Among the options have been: (1) to stylise or formalise the action (e.g., ribbons in place of blood); (2) to seek 'realism', often with an emphasis upon blood, severed heads, maiming, and brutality; (3) to focus on the bizarre features of the play, whether to single out the horrors in the Grand Guignol tradition or to treat the script as parody or burlesque (as in William Freimuth's 1986–87 production for the Source Theatre Company of Washington, DC which, according to Margaret M. Tocci [*Shakespeare Bulletin*, 5.2, March/April 1987, pp. 10–11] provided 'liberal doses of knockabout farce and cheerful mayhem sprinkled with gallons of stage gore'). To my knowledge, in pursuing these options only two directors of this tragedy have used an uncut script.

Consider first some productions in which directors, following Brook's example, chose to stylise some or many moments. Perhaps the most significant example is director Gerald Freedman's summer 1967 rendition for the New York Shakespeare Festival. In his introduction to the Folio Society edition of *Titus* (1971), Freedman notes that he had recently seen a production (directed by Douglas Seale at Baltimore's Center Stage) that 'used modern dress and weapons in an effort to draw positive and obvious parallels between the violence and wholesale murder of our times and the time of Titus Andronicus'. But, for Freedman, that approach 'failed by also bringing into play our sense of reality in terms of detail and literal time structure'. To introduce 'realism', he argues, is to introduce some damaging questions: 'How could Lavinia suffer such loss of blood and still live?' or 'Why doesn't Marcus take her to a hospital instead of talking?' or 'Titus can't really be cutting off his hand on stage – what a clever trick.' For Freedman, these questions or issues 'are obviously not those of the play or playwright, but they are inevitable if you are invoking a reality embedded in a contemporary parallel'.

So, given his sense of the limits of 'realism' or contemporary analogies, Freedman poses a telling question. If 'the Elizabethans were more receptive to blood and gore as theatre staples' and if 'they accepted all the extravagance of emotion and intensity of feeling with a passionate response', how then 'does one create a similar response to horror and violence in a modern audience?' The answer might seem easy, 'living as we do in an era where violence and destruction are presented to us daily in the newspapers and on television'; nonetheless, 'attempts realistically to recreate physical violence on the stage in the manner of the Grand Guignol now appear ludicrous or stagey'. Therefore, he argues (in a manner reminiscent of Brook), 'if one wants to create a fresh emotional response to the violence, blood and multiple mutilations of *Titus Andronicus*, one must shock the imagination and subconscious with visual images that recall the richness and depth of primitive rituals'. To find such images, he opts to build upon 'poetic conventions drawn from the ancient theatres of Greece and the Orient'; upon 'instruments and sounds that nudge our ear without being clearly explicit or melodic'; and upon 'fragments of myth and ceremony and childhood fantasies that still have the power to set our imaginations racing'.

What then emerged in the Delacorte Theatre was a highly stylised production far removed from 'realism'. To gain his effects, Freedman confesses, he 'took more liberties with the text and form' of this tragedy than he had with any Shakespeare play he had previously directed. For him such liberties were necessary to capture 'the audience's imagination in a snare of made-up theatre conventions' and to play out Titus's tragedy 'within the world of those conventions in an effort to incite the audience to identification, shock and recoil' – to make that audience 'accept the mutilations and decapitations and multiple deaths with belief instead of humour'.

To achieve such goals and solve the many problems posed by the script, Freedman found his solution in 'masks and music and ritual'. The music he chose, for example, 'eschewed electronics' (which he associated with 'our' era) but built instead upon 'sounds that are part of our inherited primitive consciousness – drums, rattles, rubbed stones, animal horns and stretched strings'. Similarly, 'the costumes recreated an unknown people of a non-specific time', with elements of 'Roman-Byzantine and feudal Japanese', so the playgoer saw leather and wool but 'no literal use of any specific detail'. The set design elicited from reviewers various 'lunar' analogies; one described it as 'a rocky construction, a cross between the lunar surface as found by Lunar Three and Lunar Five and a wall of pumice struck by shells from howitzers' (Whitney Bolton, *Morning Telegraph*, 10 August 1967). Another distinctive feature was a Brechtian narrator (played by Charles Durning) to announce what was coming in each scene.

Along with masks, narrator, a 'lunar' set, and distinctive music, Freedman provided a chorus 'whose constant presence would both cool and abstract the violence' and also lend 'volume and size' to his images. This group of actors served as the Roman populace in Act 1, then an 'earth-conscience' in Act 2, 'reflecting in sounds the agonies and strains of the "natural" moral order in the process of being torn apart'. In subsequent acts, the chorus 'became the interior manifestation of Titus' growing madness and disintegration' or 'a nightmarish fusion of Furies and Fates, a visible personification of the forces let loose by the wrenching apart of the "natural" order by acts of violence, treachery, and deception'. For example, the ensemble reacted in one voice to the news of the birth of Aaron's child and elsewhere provided similar sounds or choreographed movements.

Reviewers reacted variously to the chorus and the other stylised effects. Most found the actors' half-masks and long priest-like robes suggestive and successful, so reviewers regularly refer to the show's 'unearthly quality' or to images linked to 'Men from Mars' or the 'other side of the moon'. Several commented, for example, how speeches were often spoken hollowly, with an echo-like effect (although sometimes the actors lapsed back into 'normal' delivery). Most reacted positively to the masked Greek chorus that danced, chanted, buzzed like flies, intoned and repeated lines, and writhed around on the floor, an omnipresent group that could be soldiers, townspeople, furies, vultures, or quivering trees, all intricately choreographed and backed by rasping, percussive, musical sound effects. One less enthusiastic critic (Julius Novick, *Village Voice*, 17 August 1967) refers to Lavinia's 'Dance of the stumps' at her entrance in 2.4; before the rape, as he saw it, 'a lot of extras writhe on the ground and say "Oooo" after which they produce little stylized tree branches and impersonate a forest'. A more sympathetic Walter Kerr describes a Lavinia who 'ran headlong to the edge of the open-air stage only to be hoisted high in the arms of two neutral forces, while the ever-present chorus rolled away to the ground to huddle in sleep or in shame'. For Kerr, such staging elevated the crime 'from the level of simple shocker to that of cold, universal injustice' (*New York Times*, 6 August 1967).

Freedman used other devices to elicit larger-than-life emotions and effects. So in addition to the masks, the chorus, and the music, he also stylised the violence. Instead of swords or daggers, the actors used wands which did not touch the victim but were whirled over their heads and then flicked smartly down as the bodies fell, so a great deal was left to the imagination of the playgoer who had to fill in the actual violence. Titus's killing of Mutius, for example, was done in slow motion, with a frightened and apparently prescient Mutius calling for help in advance. As in the Brook production, Lavinia's mutilation was displayed not through blood but by means of blood-red ribbons dangling from her wrists or stumps and a third ribbon that streamed out when she opened her mouth to speak to Marcus (a moment that elicited gasps from the audience). For Walter Kerr, 'the use of thin, flying streamers where blood should be was more effective than any amount of greasepaint: we were looking at a happening, not at a painted picture'. For Mildred C. Kuner, 'what would have been, to a modern-day audience, absurd to the point of laughter-inducing, became oddly moving, as though one were witnessing a universal agony set to a formal dance pattern' (*Shakespeare Quarterly*, 18, 1967, 414).

Similarly, no severed heads were visible, nor was there a 'real' baby. Rather, Kerr notes that Aaron's child 'was an armature to which no defining plaster had yet been applied; the effect was to make us believe in the child as we would never have believed in the customary rag bundle', especially when this ribbed prop was cradled by Aaron. One of the most successful effects in the show occurred in 3.1 when the severed heads of Titus's two sons were brought slowly in on a platter. As Kerr notes, the platter 'contained the two masks, nothing more', but nonetheless the audience 'gasped aloud', because 'the shock was more intense for not being literal'. Rather, 'the masks were now *empty*; it was the emptiness itself that was felt at the pit of the stomach'.

Another distinctive effect came at the series of murders in 5.3, a moment that (as in the 1923 Old Vic production) can easily elicit unwanted laughter. As Dan Sullivan describes the effect (*New York Times*, 10 August 1967): 'a shadowy chorus envelops each figure in a billowy red cloth, which unwinds to reveal a black cloth underneath'; then, 'instead of pitching forward, the victims – head and shoulders now swathed in black – remain vertical: statues instead of corpses'. Sullivan found the moment 'powerful, dignified and almost liturgical'. Kuner, also impressed by this moment, concludes that 'symbolism rather than gory realism was what made this production so stunning'.

Unlike Brook's production, the acting here was not the strong point of the show. Moses Gunn's Aaron was most often singled out for praise (so again the potential show-stealing quality of this role was recognised), as, to a lesser extent, was Clayton Corbin's Marcus. Gunn played an expansive Aaron, with large gestures (e.g., a spreading of his hands to take in the entire stage) and a big wicked laugh that conveyed a delight in his wittiness and superiority that made his villainy appealing and appalling. His clearly demonstrated love for his baby impressed many reviewers. Corbin's Marcus projected a great deal of compassion in his voice, especially in the lyrical rendition of his lines when he finds the maimed Lavinia, so that he emerged as the most humane figure in the show. Sullivan, for one, had high praise for Olympia Dukakis as Tamora, for, in his terms, she played 'the queen not as a woman but as a perverse, abstract force momentarily inhabiting a woman's body' – an effect he found 'chilling'. As Titus, Jack Hollander received some plaudits for his mad scenes near the end, but the recurring phrase used to describe his performance was 'wooden'.

Here, then, is the most elaborate attempt in the short stage history of *Titus* to 'stylise' the play as a way of heightening the effects and avoiding various traps. That choice to stylise involved much tinkering with the script, strong design choices (e.g., masks, red ribbons, a lunar set), distinctive music, and various insertions (a narrator, an ever-present chorus). Some moments apparently did not work (e.g., the action around 'the pit' in 2.3);

if the reviews are any index, not all playgoers reacted positively to the chorus or other strong choices. But by focusing on the mythic or ritualistic side of the tragedy, Freedman (like Brook twelve years earlier) helped to bring *Titus* back into the circle of 'performable' Shakespeare plays.

More evidence about alternatives to 'realism' is provided by the three renditions at the Oregon Shakespearean Festival. The first, directed by Hal Todd, had only two performances in summer 1956 and is best remembered for its pigeons. Thus, in the promptbook at the bottom of 4.4 is a large scrawled query – 'Release pigeons?' – for, to enliven this scene, the director chose to set loose two homing pigeons at the clown's death. At the first performance in this outdoor theatre, however, the pigeons were startled by the lights and by the audience and, instead of flying home, perched on top of the lighting standards and watched the rest of the show. The next night the pigeons were left in their basket.

The 1974 and 1986 Oregon productions, in contrast, played twice a week for the three-month summer season. Both productions conveyed the raw power of the tragedy with little or no use of on-stage blood; in both, the directors chose to stylise some moments (so as not to risk unwanted audience laughter) but did not go as far as Freedman had, with his masks, chorus, and narrator. Both directors, moreover, cut heavily (though not as many lines as Brook).

First, the 1974 production, directed by Laird Williamson, had Denis Arndt in the title role (Arndt played Lear two years later) and strong performances from Eric Booth as Demetrius and Ernie Stewart as Aaron. Throughout the show Williamson skilfully blended 'real' and stylised effects. For example, the severed heads in 3.1 were lifelike, but the audience did not see the severed hand. Rather, after the amputation, they saw an object covered with a white cloth that had upon it not a bloodstain but a snowdrop pattern of red rhinestones. Lavinia was not physically abused by her two tormentors in 2.3, but the director did have her caught and manipulated in a net by which she was pulled off-stage, a striking and very powerful image. After the rape, the audience saw a dishevelled figure with wrapped hands and later a Lavinia swathed in a hood and cloak covered with a few prominent red rhinestone drops (so again stylised rather than 'real' blood).

In his programme note Williamson observes that 'in strokes as bold as the lines of an ancient woodcut, Shakespeare creates the living iconography of a world going mad'. Richard Hay's stage design built upon this 'ancient woodcut' analogue; for example, above the action was placed a scrolled banner, 'The Lamentable Tragedy of Titus Andronicus', and, on the railing of the upper stage, a scrolled *'Terras Astraea Reliquit'*. In addition, woodcut images adorned the Andronici tomb and other key places; Latin words often were chanted in the background (e.g., *'sit fas aut nefas'* at the rape); and at climactic moments two actresses appeared as winged seraphs carrying scrolls to frame the action on this wide platform stage. The fierceness of Booth's barbarian Demetrius, the mocking wit of Stewart's energetic Aaron, and the raging of Arndt's warrior Titus were thereby all contained within a framework that channelled the effect. Some scenes did not work (most notably the falls of the two boys into the pit in 2.3), but through a mixture of realism and formalism Williamson conveyed his vision of 'this bloody nightmare of disordered madness which obsesses Shakespeare's creative energies'.

Pat Patton's 1986 production also blended stylised effects and realism. In place of 'real' blood Patton used not red rhinestones in snowdrop patterns but rather red China silk streamers that seemed to flow out of the wounded figure, whether at the entrance of Lavinia in 2.4, at the cutting off of Titus's hand, or at the murders of Chiron and Demetrius (but not at the murder of Bassianus). The first appearance of these streamers, at the death of Mutius, was an electric moment that elicited gasps of surprise from the audience; subsequent use of this device was then readily accepted as a convention and helped to dampen some unwanted laughter. In the final scene the three murders were done rapidly, but, just as some spectators began to titter at the staccato action, soldiers wafting red banners appeared to cover the bodies and cut off the laugh – a stunning stage effect. Also presented in stylised fashion was Lavinia's maimed state, for, starting in 3.1, her stumps were wrapped and her missing tongue was conveyed visually by one vertical red line in the middle of her lips.

Some of Patton's effects, however, were anything but stylised. Admittedly, no stage blood was used in this production (the streamers and banners provided the only significant reds in the show), but Lavinia was badly mauled in 2.3 (actress Nancy Carlin compared playing that scene to running a mile), and the heads and hand were not tastefully concealed. Rather, the two heads were visible and, placed on poles, remained on-stage at the intermission after 3.1 (so the distinctive *exeunt* was altered). Titus's hand *was* carried off by Lavinia but attached to a platter, not in her mouth, so to accomplish this task the handless figure used specially designed handles (the tech personnel called them 'stumples'). No attempt was made to stylise the falls of the two boys into the pit. Rather, this part of 2.3, heavily cut, was played as a drunk scene with Aaron pushing the first of his two victims into the trap (a sequence that here, as in Williamson's 1974 production, did elicit some titters from the audience).

As had Williamson with his seraphs, Patton often took advantage of the width of this Elizabethan stage for strong effects. Thus, at various points he placed figures half-way up two sets of visible stairs so as to set up a distinctive stage picture (so Saturninus versus Bassianus on opposite sides in 1.1, the Goths holding Aaron in 5.1). At the end of 5.2, Chiron and Demetrius were being held some distance apart on the two sets of stairs, so Titus made a stage cross for the second murder and repeated several lines so as to set up a ritualistic sacrifice (that climaxed with the final use of the red ribbons). Lavinia *was* on-stage with her basin (so that image was included) but was not that close to the two victims, so no attempt was made to 'catch' the red ribbons as if liquid blood. Although not going to the lengths that Brook had chosen for his music in 1955, music director Todd Barton did find some distinctive and unusual background sounds – most notably what Barton termed a controlled panic scream that was heard at key moments.

Given a less than potent Aaron and a sexy rather than queenly Tamora, the strength of this production lay in fine performances by Larry Paulsen as Marcus and Henry Woronicz as Titus. To Woronicz, Titus does not develop as a character (as opposed to Lear who does have his breakthrough with Cordelia in 4.7) but rather epitomises a single-minded thirst for revenge. Like other actors who have played Titus, he characterised this figure as a military man who sees everything in clear black-and-white terms as opposed to the greys of a play like *Measure for Measure* (Woronicz was playing Duke Vincentio in the same season). To this Titus, Rome's ingratitude towards his years of military service was comparable to the American public's reaction to those who had fought in Vietnam.

As in most productions, 3.1 was the emotional centre. For Woronicz, the key moment was not 'I am the sea' but came later with the snap of Titus's mind after the messenger's arrival in 3.1 with the two heads and the hand. At this point the audience saw a kneeling, motionless Titus, his back to us, who, in response to Marcus's 'Now is a time to storm; why art thou still?' (3.1.262), starts to shake. After the raging up to this point in the scene, we, like Marcus, expect even more fireworks, but from the stillness, then the visible shaking (again, without our being able to see Titus's face) emerged a frightening laugh (Marcus asks: 'Why dost thou laugh? It fits not with this hour') and the deadly calmness of Titus's 'Why, I have not another tear to shed.'

As a final example of a stylised *Titus*, consider director Paul Barry's 1977 production at the New Jersey Shakespeare Festival. Barry took the 'ritual' approach even further than Brook, for he chose as his set a Roman temple so as to convey the sense of the stage as an extended altar. Marcus (here played as blind) was high priest; the remaining actors began as priests, acolytes, or choir chorus (the latter group all women). The actors started in similar scanty costumes with a minimum of make-up and then, as they took on various characters, put on articles of clothing. All the violence was done symbolically or ritualistically. For example, no blood was shed at the murders of Chiron and Demetrius; rather, in a manner reminiscent of a Catholic Mass, an upstage Marcus poured wine from glass decanters into a chalice held by a vestal virgin. For the rape scene, a white-clad Lavinia had her costume torn off in view of the audience. With the actual rape then masked from view by the actors, Lavinia reappeared in shreds of blood-coloured ribbons.

In his review (*Shakespeare Quarterly*, 29, 1978, 232–3), Bernard Beckerman found 'the ritual frame' ('we were purportedly witnessing an ancient rite') to be 'merely decorative' in that 'it provided tone but little emotive charge'. 'Far more effective' for Beckerman, however, 'was the handling of the physical horror', for 'without shrinking from presenting the bloody business of hacked limbs, the director succeeded in throwing attention on human reaction to horror rather than on the horror itself'. He singles out Barry's insistent use of a trap opening downstage centre that 'gradually assumed the resonance of an insatiable maw as it became increasingly tomb, pit for Bassianus, and finally indiscriminate receptacle for all the dead'. 'The relentless pressure of this abyss', he notes, 'was further reinforced by the absence of an intermission' (Barry cut roughly 640 lines so as to get a playing time of about two hours).

The productions directed by Freedman, Williamson, Patton, and Barry show one line of descent from Brook in the choice to stylise some or many of the elements in the script. This approach does not always work and, indeed, can create a new set of problems. In his review of the Riverside Shakespeare Company production in New York City (*New York Times*, 1 June 1988), Wilborn Hampton urges directors to 'proceed with caution' given the difficulties in the script, 'not the least of which is to avoid looking ridiculous in some of the more horrendous scenes' (e.g., 'the one in which Lavinia carries off her father's hand in a bag in her teeth or the bloody finale in which four bodies suddenly litter the stage in less than a minute'). Hampton praises director Timothy W. Oman for resisting the 'temptation to try to shock the audience with buckets of blood', but concludes nonetheless that 'the bright red scarves, ribbons and gloves used to denote the results of all the hacking and hewing on-stage are sophomoric'. Without strong acting (Hampton refers to the 'emotional anemia' and the consistent shouting of this production), stylised effects alone cannot provide an answer to the problems.

To demonstrate the alternative to the approach chosen by Brook, Freedman, and others, let me focus upon several very different renditions. First, in his 1967 Center Stage production in Baltimore, Maryland, director Douglas Seale observes in his programme note that Brook's production 'was most painstakingly presented to avoid too much blood'; he cites in particular the omission of 'the killing and bleeding of Tamora's two sons'. To stage the violence and horrors of *Titus*, Seale argues, the director must decide 'whether to play the nightmare for all it is worth, or spare the audience's feelings by avoiding too much realism (or seeming realism)'.

In his production, Seale opted for 'realism', so in his rendition of 2.4 Marcus ministers to a bleeding Lavinia who screams incoherently. For this director, 'Titus falls into the depths of hell because he is guilty of the cardinal sin of pride, and his pride blinds him to his own brutality, as well as the brutality of those around him, so that he and those he loves become victims of second-rate, but none-the-less skillful manipulators.' To this interpretation, moreover, Seale attaches a contemporary analogue, for he perceives a similar pride in 1939 when people found it 'inconceivable that an ex-house-painter and his gang could challenge the supremacy of the two greatest nations in Western Europe'. Seale therefore chose to set his production in the 1940s so as to remind the audience 'of the horrors of the concentration camps, the bombing of Hiroshima, and the mass executions at Nuremberg' and thereby reduce the likelihood that spectators will dismiss *Titus* 'as a blood bath of horror which might be acceptable to those coarse Elizabethans, but hardly to sophisticated, civilized, educated humanitarians like us'.

To invoke images of Fascism when staging one of Shakespeare's Roman plays was not 'new' in 1967, but Seale may have been the first to present a Fascist *Titus*. For example, Saturninus was portrayed as a shaven-headed villain highly reminiscent of Mussolini with a retinue of black-shirted followers; Titus was 'the classic Prussian officer, complete with saber scar'; the Andronici wore 'Nazi uniforms, heavily laden with swastikas'; and the Goths who accompany Lucius in Act 5 were portrayed as a liberating army in 'clothes reminiscent of the Allied Forces in World War II' (R. H. Gardner, *Sun*, 13 February 1967). The clown's scenes with Titus and Saturninus (4.3, 4.4) were played for laughs, but, when killed, the clown was turned around to reveal a Star of David on his back. Then, in the final scene once the smoke had cleared after the murders (carried out with a fusillade of rifles rather than with swords), the audience saw that swastikas had been thrown down from above.

Other 'modern' images were also invoked. For example, Chiron and Demetrius were portrayed not as Nazis but as motor-cycle gang members with leather jackets and switchblades. A recognisable version of 'Hail to the Chief' was heard at the first appearance of Titus. Some of these images troubled reviewers. Lou Cedrone did not object to Seale's adaptation until Chiron and Demetrius spoke, for, in his terms, 'verse coming from the leather boys is enough to shake anybody' (*Evening Sun*, 13 February 1967). R. H. Gardner recognised 'the poetic value of Fascist and Nazi symbols', but he also noted that the director 'has used them in a general sense without apparently giving thought to the confusion that might arise from the specific significance they represent to the contemporary mind'. Thus, if Titus 'is the most just and civilized principal in the play', then 'to present him in the trappings of the most brutal and uncivilized order in modern history is inappropriate' and sets up 'the pictorially mixed metaphors rampant throughout this production'.

When faced with a daunting script, this director's solution was therefore not to find excitement in Shakespeare's words, personae, or events but rather to transpose the action from ancient Rome to a more recent period so as to create striking, compelling images meaningful to the spectator (a solution familiar to generations of playgoers). A different set of choices and a different approach to 'realism' are provided by the 1972 Royal Shakespeare Company production of *Titus*, the fourth item to be presented in the Stratford 'Romans' season, with all four shows directed by Trevor Nunn. In his programme note for the four plays, the director set up a series of larger questions or concepts and then set each tragedy within that framework. Thus, for Nunn, 'thinking about Rome was the only way an Elizabethan had of thinking about civilisation', for Roman 'language, history, thought and literature' were at the heart of Elizabethan education and epitomised 'the model by which Renaissance Englishmen measured their own conquests, laws and arts, their public magnificence and private virtue'. Rome, however, 'was also the great Elizabethan problem', for 'if Roman power, law and virtue could fail in the end, what absolutes could men look to under heaven?'

For Nunn, then, the losses suffered by Titus represent 'the worst a Roman could fear' for 'the goddess of justice, last child of the golden age, has fled from the earth', with the result that 'Rome, once her seat, has become a "wilderness of tigers" ruled by a sadist, his Gothic Empress and her Moorish paramour'. In this early play, Shakespeare displays 'the Elizabethan nightmare', for 'even golden ages come to an end, in blood, torture and barbarism', and even 'Rome, the greatest civilisation the world had known', can fall, 'dragging mankind with it into darkness'.

Such a view of the play and of Rome then leaves many questions. 'How could subsequent Empires, no matter how splendid, evade the same fate? Was there some secret, a balance of freedom and order, which Rome had lost? Or was there an inescapable tendency, in the lives of men and societies, to revert to a Hobbesian state of nature, nasty, brutish and short?' In his conclusion, Nunn links the plays and productions to our own age, for, in his formulation, 'Shakespeare's Elizabethan nightmare has become ours.' In a final sentence (cited by many reviewers) he asks: 'have we time for answers, or are we already in the convulsion which heralds a fall greater than Rome's?'

In his own comments (as recorded by Judith Cook in *Shakespeare's Players*, 1983, pp. 88–9), actor Colin Blakely described *Titus* as 'a marvellous, tremendous play as epic as *Lear*. It is a remarkable examination of grief and madness and it looks at the very still centre of violence.' Echoing his director, he argues that 'of all the Roman plays it is the most apposite for our present time, it seems quite up to date. It takes a look at an empire in decay and a system which has become so hard, so brittle that it breaks.' To Blakely, as an Irishman, the play cut 'near the bone', for just as the figures here devour each other, so the Irish and the English have 'fed on each other' (he also saw a link between the Andronici and rigid right-wing Conservatives). Titus, moreover, is 'so severe and so domineering that his children can hardly breathe without his permission'. But all this crumbles when figures in the play 'turn and rend each other – almost literally – the stage falls to pieces and the forces of destruction take over completely'.

To stage this vision of *Titus*, Nunn broke with the precedent set by Brook, Freedman, and others and opted not to stylise the violence. Blakely, for one, much admired the 1955 production ('I still think it's the best thing Olivier has ever done') but was less enthusiastic about the 'formal, almost ritualised' style. In his terms, 'the violence was symbolic and very cold, as if it was taking place on the moon' (he cites Lavinia's red ribbons). Rather, the 1972 production went for 'realism', the only possible choice 'nowadays', according to Blakely, 'when people can see what violence is really like when they watch the news on television'. He notes: 'Whatever we did, it would never be as horrible as that picture of the officer pushing a gun into a man's head in Vietnam.'

What resulted from the stances enunciated by Nunn and Blakely was what Michael Billington termed a 'lingering, slow-motion realism', with a 'naturalistic weight and stress' (*Guardian*, 13 October 1972). Thus, in Nunn's production, as opposed to Brook's or Freedman's, when severed heads are called for, realistic replicas of the two sons do arrive (in a black box), and, after the rape, Janet Suzman's Lavinia has difficulty walking upright (unlike Vivien Leigh's elegant entrance in a white gown in 1955). In the terms of a less than sympathetic Jeremy Kingston (*Punch*,

25 October 1972), Nunn played 'all this beastliness for naturalism', but a more appreciative Irving Wardle found that the director, for the most part, had succeeded in staging the play's horrors 'without relapsing into monotony or unintended farce' by having Titus hit 'as if with hammer blows' by the events (*The Times*, 13 October 1972).

Some of Nunn's most controversial choices arose from his vision of Rome's decadence and decay at the end of its empire. Thus, the director first had his cast see the Fellini film, *Satyricon*. Then he supplied one elaborate on-stage orgy (at the beginning of 4.2) and throughout the show went to some lengths to exhibit a sick, decadent court. As might be expected, reviewers reacted variously to such choices. Almost all at least mention the '*dolce vita* atmosphere' with its 'debauched parties, abandoned dances, and other Fellini-like routines' (Wardle). Many found these scenes effective, although Harold Hobson complained that the 'bulging-breasted, big-thighed women' in the major scene of debauchery 'are enough to put one off orgies for the rest of one's life' (*Sunday Times*, 15 October 1972).

Central to the decadence was John Wood's portrayal of Saturninus. According to Benedict Nightingale (*New Statesman*, 20 October 1972), Wood provided 'not only malice' but also 'urbanity, irony, pettishness, narcissism, hysteria, and even a strange infantilism, as when he responds to disaster by relapsing into baby-talk'. This Saturninus can appear 'with golden arrow and armour, a scrawny cupid smirking priggishly at his sycophants'; elsewhere, 'he slithers across the stage and sinks his teeth into the calf of a courtier'. For this reviewer (who had qualms about both the script and the production), Wood's rendition was 'more entertaining than it has any right to be'. Other reviewers noted Wood's purple gown and ringleted wig ('like a refugee from an Andy Warhol movie', notes Billington). To B. A. Young (*Financial Times*, 13 October 1972), Wood was 'a spoilt aristocrat of hair trigger passions'; to Jeremy Kingston, he was a 'decadent and crosspatch Emperor, shooting out his fingers like a wizard flashing magic, given to angrily flinging himself to the ground and biting the legs of courtiers' .

The most positive reaction was provided by Irving Wardle who found this Saturninus 'spell-binding to watch'. Starting with his 'murderously hysterical first speech', Wood provided a 'man governed by whims' who clearly *would* suddenly drop Lavinia for

Tamora. Wardle found Wood's delivery 'endlessly mobile and unpredictable as it drops into the chatty cadences of modern English or rises into spitting fury'. For example, 'at the news of the Goth's invasion he raises a finger to his lips warning the messenger not to wake the baby'. For Wardle, this figure was a 'wonderful blend of deadly vigilance, petty rancour and buffoonery' even though ultimately only a 'poisonous gadfly at the margin of the action'.

In contrast, Michael Billington, who praised many aspects of the production, found it less successful only when Nunn 'spells out too obviously the reason for Rome's decline' (as in the Fellini-like orgy). For this reviewer, the mood was 'austere, dignified and weighty', with the keynote the 'wilderness of tigers'. Nunn presents 'an empire on which the sun has already set', so, at the start, Saturninus scrambles for his father's crown like a hysterical child. For Billington, the violence acts out the breaking down of all restraints, the absence of any moral law, and the elevation of individual will, so that the production provides 'a portrait of a decadent society crumbling into destruction'.

Colin Blakely's Titus elicited mostly positive reactions. A few reviewers agreed with Harold Hobson, who found this Titus 'a rough and shaggy bear, with whose brutality and misfortunes one has no sympathy'. But most found great power in this rendition. J. C. Trewin, who admitted his preference for Brook-Olivier, still praised Blakely's 'fine oak-cleaving, oak-splintering voice' and his 'sustained, all-out acting' (*Birmingham Post*, 13 October 1972). Other reviewers describe this Titus as 'a grizzled soldier, squat and muscular' and 'as an oak, lightning struck but still capable of crushing his enemies as he falls' (*Tipton Herald*, 20 October 1972) or as 'craggy, almost Promethean'. Billington admired Blakely's 'rocklike performance', so that eventually this 'revenge-crazed' figure, who had entered wearing a lion's head or mane in 1.1, 'becomes like some ageing jungle beast tearing to pieces those who have savaged his cubs'.

Two reviewers singled out Blakely's manner of delivering his lines. B. A. Young, who viewed this rendition as melodramatic rather than tragic, described Titus as turning into 'a sad, grey old man, as near mad as makes no difference'. According to Young, Blakely delivered his lines 'in a kind of Schoenbergian speech-song, prolonging vowels as if to music; his gestures, mostly made with both arms together as long as both his arms are complete to make them with, are bold and artificial but expressive'. Irving Wardle, who found 'continuous character growth' in this Titus, admired Blakely's grating delivery in 1.1 of 'to be dishonoured – by my sons – in Rome', in which the line was broken 'into three sentences as a crescendo of priorities'. Wardle describes Blakely's delivery as often relying 'on stabbing emphases on single words, and variations between stoic briskness and the cry of an old abandoned child'.

Various moments were singled out by the reviewers. Many mentioned the opening of the show, in Wardle's terms 'a period-defining tableau showing a black-habited throng paying court to a bloated imperial waxwork that reclines on a litter clutching the ultimate symbol of carnal indulgence – a bunch of grapes'. After this 'powerfully ironic opening', the squabbling of the heirs for the crown was contrasted to 'the sober arrival of Titus', a figure 'confident of a stable society that will reward him with an honourable old age'. Also mentioned often was Lavinia's entrance in 2.4 after the rape. For Billington, Lavinia became 'a pitiable, hunched grotesque crawling out of the darkness like a wounded animal'. Sarah Eily Wood found that the 'humiliation of her crouching body is to some extent belied by the passion in her eyes' (*Stratford-upon-Avon Herald*, 20 October 1972). Wendy Monk, who found Janet Suzman's Lavinia the strongest element in the show, describes the 'truest moment' as when 'she transforms Lavinia from radiant girl to old woman, hump-backed, almost crawling'. For Monk, 'miraculously, it is a moment of beauty' (*Stage and Television Today*, 19 October 1972).

Several reviewers cited the cutting off of Titus's hand in 3.1. Blakely only winced at the amputation 'when one hears the bone of Titus's wrist being sawn through' (overall she found the emphasis upon 'mental and spiritual agony rather than the physical'). Similarly, Billington found this and other analogous moments' deprived of their crude sensationalism by the stress on the sheer physical difficulty of the action'. When Blakely's Titus greeted the maimed Lavinia (see Figure 4), 'he clasps her between his elbows, keeping his own hands stiff and useless' (Kingston); 'as he folds her to his breast he bends his own hands outwards as if to make up for the loss of hers' (*Solihull News*, 28 October 1972); so Lavinia 'presses against her father for comfort like some terrified animal' (*Leamington Spa Courier*, 20 October 1972). For Wardle, a turning point came at the arrival of the two heads when Lavinia, 'who has previously shrunk from human contact, turns and kisses her father', an action he found 'at once deeply felt and marking a decisive point in the events', so from that moment 'the blindly loyal Titus starts to think for himself'.

As to the design, reviewers commented on the 'gaunt elder tree in one foreground' or the 'dry, wind-bent trees' as obvious symbols. B. A. Young described Christopher Morley's set as a 'sumptuous series of designs, often against a black back-drop which suggests that events down stage, subtly picked out by the lights, are taking place miles from anywhere'. For example, in 5.2 Tamora visits Titus 'under a bare windswept tree', an effect he found 'economically striking'. Throughout the show, emotions were kept taut by 'the growl and scream of brass back stage and the thunder of percussion from the Juliet balconies'.

Another 'realistic' approach to this script is provided by the 1988 Shakespeare Santa Cruz rendition directed by Mark Rucker. Like the three Oregon shows, this production was presented out of doors, but, in contrast to the large Elizabethan stage and 1,200

4 Janet Suzman as Lavinia and Colin Blakely as Titus in Trevor Nunn's Royal Shakespeare Company production (1972).

seat auditorium in Ashland, the Santa Cruz playing space is a wooded glen with the audience (up to about 400) seated upon blankets and folding chairs. The centre of the set was a stage that appeared to be made of large blocks of stone; a removable section in the stage floor served as the tomb, so that bodies could be lowered into this space in 1.1 and later the two heads and the hand were placed below in 3.1. In addition, the acting area included the ground around the platform, including a hill or rise on stage left that was associated with Saturninus and his court and a smaller patch of ground stage right backed by trees. No 'above' was available, so in 1.1 Marcus did not appear above to address the warring factions but rather, while delivering his initial speech, descended from the rear of the audience to the main stage. Similarly, in 5.2 Titus greeted Tamora-Revenge not from above but from a rise to the playgoer's right, then walked around to join her; in the final scene, lines were adjusted so Lucius and Marcus did not ascend after the murders but addressed the assembled Romans and the audience from the platform.

One distinct advantage of this outdoor theatre (an advantage apparent to playgoers familiar with London's Regent's Park) is that some scenes set out of doors, here the forest scenes of Act 2 and the capture of Aaron in 5.1, can take on a special quality when played around or, in one case, actually between 'real' trees. The cluster of trees on stage right here served as the backdrop for Aaron's tryst with Tamora in 2.3 (so that Aaron could bury his bag of gold in 'real' dirt at the base of a 'real' tree). The body of Bassianus could then be dumped into a 'real' pit among a cluster of trees; Quintus and Martius then also fell into that pit and were pulled out with some difficulty by a Lucius who was held by the legs and lowered by Aaron. Similarly, for his speech comparing the tribunes to stones (3.1.37–47), this Titus could stand close to the audience next to a large 'real' column base and finger a small 'real' stone sitting on top.

Along with 'real' trees and stones (and much sliding over 'real' leaves and dirt and tripping over 'real' roots), this production also offered a great deal of 'real' blood and violence. Lavinia's stumps were very visible during 2.4 as was the blood that gushed from her mouth (wiped away several times by Marcus). The presence of such highly visible wounds then allowed Marcus to cover parts of his long speech by offering first aid, so that, in the terms of one astute observer (Robert Miola), his highly rhetorical lines appeared to be an intellectual means of coming to terms with the unbearable but his human response was physical and immediate. In the next scene, Titus offered his hand to Aaron's scimitar but turned suddenly and cut it off himself so as to display a verisimilar fake hand (a bit of business that did not always work); later in 5.2, a great deal of blood flowed from Chiron and Demetrius who were suspended upside-down. In the final sequence, Titus killed Tamora savagely, and Saturninus shot Titus with a pistol, the only such weapon in the production which was designed for a 'Road Warriors' post-nuclear holocaust look.

Given the outdoor theatre and the small size of the company (a core of thirteen actors, with guest artists playing the clown), effects available in other productions were somewhat curtailed. Except for 1.1 where a slow procession brought in Titus, his sons, and his captives, there were few ensemble scenes, so often (e.g., the beginning of 1.1, 4.4, 5.3) the actors played to the audience as 'Romans'. Any limits in personnel, however, were offset by some strong acting in the major roles, with solid performances from Molly Mayock as Tamora, Elizabeth Atkeson as Lavinia, Bryan Torrington as Saturninus, and Brad Myers as Marcus. Mayock's initial entrance carried in a cage curtailed some effects (e.g., she could not, in that confined space, kneel and plead for Alarbus as in the Peacham drawing), but the loosing of her by Saturninus set up a powerful image of a force unleashed upon Rome, a force Mayock conveyed vividly in 1.1 and 2.3. As often happens in productions of this script, Myers's Marcus emerged as the most caring figure in the play, a quality that paid dividends in 5.3.

As Titus, J. Kenneth Campbell had some fine moments, especially in 3.1. For example, as a prelude to 'the vow is made' (3.1.278), he addressed Marcus, Lavinia, and Lucius ('you heavy people') so as to build to the climactic line: 'And swear unto my soul to right your wrongs.' With the final three words he stabbed out a gesture with his remaining hand to each of the three, pausing between words ('right – your – wrongs'), a powerful ritual that set up a strong climax to this long emotional scene. In 1.1, this Titus was not as inflexible as have been most interpreters of the role, so he seemed to listen with sympathy to Bassianus pleading his case to be emperor and then killed Mutius by accident, giving him a savage push that inadvertently drove the boy head first into a tree. Although less successful in portraying Titus from 3.2 on (especially in his sing-song pretended madness with Tamora in 5.2), Campbell provided some powerful moments in the centre of the tragedy.

But the most distinctive feature of this production was Bruce Young's Aaron, an eye-catching, show-stopping rendition very much in the grand tradition that goes back to Quin, Aldridge, Hayes, and Quayle. What was particularly interesting about this Aaron was that, although wily, witty, and intelligent, he was not so much the proto-Iago or Richard III (although such elements were present) but was rather a warrior figure. Here one key was Young's size, for among his many assets as an actor (e.g., his fine diction, his control of verse, his resonant voice) he is also 6 feet 4 inches, and weighs about 240 pounds. Such size and stage presence gave him some grand opportunities, starting in 2.1 where he towered over Chiron and Demetrius whom (here and in 4.2) he tossed around with ease (after they had struggled on equal terms with each other). With his size and presence he could get great mileage out of his asides (often delivered downstage centre with a slight turn of the head to the audience). In 2.1, and at the beginning of 2.3 with Tamora, his sexuality was also emphasised; so, after a forceful rendition of the soliloquy that begins 2.1, he reached 'to wait upon this new-made Empress', then added: 'To wait, said I? – To *wanton* with this queen ...' (20–1), with a gesture to his crotch on 'wanton'. Clearly, this Aaron was potent in various senses.

As often happens in productions of this script, Aaron got some of his strongest effects in 4.2 when defending his son. Standing with his scimitar and his baby on the hill stage left, this Aaron towered over the smaller figures below, whose figures and weapons seemed puny in comparison. His rebuttal to Chiron's 'Thou hast undone our mother' was a show-stopping 'Villain, I have *done* thy mother' (75–6), delivered with wit and panache, and was followed by a strong defence of his 'first-born son and heir' (92) and his values (e.g., 'my mistress is my mistress, this myself, / The vigour and the picture of my youth', 107–8). But the key to this interpretation lay in the soliloquy that ends the scene, for Young (who felt that Aaron at this point was leaving Rome for good, not merely finding sanctuary for the baby) placed special emphasis upon this moment, particularly the pledge to 'bring you up / To be a warrior, and command a camp' (179–80). The politician-manipulator at Saturninus's court clearly has been superseded here by the warrior who is dedicating himself to

5 Bruce Young as Aaron, Stephen Jones and Brett Harvey as Goths in Mark Rucker's Santa Cruz production (1988).

raising his son and heir in the same tradition – again, an emphasis that is readily accessible, thanks to the size and stature of the actor (see Figure 5).

The power and prowess of this Aaron was then further enforced when he arrived as a prisoner in 5.1, for he did not come in as a captive at sword-point but rather trailed behind the Goth who was carrying the baby. The clear implication was that none of these figures, Lucius included, could have captured him had not the baby been available as a hostage (the one thing Aaron valued more than his own life). Readers of the script can readily see that the baby is Aaron's one weakness but, given his size and stature, the sense for the playgoer was that this figure might have been invincible without this Achilles' heel. This sense of his power and the threat he poses then gave a particular edge to his account of his evil deeds in the big speech of 5.1 and also to his defiance of his captors in 5.3. Overall, Young provided a rendition on the grand scale that almost (but not quite) turned Aaron into the centre of the show.

Like many audiences before them, the many Santa Cruz playgoers seeing this play for the first time did not know what to expect. The falls into a 'real' pit in 2.3 evoked some titters as did the rapid murders in 5.3; at first Chiron and Demetrius, played energetically by Sheffield Chastain and David Baker, seemed to be appealing 'bad boys'. But the moments of violence, starting with the verisimilar deaths of Mutius and Bassianus, came as shocks that elicited gasps from an audience unfamiliar with the script, as did the brutal treatment of Lavinia before she was taken off in 2.3. The very bloody Lavinia in 2.4 and 3.1, the self-maiming of Titus, and the gory deaths of Chiron and Demetrius were then risky choices that produced a mixture of reactions in the audience but, for most playgoers, added up to a visceral and memorable experience, especially in 2.4 and 3.1, the centre of the play. Some moments, especially the final scene, flirted with melodrama; some problems were not fully solved (e.g., the boys at the pit, 4.3, Titus's madness); but this strenuous attempt at 'realism' (in several senses) often had a very strong impact on its audience.

Even more 'realistic' was the television production (filmed in February 1985) directed by Jane Howell for the BBC series, 'The Shakespeare Plays'. The last of Shakespeare's plays to be staged at Stratford-upon-Avon, *Titus* was also the last of the thirty-seven to be produced by the BBC. In an interview with Michael Billington (*New York Times*, 14 April 1985) Howell notes that her point of departure was the image of young Lucius in 3.1 – 'a small boy at the end of that dinner table sitting alongside people with hands cut off'. To Howell that image raises the question: 'what kind of world is he being brought up in?' She chose not to present the play as Lucius's dream (a choice that 'would wrench the structure'), but in her production 'the boy is palpably there all the time'.

For example, this young Lucius (Paul Davies-Prowles), wearing distinctive (eighteenth-century rather than Roman or Elizabethan) eyeglasses and plainly dressed, is highly visible in 1.1 as part of the ritual of welcome for Titus, as an observer of the death of Mutius (he retrieves a cloak and the murder weapon), and at the end (with his face superimposed on the screen). Later, he is part of the fly scene (3.2), at first reading a book but then seen by us in reaction shots; Titus, moreover, uses the boy's knife (not Marcus's) to stab at the fly. Young Lucius also is linked to Lavinia's writing her words in the sand, delivers the weapons to the court in 4.2 and, after helping to bind Chiron and Demetrius in 5.2, looks on at their fate, again with strong focus upon his face at the end. He then plays a significant role in 5.3: in the ritual welcome of his father; in the serving of the food; in an attempt to stop his father's stabbing of Saturninus; in the mourning; and in his strong reactions to the elevation of his father to the throne and to the death of Aaron's son. His highly visible presence and reactions (as opposed to Shakespeare's *puer* who does not appear until 3.2) were designed by Howell to encourage us to ponder: 'what are we doing to the children?' As Mary Maher notes ('Production Design in the BBC's *Titus Andronicus*', 1988, p. 146), Howell's rendition 'is in part about a boy's reaction to murder and mutilation'. Thus, 'we see him losing his innocence and being drawn into the adventure of revenge; yet, at the end, we perceive that he retains the capacity for compassion and sympathy'. For Maher, this effect 'is a privileged commentary created by the director within the television medium'.

For the most part, Howell rejected the stylised effects familiar in other productions. One exception was her choice to have her Roman people (e.g., the followers of Saturninus and Bassianus in 1.1, the courtiers in 4.4) wear blue masks. Here her goal was 'a strange, dislocating effect', for Rome to Howell 'seemed like a society where everyone was faceless except for those in power'. Maher notes that 'when the foot soldiers and servants wear masks, interestingly enough, the masks have no mouths' so as to convey the impression that this society 'is not characterised by political freedom and democratic ideals' (p. 147). Elsewhere, Howell provided some special effects only available in television or cinema. For example, Titus's blow against Mutius that initiates the visible violence was seen in slow motion. The opening image of the show was a skull which faded to reveal the dead emperor; later, 1.1, 2.1, and 3.1 ended with flames on the screen. Glimpses of other images were also provided: the face of young Lucius at several points; Aaron's baby on a platter (at the end of 5.2).

Overall, however, this director chose 'realism', for, as she notes, to the television viewer 'it would look strange to see red ribbons on the screen'. Rather, in this rendition 'when throats are cut, there are rivers of blood'. As Stanley Wells notes (*TLS*, 19 April 1985), the 'notorious horrors' of this script 'are not flinched' (he cites 'the horribly bloody stump of Titus's arm', the two severed heads, the maimed Lavinia, and the flowing blood at the murder of Tamora's two sons in 5.2). In particular, the murders of Chiron and Demetrius take place in an abattoir where the two gagged and squealing figures hang upside down alongside slabs of meat. When their throats are cut, a large quantity of blood gushes down to be collected by Lavinia in a basin held in her stumps and steadied by her lips. Maher notes (p. 149) that most of the carcasses of meat were constructed for the purpose, 'but one genuine lamb carcass was ordered from a butcher, and this one would get most of the frontal shots from the camera' (and, at the appropriate moment in the shooting, 'a stagehand spread Vaseline on the hanging meat to make it gleam under the lights').

To ensure 'real' effects elsewhere, Maher notes that 'all of the decapitated heads and severed hands' were checked for authenticity at the Royal College of Surgeons; moreover, 'the properties builders looked at cadavers and pieces of bodies from autopsies' (p. 149). The heads, the severed hand, and the stumps of Lavinia and Titus were then clearly visible on camera; this Lavinia *does* carry off Titus's hand in her mouth, although, thanks to the editing, the viewer gets only a momentary glimpse of that image. For another 'real' effect, a live baby, not a swaddled property, was used in 4.2 and 5.1.

Costumes, according to Maher (pp. 146–7) 'were designed to reflect the differences between the Romans as civilized and well governed countrymen and the Goths as lawless barbarians' (so that 'colors are sharp and defined on a Roman costume, diffuse and textured on a Goth'). The costumes of Tamora's sons were inspired by the rock-music group, Kiss, with rough, leathery material, chains around their necks, dead animals hanging from their belts, and spiked or punk hairstyles. Eileen Atkins's Tamora 'looks like a punk queen in a shock of unruly red and orange hair with small ghouls braided into it', along with 'a gold ring through one side of her nostril', overdone make-up, and 'a gown cinched with a corselet made of what looks like fish scales – a creature who has no doubt oozed from the slime'. This 'savage, animalistic effect' (especially in the first two acts) was played off against the softly draped and flowing costumes of such aristocratic Romans as Saturninus, Bassianus, and Lavinia.

With little cutting or retooling, Howell found ways to adapt many of Shakespeare's stage effects to her medium. The longer scenes (e.g., 1.1, 5.3) were broken down into sub-scenes in different places; for example, 'the Tomb' was distinguished clearly from the banquet room or the senate chamber. At key moments the director provided a strong sense of ritual. For example, she set up an impressive procession for the arrival of Titus in 1.1 and a welcoming ritual in which young Lucius presents a basin and towel, Titus washes his hands, and then lights a fire with a torch (a sequence that is repeated in 5.3 with the arrival of Lucius). While the four chained Goths look on, Titus's sons depart with Alarbus and return to throw his 'entrails' into the 'sacrificing fires', here a small dish that flares up. The movement into the tomb in 1.1 involved a long entry accompanied by drums, a viewing of the corpses, and a lighting of candles.

At times, the verisimilitude encouraged or demanded by television jarred with the presentational nature of the script. Howell found a practical solution for the always difficult end of 2.3, for here (with an eerie green light coming from below) the boy below in the pit (Martius) is heard but not seen, so through most of this sequence we see one figure above and get only a glimpse of a hand thrust up. The second boy (Quintus), with a spear in his hand, appears to fall into the pit rather than be pulled in by his brother, so the scene did retain some credibility, but the emphasis upon 'hands' in the dialogue became irrelevant.

Unlike many other productions, this Marcus did have a full speech in 2.4, but the artifice of his poetry did not mesh well with the verisimilar stumps and bloody mouth of this Lavinia. Moreover, given the camera and editing choices here, we hear Marcus but primarily see Lavinia (who is closer to the camera), so the elaborate description seems unnecessary. Even though the two actors (Anna Calder-Marshall and Edward Hardwicke) give strong performances, artifice and realism do not mesh well here (as with the boys at the pit). The same problems pertain to 3.1, with the close-ups of two maimed figures, many groans from Lavinia, and glimpses of severed hand and stumps, but the raw power of this scene did come across, thanks to the vehemence of Trevor Peacock's gritty, muscular Titus. Here and elsewhere, moreover, Hugh Quarshie's Aaron brought a distinctive flavour to his scenes, a combination of wit and violence. As at Santa Cruz, this Aaron was especially effective when spelling out the one thing he does value, his son ('This before all the world do I prefer', 4.2.109). In this production, however (as discussed in detail in Chapter V) Aaron is mistaken in 5.1 when he assumes

Lucius's belief in God and conscience and therefore accepts the Roman's oath to preserve the child.

A balanced critique of this rendition is provided by Stanley Wells, who praises many features yet concludes that 'the play's emotional impact is not fully realised', in part because 'the production's most touching figures' (Lavinia and the young Lucius) 'are its least articulate ones'. To Wells, 'the play's tableaux of grief are comparatively unaffecting, partly because the camera dwells too much on the object of suffering, too little on the sufferer' (he cites Marcus in 2.4) and 'partly because the performers do too little to move us'. Wells points to the problems in dealing with the rhetoric of the play which 'may need to be scaled down for television, but it must not be evaded'. He praises Trevor Peacock's splendid beginning as Titus ('a grizzled, sombre warrior with the authority of experience, sternly stoical in the face of grief'), but finds, 'as his sufferings take the centre of the stage', that 'his gravelly voice does not realise the emotion latent in his anguished arias' and that he does not 'create any impression of madness, real or feigned'.

One danger of too much 'realism' and too many close-ups is an overdose of horrors that can turn *Titus* into an equivalent to a slasher movie or lead to a comic-book flattening of the figures (at times Brian Protheroe's petulant Saturninus came close to this effect, especially in 4.4). Strong acting from Peacock, Quarshie, Hardwicke, Calder-Marshall, and Atkins overcame most of these dangers. Moreover, Howell's adept use of young Lucius as a framing device or barometer often screened what was happening through an on-camera consciousness so as to channel the horrors and convey vividly the logic (and the taint) of violence and revenge. Given the many problems in adapting any Shakespeare script, much less this daunting one, for television, Howell's production represents a significant achievement and provides the most 'realistic' *Titus* one is likely to see.

As a final example, consider Brian Bedford's 1978 production for Stratford Festival Canada (remounted with some cast changes in 1980) with William Hutt as Titus. Like Seale, Nunn, Rucker, and Howell, Bedford chose not to stylise the violence and horrors, but neither did he opt for brutal 'realism' with large amounts of gore, highly visible stumps, and verisimilar heads. As Mel Gussow notes (*New York Times*, 14 June 1980), 'stage blood never flows' in this production; rather, when Titus chops off his hand in 3.1, 'he discreetly turns away from the audience', so that the horrors became 'more palatable, but no less palpable'. Similarly, Lawrence DeVine (*Detroit Free Press*, 14 June 1980) praises Bedford for not resorting to 'cheap effects'; rather, the 'suggested horror is more effective than any apparition of stage blood and papier-mâché'. DeVine concludes: 'There is, in short, restraint', and that restraint 'makes the difference between drama and melodrama'. Jamie Portman (*Windsor Star*, 28 August 1978) notes that although this show 'could have been a cacophony of cheap horror', 'instead it is unexpectedly elevated to a level of tragic beauty'. For Portman, Hutt's Titus is therefore 'a miracle of tact and restraint' ('a study in madness' yet 'also a study in tattered dignity'), and Domini Blythe's Lavinia 'conveys a poignancy which is the equivalent of a thousand words'. Julius Novick (*Nation*, 16–23 August 1980) praises the director's 'courageous simplicity and consummate tact', for 'except that we see no blood, the horrors are not stylized'. Nonetheless, 'the horrors do horrify', but 'you would not know from this powerful production how easily they can become ridiculous'. According to Jacob Siskind (*Ottawa Journal*, 13 June 1980), on opening night, 'not a single giggle, not a titter ran through the house', for Bedford 'has moved his players about with such discretion, has kept them under such strict control, that the horrors of the play are that much more terrifying'. Audrey Ashley (*Ottawa Citizen*, 28 August 1978) finds 'the utmost delicacy' in Bedford's presentation of the mutilated Titus and Lavinia, and notes that 'all of these horrors seem to fit right into the dark context of the play rather than being imposed upon it for the sake of effect'.

But a significant number of reviewers saw the production with different eyes. For example, Ralph Berry notes the 'strategic gains' in the director's 'restraint' and 'control', particularly his avoidance 'of anything that might cause the audience to laugh in the wrong place', but this policy also 'incurred its losses in passages that called for greater voltage than Bedford was ready to permit' (*Shakespeare Quarterly*, 30, 1979, 171). Noel Gallagher (*London Evening Free Press*, 12 June 1980) argues that Bedford goes 'perhaps too far in sanitizing the cruel action of the play' and laments the absence of 'even a few drops of blood'. According to Gallagher, 'without that touch of realism, the play takes on a sterile tone' so that 'the final scene features four stabbing victims who might just as easily be succumbing to epilepsy'. Similarly,

Gina Mallett (*Toronto Star*, 28 August 1978) welcomes the absence of a 'stage awash with blood', but nonetheless finds Lavinia's appearance after the rape and maiming 'a little too tasteful' and notes that 'some of the bloodless stabbing evoked guffaws'. Doug Bale (*London Evening Free Press*, 28 August 1978) argues at length against Bedford's de-emphasis of the 'goriness' in a script in which 'blood and blood thirstiness are its theme from first to last'. For Bale, 'every stabbing is discredited by the unbloodied blade that is drawn back from the blow'. If one assumes, as does Bale, that Shakespeare wanted his audience to experience 'an orgiastic wallowing in blood', then it is 'hard to understand why Bedford has done so little to drive home the horrors of it, or perhaps even done so much to suppress them'. Clearly, playgoers committed to 'realism' or to a view of the play linked to 'an orgiastic wallowing in blood' will not be satisfied by what they deem half measures.

To read these widely varying reviews is to confront a basic problem in evaluating any production of this daunting script. Is there indeed a middle ground between the choice to stylise the violence (epitomised by Brook and Freedman) and the choice to provide varying kinds of graphic 'realism' (championed by Seale, Nunn, Rucker, and Howell)? Critics praised both Brook and Bedford for their 'restraint', but by 1978–80 at least some members of the audience expected – even demanded – heads, hand, and gore. Today's director may have more options to draw upon than Brook, for the attitudes of at least some playgoers to on-stage violence or horrors have changed since 1955 (or 1923). Nonetheless, as indicated by the varied reactions to Bedford's rendition, to mount a production of *Titus* in the 1980s or 1990s is still to take on a series of formidable problems and risks.

CHAPTER III

Trusting the script: Deborah Warner at the Swan

Today's director regularly cuts lines, speeches, and even entire scenes from Shakespeare's playscripts. Since modern productions usually incorporate one or more 15-minute intervals into plays originally conceived for uninterrupted 'through' performance, directors concerned with running time (and with spectators anxious to catch the last train home) often choose to streamline their acting scripts. In this process, supernumerary figures are cut or telescoped together so as to economise on personnel, and passages that are perceived as opaque, redundant, or syntactically difficult often disappear. Often the first to go are mythological allusions: so Trevor Nunn (RSC, 1972), Pat Patton (Oregon, 1986), and Mark Rucker (Santa Cruz, 1988) cut the four lines from Aaron's speech in defence of his son (4.2.93–6) that built upon allusions to Enceladus, Typhon's brood, Alcides, and Mars.

Because *Titus* poses more than the usual number of problems for theatrical professionals, its stage history is a history of cuts and other changes. Starting with Peter Brook in 1955, directors have found that one way to bridge the many gaps between the 1590s and today (or to 'translate' *Titus* into our idiom) is to omit from the playing script those passages or moments that are deemed unplayable or flawed. In her television rendition Jane Howell does very little cutting or reshaping (a major transposition in 1.1, translation of some Latin), but most stage productions involve substantial cuts. For example, Brook cut about 650 lines; Brian Bedford made equally extensive cuts; John Barton cut even more in his 1981 Royal Shakespeare Company production so as to present a 90-minute rendition as part of a double bill with *The Two Gentlemen of Verona* (an experiment that was not received favourably by the critics).

As noted in Chapter I, many reviewers of Brook's production were less than enthusiastic about the original script and therefore praised the cuts and adjustments. Daniel Scuro (p. 42) admired Brook's tasteful editing of Shakespeare's 'extravagant poetry and melodrama'. Several reviewers singled out for praise Brook's cutting of the last four words of Titus's line, 'Why there they are both, baked in that pie.' Richard Findlater argues that Brook 'has cut up the play as ruthlessly as its characters dismember their acquaintances', for 'he has lopped off Senecan quotations, hacked away at the worst improbabilities, and abbreviated *Titus* into a convincingly Shakespearean text'. To Findlater, Brook is 'not only a great director but a great bowdleriser', so his 'liberties are abundantly justified' (*Tribune*, 26 August 1955). Similarly, Bernard Levin (*Truth*, 26 August 1955) notes that the director 'has committed upon the text a butchery scarcely less severe than that suffered by most of the people in the play', but, like Scuro and Findlater, he concludes that 'Mr Brook's play is a far better one than Shakespeare's', for in this instance the director 'knew Shakespeare's business better than he did'. According to Levin, only 'by this judicious lopping' does the play gain 'a shape and a dramatic tension that simply did not exist in the original'. Although purists will have fits, 'the rest of us will recognise that a worthy evening's theatre has been fashioned out of what would otherwise have been nothing but an Elizabethan bloodbath with some good lines of poetry floating on the surface like so many rubber ducks'.

In this tradition of cutting and reshaping initiated by Brook, various moments in the script have proved especially vulnerable to the blue pencil. Thus, Brook, Nunn, and Patton all made substantial yet different cuts from the dialogue between Quintus and Martius before they both fall into the pit in 2.3 and from Titus's long vengeful speech to Chiron and Demetrius that ends 5.2. For example, in 2.3 Patton cut lines 225–36, so gone completely were Quintus's question ('If it be dark, how dost thou know 'tis he'?), the long response that identifies Bassianus by means of 'a precious ring, that lightens all this hole', and the allusions to Pyramus and Cocytus. Brook, in contrast, left in Cocytus but cut most of the rest of the scene, including most of Quintus's second speech (ll. 198–202), Aaron's speech (ll. 206–8), and most of the subsequent dialogue (ll. 209–21, 223–32, 234) but left intact the final eleven lines (235–45). Nunn also made extensive (albeit somewhat different) cuts, as did Brian Bedford (who omitted twenty-nine lines) and Mark Rucker (eighteen lines). All five directors omitted all or most of Martius's speech on how he identified the body of Bassianus in the darkness, for, as Patton observed to me, how are we to believe in a ring that glows in the dark?

Comparable heavy cutting took place at the end of 5.2. Brook cut the final nine lines (so that the murders took place off-stage); Nunn cut a total of about fifteen lines, including seven of the last nine; and Patton cut about twelve, including lines 172–9 (left in by most directors) which he felt merely repeat what the audience already knows and thereby slow down the action. In 5.2 and even more so in 5.3 the ritualistic recapitulation by Titus, Marcus, and Lucius of the horrors and indignities done to the Andronici is often pared down, for Patton and other directors find these efforts at justification or legal argument redundant and time-consuming (particularly those passages that come after the death of Titus). Clearly, behind these cuts lies a post-1590s sense of the functions of dramatic speech (and the purposes of the end of this tragedy). For example, at the end of 5.2 in Patton's script, the same point is being made about the pasty that will be served to Tamora in 5.3, but that point is being made more economically (with less spelled out for the audience) so the production *is* tighter – but at the risk of being thinner or losing an element of Titus's need to justify his actions or exult in his power.

As in other Shakespeare scripts, asides are often omitted. Thus, again in 5.2, most directors omit Titus's aside ('I knew them all, though they supposed me mad ...', ll. 142–4) that signals to us that he has not descended into madness to the extent of not being able to recognise Tamora (as she assumes) but rather is playing a part. Without these lines, the audience remains in doubt a few beats longer about Titus's state of mind or control, so that the scene's pay-off or climax is delayed. As in the speeches of recapitulation or justification, at stake here is a different sense of psychological progression or dramatic focus.

Such streamlining of the playscripts found in the quartos or the First Folio is commonplace today. What is particularly revealing about *Titus* is the widespread suppression or adaptation of various passages for reasons analogous to the rationale for substituting red streamers for blood. Certain moments in this script, even in highly stylised productions, cause severe problems for actors, directors, and spectators, so what happens to this playscript in the modern theatre can reveal a great deal about the scenes Shakespeare crafted – and about us.

Consider first Marcus's 47-line speech in 2.4 when he confronts the maimed Lavinia. Brook and Bedford omitted this speech completely; Barton cut 24 lines; Nunn cut 29; Paul Barry (New Jersey, 1977) cut 19; Patton cut 13. Why is this speech so often cut or reduced? Actor Barry Kraft, who had to play the speech uncut (Colorado Shakespeare Festival, 1967), told me it was the hardest thing he ever had to do on stage, for, as he put it, every nerve in his body was crying out 'GET FIRST AID!!!' As noted in Chapter II, Gerald Freedman singled out this moment in his argument against 'realism', for if we start thinking in 'real world' terms we must also ask: 'How could Lavinia suffer such loss of blood and still live?' or 'Why doesn't Marcus take her to a hospital instead of talking?' So here, as with Titus's speeches in 3.1, the modern interpreter must confront a different pre-realistic sense of style, an alternative approach to dramatic speech or rhetoric (typical of early Shakespeare and the drama of the late 1580s and early 1590s, including *The Spanish Tragedy*). Faced with an audience that may have seen a Neil Simon comedy or *Cats* the previous night, today's director will usually pare down such a speech which, to the modern ear or eye, seems ornate, even leisurely, rather than an anguished reaction to this horrible sight. To many today, the passage appears flawed, overdone, with lines 29–32 (the image of the 'conduit with three issuing spouts') deemed particularly offensive or problematic (e.g., critic S. Clark Hulse complains that 'Marcus might be describing a broken water main, not his niece', 'Wresting the Alphabet', p. 110).

Not all theatrical renditions, however, have been unsuccessful or problematic. Thus, Paul Barry reports that Marcus's speech 'turned out to be one of the most moving moments' in his 1977 production. Rather, given a strong actor playing Marcus (e.g., Larry Paulsen in Oregon, 1986), the moment can have considerable theatrical power. Paulsen broke his thirty-four lines into thirds, for he started above (so, initially, he saw Lavinia from a distance), then descended a staircase to confront her, and finally wrapped and nurtured her in his cloak. Similarly (as noted in Chapter II), Brad Myers (Santa Cruz, 1988) delivered the latter part of his forty lines while giving first aid (four of the seven omitted lines were linked to the maligned 'conduit with three issuing spouts'). Shakespeare, moreover, does provide here a series of scripted signals to break down the long speech into discrete moments or beats. For example, Marcus notes first the severed hands (ll. 16–21), then, after 'why dost not speak to me?', the severed tongue, at which point he invokes the Philomela story ('But sure some Tereus hath deflowered thee / And, lest thou should detect him, cut thy tongue'). Line 28 then reads: 'Ah, now thou turn'st away thy face for shame.' The modern editor's insertion of a comma after the 'ah' (not found in the quarto) masks the potential signal in the metre, for if, in keeping with the iambic foot, Marcus says 'ah *now*', Lavinia's reaction is linked closely to the preceding Ovidian analogue (she had not turned away in shame until 'now').

A further question blurred by our habits of reading or staging is: what does or should the maimed Lavinia look like at this point? Specifically, would she have been or should she be bleeding or exhibiting visible blood? Thus, if Marcus's elaborate account of the blood issuing forth is a verbal description of what a spectator is seeing, the accusation of gilding the lily would hold up (as may be true with the close-ups of the brutalised Lavinia in Howell's television version). But if the full horror lies in the combination (on an Elizabethan non-representational open stage) of: (1) a distressed but not visibly bleeding Lavinia, and (2) the words provided by Marcus, this speech performs a somewhat different function. Would or should the conduit with three issuing spouts be provided by Lavinia and blood capsules or is that image to be generated by the poetry in combination with the imagination of the spectator?

Also of interest are the consistent cuts made in 3.1. At one extreme is Brian Bedford who cut 140 of the 299 lines, including lines 103–29, 162–91 (the quarrel over who should supply the hand), and all of Lucius's final speech. Other directors have used their blue pencils primarily on Titus's impassioned speeches, for, although Olivier made famous the 'I am the sea' speech (ll. 218–32), few theatrical professionals today can resist paring down considerably the rhetoric of this long, intense scene. For example, Brook, Nunn, Williamson, Bedford, and Patton cut from seven to eleven lines of Titus's speech to Lucius on why 'I tell my sorrow to the stones' (ll. 37–47). Similarly, all five directors made elaborate (but not the same) cuts from Titus's speeches to Marcus and Lavinia before the entrance of Aaron. Brook and

Bedford, for example, took out the entire sequence involving Marcus's napkin (ll. 136–49), so Olivier and Hutt did not, in a 'sympathy of woe', interpret for Lavinia or reject a handkerchief already saturated with Marcus's tears. The Oregon actors also lost these lines and many of the preceding ones as well (e.g., ll. 114–19, 122–9), so, here as elsewhere, the rhetorical emphasis upon tears and grief was greatly diminished.

Particularly revealing in this context are the repeated modifications made in the *exeunt* in which Marcus carries one head, Titus carries a second in his remaining hand, and Lavinia carries off Titus's hand in her mouth ('Bear thou my hand, sweet wench, between thy teeth', l. 281). Here, to avoid an unwanted response, a climactic and highly theatrical image is often altered or omitted entirely (exceptions are Colorado, 1967, RSC, 1972, New Jersey, 1977, Santa Cruz, 1988, and BBC TV). Interestingly, both Brook and Freedman did not *have* to cut or change this *exeunt* because they were using the New Temple edition in which M. R. Ridley, following one editorial tradition, emended this passage so as to eliminate the reference to hand-in-mouth. Many directors today are unwilling to risk an audience's reaction to the image of Lavinia exiting with the hand like a puppy carrying off its master's slippers (although, for the original audience, the image might rather have recalled a trained hunting dog carrying its master's quarry).

Various moments in this tragedy that trouble today's directors may therefore provide windows into distinctively Elizabethan effects and procedures. To confront squarely what is deemed 'unplayable' today may lead us to a greater understanding of what was workable or meaningful then. Note also that what is 'unplayable' for one director often turns out to be 'good theatre' for another. For example, director Paul Barry (New Jersey, 1977) told me that Quintus and Martius at a very deep pit worked well for him ('the two boys, very athletic strong young men, made it frightening rather than funny').

To observe the cuts and changes can therefore be revealing in a variety of ways, especially when directors on two different continents not aware of each other's work cut the same things. All such choices involve trade-offs wherein the director decides to forego passage A in order to gain or preserve effect B. In making such decisions about most of Shakespeare's scripts, the issues at stake are usually economy and playing time, but in *Titus* the problems are linked as well to rhetoric, to seemingly inappropriate responses, to violations of 'realism' (e.g., a ring that glows in the dark, a forty-seven line speech in lieu of first aid), and to what are perceived as risky stage images or configurations. At stake as well may be our post-Elizabethan sense of emotional or psychological truth (especially in 2.4 and 3.1), and our assumptions about the function or possible functions of dramatic speech (e.g., in 5.2 and 5.3). Our notions about dramatic rhetoric, especially as a means for expressing emotional or psychological states, may not always correspond to the views or practices of an age still enraptured by *The Spanish Tragedy* and Marlowe's mighty line (as reflected in the cuts in Marcus's speech, in Titus's rhetoric in 3.1, or in various passages in 5.2 and 5.3).

To cut or otherwise to alter the received script of *Titus* is therefore to tame the beast, to translate what appears to be Shakespearean overkill or overwriting into our idiom. To include *all* the scenes, lines, and stage imagery (as in James Sandoe's 1967 Colorado Shakespeare Festival production) is certainly no sure ticket to success and may, in fact, involve considerable theatrical (and box-office) risk. So wherein lies the incentive to stage the play uncut?

An answer is provided by the 1987 Royal Shakespeare Company production at the Swan Theatre in Stratford-upon-Avon (remounted in 1988 at the Pit in the Barbican) directed by Deborah Warner. New to the RSC and Stratford, Warner was best known for her work with the Kick Theatre, a 'Fringe' group in London that specialises in minimalist productions. Thus, in contrast to Brook's meticulous advance planning for all elements of his 1955 production, Warner started with no overriding interpretation (or music or design concept), but rather assembled the best actors available, actors who *wanted* to do this script, and then went through, scene by scene, confronting each problem as it emerged, with her designer (Isabella Bywater) on hand, making sketches, so as to adjust design and costume choices to those ongoing decisions. The word repeated constantly among *Titus* personnel was 'trust': trust in the script, in the audience, in the Swan (a major component in the success of this show), in each other. What then emerged was a production vastly different from its predecessors that, like Brook's rendition in 1955, had a profound effect upon many playgoers.

Unlike most productions (whether of *Titus* or other Shakespeare plays) the design or 'look' of this production evoked no specific period. Thus, classical Roman overtones were evident in the togas and armour worn by some figures, but the hair-styles were modern as were the shoes and at least some of the clothes. The set, as noted by Charles Spencer (*Daily Telegraph* 6 July 1988), consisted 'of scrubbed wooden boards' reminiscent 'of a butcher's shop, clean and gleaming before the start of the day's business'. In addition, Warner gained some striking effects with distinctively unRoman images or objects (e.g., an aluminium ladder, a naked light bulb in 5.2 to define Titus's study, a chef's hat). Indeed, according to Robert Hewison (*Sunday Times*, 4 July 1988), a major source of the power of this production was its 'stripped simplicity of means' that 'enables us to feel the terror of a bucket, cheesewire, and a little stage-blood'.

Rather than starting with a concept, Warner predicated her production upon an uncut script (as set forth in J. C. Maxwell's Arden edition), taking the liberty only of translating '*Terras Astraea reliquit*' (4.3.4). As can be seen from Ravenscroft to the present, to tackle all the scenes and passages in this daunting play is to take various risks. To take those risks, however, is to test various hypotheses about *Titus* that have hardened into facts. Thus, to the surprise of many observers, scenes that editors, scholars, and directors have stated firmly were unplayable emerged in this production as powerful and highly meaningful. Indeed, playgoers I queried who were still feeling the impact of the show had difficulty believing that Brook and Bedford had cut all of Marcus's 47-line speech in 2.4 and Nunn and Barton had cut about half of it. Nor did such playgoers feel that Titus's speeches in 3.1 should be pared down considerably or that the arrow-shooting scene is embarrassing or that the various horrors are risible, not moving. Rather (thanks in part to the intimacy of first the Swan, then the Pit), playgoers who had not been told they should demand a scaled-down rendition of this supposedly primitive play were caught up by the narrative and at times overpowered by the total effect.

Let me start by returning to that maligned moment, Marcus's forty-seven-line reaction to the maimed and ravished Lavinia. As noted earlier, editors and readers have complained that the speech goes on interminably and only tells us, in florid and inappropriate terms, what we already know or can see for ourselves. But what if that image of Lavinia as a fountain spouting blood is not the stage picture visible to the viewer's eye but rather is a product of Marcus's poetic rhetoric in conjunction with the imagination of the audience? Thus, in this production, as H. R. Woudhuysen points out (*TLS*, 22 May 1987), 'blood is used sparingly and, almost always, on white linen': marks on the heads of the brothers after the sacrifice of Alarbus; blood on the white bag that contained Titus's hand; ample blood at the murders of Chiron and Demetrius (suddenly and shockingly visible on Titus's white apron). In 2.4, Lavinia's plight was therefore signalled not by visible blood or by silken streamers but by a coating of clay or mud, by what appeared to be hastily applied wrappings on her stumps, and by the abject posture of Sonia Ritter's shamed, half-crazed figure. As demonstrated here, Marcus's imagery *can* be theatrically potent if his words do more than merely convey to the audience's ears what their eyes have already seen.

Much depends, moreover, on how those words are delivered. For Stanley Wells (*Shakespeare Survey*, 41, 1988), one of the overall strengths of this production was that 'the rhetoric was plumbed for its deep sources, which were then brought to the surface so that even the most artificial verbal structures become expressive of emotion'. Although Marcus's speech 'may read like a heartless verbal exercise by a bright boy from the local grammar school', when 'spoken in Donald Sumpter's hushed tones it became a deeply moving attempt to master the facts, and thus to overcome the emotional shock, of a previously unimagined horror'. Wells came away with 'the sense of a suspension of time, as if the speech represented an articulation, necessarily extended in expression, of a sequence of thoughts and emotions that might have taken no more than a second or two to flash through the character's mind, like a bad dream' (see Figure 6).

Warner's potent effect was keyed as well to what we see before Marcus appears, for this Lavinia was preceded on stage by a mocking, sub-human Chiron and Demetrius (Richard McCabe and Piers Ibbotson) who not only provided the savage comments recorded in the script but also viciously mimicked her crawling on her elbows (what the three actors privately referred to as 'the snail dance'). For Mary Harron (*Observer*, 17 May 1987), the beginning of this scene crystallised the most terrifying thing about this play – the characters' absolute lack of pity. Here and elsewhere Harron finds no bonds except those between parent and child and 'even that is more like wild animals protecting

6 Donald Sumpter as Marcus and Sonia Ritter as Lavinia in Deborah Warner's Royal Shakespeare Company production at The Pit (1988).

their young' and can break down, as when Titus kills Mutius 'as casually as if he were breaking an egg'.

At Marcus's blithe entrance, Lavinia, standing but barely able to hold herself together, is in a downstage corner, her back to her uncle. What follows then, despite the appearance on the page, is a two-actor scene, wherein we observe Marcus, step-by-step, use his logic and Lavinia's reactions to work out what has happened, so that the spectators both see Lavinia directly *and* see her through his eyes and images. In the process, the horror of the situation is filtered through a human consciousness in a way difficult to describe but powerful to experience (so as to produce what many observers felt to be the strongest single moment in the show). At the first of the passages notorious among *Titus*-bashers (Why dost not speak to me? / Alas, a crimson river of

[65]

warm blood, / Like to a bubbling fountain stirred with wind, / Doth rise and fall between thy rosed lips ...'), Sonia Ritter provided the only blood of the scene – not a river (or a ribbon) but a trickle from her mouth that elicited shocked gasps from the audience. Midway in the speech Marcus finally does hold and cradle his niece, a position he maintains for the rest of the scene. His 'do not draw back' in the penultimate line sets up one last bit of stage business, for this Lavinia (both here and in 3.1) cares not only about her shattered self but also about the impact her fate will have upon her father.

If this scene works (or is allowed to work), other results follow. First, an audience that, step by step, has experienced the shock along with Marcus is better prepared to witness Titus's comparable yet different reactions in 3.1. In addition, if Marcus (especially as played by Donald Sumpter) is allowed his full range of reactions and images in 2.4, he can more readily emerge as one of the major figures in the play – a voice of reason in 1.1 (as a politician above the fray and a pleader to Titus first on behalf of Lavinia, then for the burial) and compassion who, although driven to rage at the appearance of the two heads and hand, retains his reason and detachment through most of the play, only to be shocked at Titus's entrance as chef in 5.3 and shattered by the series of murders. His rising from his chair (the same chair in which Titus had killed a Lavinia seated on his knee) and his ascent to deliver his speeches after the murders were then slow and painful. To take away all or part of the forty-seven lines in 2.4 is to change this progression and to diminish the full resonance of this important role. Often the voice of reason in the play (as with his solution for Lavinia's communication problem in 4.1), this Marcus was not unaffected by madness and revenge, whether in his passion at the appearance of the heads and hand in 3.1, his indictment of the heavens at the end of 4.1, or his shock at the (to him) unexpected events of 5.3. Overall, as noted by Michael Billington (*Guardian*, 14 May 1987), Sumpter's Marcus 'movingly embodies the ineffectualness of reason'. Indeed, Marcus as enacted here struck me as a preview of Horatio, another figure identified with reason and control as opposed to passion, who also at the climax of his play runs up against the limits of that control.

Thanks to some fine acting and inventive staging, other 'unplayable' moments also came across with great force. The clown (omitted completely by Pat Patton) as played by Mike Dowling (who doubled as Bassianus) was actually funny, especially in his encounter with Titus in 4.3. For example, Dowling got a great deal of mileage out of his basket which turned out to carry not only the pigeons but also ink, pen, paper, knife, and just about anything called for by Titus. Tamora's often-cited second description of the woods as 'a barren detested vale' (2.3.91–115) was played by Estelle Kohler as a joke or deliberate exaggeration, so that Bassianus, Lavinia, and the audience laughed as Chiron and Demetrius pantomimed the hissing snakes and swelling toads. The pay-off was an even greater shock when an apparently funny moment erupted into violence (an effect enhanced by the unfamiliarity of much of the audience with this script). Elsewhere, the scene involving two boys at the pit did not elicit audience laughter; rather, Quintus, except when actually kneeling in the attempt to pull up his brother, circled the open trap so as to use his lines to convey agitation and concern. Significant here were the excellent acoustics of the Swan and the close proximity of most of the audience, for, although below, Martius's words could be heard distinctly. Thanks to some energetic acting and forceful staging, the moment was intense, not unintentionally funny.

As noted in previous chapters, productions since 1955 have gone to some lengths to avoid eliciting unwanted laughter from the audience. This issue of when laughter is or is not elicited was also central to this show and to some of the most provocative choices made by Warner and her cast. Thus, Michael Billington notes that Warner's 'wiliest tactic is to pre-empt possible laughter at the play's grosser cruelties by launching them in a spirit of dangerous jocularity' (he cites Tamora's account of the 'barren detested vale') so 'the horror when it comes is all the greater'. Similarly, Mary Harron sees the building of 'a thrilling momentum ... in which laughter and horror become inseparable' so, for her, this Titus starts as 'semi-buffoon' who 'rises to a blackly ironic power'. For Stanley Wells, 'acknowledgement of the comedy in the situation when Titus, Lucius, and Marcus squabble over who shall have the honour of losing a hand in the hope of saving Titus' sons intensified the pain of the moment when Titus outwits the others by getting Aaron to mutilate him while they have gone to fetch an axe'. For H. R. Woudhuysen, Warner's production 'moves unerringly between high tragedy and the most painful comedy' so that 'the audience is allowed to laugh, but at the right moments' and is made to feel that here 'laughter need neither be innocent nor happy'.

Much of the credit for this distinctive tone and for the overall success of the production can be attributed to the actor playing the title role. For Billington, Brian Cox as Titus 'combines a quirky, senescent humour with a tremendous bottled danger'; he kills the fly 'with a savage table-turning zest that is a terrifying prelude to his later calculated revenge' but still manages to convey 'strong pathos'. According to Wells, 'Cox established Titus as a credible, human character by making him a bit of a card – an odd, shambling hero, very much a law unto himself.' Thus, midway in his first speech (at 'sheathe my sword', 1.1.85), he stopped and, humming to himself, absent-mindedly pawed at a Tamora whom he held by a rope attached to a slave collar. At a whispered cue from Lucius, Cox slapped his head ('Titus, unkind and careless of thine own') and focused upon the burial of his sons. This moment encouraged laughter, as did an audible grunt when Titus prostrated himself before the newly crowned Saturninus. Also in his first speech – at 'Romans, of five-and-twenty valiant sons, / Half of the number that King Priam had' – Cox 'defensively isolated the second line', as Wells notes, 'as if to counter accusations of excessive breeding'. Later, this Titus put his fingers in his ears to block out what he knows will be telling, reasonable arguments from Marcus in behalf of burying Mutius (see Figure 7). Overall, such choices yielded a curious but effective mixed tone at the outset that, especially in an intimate theatre where nuances can be noted and appreciated, set up what was to follow.

For this first appearance, Cox provided a leathery, gritty, battered field soldier (an effect enhanced by Cox's stocky muscular posture and the covering of clay on him and his sons), already more a statue than a man, who knows only killing and does everything by the numbers (so to return to Rome is to sacrifice a captive). For Michael Billington this Titus was a 'working warrior' in 'dusty, ashen, hempen costume'. To Charles Osborne (*Daily Telegraph*, 14 May 1987) Cox was 'an elderly, beaten-up Albert Finney'. For Mel Gussow (*New York Times*, 16 August 1987) Cox provided 'a peasant warrior, grizzled, plain-spoken and given to outrageous fits of temperament'. Michael Ratcliffe (*Observer*, 10 July 1988) describes Cox's Titus in 1.1 'as an old bull

7 Brian Cox as Titus in Deborah Warner's Royal Shakespeare Company production at The Pit (1988).

and warrior – eccentric, bloated on victory over the Goths, eyes wild and mind unfocused by exhaustion' with a face that 'is a muddy, grizzled map of blind service and catastrophe'. Cox's voice, continues Ratcliffe, 'makes a sound like a strangled brass: a gentle persuasiveness rises to a pitch of ringing hysteria and beyond to wild cackles of disbelief that break all the rules of melody and expressiveness with idiosyncratic confidence and success'.

When taking action, this Titus, in Gussow's terms, became 'a tank on the warpath'. Faced with the rivals for the crown, he proves a believer in primogeniture so to him the choice is obvious. He cannot see his children or anyone else as individuals (Mutius merely represents an object in his path and Tamora a plaything, not a person), so not until 3.1 does he see what is happening to *his* sons and daughter. Rather, he expects, even takes for granted, Rome's gratitude. The covering of clay on Titus and his sons was never washed off (clay rather than visible blood was the keynote for this show) so as to convey a primitive quality, a Rome on the edge of civilisation. Rather, other figures (first Lavinia in 2.4, later Marcus, gradually, as his 'reason' is affected) added the clay to themselves.

One pay-off from such distinctive choices in 1.1 comes in later moments with comic or ironic potential. For example, Titus often evokes laughter when he first chastises, then praises Marcus for killing the fly in 3.2, so the scene can seem an unintended comic intrusion into the world of tragedy (as was the case in the 1974 Oregon production where audience laughter punctuated and undercut this moment in a damaging way). Cox, however, not only accepted such laughter but, at the point of stuffing bread in his mouth with his one good hand, compounded the effect by diving over the table and scattering food and utensils in his anarchic thrust to destroy this stand-in for Aaron. To Wells, 'Cox made a marvellous moment of the transition, represented in the text only by "O, O, O", from the tragicomic absurdity of his initial reaction, through dawning acceptance of the validity of Marcus' excuse, to the ferocity of frustrated despair with which he cast himself on the table, repeatedly stabbing at his enemy's surrogate.' Wells concludes: 'This was masterly acting.' Similarly, in the final scene Cox not only entered dressed as a cook (in white with a chef's hat) but, carrying the meat-pie, he walked in *over* the banquet table so as to startle those on stage and in the audience. Again, in the arrow-shooting of 4.3 this Titus managed to combine humour, madness, and some telling truths, as was also true in his sparring with Tamora in 5.2. By allowing or calling forth laughter as early as 1.1, Cox therefore made possible a wide range of effects or reactions later in the play. Indeed, without such humour (or without disarming the playgoer in 1.1), some subsequent scenes (especially 4.3) become extremely difficult to bring off (as attested by other productions).

The key scene, the ultimate test for any Titus (as demonstrated by Olivier) is 3.1, but, to my knowledge, since 1955 only James Edmondson (Colorado, 1967) had played all the lines. But Cox felt strongly that a Titus must go through *all* the steps to expose as much as possible and thereby set up the full effect (for him, the equivalent of a pustule breaking). Since, in his terms, all the lines are earned, to cut a line is to short-circuit the process. At the outset, in his hapless appeal to spare his two condemned sons, Titus was still connected to Rome, still a believer in justice and the state. But after seeing Lavinia, this Titus disconnected himself, as signalled by his discarding the armour that he had worn since 1.1 (at 'for hands to do Rome service is but vain'). The effect was enhanced by some shrewd staging. For example, the messenger who brings in the heads and hand did so slowly, put the three objects (in white bags) on the floor upstage, and then paused so as to set up a strong moment that enhances our sympathy for Titus (and provides a sense of some Romans who support him). As in other productions, Lavinia's move to comfort Titus (after all that has been done to her) was also a powerful moment.

The 'I am the sea' passage made famous by Olivier was also very powerful here and was enhanced by a Lavinia whose heaving sighs provided a sea-like sound, but the climax came after the return of the heads and hand when Cox, his back to the audience, first delivered his powerful one-line speech ('When will this fearful slumber have an end?') and then, after the raging speech of the previously reasonable Marcus, provided a long, chilling laugh that signalled his total break with Rome and with ordinary humanity ('Why, I have not another tear to shed'). The scene ended with the three figures exiting and then standing upstage with their backs to us; Lucius (Derek Hutchinson) then delivered his strong speech, part of it on his knees; then, after his exit, the three put down the heads and hand (which stayed in view upstage) and moved downstage to the 'table' (created by a rising lift in the trap, the same centrally placed trap that had been the tomb and the pit) to set up 3.2. The ritual that climaxed the scene – a flip of one head to Marcus and the giving of the hand to Lavinia (placed in her mouth and quickly wrapped round by her stumps) – did elicit some audience laughs, but, given the preparation in 1.1 and the long build-up in this scene, by this point shock, irony, and laughter were so intermingled that no 'normal' reactions were possible. The effect was stunning.

In the next movement, Cox chose to undergo a gradual stripping in Act 4 (although his intent was not to emulate Poor Tom or Lear). Thus, in 4.3 he appeared for the arrow-shooting with rolled up trousers and with a knotted handkerchief on his head (so as to prepare for the cook image in 5.3), an image that drew upon the images of both 'Grandfather at the Sea' and a road-digger (in keeping with the desire set forth in the dialogue to reach to the centre of the earth). When he next appeared in 5.2, Cox was above, wrapped in a cloak, surrounded by reams of writing, with bloody words revealed to be etched on his chest. To Cox, the series of steps or stages that starts with the shocks of 3.1 is necessary for Titus, who must go through everything in order to face his impotence and realise there is no justice. Marcus was thereby the Gloucester to his Lear, a figure who can go down the road with him but is not a man of action. Indeed, this Titus at times patronised Marcus as a younger brother (e.g., 'a young huntsman', 4.1.100) not equipped to understand the harsh realities of revenge, violence, and politics.

As to Titus's madness, Cox saw an analogy to Hamlet where at times the line between madness and control is very thin, sometimes invisible. At the outset, Titus can kill without thinking, almost as a reflex (as with Mutius), but soon he has no children – only a banished Lucius and a sub-human Lavinia who in the final two scenes (as played by Sonia Ritter) has lived so long with the memories of Act 2 as to become catatonic. The long process acted out in 3.1 is then a digging into self, a movement to a deeper level that is first signalled in the appalling laugh (instead of the rage anticipated by Marcus), then the arrow-shooting speeches of 4.3, and finally the chef image of 5.3. To Cox, however, Titus is sane enough to recognise Tamora in 5.2 and to outfox her so as to set up his revenge.

In addition to Cox's Titus and Sumpter's Marcus, the two women also were distinctive presences in this show. Mel Gussow describes Estelle Kohler's Tamora 'not as a wicked witch but as a queenly bird of prey, at once sensual and manipulative'. For Charles Spencer, Kohler was a 'splendidly sexy Tamora, a woman who finds violent death the most erotic sexual turn-on of them all'; for Annalena McAfee (*Evening Standard*, 7 July 1988) this Tamora 'stalks the stage like a hungry cat, more claws than paws'.

Equally distinctive was Sonia Ritter's Lavinia. Initially a loving daughter in a golden gown, she appeared in 2.4 as a drab, crawling sub-human creature, caked with clay, characterised by intermittent, jerky movements (Ritter here drew upon the image of a wounded bird or horse that alternates between stillness and flight). The power of this image carried over into 3.1 and greatly enhanced the sense of Titus's tragic situation (as in Ritter's keening sea sound during 'I am the sea' or her slow, painful stage cross in order to kiss Titus). Especially potent was her frustration in 4.1 at her inability to communicate what had happened to her, for here she repeatedly thrust her stumps into the air (as in the American signal for a football touchdown) so as to signify two attackers, but little or nothing got through to Titus and Marcus. When she did communicate by means of the three words written in the sand (using her stumps but not her mouth to guide the staff – a choice many playgoers found suggestive and troubling), she conveyed vividly a sense of euphoria at this breakthrough, an initial reaction that was soon followed (once events had passed her by) by a let-down that was acted out in a slow, shambling exit upstage during Marcus's closing speech.

In her Act 5 appearances, this Lavinia then showed neither shock nor relish but rather seemed neutral, above the fray, nearly catatonic (she played her part in Titus's plans but left it to the men to make the decisions). Another slow exit carrying the bucket filled with the blood gleaned from Chiron and Demetrius was accented by Ritter's obvious difficulty in carrying what, thanks to the added weight of the liquid, had become a heavy object. Overall, Ritter responded to the challenges in Lavinia's silences in a powerful and often disturbing fashion that signalled her status as a reflection and, as a result, a victim of the men in this Rome.

To work with an uncut script of *Titus* is to take on other challenges as well. Thus, given the intimacy of the Swan and the Pit, a strong feature of this production was the potency of the asides, not only the mocking ones from Aaron but also those from Titus (in 5.2), from young Lucius (in 4.2), and particularly from Tamora (the end of 1.1), where Estelle Kohler found some Richard III-like dimensions in her asides that I would not have believed possible from my reading of the script. Given the proximity of the audience and the absence of any illusion of 'realism', actors in the Swan and the Pit can reap large dividends from their asides and other conversations with the spectators.

Working with a cast of limited size, Warner had to find inventive alternatives for densely populated ensemble scenes. So, at the outset, first Saturninus, then Bassianus raced on to the stage to address us with great intensity as if we were their 'factions'. Marcus (but no senators or tribunes) then appeared above to resolve the conflict. Thanks to the intimacy of the two theatres and the clarity and force of the presentation, most playgoers were immediately caught up and involved in the developing action so as to feel themselves part of an event (an effect particularly strong at the Pit where actors could be placed in the aisles between the wedges of spectators) and therefore did not miss an on-stage crowd of Romans. Some of the scenes that followed did involve a significant number of actors (most notably Titus's spectacular Tamburlaine-like entrance in 1.1 seated on a ladder held horizontally by Aaron and Tamora's three sons), but, in general, Warner avoided ensemble scenes. For example, when Saturninus entered in 4.4 irate at the arrows shot by Titus, he was addressing not a full court but only Tamora and her two sons, all of whom had obviously been rousted out of bed. Elsewhere, some effects were curtailed. For example, at the beginning of 3.1 Titus did not have tribunes to address; at the end of 2.3 the two boys and the body were not taken out of the trap and off-stage (so omitted was a possible link to Titus's entrance in 1.1 with prisoners and a body, the latter deposited in the trap).

The most controversial choices then came in the final sequence. To set up the banquet table, Warner brought on a full complement of actors – whistling, in a minor key, the work song of the seven dwarves. These eight actors then sat in two rows of four, facing each other, to serve as a chorus that reacted to the series of murders with sounds and motions (a stylised effect, the only such in the show, that blunted any laughter at the staccato killings). But, after the four deaths, this group of eight exited, so that the remainder of the production focused upon a small group of figures rather than a crowd of on-stage 'Romans'. Aemilius did speak his lines from behind the spectators; several actors, also in the back, shouted out 'all hail' as needed. But the appeals by Marcus and Lucius for vindication from Rome were delivered not to an on-stage crowd but to the audience and to a few actors scattered around the theatre (so that the spectators were enveloped by the action or situation).

The effect of this staging was mixed. On the plus side, the final movement was handled smoothly and economically, with a strong focus upon family ties and on putting the pieces back together. As H. R. Woudhuysen points out, moreover, the Swan audience 'is clearly implicated in the action by the opening and closing scenes'. This climactic sequence, however, did not display to us an on-stage group being swayed (or not swayed) by the rhetoric and arguments of the surviving Andronici. As a result, even though the moment did work in its own terms, some of the potential political tension was blurred or lost.

To see a strong rendition of this script without all the familiar cuts can therefore be very enlightening. According to Woudhuysen, this production 'keeps theatrical tricks to a minimum' and 'takes refuge in neither a ritualistic, nor a symbolic, nor an abstract approach, yet its naturalism is kept in check'. In Billington's terms, if this production works, it does so 'because it throws the burden on the acting and the language', and because Warner renders it 'with burning conviction of its worth and discovers the humane values under the mountainous horrors'. Wells notes as well that, 'like any strong production, this one impelled its audience to revalue the play'. Since this script 'stood in greater need of revaluation than most of its author's works', he concludes that 'this production gave it what it needed at this point in its history', so that *Titus* 'emerged as a far more deeply serious play than its popular reputation would suggest, a play that is profoundly concerned with both the personal and the social consequences of violence rather than one that cheaply exploits their theatrical effectiveness'. According to Wells, 'subsequent directors will have far less excuse than before for evading its problems by textual adaptation or by evasive theatricalism'. In terms of this and previous chapters, twin insights emerge: that laughter (when under control) *can* mix with tragic effect in renditions of this script; and that, given the right conditions, the 'unplayable' can become the theatrically potent.

CHAPTER IV

Problems then and now

Every staging of *Titus* elicits comments about the daunting nature of this script. For example, in his reaction to Trevor Nunn's 1972 rendition, Irving Wardle argues that a major problem in any production is how to present the 'succession of horrors' in *Titus* 'without relapsing into monotony or unintended farce'. Similarly, in his review of the Swan production, Stanley Wells notes the 'twin problem' posed by this script.

> How do you stage its horrors – murder, rape, mutilation, cannibalism – without driving the audience over the bounds of credulity into giggling hysteria? And how, on the other hand, do you cope with its self-conscious literariness – the Latin quotations, the extended similes, the long, rhetorical speeches uttered by characters who according to any normal standards of behaviour should be capable of nothing but shocked speechlessness or gibbering idiocy?

Starting with Ravenscroft, directors, actors, and adapters have wrestled with such questions or problems and have arrived at a variety of strategies to stage or contain this script. Many of these strategies involve substantive changes; a few do not. Thus, for many playgoers at the Swan and the Pit Deborah Warner's production worked – with no cutting of the script and very little stylised action. Given the right variables, Titus is indeed playable, as has also been demonstrated by other productions, most notably Peter Brook's (with its very different approach to the original script and to music, set, design, and style).

However, as seen in the widely varying approaches taken by Brook, Warner, Douglas Seale, Gerald Freedman, Trevor Nunn, Brian Bedford, Pat Patton, Mark Rucker, and Jane Howell, various problems continue to bedevil the theatrical professional who takes on *Titus*. A director or actor may succeed in avoiding unwanted laughter at a potentially grotesque moment (or, in the case of Brian Cox, may elicit such laughter so as to gain a striking effect), but, even in a highly stylised production, the actors still must present a 'reality' that makes sense to their audience in psychological, political, or familial terms or risk losing the attention of that audience. Questions about 'consistency' or 'truth to life' recur in reactions to all of Shakespeare's plays but those questions become especially prominent in reactions to *Titus*.

To stage *Titus* today is therefore to take on a series of challenges. In addition to the problematic areas cited in previous chapters, theatrical professionals point in particular to the difficulty in bringing off the first scene. Admittedly, some problems (or silences) apparent to the first-time reader can readily be resolved on-stage. For example, Saturninus's choice of Lavinia as his empress and the subsequent interference by her brothers, Marcus, and Bassianus are not prepared for in the dialogue but can easily be signalled by the actors. In Patton's production, for example, Bassianus and Lavinia were visibly linked as lovers (a union evident to everyone except Titus), so that Saturninus made his choice so as to spite his brother-rival, a choice that clearly shocked Lavinia and her group (although Titus in his blindness welcomed it as an honour).

But Titus's series of choices in 1.1 are not as easily resolved, so every actor must work out his rationale, a rationale that, in turn, will condition if not control the rest of his interpretation. Particularly instructive here are the comments of Patrick Stewart, who played Titus in John Barton's 90-minute 1981 rendition for the Royal Shakespeare Company. To Stewart, one of the two major difficulties in playing Titus is getting Act 1 right. As with several actors I talked with (perhaps influenced by Maxwell's introduction to his Arden edition, the scholarly text most often used as a script), he was not convinced that Act 1 was written by Shakespeare. Rather, in his terms, performing Act 1 is like being a handicapped runner in a race, with the language, images, and rhythms the weights that hold you back. In contrast, as one moves into Act 2 he feels the play tighten and gather pace as various restraints fall away, so that the actor can take off and fly in Act 3 when the language begins to soar. Thus, to Stewart, one of Shakespeare's greatest moments comes when, after hammer blows of horror have fallen on Titus's head, he can respond from his waking nightmare: 'When will this fearful slumber have an end?' (3.1.251). At the height of a character's suffering, Shakespeare here finds a simple phrase that locks tragedy into the everyday human experience.

Not only the poetry poses a problem, for, more important, Stewart finds Titus's actions in Act 1 hard to justify. As he sums it up, here we have a protagonist who returns a conquering hero and at once, from a position of power, makes some stupid and quite potty mistakes, so that his irrational behaviour, hubris, and stubbornness set in motion the train of horrific events. Titus shows no compassion for Tamora; he refuses the crown (his only sensible act); in his position as kingmaker he then chooses an unsuitable, unstable hysteric; he kills his son, refuses him proper burial, insults his few friends, and, having been humiliated, then patronised by the Emperor, invites him to go hunting.

The problem then for both the actor and his audience is: who cares what happens to a cruel, stupid, reactionary old man? Like other actors, Stewart found his answers in Titus's warrior past. To him, this returning hero is first and foremost a soldier and, moreover, an arch conservative, who has spent his life at the outposts of the Empire. For the last ten years he has been fighting Goths; twenty-one of his twenty-five sons have been killed (the allusion to half the number of Priam's sons in line 80 provides an indication of how he sees himself). He therefore anticipates general respect for his accomplishments when he returns, but, in fact, he is a child in the ways of Rome, politically naive, particularly in his expectation that everyone else shares his warrior's sense of honour. Because he is so out of step with the times, one mistake leads to another, so that we come to see and pity the vulnerability of this unworldly figure in this Rome as he helps to unleash the wilderness of tigers that in turn will prey upon him and those he loves.

Stewart therefore chose to play Titus as, in Michael Billington's terms, 'a ramrod-backed Roman Monty' (*Guardian*, 4 September 1981), a figure with a white moustache (but Jacobean doublet and hose) and an upper-class, military bearing who has totally lost touch with current politics but rather lives by the old, traditional values (and hence appears to be an antique in the eyes of the 'new' Rome). When Tamora (kneeling in chains) pleads for the life of her son Alarbus, this Titus cannot understand why she is making such a fuss. Rather, to him such a sacrifice is necessary, obligatory, a fact of nature (so why argue about it?); indeed, he sees Alarbus as being dignified by this sacrifice so, in a sense, the Romans are doing this Goth a favour by so ennobling him (hence Stewart can justify Titus's belief that Tamora at the end of 1.1 will be on his side). In his burial speech, moreover, Stewart notes that Titus talks of the dead as being better off than the living (e.g., 'here lurks no treason, here no envy swells ...', l. 153). To Titus and his sons, the necessary rituals (here the 'Roman rites' of lopping Alarbus's limbs) and the sense of honour are 'real' whereas the young Saturninus and the Romans who have stayed at home (including Marcus) are not. Both Stewart and Brian Cox see a huge generation gap between Titus and Saturninus-Bassianus (who were only children when he last was in Rome), so, as Cox argues, Titus would without question pick the elder to be emperor because he assumes the eldest son would be the best trained (as is true of his own Lucius).

Stewart, like other actors who have played Titus, therefore found a major key to the choices of 1.1 in this warrior's rigidity, his adherence to a code by which he lives, however much that code may be out of phase with the 'new' Rome. An anecdote from James Sandoe's 1967 Colorado Shakespeare Festival production can illustrate this rigidity, for actor James Edmondson wanted to deliver line 92 from Titus's first speech – 'O sacred receptacle of my joys' – with the modern pronunciation of 'recep*tacle*'. The director, however, insisted on '*recep*tac*le*' in keeping with the metre, for, as Sandoe argued and Edmondson came to agree, a rigid Titus, who did everything 'by the numbers' and according to the rules (as in his choice of Saturninus to be Emperor), would never break the metre but rather would bend the word to fit it.

That rigidity is also singled out by Alexander Leggatt in his unpublished account ('Playing Titus') of the 1985 Trinity College Dramatic Society production at the University of Toronto. For Leggatt, the opening scene sets up the basis of this character that he describes as 'conservative and hidebound, unreflective and unfeeling: a hard surface that later events will shatter'. Drawing upon Kenneth Tynan's account of Olivier (cited in Chapter I), this Titus was 'dog-tired from his umpteenth campaign' and therefore, like Lear, begins the play 'assuming that he's finished, assuming that his life is settled and complete'. The initial speeches and the decision about Alarbus, characterised by a 'formal, unreflective quality', were therefore merely formulas, matters of routine that did not seem momentous. For Leggatt,

Act 1 'creates a character: narrow-minded, a bit dense, automatically dedicated to state and ruler' so the method here 'is quite different from that of the rest of the play' where 'we watch the wrenching transformation of a slow and stubborn nature'. At the outset, Titus may be shocked or bewildered by the actions of Lavinia, Marcus, or Saturninus, but he does not feel 'strongly or deeply', for 'his hide is too thick'.

The second major problem in playing Titus, according to Stewart, is that of endurance. Building upon a comment from Olivier, he notes that Titus is 'a punishing role' not because of its size but rather because of the suffering the figure must undergo, for it can be exhausting when a character is a victim rather than a motivator. For the bulk of the play Titus is, in effect, saying: 'Oh, please don't do that to me. No, No. Oh, you've done it and it's all dreadful. It can't be any worse. Yes, it is. Now this has happened and it's very much worse.' Similarly, in his review of the Swan production (*Shakespeare Bulletin*, September/October 1987), Gerald M. Berkowitz observes that 'it is Warner and Cox's insight that Titus thinks he has reached bottom in act one; he is feeling the greatest amount of pain he has ever felt', but the play proceeds 'to rain more and more pain upon him' so as to test 'how such a man will cope when the unbearable is continuously made worse' (p. 16).

Such bearing the unbearable, according to Stewart, is especially trying and relentless for the actor who has to find variety and freshness, line by line, so as to prevent his speeches turning into one long complaint or a series of shouts (as can also happen with Timon of Athens). In addition, since Titus is old (like Lear but unlike Othello and Macbeth), his stamina is limited and his capacity to take punishment is low, so he is quickly pushed to his physical limits. If the actor is not watchful, notes Stewart, he can exhaust his resources too; so director John Barton, citing the danger in allowing the emotion to take over, told Stewart: 'Stay cool within the part.' Stewart recognised this dictum as good advice, but found it hard to accomplish in acting terms, especially when you have just had your hand chopped off and your children are being dismembered around you. Stewart did find it possible to find such 'coolness' in his first reaction to Lavinia in 3.1, for the shock of seeing her, maimed and tongueless, numbs him, so that for this segment it is as if he is standing outside himself, watching the events as if they were happening to a third person (he also finds here a sense of detachment in the language). But how does one stay detached during what follows, especially in the overflowing emotions that build to 'I am the sea'?

For Stewart, Titus can never become a truly tragic figure – in contrast to a Lear who passes through madness to insight. Rather, Titus's suffering only leads him to the ultimate in revenge, so retribution and retaliation become his philosophy. His Titus (again, in a streamlined version) therefore had no larger recognition or breakthrough and was in essence mad after 3.1, so that the fly scene, the arrow-shooting, and even parts of the final banquet (where he appeared in an apron with a chef's hat and flour on his face) were played so as to encourage bizarre laughter.

Stewart's formulation aptly sums up some major problems facing the actor who takes on Titus today. Other problems also emerge in staging Titus or *Titus*, some of them generated by the gap between us and the 1590s. Since many difficulties arise when we interpret plays of our own age scripted in our idiom with many revealing stage directions, how much more difficult is it to read and interpret a script from another age written in what is often a lost language of the theatre with few authentic stage directions to guide us. As noted in previous chapters, when faced with the anomalies that inevitably result, directors often cut or adapt such a script or stylise the action so as to sidestep unwanted effects. James Sandoe (Colorado, 1967) and Deborah Warner, in contrast, did choose to play the received script, warts and all, but still with modern actors and modern playgoers in mind.

In the light of the performance history set out in Chapters I–III, consider then this question: to what extent would those moments that have puzzled or antagonised adapters and directors since Ravenscroft have made more sense or have 'worked' in the 1590s? A Shakespeare early in his career crafted this script for playgoers, players, and theatres that no longer exist, so what happens when today's theatrical professionals reconceive that script for another, very different space or medium (with the translation to television more extreme than that to the modern stage)? To what degree, then, are our problems with *Titus* a result of such a reconception or translation and therefore linked not solely to the play's defects but also to the passage of time and to the consequent changes in notions about theatre, imagery, decorum, and 'realism'? Thus, some of the supposed anomalies or howlers perceived by actors, directors, editors, and teachers may seem less daunting when viewed as integral parts of a larger pattern or sequence easily blurred by post-Elizabethan theatrical practice.

As a point of departure, consider one gap between then and now that playgoers today take for granted (as part of *our* unacknowledged assumptions about 'going to the theatre') that in turn poses a problem for the director: where to place an 'Interval' (UK) or 'intermission' (USA)? Throughout most of his career, Shakespeare would have seen his plays performed continuously, from start to finish, with no breaks between acts or scenes. Around 1610, however, the fashion changed, so that performances in the public theatres gradually began to follow the practice of the private theatres in having brief pauses, with musical interludes, between the acts. Elizabethan and Jacobean audiences would therefore have been comfortable with either procedure (continuous flow or act pauses) but would have been surprised by the single 15-minute break that playgoers today take for granted. As a result, the imposition of such a break on a dramatic strategy predicated upon a continuous flow of action will of necessity introduce changes and often a new set of problems. For example, in making such a decision today's director must not only be concerned with where to stop (some kind of climactic moment) but also where to start up again, for the dramatist, who was not thinking in terms of such a decisive stop and start, did not provide that director with a scene that would re-engage an audience once again settling into their seats after a chat and a drink.

An occasional modern stage production of *Titus* may be played with no break (e.g., Oregon, 1974, New Jersey, 1977, Barton, 1981), but, given the expectations of today's audiences, most directors will introduce an interval after either 3.1 (so the closure of part one comes with the ritual involving hand and heads and with Lucius's soliloquy) or 3.2 (so the closure comes with Titus's attack upon the fly). If the break comes after 3.1, the director will usually make some adjustments so as to smooth over a potentially awkward transition, for in the Folio at the end of 3.2 Titus leaves the stage with young Lucius who at the outset of 4.1 enters pursued by Lavinia. As part of his streamlining, Brook cut the last two speeches of 3.2 (ll. 79–85) and the first twenty-nine lines of 4.1, so this Titus moved directly from his gloating over his ability to kill the fly to his question: 'How now, Lavinia? Marcus, what means this? / Some book there is that she desires to see' (4.1.30–1). In his Oregon rendition, Pat Patton made fewer cuts but did rearrange some lines from the end of 3.1 and the beginning of 4.1 so as to have Titus start to exit, then sit on the stairs with young Lucius, who is then frightened by Lavinia.

The transition between 3.1 and 3.2 has also been managed in a variety of ways. In the abbreviated Barton rendition (with no intermission), after Titus put the severed hand in Lavinia's mouth, he and Marcus (carrying the heads) then exited with her in a Dance of Death effect with Lavinia leading the way and Titus behind her with his hand on her shoulder (young Lucius was also involved in this procession). The four figures did a half-circle and were briefly out of sight behind a screen (so as to drop the heads and hand) during Lucius's speech, then immediately returned for 3.2. Similarly, Warner had her three figures with heads and hand move upstage, put down their objects, stay silent with their backs to the playgoers during Lucius's speech, then turn and return to begin 3.2. To quiet the spectators and bring them back into the mood or flow of the show (no easy matter after the intensity of 3.1–3.2), Warner had her Titus in deep concentration start to trudge from side to side upstage while the lights were still up during the interval (which came after 3.2), gradually covering the terrain and moving closer to an audience that, in his self-contained deliberation, he did not acknowledge.

The need for an interval/intermission, along with a potential problem in the transition between 3.2 and 4.1, therefore leads to a series of adjustments. Of the various issues at stake here, perhaps the most interesting is the question of elapsed time. One assumes when Marcus brings the maimed and ravished Lavinia to Titus in 3.1 that there has been no significant lapse in time between this moment and the end of 2.4, so Lavinia here is usually presented as we saw her in 2.4. But how much time should be felt to elapse between 3.1 and 3.2 or between 3.2 and 4.1? In such spaces, do the characters (or actors) have an opportunity to wipe off the blood, change to other garments/costumes, and come to terms with some of their woes, or are we meant to feel a thrusting forward of events with no respite? To cite two extremes, in Howell's television version Lavinia remains the same bloodied figure from 2.4 to 4.1, so the viewer gets the impression of a continuous, headlong action. In contrast, Mark Rucker and his actors at Santa Cruz, keying their sense of elapsed time to Tamora's bearing a child in 4.2 that Saturninus would accept as his own, felt the need for a significant gap between 3.1 and 3.2, so after the intermission (placed after 3.1) Titus and particularly Lavinia appeared in fresh costumes with bound, unbloodied limbs.

Such choices present to the spectator very different senses of the amount of time taken by Lavinia (and Marcus) to find a way to communicate what has happened and, equally important, the amount of time Titus has been brooding over his wrongs. The quarto, which lacks 3.2, shows no signs of any space between 3.1 and 4.1; the Folio, where 3.2 first appears, does have an act break between 3.2 and 4.1, but neither quarto nor Folio would support the kind of decisive punctuation signalled by a 15-minute interval. Warner's choice to have a visible pacing Titus was ingenious and, given the intimacy of the Swan, highly effective, but whether in terms of theatrical rhythms or an audience's sense of elapsed time a later playgoing convention has subtly impinged upon the original strategy or effect. Indeed, the more powerful the rendition of 3.1 and 3.2, the more significant (and potentially damaging) is this break in the flow.

As a second example, consider the moment in the Swan production that worked least well for me – the appearance of Tamora, Chiron, and Demetrius in 5.2 disguised as Revenge, Rapine, and Murder. This lapse into allegory or near allegory poses problems for every production, even if (as was the case here) the actors are assuming a mad or nearly mad Titus and a Tamora so confident in that madness that she is willing to take on a disguise that clearly would not 'work' for a sane figure. To enhance the credibility of the moment, directors usually resort to a darkened stage (to heighten the possibility of concealment), heavy make-up, and some kind of outlandish disguise for the three figures. For example, in Howell's television rendition the costumes, according to Mary Maher, 'connote a kind of morality-play feeling', with Tamora 'in a dark-purplish silk robe that was dyed to create the effect of dried blood' (p. 148). Masks for the three were considered but rejected; instead 'the faces of the characters were made up to look like masks' so that 'Tamora's make-up is white with grey shadows that shape her face into a skull' and her sons have slanted black slashes across their eyes. For Maher, the impression created is 'of forest animals, perhaps raccoons or wild birds of prey'.

In the Swan production, however, the Revenge disguise was a white laced shawl for Tamora and no change in costume for the two boys; moreover, by the time Titus (with lines on his chest written or carved in blood) came down from above (see Figure 8), Tamora had discarded the shawl. Titus's aside (5.2.142–4), cut by most directors, can be important here, for the audience too could easily assume he is mad and has totally lost control (to Brian Cox, he *is* mad, but can still tell Tamora from Revenge).

According to Estelle Kohler, a great deal of thought was given as to how to play Tamora's disguise as Revenge but, taking her cue from the reference in the script to 'this strange and sad habiliment' (5.2.1), she took the view: why bother with an elaborate costume to deceive a figure assumed to be mad? For her and the other actors, the overriding political dimension of the scene (the need to lure Lucius back to Rome) took precedence, so the soon-to-be-discarded shawl was chosen so as not to deflect from that focus.

At least part of the point of the moment as scripted in the quarto, however, lies not in Tamora's attitude to disguise or Titus's presumed madness but in the 'image' of Revenge (along with Rapine and Murder) set up for the playgoer. What Shakespeare provides, at least in his terms, is an individual (here Tamora) who for a moment 'becomes' Revenge, a process certainly not irrelevant to Titus himself (whether mad or not) in the last two scenes of this revenge tragedy. In *The Spanish Tragedy*, perhaps the single greatest influence upon this play, Revenge appears with Don Andrea at the outset and remains onstage throughout. We do not know how that figure was costumed either (that Prospero sets up Ariel as a harpy for a major revenge speech in *The Tempest* 3.3 *may* provide a clue), but the presence of a figure of 'Revenge' in the 'real world' of Titus's Rome was at least possible in the theatre of the early 1590s.

Several apparently incompatible elements are at work here. On the one hand, actors today working within our available theatrical vocabulary make their many interpretive choices with modern playgoers in mind, but they are working with scenes and speeches originally scripted in what can be a different, even alien shared vocabulary for actors, playgoers, and theatres of another age. Our dominant mode of psychological realism (would such a 'character' say or do x in this situation?) does not mesh comfortably with a figure posing as Revenge, even if that pose is to

8 Brian Cox as Titus, Estelle Kohler as Tamora, Richard McCabe as Chiron, and Piers Ibbotson as Demetrius in Deborah Warner's Royal Shakespeare Company production (1987).

deceive a supposedly deranged figure with 'miserable, mad, mistaking eyes' (5.2.66). But given the theatrical vocabulary available in the 1590s, Shakespeare may have had more rather than fewer options than a dramatist confined to 'realism'. For example, in a dramatic romance published at about the same time as *Titus* (*A Knack to Know an Honest Man*) a banished figure in disguise as a hermit announces his name to be Penitential Experience. In the early 1590s such mixing of allegorical nomenclature and 'literal' action, if not widespread, is at least possible.

Consider then the assets of having this visible epitome of Revenge, however costumed, announce that she has been 'sent from th'infernal kingdom / To ease the gnawing vulture of thy mind / By working wreakful vengeance on thy foes' (30–2). Of particular interest here is her demand: 'come down and welcome me to this world's light' and, a few lines later, 'come down and welcome me' (33, 43). Here, in a simple yet highly emphatic fashion, Titus's acquiescence to Tamora-Revenge's twice repeated 'come down' clearly brings him from some removed position above to her level below. Such a movement downward is characteristic of many Revenge plays (whether that 'below' is Hell or subterranean psychological forces) and, moreover, is set up forcefully in this play in the arrow-shooting scene where Publius brings word to Titus that Justice is not available (being employed 'with Jove in heaven, or somewhere else') 'but Pluto sends you word / If you will have Revenge from hell, you shall'. Titus responds that Jove 'doth me wrong to feed me with delays'; rather, 'I'll dive into the burning lake below, / And pull her out of Acheron by the heels' (4.3.38–45). Most editors gloss 'her' in line 45 as 'Justice', but equally likely is a confusion between Justice-heaven and Revenge-Acheron-hell, a confusion that feeds into Tamora's appearance in disguise with her request for Titus to 'come down'. The link, moreover, can be enforced in the theatre; for example, in the Santa Cruz production Tamora-Revenge entered bearing an arrow with the message still attached, thereby suggesting that her appearance was in response to his quest in 4.3. Here, Titus can therefore act out his literal and figurative descent to the level of Revenge, a descent that, by the end of 5.2, yields the bloodiest moment in a bloody play and leads to the ultimate in revenge, the Thyestean banquet of 5.3.

To focus upon Tamora's overconfidence and Titus's madness (or, in other productions, upon darkness and a well-crafted disguise), then, is to provide a workable scene in terms that make sense to playgoers today but, perhaps, to diminish the full range of the original effect. Although perhaps distant or even inaccessible today, the acting out of Revenge as a force that can take over an individual, along with the descent of the title figure to the level of that Revenge, has a stark power and elegant simplicity that anticipates and feeds into the events of the final scene.

To see other potentially meaningful signifiers in that theatrical vocabulary available in the 1590s, consider also the links between 'imagery' and 'place'. Thus, when we read of a scene involving a tomb (1.1), a forest (2.3–4), a bloody pit (2.3), or a study (5.2), we readily conjure up (in the theatres of our minds) appropriate pictures; directors often will then provide us with some version of those images in their productions. But, given the exigencies of Elizabethan playing, a spectator in the 1590s would not have seen a 'set' or other elaborate representation of tomb, forest, or study but rather would have watched some mimed action involving minimal properties (e.g., books, perhaps a table for Titus's study) and the permanent parts of the stage (e.g., the doors or trap-doors). As is true throughout Shakespeare's plays, the creation of 'place' is a joint effort by the actors (who provide signals in their words, properties, and gestures) and the spectators, who with their 'imaginary forces' piece out or eke out the rest (a process Shakespeare calls attention to in a series of choric passages in *Henry V*).

Consider then some theatrical signals found in the quarto: for example, in 1.1, *'They open the Tomb'* (A4v); *'Sound Trumpets, and lay the Coffin in the Tombe'* (B1v): and *'they put him* [Mutius] *in the tombe'* (C1r); and in 5.2: *'They knocke and Titus opens his studie doore'* (I3r). Most readers today will readily infer on-stage objects or structures from such stage directions, but, as Richard Hosley points out, Elizabethan dramatists often provide 'fictional' rather than 'theatrical' signals that help to tell the story to a reader (*Enter on the walls*) rather than providing purely theatrical instructions for an actor (*Enter above*). Two obvious 'fictional' stage directions in this play are: *'They goe up into the Senate house'* (A4r) and the judges *'passing on the Stage to the place of execution'* (E3r).

If we do take seriously such signals about 'place' in the quarto, what difference do they make to our understanding of the script? Here, the choices made by Jane Howell are especially revealing, for she consistently broke down the original scenes into smaller segments so as to provide changes of place more suited to the naturalism encouraged by television. For example, in both the first and last scenes of her production the 'tomb' (where bodies are deposited) was a distinctively different 'place' from the Senate house or throne room or Titus's house. Moreover, the forest (with a tree, a grassy carpet, and a pit) was visually distinct from the city, as was the locale for 5.1 where Lucius and the Goths confront Aaron. But in his original script Shakespeare crafted all these scenes for the same neutral (or potentially neutral) space so that the distinctions among such moments were not based upon such detailed scenic 'realism'. For example, Tamora's two speeches that present diametrically opposed descriptions of the same woods ('the birds chant melody on every bush' of 2.3.10–29 versus the 'barren detested vale' of 91–7) will 'mean' something different when spoken on a forest 'set' replete with trees and greenery (so one of the two passages appears to be wrong or a deliberate exaggeration) as opposed to when spoken on an unadorned platform stage (where, in a variety of ways, both passages can be 'right' – e.g., as descriptions of psychological as opposed to physical environment). On television and in many stage productions, post-Elizabethan approaches to staging supersede the original rationale in which the 'place' was neutral until defined by the poetry and the actors.

Similarly, the absence of a clearly delineated tomb or study and the reliance instead upon the 'imaginary forces' of the audience can change the actual stage picture available to a spectator and, in turn, change the 'imagery' of the production. For example, many directors today like to set up linked scenes wherein a striking image or configuration at one point in the production is clearly echoed or recapitulated elsewhere. Such analogous actions can also be seen or inferred in Shakespeare's (and other Elizabethan) plays, but today's reader or playgoer is less likely to catch such links as originally scripted when the original signals are not heeded. To cite one possible example (noted by some readers), if the tomb in which two bodies are placed in 1.1 is, in fact, a stage trap-door (as at the Swan), that same 'place' could also become (1) the 'pit' in 2.3 for Bassianus, Quintus, and Martius and (2) the place for Aaron's final punishment as indicated in the dialogue (all distinctly different 'places' in Howell's television production). The option also exists in the final scene of placing one or more of the murdered figures in the trap-tomb-pit. For example, in 5.3 of Williamson's 1974 Oregon production Tamora's body was thrown into the trap and Aaron was tied to a grated trap-door and lowered below. Such possibilities, however, although consistent with the signals and silences in the quarto, are easily blurred by today's stage pictures and assumptions about 'place'.

Other suggestive stage directions also set up images or potential links. Consider some details in Act 2 linked to the hunt or chase: '*Enter* Titus Andronicus, *and his three sonnes, making a noise with hounds & hornes*'; then '*Here a crie of Hounds, and wind hornes in a peale*' (D1r); so eventually, just before he discovers the maimed Lavinia, '*Marcus from hunting*' (E2r). Elsewhere in the age of Shakespeare, hunting scenes are common, with the woods or forest suggested not by a 'set' but by the green costumes of the hunters, their horns and characteristic sounds, and the weapons they carry (usually bows or javelins).

As many critics have pointed out (especially Alan Sommers and Albert Tricomi), the image of the hunt and the forest is central to this play, as set up by Aaron ('The woods are ruthless, dreadful, deaf, and dull. / There speak, and strike, brave boys, and take your turns', 2.1.128–9) and summed up powerfully in Titus's lament that Rome has become 'a wilderness of tigers' and 'affords no prey / But me and mine' (3.1.54–5). The manner in which the literal on-stage hunt is established in Act 2 can then determine how effectively the metaphoric sense of the hunt is realized and appreciated in Act 3 and thereafter.

Of particular interest here, in terms of 'imagery', is how we are to interpret '*Marcus from hunting*'. If he is carrying the carcass of an animal, that summary image of what he has been doing offstage would provide a jarring comment upon the state of the Lavinia he discovers. If he is carrying a bow (with bows also evident earlier), that property highly visible here in this charged context with Lavinia could anticipate the arrow-shooting of 4.3. Indeed, given appropriate costumes and properties, the action in the often puzzling 4.3 could seem, according to the stage conventions of the 1590s, to be a second hunt scene (just as 5.3 is a second banquet scene after 3.2), with the target not the deer or even Lavinia, 'this dainty doe' (2.1.118) for Chiron and Demetrius, but (1) Astraea-Justice, (2) Revenge, and (3) Saturninus and his court. But many of these links or associations remain blurred or strictly on-the-page notions if the sequence in Act 2 is anachronistically translated into a 'forest scene' in our terms so that the original 'images' (that established that 'forest' in Elizabethan terms) are gone or diminished.

Of similar potential interest to the imagist is the stage direction that Titus appear *'like a cook, placing the dishes'* (5.3.25), an odd costume immediately called to our attention by Saturninus's question: 'Why art thou thus attired, Andronicus?' Titus's answer ('Because I would be sure to have all well / To entertain your highness and your Empress') has not satisfied many directors (e.g., Howell and Patton) who therefore do not present a decidedly different image here of the revenger; in contrast, Patrick Stewart and Brian Cox used this appearance as cook or chef to elicit laughter. For the original audience, such a costume (along with 'placing the dishes') would have served as part of a theatrical shorthand to denote the 'place' (a banquet room) and would have suggested (wrongly) a subservient Titus debasing himself in degree in order best to serve his Emperor and Empress.

But to ignore this distinctive costume or to play it for laughs may be to blur a climactic image that brings into focus various motifs in the play linked to appetites, feeding, and revenge. Thus, the Folio stage direction for 3.2 indicates *'a banquet'*, but Titus opens that scene with the order: 'So, so, now sit, and look you eat no more / Than will preserve just so much strength in us / As will revenge these bitter woes of ours' (1–3). By the end of the play, however, revenge has become linked not to abstinence but to feeding and appetite, usually in dangerous or self-destructive terms. For example, in her overconfident claims to Saturninus, Tamora promises to 'enchant the old Andronicus / With words more sweet and yet more dangerous / Than baits to fish, or honey-stalks to sheep'; the fish, she notes, 'is wounded with the bait', and the sheep 'rotted with delicious feed' (4.4.88–92). The most potent orchestration of 'appetite' or feeding is found in Titus's long speech at the end of 5.2 (a passage referred to by the cast in Leggatt's Toronto production as 'the recipe'). Here the revenger first torments the muted Chiron and Demetrius with a detailed account of what he is going to do to or with them (e.g., 'I will grind your bones to dust, / And with your blood and it I'll make a paste'), then promises to 'make two pasties of your shameful heads', and finally announces that he will 'bid that strumpet, your unhallowed dam, / Like to the earth swallow her own increase' (186–91). After his command that Lavinia 'receive the blood' and a second reference to paste and heads, Titus '*cuts their throats*' and announces 'I'll play the cook' so as 'to make this banquet, which I wish may prove / More stern and bloody than the Centaur's feast'.

When Titus enters to set up the banquet in 5.3 (with or without a cook's costume), the spectator is therefore well prepared. The savage ironies in his lines, moreover, are anything but subtle: starting with 'although the cheer be poor / 'Twill fill your stomachs; please you eat of it' (5.3.28–9); building to 'Will't please you eat? Will't please your highness feed?' (53); and climaxing, in response to the Emperor's command to fetch Chiron and Demetrius: 'Why there they are, both baked in this pie, / Whereof their mother daintily hath fed, / Eating the flesh that she herself hath bred' (59–61). Indeed, these lines and the overall effect have seemed excessive to some directors; Brook, for one, omitted 'baked in this pie' and moved line 53 ('Will't please your highness feed?') earlier (after line 34).

But what is (or would have been) the effect if Titus does appear '*like a cook*' (as predicted in the closing lines of 5.2) and, in this odd costume, does call emphatic attention to his culinary role as he hovers around the banqueters? In imagistic terms, what has so far been primarily verbal or aural (animals 'rotted with delicious feed') now is being displayed visually, not only in the pasties being consumed by Tamora and others but also in the purveyor of such delicacies, Titus, who sets up the feeding of (and himself feeds upon) his enemies so as to become a visible part of the appetitive revenge process (just as Tamora had 'become' Revenge in 5.2). The image of the revenger as cook builds upon what has gone before (as with Barabas and his carpenters at the end of *The Jew of Malta*) and, especially as italicised here by both the costume and Saturninus's question, brings to a climax the feed-and-be-fed-upon imagery earlier linked to the hunt and to the 'wilderness of tigers', a wilderness in which *both* families have now become prey. The same man who in 3.2 had urged his family to refrain from eating now sets up the meal for others and feeds upon his revenge. Moreover, if Aaron, or Tamora's body, is placed in the trap-door, this cook-revenger has generated a feast that parallels and supersedes the 'detested, dark, blood-drinking pit' and 'fell devouring receptacle' (2.3.224, 235) that had claimed Bassianus, Quintus, and Martius. In short, at the climax of this revenge process, 'Titus like a cook' makes very good sense indeed.

Note that the 'images' singled out here have been blurred or eclipsed for different reasons. In some instances, the evidence about the original stage picture is thin or non-existent. Thus, without a videotape of a production from the 1590s, no one can prove that the absence of a visible 'tomb' in 1.1 made clearer a link to the three figures in the pit of 2.3 or that the absence of a clearly delineated 'forest' enhanced the hunt as an image (including the arrow-shooting of 4.3). In contrast, other moments that appear odd or anomalous to the director today (e.g., Titus as cook) *are* signalled in the quarto. That such signals do make sense in terms of theatrical or climax imagery should therefore alert us to a rationale at work that may prove awkward in today's theatre but, nonetheless, does have an integrity of its own. As is also true in the directorial streamlining of this play's rhetoric and verbal imagery (e.g., in 3.1), theatrical professionals (and many other interpreters) place great emphasis upon 'realism' in the narrative and in the motivation of the characters, but, especially in this early Shakespeare script, the images (for both the ear and the eye of the spectator) can be especially strong and can exhibit their own logic and consistency. Our sense of theatre or staging, often controlled by unacknowledged assumptions about naturalism, can at times collide with the rationale behind a playscript designed for a pre-realistic stage without any pretence to 'theatrical illusion' at a time when the major literary event was the appearance of Books I–III of *The Faerie Queene*.

By far the best example of such theatrical imagery is provided by some obvious and not so obvious on-stage images linked to hands and parts of the body (perhaps the most often cited recurring image in this play). First, Lucius asks Titus for Alarbus: 'Give us the proudest prisoner of the Goths, / That we may hew his limbs', a request that is countered by Tamora's plea on behalf of her son. The artist who supplied the so-called Peacham drawing (see Figure 1) here depicts a kneeling Tamora, her hands together in the traditional posture of imprecation. But after the mother's plea is rejected, Lucius returns to report: / See, lord and father, how we have performed / Our Roman rites. Alarbus' limbs are lopped, / And entrails feed the sacrificing fire.' As used here 'See' may direct the eyes of Titus and the spectator to actual lopped limbs or to a sacrificial fire or to some neutral space to be enhanced by our imaginations; regardless, Tamora's plea on the basis of family bonds ('And if thy sons were ever dear to thee, / O, think my son to be as dear to me'), probably linked to hands clasped in prayer, is rejected in favour of lopping limbs ('And with our swords upon a pile of wood / Let's hew his limbs till they be clean consumed'). If our reaction to this sequence corresponds to Tamora's ('O cruel, irreligious piety!'), that reaction will then condition our understanding of Marcus's plea to Titus to take on the empery 'and help to set a head on headless Rome' (he responds: 'A better head her glorious body fits / Than his that shakes for age and feebleness').

The pleading hands (here rejected) and the lopped limbs then set up the revenge sequence of Act 2. Clearly, Lavinia's plea to Tamora echoes Tamora's earlier unsuccessful plea to Titus, a parallel noted by Tamora herself ('Remember, boys, I poured forth tears in vain / To save your brother from the sacrifice, / But fierce Andronicus would not relent', 2.3.163–5) and one that can be enhanced (especially on a bare stage without a forest 'set') by having this second pleading woman kneel with clasped hands. The fate of Alarbus now becomes the fate of Lavinia (*'her hands cut off, and her tongue cut out, and ravished'*), a violation that receives extended commentary first from Marcus (in the forty-seven line speech) and then from Titus in 3.1.

A less obvious link to the emphasis upon hands and failure of bonds, however, is to be found in the intervening passage when first Martius falls into the pit that holds Bassianus's body and then, after much emphasis on the reaching of hands, Quintus falls in as well. As noted in Chapter III, however, this moment poses severe problems in modern productions geared to the 'logic' or yardsticks of 'realism' or 'naturalism'. A director will reason: the scene is to demonstrate the failure of one brother (Quintus) to pull another (Martius) out of a hole in the ground. Therefore, if the audience is to believe in the attempt and the failure, that audience must have a sense of the depth of the pit and the difficulty of the task. In Oregon, 1974, Laird Williamson therefore placed Martius out of sight beneath the stage (with the result that his lines were muffled) and Quintus on his knees reaching down into the trap (with the result that some of his lines and most of the action were lost to the viewer). Such a staging may then satisfy the logic of realism, but the scene fails. The audience sees only the ignominious, unintentionally funny fall of the second brother with no apparent point at stake.

But what if this moment brings into focus not only the fall but, equally important, the hands emphasised in the dialogue ('help me with thy fainting hand ... reach me thy hand, that I may help thee out ... thy hand once more')? What if the joined hands are not only visible but are central to the action? Consider the effect if Martius, regardless of 'realism', is visible from the shoulders up so as to display clearly the link to a kneeling (perhaps even standing) Quintus. The eye of the spectator would then be focused on the joined hands, a familial bond that not only fails to rescue the fallen figure but brings down a second figure as well. That this failure is sandwiched between Lavinia's unsuccessful plea to Tamora and her re-entry without hands makes the link even more compelling, especially if we remember Tamora's ineffectual plea in 1.1 and the subsequent lopping of Alarbus's limbs.

The emphasis upon Lavinia's plight is furthered by Marcus's forty-seven lines and Titus's reactions in 3.1 and then pushed to the extreme by the introduction of the two heads and Titus's severed hand. The *exeunt* in 3.1 that troubles so many interpreters can then epitomise, in one strident image, all that has gone before, for how better to act out the violation of the personal, family and political body than to have severed heads carried in the hands of two old men and the warrior's severed hand carried off in the mouth of the violated woman? How better express the Andronici as prey to the wilderness of tigers or the chaotic disorder of the body politic or the failure of traditional norms?

This set of images has thus been orchestrated for both the ear and the eye of the spectator during the first three acts. We hear more about 'hands' when Titus castigates Marcus for his reference to Lavinia laying violent hands upon herself (3.2. 22–30) and see another relevant image in 4.2 when Aaron takes the baby from the nurse and holds his child in one hand, his sword in the other, to counter the threat from Chiron and Demetrius. Titus again calls attention to his handless state when facing Tamora as Revenge (5.2.17–22) and, in reducing Tamora's two sons to blood and paste, pushes beyond the previous violations of hand, head, and chastity to act out his revenge.

The climax of this sequence in 5.3 then comes not with the four murders but with Marcus's appeal to the Romans ('have we done aught amiss?') and his offer, if judged guilty, that 'the poor remainder of Andronici / Will hand in hand all headlong hurl ourselves, / And on the ragged stones beat forth our souls.' He concludes: 'Speak, Romans, speak, and if you say we shall, / Lo, hand in hand, Lucius and I will fall.' The response is: 'Come, come, thou reverend man of Rome, / And bring our emperor gently in thy hand, / Lucius our emperor.' Marcus here seeks to counter the previous disjunction of hands and parts of the body: 'O, let me teach you how to knit again / This scattered corn into one mutual sheaf, / These broken limbs again into one body.' The image of this 'reverend man of Rome' hand in hand with the future emperor can (in one interpretation) provide a theatrical answer to the failure of just such a union at the pit of 2.3.

To cite this patterned development of the parts of the body is certainly not to 'solve' the many problems facing today's interpreter of this script nor does this analysis take into account all the possibilities in this linked group of images. But this sequence does include some of the most bizarre actions in the play (e.g., the hand-in-mouth exit, the two boys at the pit) and calls to our attention a rationale that, at least for the original actors and audience, may have informed a series of moments. As witnessed by the achievements of some fine actors and directors, this daunting playscript *can* be brought alive and *can* convey much of its original power today, but, as with all of Shakespeare's plays – but especially with this one – some effects and strategies may not translate smoothly or readily into our idiom. At least some facets of Shakespeare's *Titus* are likely to remain of an age and not for all time.

CHAPTER V

The sense of an ending

Although many different areas of *Titus* have posed problems on the stage and on the page, without question, the densest concentration of such problems and anomalies (as perceived by today's directors, critics, and editors) comes in the final scene. These moments or choices, moreover, vary widely in nature. Some are linked to grotesque or violent actions (Tamora eating the meatpie, the three rapid murders); some arise from problems perceived in the quarto text (e.g., who speaks several speeches); some result from pregnant 'silences' wherein matters important to any interpretation are unresolved in the script. Several of these problems are masked from the casual reader, for, with little fanfare, editors make emendations or insert stage directions that can have major interpretive significance for the users of their editions (who are often unaware that such decisions have been made). Other choices that can have large interpretive significance, moreover, are easily ignored by the reader or even the director (e.g., what happens to Aaron's child). A close look at some features of 5.3 can therefore provide a useful conclusion to a 'Shakespeare in performance' approach to this difficult script.

First, consider the segment up to the deaths of Lavinia, Tamora, Titus, and Saturninus. For obvious reasons, spectators will be more than usually alert to Tamora's approach to the cuisine, so directors often find ways to heighten the suspense. Thus, as Richard David described Peter Brook's production, 'A slow see-saw of two bass notes, a semitone apart, wrought the tension of the final scene to an unbearable pitch, and ceased abruptly, with breath-taking effect, as the first morsel of son-pie passed Tamora's lips.' In Pat Patton's 1986 Oregon rendition, only Tamora and Saturninus sat at the table to partake of the banquet, so these two figures were highlighted while the audience and the remainder of those on-stage (including Lucius) looked on.

Exactly how Tamora eats the meat-pie poses a problem. In Patton's production, Joan Stuart-Morris (presumably taking her cue from line 60 where Titus recounts how the mother 'daintily hath fed' upon her sons) picked elegantly with her fingers at the food set before her. Similarly, Ralph Berry describes Brian Bedford's 1978 Tamora who 'daintily prepared a small portion of the pie and ate it' while 'Saturninus, conceiving it to be poisoned, watched her intently'. As an alternative, given the heavy emphasis in the earlier dialogue upon appetites, tigers, and beasts of prey, to see Tamora as a voracious feeder here can make a strong statement and even control how we 'see' this mother's predicament. Thus, in the Santa Cruz rendition, Molly Mayock's Tamora (who had started the play as a caged animal) not only fed heartily upon the pie but managed to feed some morsels to an appreciative Saturninus. In the Swan production Estelle Kohler's goal was to 'feed' as much as possible on the pie, but, in practical terms, she found it difficult to get in more than a few mouthfuls because her Tamora was distracted by her first view of Lavinia, astounded when Titus kills his daughter, and finally had a delayed reaction to the revelation about what she had been eating (for Kohler, first laughter, then shock, then a reflexive movement of hands to mouth as if to pick out the fragments in her teeth).

For the director, a more severe problem is how to deal with the staccato murders so as to avoid an unwanted audience reaction (as at the 1923 Old Vic production) that might undercut the finale. Peter Brook opted to streamline the script and speed up the action. For example, he cut the opening sixteen lines of 5.3 so as to start his scene with the entrance of Saturninus; he also cut line 47 and 'baked in this pie' that ends line 60 and moved line 54 ('Will't please you eat? will't please your highness feed?') so it preceded the Virginius passage that starts at line 35. The murders then came rapidly in varied fashion, so, according to J. C. Trewin (p. 85), 'Michael Denison's Lucius killed Saturninus from above with a dagger-cast strongly aimed.' Daniel Scuro notes (p. 44) that in Brook's rendition the four murders 'all occur with such suddenness that the sensationalism of the actions scarcely has time to make itself felt'. Indeed, given the heavy cuts in what followed, 'Brook literally emptied his stage and the auditorium in a matter of minutes.' As described by Richard David, 'in the glare of the torches the victims topple forward in succession across the dinner-table like a row of ninepins skittled from behind'.

In contrast, in Gerald Freedman's highly stylised rendition, Olympia Dukakis as Tamora, after hearing what she had eaten, rose to vomit only to be killed by Titus with a slow motion blow. Each murdered figure was then enveloped by the chorus in a red cloth which unwound to reveal a black cloth underneath. Then the victims, swathed in black, did not pitch forward but remained vertical, frozen like statues. In another stylised effect, immediately after the murders Pat Patton brought on soldiers wafting red banners to cover the fallen bodies (and cut off the laughter). Patton's Titus, Henry Woronicz, moreover, felt strongly that, even though he is stabbed by Saturninus before the latter is killed by Lucius, Titus should be the last to die, for, in his view, the warrior-protagonist should hold out so as to see his revenge completed. At the opposite extreme is Ravenscroft's choice to have both Tamora and Saturninus live on and make speeches after Titus's death.

Deborah Warner, in contrast, encouraged laughter at the outset of 5.3 not only by having Titus enter wearing a chef's hat but also by having Brian Cox literally walk in over the banquet table. The figures who set up the banquet then remained in view, facing each other in two rows of four as an on-stage chorus that reacted to the four deaths. Stanley Wells observes: 'I should never have imagined that the subsequent stretch of action [the series of murders] could have been so chilling in its effect'; he describes the chorus, 'stretching forward in horror at the death of Lavinia, bending as Titus stabbed Tamora, gasping as Saturninus killed Titus, and finally rushing off through the audience as Lucius killed the Emperor'. For Wells, this on-stage response 'both directed and channelled off the audience's reactions'.

Exactly how Titus kills Lavinia and our sense of her role, if any, in her own death, also presents a problem, one linked to a significant silence in the quarto. Lavinia, so central to the horrors and pathos of this tragedy between 2.3 and 4.1, is off-stage between her writing the words in the sand (4.1) and the end of 5.2 when, according to the stage direction, she enters *'with a basin'* and is then told by Titus to 'receive the blood' of the two men who raped and mutilated her. To avoid excessive gore, Brook banished the basin and the murders from his stage, but such a choice (although applauded by many reviewers) eliminates some significant opportunities and some potentially meaningful signals.

Obviously, both here and in 5.3 the spectator can only infer

Lavinia's state of mind from her facial expression and body language. Is she eager for revenge? Is she reluctant to participate in this grisly action? Or is she so far gone in her grief as to be oblivious to what is happening around her? Many actresses (e.g., Nancy Carlin in Oregon, 1986) have chosen to play her as catatonic, no longer really human, so, according to this interpretation, in her final two appearances she plays her role in Titus's revenge in a zombie-like fashion. A second option is a figure who is aware of what is happening in her final two scenes and who somehow registers that reaction. For example, Domini Blythe (Ontario, 1978) played a Lavinia who, starting in 3.1, lived consciously with the horrors and (like some Lady Macbeths in the sleepwalking scene) literally did not blink, so that, given the bright stage lights, her eyes were continually watering. In 5.2, this Lavinia was neither oblivious nor eager for revenge but rather was submissive to her father's will and therefore resigned to what was happening, so here and in 5.3 Blythe conveyed a dignity that several reviewers found very moving. A third option is to have Lavinia visibly enjoy the revenge upon Chiron and Demetrius (a glimpse of this relish may be sensed in Anna Calder-Marshall's face in Howell's television production) and then be seen as a willing, even enthusiastic participant in the plot against Tamora and Saturninus in 5.3.

For the playgoer's assessment of Lavinia much therefore depends upon what we see in the moment involving the basin and blood (some directors – e.g., Brian Bedford – include the basin but no blood), then in and after her entrance to the banquet (with or without the veil specified in the script). If that earlier moment is cut (as in Brook's production), that cut removes a major signal to us (whatever that signal may be); if we do see Lavinia and her basin, her reaction can set up one of several possible scenarios for 5.3. After seeing the completion of the revenge plot when Tamora feeds upon the pie, does Lavinia welcome death (in 2.3 she had not pled for her life because 'I was slain when Bassianus died', 171) or has she by now been driven mad by the earlier horrors, by the holding of the basin to catch the blood of her tormentors, and by the sight of what her father has become? Choices must be made, starting in 2.4 and 3.1, but what Lavinia, after a long absence from the stage, conveys to an audience at the end of 5.2 can make an enormous difference to the final effect of this tragedy (for an analogy in a later play, consider the comparable problem in *Coriolanus* of what a silent Volumnia should convey to an audience when she returns to Rome in 5.5 to hear herself praised for having saved her city but at the cost of her son's life).

How then should Titus kill Lavinia? Olivier as Titus first kissed Lavinia, then stabbed her, then laid her out gently on her back on the banquet table while the seated banqueters rose in shock. Often this murder comes as a surprise to the audience as well as to the on-stage banqueters. Thus, in Patton's Oregon production Titus embraced his daughter, then slowly put her down, so that only afterward did we see the knife he had used (Patton, Williamson, and Nunn cut most or all of lines 50–2 in which Titus compares himself to Virginius). Here actress Nancy Carlin conceived of her Lavinia as a half-crazed figure who had had no sleep since the events in the woods; this Lavinia also understood that Titus was soon to die so could no longer protect her; she was therefore awaiting her death; indeed, now had nothing to live for. Domini Blythe's Lavinia (Ontario, 1978) appeared in 5.3 (on a stage lit mainly by flickering candles) in a white flowing robe (a new bride-like look for her) and with a white veil. The veil remained in place until after the Virginius passage, at which point Lavinia moved to Titus who lifted the veil gently, as if in a ritual, and then stabbed her slowly, lovingly, so that she died in his embrace. For Julius Novick, 'when he folds his ravished daughter in his arms and stabs her to wipe out the stain on his honor, what we feel is the lovely tenderness with which he does it'. According to Novick, such a moment 'leads the play to a transcendence of its own horrors' and 'makes it a magnificent affirmation of the persistence with which human beings can remain human'.

At the Swan the death of Sonia Ritter's Lavinia came as a particular shock, for at this point Titus was seated on a chair in front of the banquet table with Lavinia in his lap. This image was especially effective because the apparent daughter–father relationship would seem to suggest tenderness but produced instead sudden unexpected violence. Before the murder, Brian Cox paused, made a long sweep of his hand towards the seated figures at the banquet table (at the Pit, this gesture included the audience as well), then gave a sudden wrench of his daughter's neck (not at 'die, die, Lavinia' but at the end of the next line) that produced an audible snap, at which point the on-stage chorus extended their hands. Michael Coveney (*Financial Times*, 14 May 1987), who admired the Sweeney Todd side of Brian Cox's deeply sinister Titus, saw Cox breaking Lavinia's neck 'as though she were a discarded dummy on a ventriloquist's knee'. For Coveney, this action supplied 'the merciful release of a young girl who has lived too long without feeling'. A similar effect was achieved in Barton's 1981 production where Patrick Stewart's Titus was (with Lavinia's help) an attentive host who poured wine and made sure all was well with his guests. After much embracing of family members throughout the play, at the end he once again wrapped his arms around Lavinia (like a father with a baby), an embrace that became a kiss on 'die, die, Lavinia', at which point he broke her neck with a caress.

At least two productions have made Lavinia an active participant in her own death. First, in Santa Cruz Elizabeth Atkeson was not a catatonic figure or even a passive bystander in 5.2. Rather, director Mark Rucker brought her on (quietly, in the background) not at Titus's re-entrance, as directed in the quarto, but during his previous speech ('And therefore bind them ...'). At this point Chiron and Demetrius were standing in a sandy area stage right; at the appropriate moment during Titus's speech, Atkeson's Lavinia stamped her foot so as to spring a trap (ropes buried in the sand that caught the feet of the two boys). Her two tormentors were then overpowered, tied, and suspended upside down so that she could catch in her basin the ample blood that cascaded from their throats. By such stamping of her foot to initiate the action, this Lavinia signalled to the audience that she was not a catatonic supernumerary but rather a knowing agent in the revenge process. This choice then set up a moving death scene (one of the most powerful moments in this show), for at the outset of Titus's last speech to her, Atkeson rose and, with her arms raised and outstretched, slowly walked towards her father and his visible knife as if walking towards an embrace. Now that Chiron and Demetrius are dead and Tamora has eaten the meat-pie, this Lavinia was clearly choosing to walk to her death as a release from shame and pain. Given the preparation in 5.2, this moment emerged not as yet another senseless killing but as a visibly willed action that conveyed a poignancy, even a strange kind of beauty, not found in the three murders that followed.

In her television rendition, Jane Howell provided an equally distinctive sense of Lavinia's death. At the outset of 5.3 Lucius enters in a manner that clearly echoes that of Titus in 1.1 (so he washes his hands with a basin and towel supplied by young Lucius, then lights a flame); meanwhile, Aaron laughs mockingly in the background and then creates a furore at his forced exit, first struggling, then throwing wine at Lucius along with a great deal of shouting (so as to elicit a savage response from Lucius). As the banquet begins (after a procession to another room), Titus, a veiled Lavinia, and the boy Lucius are at a separate table where Titus with his one hand cuts up a meat-pie so as to present two plates to Tamora and Saturninus. Howell here provides some very long pauses, so that Titus, Lavinia, and the boy silently sit and stare at the two diners (Titus, it should be noted, is now wearing a different costume so as to elicit Saturninus's query, but not a modern cook or chef's outfit). After a few beats, the boy hands a knife to Lavinia; she then pulls back her veil (she is dressed in black, also a new look for her as opposed to previous scenes), presumably as a signal (after watching Tamora eat) that her, or their revenge, is complete so she is now ready to die. After Titus asks his question about Virginius, Lavinia very deliberately hands the knife to Titus and waits for the blow, so that the murder seems like an embrace. Titus then grabs a knife from the table to kill Tamora with one blow; an enraged Saturninus throws over the table and kills an unresisting Titus; a raging, out of control Lucius then keeps driving blows at Saturninus to the point that the boy jumps on his neck (crying 'No! No!') in an unsuccessful attempt to make him stop. Clearly, an obsessive overpowering revenge is here being acted out.

Owing to the significant silences in the quarto, all of these Lavinias are in keeping with the original signals. Many directors, in making their choices, dispense with both Lavinia's veil and Titus's cook's costume, items clearly signalled in the script ('*enter Titus like a cook, placing the dishes, and Lavinia with a veil over her face*', 5.3.25, s.d.), although Howell used the veil to convey a major signal from Lavinia to Titus and the audience. Some productions have brought on a veiled Lavinia at an earlier point so as to anticipate this moment: in both Ravenscroft's adaptation and the Toronto rendition described by Leggatt, Marcus leads in a veiled Lavinia for her encounter with her father in 3.1 after the rape and mutilation. With or without the veil (at the least, a provocative signal), actress and director must decide if Lavinia at this point is a half-crazed figure (as befits our sense of what has been done to her) or, at the other extreme, a knowing participant in her, and her family's, revenge (so, after that impulse is satisfied, she can die with no regrets).

Although not of equal concern to most critics and editors, a second set of problems or issues is evident to directors and playgoers: how much of the 134 lines after the death of Titus should be included? For many readers, playgoers, and theatrical professionals, interest in the events wanes considerably after the protagonist's death, so, as in *Romeo and Juliet*, a modern 'sense of an ending' can lead to the omission of a large body of material that follows the deaths of the central figures. Indeed, some of the playgoers who praised Brook for eliminating much of this material (a practice followed by many subsequent directors) objected to Warner's playing the script uncut. J. C. Trewin, for example, argues that 'Miss Warner should have hesitated before letting Marcus and Lucius have the entire post-banquet passage which tells us all we know already' (*Birmingham Post*, 14 May 1987).

Most directors (unlike Warner and James Sandoe) have agreed with Trewin, so these final 134 lines are often heavily cut and sometimes rearranged – again as with the comparable part of *Romeo and Juliet*. As noted earlier, to empty the stage and the auditorium as quickly as possible after the death of Titus, Brook cut most of this section. Indeed, all that *was* included were (1) a speech patched together for Marcus made up of his lines 67–72 and three lines taken from Aemilius (138–40), and (2) most of the final twenty-five lines of the play, starting with Aemilius in line 176. At Oregon, both Laird Williamson and Pat Patton not only made substantial cuts but also rearranged the passages that were kept so as to end with a ten-line coda from Marcus (ll. 67–76). Gone therefore from both of these productions was the hand-in-hand offer from Marcus and Lucius to fall and the positive response from the Romans below, so no attention was devoted to such issues as legitimacy and the transfer of power.

The most extensive changes were provided by Brian Bedford in his Stratford Festival Canada production. In what amounts to radical surgery rather than mere cutting, Bedford (like Brook) first omitted the opening beat involving Lucius, the Goths, and Aaron (ll. 1–16) and then, more significantly, ended quickly after the four deaths by omitting lines 66–199 (all of the dialogue after the death of Saturninus). In the place of these 134 lines was a new ten-line speech from a Sybilline Oracle that was played over the public address system with the on-stage action frozen, the lights gradually dimming, and Aaron visible in a commanding position above. This speech announced that 'inexorable wrath shall fall on Rome', prophesied woe to Italy, and concluded: 'Thou shalt be plundered and shalt be destroyed / For what thou didst, and wailing aloud in fear / Thou shalt give until thou shalt repay.'

Behind this short but potent scene (minus 75 per cent of Shakespeare's lines), lay a strong directorial concept. This rendition of 5.3 started with dancing girls writhing exotically to the sound of tiny chimes while servants set the stage and lit the candles that were the primary source of light. Lucius and the Goths arrived in golden costumes that recalled the entrance of Titus in 1.1 (an initial golden moment noted by many reviewers, which masked a corruption that soon became apparent). Titus and Lavinia acted out the loving embrace that led to her death (as described earlier); Titus then for the first time lost control and stabbed Tamora repeatedly (according to Ralph Berry, 'virtually the first touch of uncomplicated, gratuitous brutality in the production, and the one real glimpse of the savagery at the heart of Titus'); though dying, he still had the strength to strike Saturninus. 'And that was it', notes Berry, for gone for the Ontario audience were the subsequent speeches from Lucius and Marcus, the mourning over Titus's body, and the final disposition of Tamora and Aaron. Rather, Aaron stood almost in triumph on the balcony, surveying the carnage, an image that was chosen to signal that the barbarism within Rome, perhaps the barbarism within us all, has won. Bedford then ended his abbreviated scene with the Sybilline prophecy of doom to indicate that the play has come full circle. In this interpretation, at the tragedy's conclusion Rome has yielded to barbarism – indeed, the barbarians are within the gates – so that the decline of this society is apparent, its fall inevitable.

The director's concept, however, did not get across to all of the reviewers. A positive assessment is provided by Audrey Ashley who describes this last scene as 'one of the most stunning' in the play; for this reviewer,

> candlelight, and Gabriel Charpentier's atmospheric music, create an atmosphere of inexorable menace, and after the last terrible deeds are done, Bedford has huddled his cast to one side of the stage, while the light remains on the chained figure of Aaron

standing on the balcony – an image that remains in the mind's eye long after the play is done.

For Ralph Berry, 'this was an abrupt and ominous ending, shorn of the restorative elements in Shakespeare's design', that climaxes 'a cerebral and finely wrought exposition of a difficult text'. In contrast, another reviewer (Marion I. Duke, *Listowel Banner*, 6 September 1978) notes that a spectator who 'did not know the play, or was not supplied with program notes' might readily conclude 'that Aaron reigns supreme at the end of the play' as this majestic figure 'stands alone on the balcony, surveying the barbarism of the once mighty Rome'. For Duke, such a conclusion 'robs the play of its sense of justice – albeit grim justice'. Even less sanguine is the reaction of Doug Bale who (after listing other directorial cuts and alterations) notes sarcastically that Shakespeare's 5.3, 'in which Titus's son becomes emperor and orders Aaron buried chest-deep and publicly starved to death, is replaced by one in which Aaron alone is left onstage, standing bound in a darkening spotlight while a disembodied electronic voice foretells the fall of Rome in a speech culled from God knows where'. To lop off the final 134 lines is here to set up a striking theatrical moment but also to cause potential confusion and to omit various elements important for Shakespeare's sense of closure.

Such cuts and changes raise the question: is the play 'over' when Titus (or Juliet) dies? Wherein lies or should lie the closure or climax of this tragedy? Do we need or want, as Trewin asks, a recapitulation of what we already know, especially after the intensity and violence of 5.2 and 5.3? When many, most, or all of these lines are included, it should be noted, the effects can vary widely. The end chosen by Bedford by means of the Sybilline prophecy and Aaron's highly visible presence is a theatrically heightened shorthand version of the ending envisaged by many critics: a decline of a Rome that has yielded to barbarism. But if the play stops shortly after the murders, how are we to know what the future is to hold for those who *have* survived? Brook, Bedford, Williamson, and Patton chose to omit the interplay between the surviving Andronici (Marcus and Lucius) and the remaining Romans (lines that appear to them and others to be redundant), but these lines can yield a variety of effects (e.g., a very negative view of Lucius, as in Howell's television rendition, or a very positive one, as in Trevor Nunn's 1972 or Paul Barry's New Jersey 1977 productions). To omit the justification, the plea, and the response is to change drastically the logic and rhythm of the final movement and, as noted in Chapter IV, to lose a rich pay-off set up by the previous disjunction of hands and parts of the body, a disjunction enunciated by Marcus: 'O, let me teach you how to knit again / This scattered corn into one mutual sheaf, / These broken limbs again into one body.'

At this point, moreover, occurs the major textual problem in the scene, so, in treating this segment, not only is some comparison shopping among post-1955 productions profitable, but some comparison shopping among post-1594 or post-1623 editions is recommended as well. Most significantly, the problem of how to stage the action after the deaths in 5.3 (given the dearth of stage directions) is compounded by a series of editorial changes. Thus, in the quarto Lucius's couplet that accompanies his killing of Saturninus is followed, with no intervening stage direction, by a six-line speech from Marcus. In Maxwell's Arden, Cross's Pelican, and Waith's Oxford editions, however, that speech extends for another twenty-three lines, until Lucius speaks ('Then gracious auditory ...') with line 72 beginning 'lest Rome ...' But in the quartos and the Folio, a new speaker takes over after the six lines from Marcus ('*Romane Lord*' in the quartos, '*Goth*' in the Folio) and his speech begins 'Let Rome ...' Again, after Aemilius has called for Marcus to descend with Lucius, editors Maxwell, Cross, and Waith (along with Evans in the Riverside) give 'Lucius, all hail, Rome's royal emperor!' and 'Lucius, all hail, Rome's gracious governor!' to '*All*' or '*Romans*'. The quartos and the Folio, however, give both 'all hail' lines to Marcus as part of one continuous speech.

The editors of three of the most important texts of this tragedy have thereby taken out a '*Romane Lord*' where Shakespeare put him in and then put in '*Romans*' at a later point when Shakespeare gave the lines to one speaker, Marcus. Such changes: (1) reconstruct the role of Marcus (see Waith's long note on p. 189), both giving and taking away lines; (2) complicate decisions about staging (e.g., when Marcus should move above); and (3) close down some meaningful options about the reactions of 'the Romans' to what has happened. As with Ridley's emendation that eliminates the hand in Lavinia's mouth, these changes seem to smooth out rough spots in the play as presented in the quarto but may, in fact, blur distinctive effects. Thus, if a Roman lord (Aemilius in the Riverside) does intervene after Marcus's first speech, the latter has time to ascend (and perhaps, off-stage, collect Aaron's child) so as to set up the climactic speech that builds to the 'hand in hand' image. Moreover, at the outset of the Roman lord's speech the 'let' need not be emended to 'lest' (see, e.g., the Riverside) if the lines as printed in the quarto are understood as one bystander's angry reaction to the murders and to Marcus's first attempt at a resolution.

So consider the following reconstruction of the scene as found in the quarto with no editorial intervention. Titus kills Lavinia, then Tamora; Saturninus kills Titus; Lucius kills Saturninus. Four bodies (and the remains of the pie) are somewhere on-stage. The same Marcus who in 1.1 spoke for the senators and tribunes makes his first attempt at ordering the chaotic situation by addressing the 'sad-faced men, people and sons of Rome, / By uproars severed' and offering his alternative: 'O, let me teach you how to knit again / This scattered corn into one mutual sheaf, / These broken limbs again into one body.' The 'this' and 'these' can refer specifically to the four bodies, for, in his first six-line speech, Marcus (with a gesture) may be offering a response to the still visible on-stage carnage. If the speech prefix attributing the next passage to a Roman lord (or a Goth) is eliminated and 'let' changed to 'lest', the next four lines then spell out Marcus's vision of the consequences should the Romans not heed his advice, for he would be saying, in effect, let us knit things back together 'lest Rome herself be bane unto herself' and, in the process, 'do shameful execution on herself'. The passage, as emended, does make sense, for Marcus, speaking on behalf of the 'new' post-Saturninus Rome, would be pleading: listen to me, help put things back together, lest Rome destroy herself.

But what happens when we follow the quarto? Here Marcus's first attempt to provide an answer ('O, let me teach you ...') is rejected by Aemilius or some other figure who cries out angrily: 'Let Rome herself be bane unto herself, / And she whom mighty kingdoms curtsy to, / Like a forlorn and desperate castaway, / Do shameful execution on herself.' If the speech reads 'let Rome' rather than 'lest Rome', Marcus, an obvious part of the family involved in this yet-to-be-explained carnage, is not accepted as a source of answers or alternatives. Rather, the Roman lord's sentiments would be: if this kind of carnage is what Rome has been reduced to, then let Rome go ahead and destroy itself. Why should we try to preserve such a society? Let it go down the drain. The subsequent lines from this Roman lord are then less angry, more sorrowful or bewildered, as would be expected from someone who had just heard about the rape and mutilation of Lavinia, is not yet privy to the plotting of Aaron and Tamora, and is reacting primarily to the murders and to the revelation of the presence of Chiron and Demetrius in the meat-pie. That lord then turns not to Marcus (who, for all this Roman knows, may have been an integral part of these events) but to the banished Lucius ('Rome's dear friend' and 'Rome's young captain') for an explanation ('Tell us what Sinon hath bewitched our ears').

Lucius (who has had time to move above) now delivers a twenty-three-line speech that, like Friar Laurence's comparable long speech at the end of *Romeo*, recounts what the audience already knows. But both of these climactic speeches are directed not at us but at the on-stage figures, here the 'Romans' not involved in the plots and counterplots. To complete the case on behalf of the Andronici, Marcus speaks for a second time, using as a symbolic property Aaron's child (as played at the Swan, held in his arms rather than in the hands of a distant attendant). In this version, Marcus's first attempt to knit things back together was rejected by the angry Roman lord, but his second attempt is buttressed first by the revelations provided by Lucius and then by the presence of the child ('the issue of an irreligious Moor, / Chief architect and plotter of these woes'). In his final twelve lines, Marcus hammers home his message. First, he sums up: 'Now judge what cause had Titus to revenge / These wrongs unspeakable, past patience, / Or more than any living man could bear'. Then, given the evidence presented, he asks: 'Now have you heard the truth; what say you, Romans? / Have we done aught amiss?' Shall we, he goes on, at your command 'hand in hand all headlong hurl ourselves' on the stones below so as to 'make a mutual closure of our house'? He concludes (perhaps holding the baby in one hand, Lucius's hand in the other): 'Speak, Romans, speak, and if you say we shall, / Lo, hand in hand, Lucius and I will fall.'

It is to this second speech by Marcus that Aemilius responds: 'Come, come, thou reverend man of Rome, / And bring our emperor gently in thy hand, / Lucius, our emperor; for well I know / The common voice do cry it shall be so.' That confidence is reinforced by most modern editors who give the next line ('Lucius, all hail, Rome's royal emperor!') and the similar line 145 to *'Romans'* or *'All'*. But if both 'all hail' lines are spoken by Marcus (perhaps as cheerleader), various interpretive options follow for the other 'Romans' on stage (some of whom may still be in shock from all the revelations), options that are precluded by the editorial choice to redistribute the lines. The effect *could* be the same as that desired by the editors, but, conceivably, the Romans could respond not to the first but to the second 'all hail' from Marcus or could respond feebly to both. In the theatre, Lucius's 'Thanks, gentle Romans' can be played a variety of ways, depending upon the strength or weakness of the reaction from the on-stage crowd. Given the range of options in the quarto, the user of these modern editions should ask: is making such a choice – on the page, without the benefit of the trial-and-error of rehearsal – the function of the editor? Where does 'editing' end and interpretation or re-scripting begin?

At the risk of trying the patience of the reader, let me note one more emendation, for of those editors who do retain the quarto's *'Romane Lord'* (rather than Marcus) and 'let Rome' (rather than 'lest Rome'), some (e.g., G. B. Evans in the Riverside) print as the speech prefix not 'Roman Lord' but 'Aemilius'. For reasons of economy and efficiency such an equation makes good sense, for Aemilius is set up as an independent figure in 4.4 and 5.1 (as go-between between Saturninus and Lucius) and is therefore clearly identified as a respected figure – the only such 'named' Roman available as a non-aligned spokesman. Nonetheless, several interesting theatrical options follow if 'Roman Lord' and 'Aemilius' are *not* conflated if: (1) that lord is identified only by costume so as to be a representative Roman voice, someone not associated with the Andronici *or* Saturninus-Tamora; (2) he says 'let Rome', not 'lest Rome' in an angry fashion; (3) another figure, Aemilius, not this anonymous Roman Lord, then calls for Marcus to descend with the new emperor, Lucius; and (4) both 'all hail' lines are spoken by Marcus, not by *'Romans'* or *'All'* as in all modern editions (including the Riverside which has Aemilius-Roman Lord, not Marcus, give the earlier speech).

What is the difference? The answer lies in the new theatrical question: how does the previously angry unnamed Roman lord react (1) to Aemilius's decision on behalf of him and the other Romans (e.g., what if Aemilius is played as a time-server, an Osric or a Rosse?); (2) to Marcus's first all hail; (3) to Marcus's second all hail (for me, the presence of the *two* 'all hails', both spoken by Marcus, carries considerable theatrical potential)? When Aemilius 'orders' the events by naming Lucius as the successor to Saturninus, is the 'Roman' response (1) quick and firm; (2) gradual; (3) grudging or (4) do some on-stage Romans remain dubious? No 'right answer' is to be found in the quarto; indeed, a strong case can be made, given one interpretation of the climax, for assigning the 'Romane Lord' speech to Aemilius. But do students, critics, actors, and directors want from their editions (that are to serve as playscripts) a plausible but iffy decision that may in turn close down equally valid or theatrically interesting options of which the reader is no longer aware? For me, the most fruitful answers will arise not from editors working on the page but rather from 'field-testing' the script that survives in the 1594 quarto.

If one does take seriously the final 134 lines, other significant interpretive options also arise for presenting the ending or closure of this tragedy. For example, much depends upon how the spectator perceives Lucius and what happens to Aaron's child. Of the productions that do include more than a fraction of this final segment, several have offered a highly positive view of Lucius. Trevor Nunn's 1972 Lucius (Ian Hogg) was a Christianised figure, a clear alternative to John Wood's decadent Saturninus. This contrast was enhanced by Nunn's rewriting of a key speech. Thus, in the script Lucius's thirteen-line soliloquy that ends 3.1 is constituted of farewells to his father, Rome, and Lavinia followed by a vow, 'if Lucius live, he will requite your wrongs' so as 'to be revenged on Rome and Saturnine'. Nunn adapted a few of these lines but, in effect, created a new fifteen-line speech which also ends with a vow and with the plan to go to the Goths in order to 'raise a power / To overthrow the emperor Saturnine / And bring back justice to the lives of men'. But, in place of the farewells in the quarto, this Lucius begins by asking: 'Is there no power that sees all things on earth / And takes revenge for evils that men do?' and then asks again 'If such a power shall be, as I believe, / Why does not heaven's vengeance fall on Rome?' Since 'no vengeance comes', Nunn's Lucius concludes: 'The heavens are silent, pitiless and dark'; his response is: 'Then here before my God I make this vow / If Lucius live, he will requite these wrongs.'

Deborah Warner's Lucius (Derek Hutchinson) was also a forceful, appealing figure who took full opportunity to win support from the audience in his version of the soliloquy that ends 3.1 and in his moral outrage at Aaron's revelations in 5.1. Hutchinson, moreover, lifted and carried the body of his father in the final moments, a 'strong' image given Cox's hefty Titus. With a Lucius who is strongly associated with heaven and Christian ritual (Nunn) or who, as a positive and trustworthy figure, will obviously keep his oath to Aaron and nurture the child (Warner), the playgoer can come away at the end of this tragedy with a sense of ordering, of knitting the scattered limbs back together, especially if Lucius has the strong visible support of his own family and the assembled Romans.

In contrast, Jane Howell's television production provides a stark, unrelenting alternative. After the image fades of a maniacal Lucius, repeatedly stabbing Saturninus (while young Lucius tries without success to stop his father), we find ourselves in a new place, a throne-room, with Marcus above to deliver the long reconstituted speech (with no Roman lord) and the boy Lucius at some distance from his father and uncle (next to the body of Titus). The older Lucius (who, as played here by Gavin Richards, has shifty eyes, an oily look, and the physical characteristics of Mussolini) kneels in front of Aemilius in a formal, religious moment, then moves to join Marcus above. Aaron's child, now dead, is in a small coffin (seen by Aaron at his entrance), so, here and later, the boy Lucius reacts silently to this death. The coffin is handed to Marcus above and displayed at 'behold the child ...' (5.3.118), although we never see what is inside; Marcus and Lucius then raise their hands aloft together. The boy shows surprise at his father's becoming emperor, moves back to the coffin (which has been handed below) while Lucius moves to the throne, and is called away to the side of Titus, but, as we hear the last speech, what we actually see is young Lucius staring at the coffin; Marcus then closes it, the boy looks up, and the production ends with an image of skulls and smoke.

As noted in Chapter II, a distinctive feature of Howell's production was the filtering of much of the action through the point of view of this boy, young Lucius, who is a continuing presence (unlike his late appearance in the quarto). Here Howell gets a particularly strong pay-off from this approach, for, after all the horrors of the play (many of them witnessed by this boy), he is visibly shaken one last time by the fate of Aaron's child and, by extension, by the choices made by his father to gain the empery. No trust is to be found in these times, including the times to come under this successor to Saturninus. This older Lucius clearly has not changed very much from the figure who in 1.1 proposed the ritual sacrifice of Alarbus. Presumably, the more positive versions of Lucius in other productions *have* learned something from what they have undergone and so have grown in the process, but, with the dead baby and the consequent violation of the oath of 5.1, Howell's rendition provides a Lucius who is not far removed from an Aaron and therefore emerges as one more figure clearly tainted by violence and revenge. When combined with Trevor Peacock's grim, savage Titus and a Lavinia who silently welcomes death once she has seen her revenge enacted, the result is an exceptionally bleak, unforgiving ending.

As Howell demonstrates, the fate of Aaron's child, although left open by the silences in the quarto, can make a substantial difference to any interpretation. If the child clearly has died or been killed, that disposition serves as a significant comment upon Lucius, the supposed new figure of hope and order, for a dead baby violates Lucius's oath to Aaron in 5.1 (and recalls the barbarous 'Roman rites' of 1.1). In contrast, if Marcus actually holds the child ('Of this ...' of line 119 could indicate an object close at hand), the spectator would have a striking image of the two Andronici 'hand in hand' bearing as well the child of their enemy, an alternative to the violations of family bonds that start with the lopping of Alarbus's limbs and permeate the play. Like many other potentially rich symbols, this on-stage object (only Howell, to my knowledge, has used a live baby) can be interpreted variously. Are we to associate the baby with innocence, with family, with the future, perhaps with a break in the seemingly unending cycle of vengeance (so that cycle will be completed and broken with the disposal of Tamora's body and the execution of Aaron)? Or is this child of Aaron and Tamora to be seen as a potential cancer within Rome, a ticking time-bomb with ominous overtones for the future health of the state? Whether the child is displayed impaled on a pike or being nurtured by Marcus, a climactic and potentially meaningful stage image is available here, an image easily obscured by both theatrical and editorial tinkering linked to a distrust of the quarto and the dramaturgy behind it.

To deal with the final movement of this tragedy is then to get entangled in a series of knotty problems involving not only the usual interpretive options but also significant textual and theatrical choices. Rather than facing squarely the ending of the play as printed in the quarto, most directors have chosen to make substantial cuts or to reconstitute this section. But the purist who leaps to fault such directors should be aware that editors too have tinkered with this sequence, with the result that critics and directors often have been dealing unwittingly with a reconstituted scene, a reconstitution, moreover, that closes down various valid and interesting options.

With these variables in mind, consider then the larger sense of an ending that arises from the components discussed so far as well as the stature (or lack of stature) of the key figures. Thus, few interpreters of *Titus* on the page or on the stage disagree about the importance of revenge, of violence, even of the degradation of the human body, but these same readers, playgoers, and theatrical professionals disagree widely about how to interpret the end of the play. Indeed, where *do* we end up after the murders? Is there or is there not a 'new' Rome?

At one extreme consider the sense of the ending espoused by director Paul Barry (New Jersey, 1977) who did cut approximately forty lines from the final segment but nonetheless stressed the importance of this material. For Barry, the pattern of the play (which he compares to rite-of-passage myths, the seasons of the year, and the circle of life) moves from the death of the emperor to the crowning of Lucius. In this formulation, at the outset there are three contenders for the throne (Titus, Saturninus, and Bassianus) but none of the three is worthy to be emperor. The action then presents (in part) the emergence of the rightful emperor, Lucius, out of the initial and subsequent deaths, so that Lucius, in the process, is put to the test and learns his lessons, with the result that the balance (lost since the outset) is restored. This approach would then correspond to the more optimistic, positive readings of the ends of comparable plays such as *Richard III*, *Macbeth*, and even *Hamlet* (given a positive interpretation of Fortinbras).

The alternative view of the ending is best summed up by Trevor Nunn's questions cited in Chapter II. Are we to sense in both the centre and the end of this tragedy Shakespeare's display of 'the Elizabethan nightmare', wherein 'even golden ages come to an end, in blood, torture and barbarism', and even 'Rome, the greatest civilisation the world had known', can fall, 'dragging mankind with it into darkness'? Can 'subsequent Empires, no matter how splendid, evade the same fate?' Is 'there an inescapable tendency, in the lives of men and societies, to revert to a Hobbesian state of nature, nasty, brutish and short?' Has 'Shakespeare's Elizabethan nightmare' indeed 'become ours'? Or, in Colin Blakely's terms, when we see figures in the play 'turn and rend each other – almost literally', are we to conclude that 'the forces of destruction take over completely'?

The theatrical realisation of such a negative vision is best represented not by Nunn's production (which provided a positive, Christian Lucius and, although cutting many of the final 134 lines, did keep the original sequence) but by Howell's where clearly nothing has been learned or gained by the end of the play, so that Lucius and the 'new' Rome are no more than debased versions of what we have been seeing all along. That sense of an ending has a strong effect upon the individual tragedy of Titus, for only one of his twenty-six children is alive by the end of 5.3. If this one has achieved empery but is difficult to distinguish from Aaron or Saturninus, then the sense of tragic waste or sacrifice is immense, especially if, as several actors have argued, Titus (as opposed to Lear) never really learns anything or breaks through to some wider grasp of himself, his family, and his society. Brian Cox, for one, describes Titus as an unforgiving play in which Rome does not move a jot forward, so, in a sense, those left standing at the end must reinvent Rome (he, for one, was not convinced of any positive associations with Aaron's child as part of this ending). If Titus is played as mad or nearly mad starting in 3.1, the ending (especially if heavily cut) acts out Rome's nightmare with little sense of a return to the sanity of the morning after.

Much therefore depends upon what are the final 'images' witnessed by the audience and what they convey. For example, a strong emphasis upon family can emerge if most or all of the final 134 lines are included, especially lines 150–74 in which Lucius, Marcus, and young Lucius pay tribute to the corpse of Titus. Thus, in his 1972 production, Trevor Nunn cut this section heavily (only three lines were retained); nonetheless, in contrast to the orgies and decadence of the court identified with John Wood's Saturninus, this sequence over the bodies was played in religious, even sacramental terms with clear Christian overtones reminiscent of a communion (and both Ian Hogg's Lucius and Tim Pigott-Smith's in the 1973 remounting at the Aldwych did hold Aaron's child). In this rendition, moreover, Lucius was not involved in the final sequence of murders (John Wood's Saturninus killed himself by taking poison) so was not tainted in the manner of Howell's violent avenger.

In her Swan production Warner did include all 134 lines but as constituted in the Arden edition (so no 'Roman Lord'). Donald Sumpter's Marcus (who by this point was also covered with the clay that had characterised first Titus, then Lavinia) was not privy to Titus's plot against Tamora and her sons, so after the murders (done behind the banquet table), his Marcus moved slowly to the chair in front of the table in which Titus had sat to kill Lavinia, first to mourn and put a veil on Lavinia and then to deliver his first speech (including the Roman lord section, as in the Arden). Lucius ascended the ladder to recite his speech above, during which Marcus moved above but very slowly, not by the ladder but by means of the stairs off-stage; when he appeared above for his second speech he was holding the baby in a manner that suggested nurturing, not further revenge. He did not, moreover, take Lucius's hand until the final lines of his speech (even after the 'hand in hand' reference). Since the Romans who are not Andronici (including Aemilius) were not in view (the actors delivered their lines from the back or side of the auditorium), the audience could not watch the reaction of 'the Romans' to the story as revealed, an omission that cut down the political emphasis of this section but, in turn, increased the focus upon the Andronici as family. With a particularly strong performance from Sumpter as Marcus, moreover (as was also true of Mark Dignam in the Nunn production), a sense of the price paid for revenge and for the 'new' Rome came across forcefully.

With the focus primarily upon Marcus and Lucius (as at the Swan), a sense of the Andronici – past, present, and future – emerges as a strong final image. Given the Roman lord and the 'all hails' in the original script, various options also exist for a focus upon the Romans and the state. Also to be factored in is the presence of Aaron (not a strong point in the Warner production), for, as early as Ravenscroft's adaptation, this figure's strident presence has been recognised as theatrically potent. At the Swan, Aaron was above at the end with his hands tied to a board. In Williamson's 1974 Oregon rendition, Ernie Stewart's defiant

Aaron was chained to a grated trap-door and then lowered below. In Howell's production, Hugh Quarshie's Aaron is also defiant to the last, both at the beginning and end of 5.3, although obviously affected by the death of his son. Here, however, with a clearly tainted Lucius who is linked to the death of the child, no sense emerges of Aaron (and Tamora) being superseded by a 'new' society that can emerge from the ashes of the old.

Howell's series of choices, especially in the abattoir deaths of Chiron and Demetrius and the series of events of 5.3, produce an overall effect far removed from the highly positive endings epitomised in the figure of Lucius espoused by Nunn and Barry or the familial emphasis developed by Warner. Thanks in part to television's propensity for naturalism, a strong emotional logic leads Trevor Peacock's Titus through the errors of 1.1, the horrors of Acts 2 and 3, and the movement towards retribution that starts in 4.3 and climaxes first in the abattoir, then in the long pauses during the banquet, and finally in the eruption into violence (including the repeated blows this Lucius gives Saturninus). Howell's rendition is therefore not only the most 'realistic' of the productions surveyed here but also, in many respects, the most brutal and unforgiving. Warner, in contrast, provided much more of a demonstration of the coming back together of the family as unit, with a visible baby, a strong, caring Marcus, and a Lucius who lifts and holds his father. None of the productions made full use of the options in the quarto that might enhance the political give-and-take of the final sequence (i.e., how 'the Romans' did or should react to the various revelations).

To present the many options presented by the script as it survives in the quarto is perhaps to frustrate the reader who prizes fixedness in interpretation and to give the impression of a Shakespeare play as a do-it-yourself kit. But without a videotape from the 1590s, we have no 'authentic' or 'authoritative' account of how to stage this tragedy, particularly the final scene. Today's theatrical professionals will continue to make their own choices based upon their sense of their personnel, resources, and audience. My goal in this chapter, especially in my treatment of the final 134 lines, is to expand the reader's or director's sense of those options and to argue as well on behalf of the theatricality and range of meaning in the original (as opposed to the edited or adapted) script. When all the components are taken into account, the quarto's sense of an ending can be rich indeed.

CONCLUSION

What price *Titus*?

To focus upon directors' solutions to the problems posed by the final scene is to call attention to the differing strategies that have been used to deal with (or tame) this troubling, formidable tragedy. In conclusion, let me concentrate again upon those strategies.

One long-standing response to the discomfort caused by this play (as witnessed by the dearth of productions between the age of Shakespeare and 1955) is to ignore it or to pretend that it does not exist. An analogous response to such a 'dangerous' script is to joke about it (so that *Titus*, like Falstaff, becomes 'the cause that wit is in other men'). To cite but two of the many *Titus* jokes, Kenneth Tynan, 'with acknowledgments to Lady Bracknell', quips: 'to lose one son may be accounted a misfortune; to lose twenty-four, as Titus does, looks like carelessness'. Equally witty is Noel Coward's reported post-show greeting to a Lavinia who had dropped the staff when writing the words in the sand: 'Hello, Butterstumps!' On stage such an irreverent approach takes the form of burlesque, as in William Freimuth's 1986–87 Source Theatre Company production in Washington, DC. For example, Freimuth opened his show with a janitor who, carrying a push broom and a blaring radio, placed large rubbish bags and protective bibs over playgoers adjacent to the stage; loud sounds of sawing were then heard at the suggestion that Alarbus's limbs be lopped; the fly scene featured the frustrations of a handless Lavinia trying to join the other Andronici in their meal of chips and dip; and in 5.3 Titus wore an apron with a banner that read: 'This is no dress rehearsal. This is it.'

Such witty remarks and burlesque choices signal a larger theatrical problem that must be faced by actors and directors. At the Old Vic in 1923 some playgoers laughed at the climactic murders in 5.3, a reaction that apparently had much to do with the absence of *Titus* from the repertoire before 1955. Subsequent directors have therefore gone to considerable lengths to avoid unwanted laughter and, at least in some instances (e.g., Laird Williamson in 1974), have felt frustrated when their audiences tittered at the boys falling into the pit, the fly scene, or the staccato murders. One of the many virtues of the Warner production was Brian Cox's purposeful evocation of such laughter for striking effects. But despite Cox's success and despite the growing recognition of the potential power of this tragedy, many theatrical professionals remain skittish about the risks posed by this play's violent or grotesque moments and worry in particular about evoking a raucous or dismissive laughter that will pull some (or, by a kind of infection, many) spectators out of the show.

As a result, many of the strategies cited throughout this book grow out of attempts to avoid such laughter. Of interest here is a choice made by Mark Rucker in his Santa Cruz production, for if significant laughter followed the four murders in 5.3, his Marcus (Brad Myers) had the option to omit the first three words of his response ('You sad-faced men, people and sons of Rome') so as not to provide a further source of amusement. As noted in Chapters I and II, to counter or sidestep this problem, some directors (most notably Gerald Freedman) have chosen to stylise some, many, or all scenes and to cut what they perceive to be risky passages or moments. So J. C. Trewin observes that Peter Brook (like Brian Bedford some twenty years later) manipulated his script 'so that his actors could let fly without dread of mocking laughter'. As Trewin notes, 'whenever he spied a possible laugh, he either cut the offending phrase or unmasked his protective atmospherics'.

Along with such cuts and adjustments (and the superb acting by Olivier and Quayle), an essential feature of Brook's success lay in his sense of 'ritual'. Recognising a 'primitive strength' and 'a barbaric dignity' in this tragedy, Brook felt that his production 'touched audiences directly because we had tapped in it a ritual of bloodshed which was recognized as true'. For him, the 'completeness' of the play 'is linked to a dark flowing current out of which surge the horrors, rhythmically and logically related' so as to produce 'a powerful and eventually beautiful barbaric ritual'. Freedman also sought to achieve his announced goal (to make his audience 'accept the mutilations and decapitations and multiple deaths with belief instead of humour') by means of 'masks and music and ritual'. The alternative, according to Freedman ('to recreate physical violence on the stage in the manner of the Grand Guignol'), would only 'appear ludicrous or stagey' in our age 'where violence and destruction are presented to us daily in the newspapers and on television'.

Such a 'ritual' approach has its advantages, as witnessed by the reception given to Brook's landmark production, but, for some playgoers, also has its liabilities. So Rosemary Anne Sisson praises the many achievements of Brook's rendition but then observes that 'what he has lost – and it is a dangerous loss – is the physical release of shock upon the audience'. According to Sisson, 'the symbolic scarlet ribbons of blood grieve us, but calmly', so that 'we can neither laugh nor gasp, but only watch and wonder, so that as great demands are made upon the audience as upon the actors'. As noted in Chapter I, this minority view was also espoused by Evelyn Waugh (who complained of Brook's 'squeamishness') and Richard David (who noted that Shakespeare's bloody effects were 'turned to favours and to prettiness'). Similar reactions were registered by some reviewers in 1978–80 to Brian Bedford's 'restraint' in omitting or playing down the blood and visible horrors and in making substantial cuts from the received script. To some playgoers, especially in the 1970s and 1980s, the choice to stylise or to ritualise this script so as to transform the horrors and avoid unwanted laughter has seemed a poor trade-off, a diminution rather than an enhancement.

To stage those horrors, however, is to take even greater risks. As Douglas Seale notes (in offering a rationale for his Fascist rendition), the director of *Titus* must decide 'whether to play the nightmare for all it is worth, or spare the audience's feelings by avoiding too much realism (or seeming realism)'. Seale, Trevor Nunn, Jane Howell, Mark Rucker, and Deborah Warner chose to present that nightmare ('when will this fearful slumber have an end?') without recourse to red ribbons, red China silk, masks, or ritualised action. Thus, Colin Blakely, who had reservations about the 'formal, almost ritualized style' and the 'symbolic and very cold' violence of the Brook production, argued that in an age 'when people can see what violence is really like when they watch the news on television', any on-stage action 'would never be as horrible as that picture of the officer pushing a gun into a man's head in Vietnam'. One facet of this 'realistic' approach to the nightmare element in *Titus* is signalled by the printed sign that greeted playgoers walking into the Pit to see the 1988 remount of the Warner production: 'This play contains scenes which some people may find disturbing' (a caveat borne out by the scattering of empty seats after the interval).

The move to 'realism', however, has not solved the problems posed by Titus and *Titus*, for, even in a very strong production such as Warner's, some scenes on some evenings prove risible rather than powerful. With such risks and solutions in mind, let me return to the provocative question posed by Freedman (as part of his argument on behalf of the stylised approach). If 'the Elizabethans were more receptive to blood and gore as theatre staples' and if 'they accepted all the extravagance of emotion and intensity of feeling with a passionate response', how then 'does one create a similar response to horror and violence in a modern audience?' Brook and Freedman respond in terms of 'ritual': Seale, Nunn, Howell, Warner, and Rucker opt for various forms of 'realism'. Clearly, much depends upon the available theatrical personnel, the audience, the theatre, and the mood of the time.

But, as Freedman implies, a significant part of the problem lies in the many (and sometimes subtle) gaps between us and the 1590s, a situation facing interpreters of all of Shakespeare's plays but especially those confronting this early tragedy of blood. The play's literariness (as in its mythological allusions, formal rhetoric, and sometimes leisurely style), its pre-realistic approach to psychological and emotional truth, and its distinctive imagery set up a variety of hurdles that must be surmounted by the actor or director who wishes to avoid that damaging laughter so feared by theatrical professionals. Shakespeare, after all, was himself a theatrical professional, but he crafted his playscripts not for us but for actors, playgoers, and theatres that he knew intimately but no longer exist. The problems that arise from such a gap may pertain to all thirty-seven plays but are particularly acute and highly visible in any theatrical interpretation of *Titus*. A scholarly on-the-page demonstration of an imagistic coherence that links the boys at the pit, Titus's hand in Lavinia's mouth, and Marcus's speech after the murders in 5.3 is *not* a solution to the problems facing today's actor and director. Compared to audiences at the Old Vic in 1923 and Stratford in 1955, fewer playgoers today would agree with Ravenscroft that *Titus* 'seems rather a heap of Rubbish then a Structure', for a series of successful renditions *have* made a dent in the pejorative view of the script widely held in the theatrical community (as witnessed by the number of productions springing up in widely scattered places in the late 1980s). Such a burgeoning of on-stage renditions cannot help but expand our understanding of the potential in this script. Stanley Wells argues, moreover, that, after the example set by Deborah Warner, 'subsequent directors will have far less excuse than before for evading its problems by textual adaptation or by evasive theatricalism'. Progress has been and is being made.

Nonetheless, the long tradition of *Titus*-bashing has left its mark. The jokes and burlesques continue. Few theatrical professionals are willing to emulate Warner and her cast so as to 'trust' the script and their audiences. The gaps between the 1590s and today, moreover, will not go away. No amount of 'historical' argument or directorial ingenuity will fully resolve 'the *Titus* problem' for today's actor or playgoer.

In response to Brook's 1955 production, Richard David posed the telling question: 'Has Shakespeare's *Titus* really any life left in it?' The answer provided by more than thirty years of theatrical experimentation is clearly 'yes'. Those fortunate enough to have seen a strong production can attest that this tragedy is not merely a museum piece only of interest to scholars and historians familiar with *The Spanish Tragedy* and Ovid's *Metamorphoses*. Like other Shakespeare plays, moreover, *Titus* exists to be appropriated by the director or any other interpreter as part of some social or political agenda (as witnessed by Seale's images of Fascism, Nunn's elaborate programme note, and Bedford's abbreviated final scene).

So what price *Titus?* Clearly, this tragedy is 'playable' today and can provide a powerful experience for a playgoer – as vividly demonstrated by Brook and Olivier in 1955 and again by Warner and Cox in 1987–88. The price tag, however, involves some form of 'translation' wherein some significant features of the original script (the two boys at the pit, Marcus's forty-seven lines to Lavinia, Titus's rhetoric in 3.1, the hand in Lavinia's mouth, Tamora as Revenge, the final 134 lines) are metamorphosed into images and effects deemed suitable or safe for today's audiences. Like the Philomela who is so much a part of this story, *Titus* can live on, even take wing in our theatres but, apparently, only at the cost of subtle or, in some cases, radical changes in its original shape.

PART TWO

SEGUE

In the two decades since the publication of Alan C. Dessen's first edition of this volume, a theoretical shift within Shakespearean performance criticism has called into question some of the central assumptions upon which Dessen's book depended. Specifically, two collections of essays published in 1996, edited by James C. Bulman and Edward Pechter, marked this change by distinguishing between an 'essentialist' performance criticism epitomised by J. L. Styan's *The Shakespeare Revolution* (1977) and a post-modern performance criticism best represented, perhaps, in several articles by William B. Worthen, later incorporated into *Shakespeare and the Authority of Performance* (1997). As Bulman notes, Styan

> subscribed to the notion that Shakespeare's texts are stable and authoritative, that meaning is immanent in them, and that actors and directors are therefore *interpreters* rather than *makers* of meaning. He believed, too, that audience responses to the plays are not historically particular, but universal. What *The Shakespeare Revolution* failed to take into account was the radical contingency of performance – the unpredictable, often playful intersection of history, material conditions, social contexts, and reception that destabilizes Shakespeare and makes theatrical meaning a participatory act. (1)

In contrast to Styan, the new generation of stage-centred Shakespearean scholars believe that 'the interpretation of Shakespeare consists not so much in uncovering the meanings already embedded in a more or less stable and self-explanatory text, but in constructing meanings which have themselves been provisionally constructed and reconstructed in socially specific and ideologically motivated ways' (Pechter, 2). Such a principle leads to a performance criticism less concerned with recovering stageable meanings latent in the original printed texts than with exploring the processes by which actors, directors, and other theatrical personnel collaborate with Shakespeare in the production of new meanings particular to their cultural and historical contexts.

Like Styan, Dessen presupposes a stable original text, albeit a problematic one, which modern directors tend to cut, alter, or reshape in an attempt to make it playable according to contemporary stage conventions of realism and psychological plausibility. Dessen does not censure such modifications, which often achieve memorable results, but he displays a clear preference for stagings that derive from a reading of the unaltered quarto or Folio texts, produced through an informed understanding of the Elizabethan theatrical conventions encoded in these printed documents. By privileging the original texts, along with the kinds of performance effects he imagines occurred on Shakespeare's stage, Dessen situates the significance of the play primarily in its Early Modern context. As Cary M. Mazer points out, 'Dessen's project is essentially historicist: it locates a work of art's meanings, its strategies for creating meanings, and its larger function within the formation of culture, in its historical moment, as distinct from the way culture is formed and meanings are generated in other historical periods, including the present' (154). What Dessen's approach therefore lacks is a full appreciation of the ways in which meaning is also created within a contemporary ideological framework, shaped by the form and pressure of the moment of its production.

For Dessen, the stage history of *Titus Andronicus* culminated in Deborah Warner's 1987 RSC production, which 'trusted' the script not only by playing it uncut, but also by paying due attention to the Elizabethan theatrical effects enshrined in its stage directions, such as *'Enter Titus like a cook'* (Mazer, 163). Observing this return to the unadulterated Renaissance text as a basis for modern performance, Dessen concludes that, 'Progress has been and is being made', but he also admits that few theatrical professionals 'are willing to emulate Warner and her cast so as to "trust" the script and their audiences'. Owing to the chasm between Elizabethan theatrical practices and today's staging conventions, most directors, Dessen predicts, will be able to make *Titus Andronicus* playable only with the 'price tag' of 'some form of "translation" wherein some significant features of the original script ... are metamorphosed into images and effects deemed suitable or safe for today's audiences' (see p. 122).

Dessen sees alterations to the text as a cost because he views the original playscript as an integrated artefact whose value is diminished by theatrical meddling. As Mazer puts it, 'Tamper with the theatrical fabric of the organic work of art: cut, delete, or transpose the text; impose a directorial interpretation or overriding metaphor, and you interfere with the integrity of the work, throw the ecosystem out of balance, unravel the fabric of the whole.' But according to Mazer, such organic unity depends upon the existence of a solitary creator: 'For if the script is a unified and integral work of art, then there must be, behind it, an authority: the artist, with a single artistic mind and imagination, who gives the work organization, unity, and integrity, who makes the play, in theatrical parlance, *work*. For Dessen, this artistic authority is the playwright' (163, italics original). Since the early twenty-first century, the assumption that there is a 'single artistic mind and imagination' behind *Titus Andronicus* has become increasingly problematic, with the gradual acceptance of the overwhelming evidence that all of Act 1 and three other scenes in the play were most likely written by George Peele (see Epilogue). If, therefore, the playtext owes whatever unity it displays to a collaborative effort, there is no inherent reason to discount the artistic collaboration that occurs when modern theatrical personnel interact with a Renaissance text to construct a playscript tailored to the particular cultural and historical circumstances of a given production.

Indeed, Dessen's prediction that few theatrical professionals would be willing to follow Warner's 'progressive' example and play the text of *Titus Andronicus* uncut has come true. According to my research, all twelve major stage productions (and one feature film) produced between 1989 and 2009 have included cuts and/or transpositions, many of them extensive. Although Warner's production achieved wide popular and critical acclaim, it has not had nearly the level of influence on subsequent stage and film versions as its success might have foretold. Rather, it typifies only one of four active lines of descent in the performance history of *Titus Andronicus*, three of which spring from twentieth-century productions described at length by Dessen: Peter Brook's in 1955 at the RSC, Jane Howell's in 1985 on BBC-TV, and Warner's two years later. The fourth line of descent, which has proved quite fertile in the past twenty years, appears to originate in a rendition given relatively brief attention by Dessen, Douglas Seale's 1967 production at the Center Stage in Baltimore, which 'may have been the first to present a Fascist *Titus*' (see p. 38).

Dessen reports that Brook gained his distinctive effects, which influenced succeeding performances, by making two key decisions: to cut the script heavily and to stylise the play's violence within a ritualistic framework (see p. 25). I would add that this stylisation drew upon techniques from Asian theatre, which reappear as Japanese elements in two of the three productions stemming from Brook's example: Jeannette Lambermont's 1989 Stratford, Ontario version, Daniel Mesguich's production at the Theatre de l'Athénée in the same year, and Yukio Ninagawa's revival for the RSC's Complete Works Festival in 2006. Howell's BBC version, which Dessen calls 'the most "realistic" of the productions surveyed here' (see p. 117), featured literal representations of the text's violence and a serious, tragic tone. Directors who follow in this vein (Michael Maggio at the 1989 New York Shakespeare Festival, Bill Alexander for the RSC in 2003, and Gale Edwards at the Washington, DC Shakespeare Theatre Company in 2007) tend toward a restrained, dignified approach that eschews the play's comic elements and labours to avoid the laughter that sometimes accompanies the performance of the text's atrocities. Warner's branch of the play's stage history, which conversely embraces the darkly comic undertones within the tragedy, has produced only one direct descendant, Lucy Bailey's 2006 production at Shakespeare's Globe Theatre.

And yet, some comic elements do occasionally reappear in the fourth line of descent, which I am calling the 'political' approach. By associating the Rome of Saturninus with an oppressive, Fascist regime, Seale inaugurated a stance toward *Titus Andronicus* that sees the play in performance primarily as a means to comment on contemporary attitudes toward violence, warfare, and repressive governments. Dessen, who locates the ultimate significance of the play in the past era of its creation, expresses a distaste for the emphasis on the present in productions such as Seale's, which he offers as an example of the way in which '*Titus* exists to be appropriated by the director ... as part of some social or political agenda' (see p. 122). To this objection I would reply that all modern performances of the play, even Warner's uncut rendition, are, in some sense, appropriations of the original text for contemporary purposes. Some productions simply signal this modern appropriation more overtly through the use of costumes and scenery that locate the action of the play in a Rome portrayed as current rather than (or as well as) ancient. Among the directors who have chosen this path are Peter Stein (Rome's Teatro Ateneo, 1989–90), Silviu Purcarete (Theatre National de Craiova, Romania, 1993–97), Gregory Doran (Market Theatre, Johannesburg, South Africa, 1995), and Richard Rose (Stratford, Ontario, 2000).

However, the best known 'political' rendition of *Titus Andronicus* is the stage production directed in 1994 by Julie Taymor, for New York's Theatre for a New Audience, and later made into the feature film *Titus* (1999). Taymor's version of the play not only stressed a modern preoccupation with violence as entertainment, but it also incorporated vital aspects of the other three lines of descent in the performance history of the text. Like Brook, Taymor cut a considerable number of lines and stylised some of the violence, particularly with regard to Lavinia's rape and mutilation. From Howell, Taymor inherited a realistic portrayal of the play's murders, especially that of Chiron and Demetrius, as well as the use of Young Lucius, Titus's grandson, as a filter through which to 'channel the horrors' of the tragedy (see p. 53). Finally, like Warner, Taymor did not hesitate to treat some of the play's absurd events, such as the battle among the Andronici over whose hand would be lopped off, in the manner of black comedy. As a result of this mixed, yet impressive, pedigree, and its wide distribution throughout the world, Taymor's version of the play is both the most characteristic and the most influential of the major productions of the past two decades.

Therefore, my study of the most recent twenty years of the play's performance history is divided into three parts structured around Taymor's central contribution. The opening section of three chapters is devoted to productions appearing in the first decade since the publication of Dessen's volume, excluding Taymor's stage production. The second section concerns Taymor's dramatic work at Theatre for a New Audience, as well as the film deriving from that theatrical event, which appeared at the midpoint of the era covered by my contribution. The third section takes up performances occurring since the cinematic release of *Titus*, many of which exhibit the pervasive influence of that film. Within each section, I hope to delineate the lines of descent that incline toward Taymor's version of the play and then radiate from it, investing the stylised, realistic, and political approaches with renewed vigour. When possible, I also pay close attention to the cultural and historical circumstances surrounding each production that helped to shape the specific meaning generated through the collaboration of contemporary theatre professionals with Shakespeare through his text.

Although my portion of this book stresses the contingent, rather than universal, quality of the play in performance, I simultaneously follow Dessen's precedent in examining recent productions by way of their solutions to the various 'problems' presented by *Titus Andronicus*. Questions about how to handle the play's violence, how to deal with its rhetorical language, and how to stage its macabre events continue to bedevil the intrepid actors, designers, and directors who take on this challenge. Since all of these theatrical professionals have chosen to cut, transpose, and occasionally add to the script of the play, I continue to analyse the specific results achieved by such changes, but without recourse to Elizabethan staging effects precluded by such alterations. With the exception of a few silent corrections, Dessen's first half of the volume has been reprinted unchanged as a testament to its crucial place in the study of *Titus Andronicus* on stage and screen.

CHAPTER I

Jeannette Lambermont, Daniel Mesguich, and Michael Maggio

During the years immediately following Deborah Warner's acclaimed 1987 RSC production, succeeding directors of *Titus Andronicus* declined to follow her example of playing an uncut script and making the most of the text's opportunities for dark comedy. Three of the four productions that opened in 1989 (directed by Jeannette Lambermont, Daniel Mesguich, and Michael Maggio) cut and rearranged the text liberally, often in an attempt to avoid the laughter that Warner had welcomed. Emulating a more distant predecessor, Lambermont and Mesguich modelled their productions on the stylised efforts of Peter Brook, while Maggio cautiously imitated the realistic presentation of Jane Howell's BBC-TV version. Owing in part to their preoccupation with the potentially offensive nature of the play's violence, neither Lambermont nor Maggio achieved much critical success in their efforts, but Mesguich attained a notable triumph in his native France with his surreal and inventive production.

Stratford, Ontario Shakespeare Festival, 1989 – Dir. Jeannette Lambermont

Peter Brook's most memorable choice in his stylisation of the violent action in *Titus Andronicus* was to employ scarlet ribbons in place of blood, a technique he adapted from Asian theatre. In 1967, Gerald Freedman's New York Shakespeare Festival production borrowed the same strategy and made the Asian connection explicit by using costumes that "'recreated an unknown people of a non-specific time" with elements of "Roman-Byzantine and feudal Japanese"' (see p. 30). Director Jeannette Lambermont, in her Stratford, Ontario production, pursued a similar strategy by mixing ancient Roman design with colourful and ritualistic aspects of Eastern theatre: 'By combining elements of several cultures I hope to reveal the universality of the story ... With some "poetic license," I have given the play a bit of a fantasy setting which combines Roman, European and especially Eastern/Oriental (specifically feudal Japanese) elements' (1). Observing the 'vaguely samurai' society created in this production, reviewer Christopher Rawson remarked that the 'Oriental stylization moderates the effect of the bloody cruelties for which *Titus* is notorious – torture, dismemberment, rape and cannibalism' (18). While Lambermont's cross-cultural mixture did help to tone down the impact of the play's violence, her intent to create a 'fantasy setting' that might reveal 'the universality of the story' was inevitably foiled by the local circumstances of her production.

On the bare, multi-levelled Festival Theatre main stage, the burden of creating a quasi-Asian setting fell to the music composed by Berthold Carriere and the costumes designed by Patrick Clark. The performance began with a '*Ran*-like' effect by which 'pounding drums' and 'discordant woodwinds' hinted at 'mannered forms of social interaction that seemed highly civilized but failed to contain the viciousness of people' (McGee, 'Stratford', 13). Lambermont's promptbook contained music cues for numerous Asian instruments, such as a low gong, a koto, a moaning flute, and what the bookholder called a 'cacophony of conch'. Clark's oriental-style costumes clearly differentiated between the Goth and Roman factions. Titus (Nicholas Pennell) and his sons sported light-coloured robes in grey or beige, and Lavinia, in her initial appearances, wore a simple cream silk kimono with broad and extended sleeves. By contrast, Tamora, once she became an empress, donned a flaming orange and red brocade dress with a long train, an elaborate gold headdress, and extra-long fingernails, while her sons were dressed in blood-red silk trousers and red suede tunics without shirts. Aaron's status as an outsider was signalled by his brown V-neck robe covered in circular medallions and his single dangling earring.

Lambermont's production employed several features borrowed from traditional Japanese theatrical forms. In the manner of Kabuki theatre, guards and attendants (called 'Ninjas' in the promptbook) moved silently among the other characters wearing white masks. At the beginning of 5.2, the promptbook records that Tamora and her sons entered as Revenge, Rape, and Murder carrying torches. A publicity photo (see Figure 9) reveals that Tamora's face was covered, down to her upper lip, with a death's head mask, and her body was wrapped in a hooded scarlet robe. Chiron and Demetrius were costumed as ancient demons, wearing fearsome masks similar to those used in the Japanese Noh theatre. Subsequently, before Titus's banquet in 5.3, a dumb

9 Andrew Jackson as Chiron, Nicholas Pennell as Titus, Goldie Semple as Tamora, and Juan Chioran as Demetrius in Jeannette Lambermont's Stratford, Ontario production (1989).

show choreographed by Robert More was performed in the traditional Bunraku style, which involved black-robed puppeteers manipulating large wooden puppets. Like 'The Mousetrap' in *Hamlet*, this dumb show depicted the crimes of a guilty party in attendance, namely Tamora, who had ordered the murder of Bassianus and the defilement of Lavinia.

In staging Lavinia's entrance after her rape and dismemberment, Lambermont did not follow Brook by employing scarlet ribbons in place of blood, but many of her performance choices emulated Brook in toning down or stylising the play's violent actions. For example, she began 2.4 with Lavinia's arrival: 'Lucy Peacock captured Lavinia's suffering powerfully; her breathing alone, which released some of her torment while containing some, filled the Festival Theatre as she dragged herself from the darkness back beneath the balcony across the platform to the front right corner' (McGee, 'Shakespeare', 115). This account mentions no stage blood; rather, it concentrates on Peacock's tormented portrayal of Lavinia's suffering and shame. Later, as in Brook's production, Aaron strangled the Nurse with a chain, and Chiron and Demetrius were killed off-stage without Lavinia's direct participation (see p. 25). In the final scene, Lambermont went even further than Brook in reducing bloodshed; whereas Olivier's Titus kissed and then stabbed his daughter, Pennell in the Stratford production gave Lucy Peacock a poisoned drink before crying, 'Die, die, Lavinia' (5.3.45). Lambermont later defended her choice to minimise the tragedy's carnage: 'It's a play for mankind, for all time ... We live in this endless chain of violence begetting violence. *Titus* is very much a play against violence, even though that message is sometimes confused because of all the gore and amputated limbs. But in the end, Shakespeare shows that this kind of violence doesn't do any good' (quoted in McMahon, A5).

Despite Lambermont's concern for the play's timeless 'message', many aspects of her production were determined by its local and immediate circumstances, particularly the fact that it was scheduled as half of an evening's double bill with *The Comedy of Errors*. Both plays were cut extensively, but according to Mel Gussow, '*Titus* suffer[ed] more in the abridgement – and in contrast to Deborah Warner's stunning production for the Royal Shakespeare Company, Jeannette Lambermont's ninety-minute, quick-script version rushe[d] from mayhem to murder, littering the stage with lost digits and limbs' (13). While Warner's uncut rendition allowed for rhetorical breathing space between the play's atrocities, Lambermont's abbreviated version had the effect 'of condensing even more densely together an already overrich evening of murder, rape, tongue-cutting-out, inadvertent cannibalism and so forth' (Conlogue, Jeannette, A13). Ironically, Lambermont's need to shorten the play conflicted with her goal to reduce the violence that she saw as an obstruction to Shakespeare's universal pacifist meaning, for by paring the play down to its essential plot elements, she left her cast little else to perform but violent actions.

Lambermont began her adaptation process with a rather low opinion of the play: 'It's the work of a writer who doesn't have his tools in line yet, who knows what he wants to do, but is a bit ham-handed about it ... But it has some beautiful poetry' (quoted in McMahon, A5). Given Lambermont's appreciation for the play's verse, it is surprising that her script 'retained virtually all the plot and characters and dispensed with an immense amount of the rhetoric' (Sidnell, 152). She shrank all of the main characters' roles, cutting some of the play's most celebrated lines, such as the speech containing the phrase 'I am the sea' (3.1.218–32) for which Olivier was so extravagantly praised (see p. 22). Tamora also had many of her long speeches reduced, including her appeal for the life of Alarbus, her reconciliation of Titus and Saturninus, and her description of the 'barren detested vale'. As a result, in the opinion of Christopher Potter, 'these personages parade[d] before us in such hurried hello–goodbye fashion that they fail[ed] to register with any depth whatever'. Aaron, played by Hubert Baron Kelly, suffered the most damaging cuts in the adapted script, which obliterated his function as a vice-like villain by minimising his soliloquies and asides. Significant cuts in the latter half of the play considerably reduced both the sympathy that he potentially earns from an audience for his defence of his son and the awe he often inspires as a result of his defiance in the face of punishment. His appeal to Lucius for the life of his baby in 5.1 was taken out entirely, along with the exchange in which Lucius swears to bring up the child. Lambermont trimmed Aaron's Marlovian recital of his past atrocities down to its first line alone, and she relocated Lucius's order to bury the Moor alive (5.3.178–81) from the conclusion of the play to the end of 5.1, obviating the need for Aaron to appear in the last scene at all. This transposition cost Aaron his final defiant speech in which he refuses to repent the evil deeds he has done and wishes that he could perform 'Ten thousand more' (5.3.183–9). Quite unfairly, Kelly was lambasted by the press for not having done much with his eviscerated role.

Although some critics applauded Lambermont for doing 'a particularly neat and concise job of editing *Titus*' (Hayman, 3D), the majority complained that the abridged script made 'cardboard characters' out of many of the play's figures (McGee, 'Shakespeare', 115). For instance, Wallace Sterling insisted that Goldie Semple as Tamora was 'hampered in her attempt to present a full portrait of the powerful Queen of the Goths' by the reduction of her role. Sterling also decried the two-minute Bunraku puppet show as 'an unnecessary appendage' (18), and indeed, since no one on stage reacted to the dumb show in any verbal way, it lacked the impact that might have justified its inclusion at the expense of potentially powerful rhetorical passages. The final scene of Lambermont's production came to an even more abrupt conclusion than Brook's (see p. 104), with Aemilius speaking the two lines inviting Lucius, who had just killed Saturninus, to become the new emperor (5.3.138–9). In response, Lucius delivered one fourteen-line speech (incorporating 5.3.146–52) in which he vowed to heal Rome's harms, gathered his family members together to mourn for Titus, and announced (in interpolated lines) that he had sworn an oath to care for Aaron's child. The baby ended up in the arms of Lucius's wife, who appeared as a silent figure in both the opening and closing scenes. Lucius's family and Marcus then ascended to the balcony and exited through a central door, while the remaining characters prostrated themselves on the stage below. On the whole, even though Lambermont followed Brook's approach by cutting the text severely and formalising the violence within an Asian style, her too heavily edited script unintentionally validated Warner's use of the full text and prevented Stratford's stage version from rivalling either Brook's or Warner's critical success.

Theatre de l'Athénée, Paris, 1989 – Dir. Daniel Mesguich

In order to create a timeless world distinct from any specific era or location, Jeannette Lambermont reinvented *Titus*'s Rome as a cross-cultural mélange within an Asian register, which also had the effect of moderating the visceral impact of the play's violence. During the same year, director Daniel Mesguich achieved comparable effects by presenting his French version of *Titus* in the mode of surrealism, which removed the action of the play from a realistic domain and recast it in the realm of dreams. This approach was signalled by a brief opening scene featuring a mysterious figure identified in the programme as 'Le Monsieur' (The Man), who lay crumpled on the stage floor as the curtain rose. As Marvin Carlson records,

> In the bookcase above his head, which formed the ceiling of the set, a book caught fire and dropped flaming to the floor beside him ... suggesting an image from a Surrealist painting ... The figure arose, revealing itself as a thin, bowler-hatted turn-of-the-century gentleman, holding a dove in his hand, an image strongly suggesting a painting by the Surrealist Magritte. (225)

This curious figure had 'time to say: "Tout va finir, tout va peut-être finir / Au bout de quelques secondes, tout reprend" ("The end is nigh, perhaps the end is nigh / In a few seconds it will all begin again") before the curtain [fell] swiftly, heavily' (Baal, 115). Within these initial moments, Mesguich established that, like Peter Brook's production, his version would not only present a stylised rendition of the play's events, but also take interpretive liberties with the text, adding to it (or subtracting from it) at will.

A bookcase loomed over the head of Le Monsieur because Mesguich's surreal setting, designed by Louis Bercut, was a baroque library tipped over on its side, with the back wall representing the oval-windowed roof of the building and the invisible fourth wall replacing its floor. The decaying library 'was seen to self-destruct during the course of the play, as the books caught fire and dust and plaster regularly fell from the cracks in the walls and from the ceiling above the stage' (Fayard, 48). This decrepit library setting formed a nightmarish 'metaphor of lost capability' (Kennedy, 70), standing in for the decline of Roman society: 'The rituals and the culture of that civilization are preserved in the books from which the characters of [*Titus Andronicus*] quote so freely ... In this crowded, claustrophobic setting, the characters used the piles of books as steps, partitions, and hiding places, they threw them in rage [or] tore them apart in despair' (Tempera, 30). What the characters in Mesguich's production did not, or could not, do with the books was *read* them, for these Romans had forgotten how to access the heritage of civilised wisdom contained within the library's dusty volumes. For example, as Bassianus died, 'the horrified Lavinia kept thrusting a book at him, as though she felt somehow it had the power to cure him if she only knew how to use it. When this failed, she cast the useless book aside, and over his dead body opened her mouth in a silent scream' (Carlson, 226). At the final banquet, as Titus revealed the crimes of Chiron and Demetrius, thick smoke began to filter across the stage, and by the end of the scene, the books had all burst into flame, turning the library into an apocalyptic inferno that symbolised the end of civilisation.

The sides of Bercut's set also featured two large rectangular glass tanks that contributed an element of the supernatural to this unrealistic setting. At first, it seemed as if these aquariums contained some sort of natural history exhibit, but as Carlson recalls, it eventually became clear that they served as a repository for the corpses of the play's murder victims:

> After Bassianus' death, he appeared among the 'specimens', which we then realized included bones and skulls, in the large glass case to our right. The previously killed son of Tamora also appeared, in the opposite case, his makeup suggesting that decomposition had begun, and in many of the subsequent scenes both corpses watched with interest from these enclosures. They were soon joined by others, such as the two sons of Titus, one falling into each glass case when they were trapped in the pit. (226)

These dead characters occasionally left the aquariums to partake in the affairs of their living relations. At the start of 3.1, the corpses joined the rest of the cast as they filed diagonally across the stage, past the seated Titus, while he appealed in vain to the 'tribunes' to spare the lives of his condemned sons. In the following act, 'it was the corpses, at Titus's instruction, who shot the arrows with threatening messages into the city, after which they joined in a round of ghastly laughter, like the crackling of dry leaves' (Carlson, 226–7). Although the reappearance of the ghosts of murdered figures is certainly characteristic of revenge tragedies, no such supernatural event occurs in Shakespeare's version of the play. Mesguich's insertion of surreal sequences of decomposing corpses walking among the living suggested that the memory of these departed figures haunted the relatives they had left behind to suffer the fall of Roman civilisation.

Mesguich's interest in civilisation's decline into barbarism prompted his choice to favour Brook's stylisation of the play's violence over Warner's realism:

> He found the recent RSC production of the play (directed by Deborah Warner) disappointing, in that it stressed the barbarism in costume and gesture, but in a deracinated way, without reference to the civilization from which this barbarism had departed. Mesguich considered it critical that ... *Titus* ... shows a late Rome, in which this culture and civilization have created their own barbarism, and a new surge of cruel and elemental forces springing up amid, and in part defined by, the no-longer-understood relics and ruins of the past. This is not a pre-civilized barbarism, but a post-civilized one. When rituals are retained, their 'civilized' meanings are forgotten, and they become elemental acts – the symbol becomes flesh, the cooked becomes the raw. (Carlson, 223)

Mesguich utilised Lévi-Strauss's categories of the 'raw' and the 'cooked' to distinguish between barbarous practices, such as human sacrifice, and civilised rituals, which protect against the consequences of barbarism by enacting its rites in a symbolic way. As Dominique Goy-Blanquet explains, Mesguich located the beginning of the decline of Rome in Lucius's request to hew the limbs of Alarbus to appease the souls of the dead Andronici:

> By substituting the 'raw' (i.e. human sacrifice) for the 'cooked' (its symbolic figuration), Rome betrays a lack of trust in its time-honoured rituals and reverts to bloodshed, thus initiating its own decline into savagery. The revenge story and chain mutilations are but side-effects of the one and only tragedy of humanity, which is loss of faith in its civilized values. (50)

The universality suggested by Mesguich's notion that the 'loss of faith in civilized values' is 'the one and only tragedy of humanity' was echoed by the production's costumes, which were 'neither historical nor [did] they belong to a fixed period of time' (Baal, 114). While Le Monsieur's black suit and bowler hat placed him at the end of the nineteenth century, the Andronici wore 'Hebrew robes and 1930s waistcoats' (Goy-Blanquet, 51) topped by headgear that gave them the look of modern nomads emerging from the Old Testament.

The Hebrew element in these costumes coloured Mesguich's staging of the sacrifice of Alarbus in 1.1 by evoking the climax of the story of Abraham and Isaac. In the Bible, at the moment when Abraham is about to forfeit the life of his son Isaac to God, an angel stays Abraham's hand and orders him to sacrifice a ram instead. This moment, when the Jews adopted a symbolic, civilised equivalent to human sacrifice, was reversed at the beginning of Mesguich's production. Titus, wearing a tallis (prayer shawl), knelt to salute the remains of his sons slain in battle, and a small statue of a ram's head was placed on the floor in front of him. As Titus was about to stab the sacrificial ram, Lucius grabbed his father's arm and suggested the slaying of Alarbus instead. After rejecting Tamora's pleas for mercy, Titus approached her son, his arms pinioned by Martius and Quintus, and drove a spike into his back. According to Goy-Blanquet, Mesguich's need to distinguish the 'real' violence of this segment from the 'figurative bloodshed' throughout the rest of the performance led him away, in this particular case, from the 'sterilized symbols' used by Brook:

> Mesguich was not much given to bloody excesses, yet the recourse to signs like red ribbons – Peter Brook's answer to the problem – would obviously have been self-defeating in his case ... So Titus' hand was torn off like bread, his sons' heads were sent back wrapped up in red velvet, but Alarbus' ritual murder was executed with realistic blood-letting to make Mesguich's point: Titus hopes to add potency to the ritual with a drop of human blood, but to Tamora there is no symbolic value attached to the murder of her son. (52)

Although the killing of Alarbus was depicted 'with realistic blood-letting', the violence in the rest of the production, such as the chopping off of Titus's hand, was stylised, but not in the same clean, aestheticised way that Brook presented the bleeding of Lavinia. Rather, Mesguich's Titus had his hand ripped off, a messy and nightmarish form of brutality in line with the surreal mode of the rest of the production.

Mesguich's portrayal of the Andronici in the trappings of Judaism may have arisen from changing attitudes toward Jews in his home country during the decade of his production: 'In France in the 1980s, rather suddenly the Holocaust replaced almost all of the Second World War history in collective memory. Thereafter the image of the Jew as the victim, the person with whom one should commiserate as a matter of principle became dominant'

(Trigano). Georges Baal perceived a strong connection between the Holocaust and Titus's Hebrew family in the sacrifice of Alarbus:

> Thus when Titus says (I, i): 'votre fils marqué par cet holocauste' ('to this your son is mark'd and die he must'), he is not only spelling out the stage picture which is reminiscent of Auschwitz, but he is also marking Shakespeare's text with the forecast of tragedies to come: the extermination of Titus's family, of which we (but not he) are aware, the genocide of the twentieth century about which we cannot be unaware and which today realigns our view of the past. (112)

By setting the murder of Tamora's eldest son in the context of the Holocaust, Mesguich may have pre-empted some of the disapprobation that could have fallen upon the Andronici for their barbaric deed in the minds of French spectators, who may instead have sympathised with Titus's family as forerunners of the victims of the Nazi death camps.

The spike wielded by Titus in the slaughter of Alarbus reappeared in the hands of Chiron and Demetrius throughout the performance. As the two brothers expressed their desire for Lavinia, Chiron used his spike to desecrate a book, while Demetrius impaled a dove. Aaron later crushed this dove within a book 'to illustrate his suggestion for Lavinia's fate' (Tempera, 129). The dove's function as a symbol of Lavinia was reinforced at the beginning of 2.4, which opened with Chiron and Demetrius sitting on the floor, again piercing a dove and a book, as Lavinia writhed on the ground in the aftermath of her rape and mutilation. The purely stylised nature of the violence inflicted by these weapons was most memorably demonstrated in 4.2. As Aaron held his baby boy, Chiron and Demetrius gouged the Moor repeatedly with their spikes, but Aaron merely laughed at their attack. He then took the spikes from Tamora's sons and walked alongside the nurse, who turned to display both spikes plunged fatally into her back. Advertising for the production visually stressed the 'tension between barbarism and civilization' through the conjunction of spikes and books:

> The posters for *Titus* showed rows of ancient, leather-bound books on the shelves of a library and two huge nail-like spikes propped against them. These books and spikes served as a kind of visual polarity in the production, the books recalling the almost-

forgotten past civilization in the ruins of which this barbaric action unfolds, and the spikes the all-too-physical reality of the present, as the weapons of choice for the play's multiple murders and assassinations. (Carlson, 223)

Baal reported that, as the dove killed by Demetrius's spike was crushed in Aaron's weighty volume, spectators saw 'the blood dripping from the pages of the book' (118). For Mesguich, this horrifying image encapsulated the contamination of civilisation by savagery: '"Blood on a book" he has said, "is more frightening than the worst of slaughterhouses"' (Carlson, 225).

The barbaric violence perpetrated during the hunting scenes, however, was represented without recourse to blood. The forest was created within the library by swathes of white cloth draped around and criss-crossing the set. Chiron and Demetrius appeared unexpectedly from behind these bands of fabric and stabbed Bassianus with their spikes, but he continued moving about the stage and attempting to embrace Lavinia for the duration of his long interpolated death speech. While Lavinia pleaded with Tamora, one of her sons waltzed merrily with the corpse of his murder victim. Finally, 'the rape of Lavinia was represented by her being caught in the center of the stage by the sons, and all three wrapping themselves in the fabric, torn loose from its fastenings at the edges of the stage' (Carlson, 227). Mesguich twice repeated this image of captivity later in the play. Rearranging some scenes, he followed Tamora's hatching of her scheme against Titus in 4.4 with her arrival as Revenge in 5.2. Then, the curtain opened for 5.1 with Aaron standing on a pile of books centre stage, 'wrapped in a spider-web of chains that stretched away in all directions' (Carlson, 227). After another curtain, Chiron and Demetrius also found themselves in chains, but as in Brook's production, their deaths were not dramatised. Aside from the death of Alarbus, all of the play's violence was either rendered in a stylised fashion or relegated to off-stage action.

As such rearrangements to the plotline suggest, Mesguich adopted a postmodern attitude toward Shakespeare's text as a point of departure for his directorial creativity. He adapted the script himself, in 'rough, angry, rugged' French prose, using the standard translation by François-Victor Hugo as his touchstone (Baal, 110). Mesguich did not 'feel committed to any slavish submission' to the original text (Goy-Blanquet, 37); in fact, he once 'characterized as "grotesque" the idea that a work, especially a rich work like [a play by] Shakespeare, was possessed of some self-sufficient and hermetic meaning with which each new production must be in harmony' (Carlson, 228). Since he believed that 'outsiders know Shakespeare better than the British' and that 'foreign spectators are better prepared to accept the significance of *Titus*, precisely because they do not have the same reverence for its author' (Kennedy, 69), Mesguich felt free from any taboos against refashioning Shakespeare's work. Through his cuts, additions, and other structural changes to the script, Mesguich far surpassed Brook in his manipulation of the text to serve his interpretive purposes.

Mesguich eliminated approximately one third of Shakespeare's text, 'partly to let the text breathe and to leave room for the actor[s'] skill without imposing a rhythm which would be difficult to reconcile with contemporary Paris' (Baal, 110–11). By making extensive cuts to passages he 'judged needlessly repetitive or prosy', he reduced the running time of his production to slightly more than two hours (Goy-Blanquet, 37). One of the most noticeable omissions was Marcus's long speech upon discovering the ravished Lavinia, also cut by Brook in its entirety. In addition, Mesguich sacrificed various minor characters, including Aemilius and Young Lucius, whose role, as we shall see, became crucial to the interpretations of several succeeding directors. Since Mesguich considered Shakespeare 'a poor director by modern standards', he 'made short shrift of the stage directions so generally revered by the majority of his colleagues'. From Mesguich's perspective, such textual signals are now 'obsolete', and 'their only interest nowadays is to indicate the place where a piece of business is required, a plain invitation to directors to use their imagination' (Goy-Blanquet, 49–50).

Mesguich also invested considerable imagination in his addition of new dialogue to his production. Le Monsieur, who incorporated the roles of Shakespeare's Messenger and the Clown, spoke several quotations from Beckett and Kafka. One Kafka extract was printed in the programme and spoken by Le Monsieur during the performance: 'Life is an eternal detour which does not allow us to understand even the direction from which it departs' (quoted in Carlson, 226). Along with sayings from 'unknown Jewish or Tibetan sages' (Goy-Blanquet, 37), Mesguich also added lines from other Shakespeare plays, such as the brief quote from *Richard III* (3.4.107) that appears at the end of Mariangela Tempera's translation of the death speech of Bassianus: 'Lavinia, Lavinia, Lavinia ... O pity, justice, peace, laws, lose yourselves in your contraries! Confusion fall! ... Why are you so beautiful Lavinia? ... They smile at me who shortly shall be dead' (196). Besides French, the characters in this production spoke three other languages:

> Latinate and English sentences appeared in direct quotations from Shakespeare's original, and Aaron the Moor spoke [insults in] an African language that the French-speaking audience could not understand. Mesguich further exacerbated the confusion of tongues by interpolating a scene in which the Monsieur ... talked with Aaron ... in this African language. (Fayard, 48, 50)

Nicole Fayard calls Mesguich's multilingual script a 'linguistic Babel' and connects it to the production's setting: a toppled library whose eventual destruction in flames represents the notion that '[l]anguage is obfuscated and linguistic as well as narrative confusion rules' (48).

Another way in which the staging of this production metaphorically reflected the thematic content of the play involved Mesguich's choice to fragment the action. As Dennis Kennedy put it, 'a play about lopping off was itself chopped into tiny fragments of scenes, each cut off by a rapid drop of the curtain, like a guillotine' (70). Carlson recounts that

> Mesguich divided the play into approximately twenty-five brief scenes, some exactly corresponding to scenes in the original, but most shorter, and a few totally of the director's invention. After each of these the curtain fell rapidly, and the audience sat a moment in darkness registering the invariably striking visual images of the scene just completed. (227)

The staccato rhythm produced by such quick scene changes tended both to break up the narrative and to make spectators more aware, in a Brechtian sense, of the theatrical conventions at work in this presentation. At some points, the curtain came down in the middle of a scene, only to rise again momentarily for a variation on what had just occurred. For example, 'When ... Saturninus turned from Lavinia to Tamora as his Empress, he first made a sweeping exit up-stage left with Lavinia. The curtain fell, then rose on the same configuration, and the exit was identically repeated, but this time with Tamora' (Carlson, 227). Such repetitions echoed the play's own numerous variations on the act of violent revenge for harm done to a family member.

As in Lambermont's production, Mesguich's script brought the play to an end very abruptly after the death of Titus (who simply handed Saturninus the knife with which he had just stabbed Tamora and waited passively for his death blow). As fires erupted all over the library, Lucius advanced downstage and gave a single impassioned speech directly to the audience, but the conflagration behind the would-be emperor did not offer any assurance that Rome would survive to be ruled by him. As the performance concluded, 'Grotesque waltz music was heard under the riot of destruction, and over it the voice of Marcus with a final question and a challenge: "Now judge what cause had Titus to revenge / These wrongs, unspeakable past patience, / Or more than living man could bear"' (Carlson, 228). Ultimately, the brevity of this closing segment resembled the truncated ending of Brook's version, which quickly emptied the stage and auditorium after Titus perished (see p. 98).

English-language reviews and critical analyses of Mesguich's production barely mention the performances of the actors in their title roles. Mesguich himself 'does not believe in characters' (quoted in Goy-Blanquet, 40), and in previous Shakespeare productions, his habit of reallocating lines and dividing roles up among various performers made it difficult for individual actors to inhabit a character, as Olivier famously did for Titus. By contrast, 'it was quite meaningless to detach Mesguich's Titus from the rest of the cast, and difficult to remember its interpreter Christian Blanc as an independent performer' (Goy-Blanquet, 41). Nevertheless, the production received critical and popular acclaim in France, and the leading Parisian theatre reviewers dubbed it 'one of the most brilliant and challenging on the contemporary French stage' (Carlson, 222). Michel Cournot of *Le Monde* named it 'the best production of one of Shakespeare's early plays' (quoted in Fayard, 45n), and in *Figaro*, Marion Thébaud claimed that it was 'by far the outstanding production' of *Titus Andronicus* 'among those stagings in a number of countries over the past twenty years' (quoted in Carlson, 222). Owing to its success in Paris, Mesguich's production was revived for a month-long run at the Théâtre National de Lille and filmed for television in 1992, but it appears not to have had any significant influence upon subsequent productions of the play outside France.

New York Shakespeare Festival, 1989 – Dir. Michael Maggio

Jane Howell's BBC version of *Titus* responded to the verisimilitude encouraged by the medium of television by offering a realistic rendition of the play that not only eschewed the stylisation of violence, but also portrayed a more traditional vision of Rome than the Asian setting of Lambermont or the surreal library of Mesguich. At New York's Delacorte Theatre in Central Park four years later, Michael Maggio followed Howell's lead and emphasised the 'strong reality' that he discovered in Shakespeare's early modern version of 'a B-movie thriller' (quoted in Rothstein, 5). Maggio set his production in a recognisable version of ancient Rome, but to avoid turning *Titus* into the equivalent of a slasher movie, he refrained from gruesome depictions of maimings and murders. 'Gore', he told an interviewer before the show opened, 'is kept to what I hope will be a potent minimum' (quoted in Rothstein, 5). Such restraint pervaded every aspect of this run-of-the-mill production's design and execution, demonstrating that a successful performance of *Titus Andronicus* requires a bold and imaginative directorial stance.

Although Maggio initially considered 'updating or changing' the play's setting, he ultimately 'felt most comfortable with the material dealing with it in terms of ... fourth-century Rome' (quoted in Rothstein, 5). This orthodox choice led Frank Rich to describe the production as a 'routine sandal-and-toga recital' (C13), which, like Howell's version (see p. 51), distinguished between the civilised Roman warriors in 'padded jerkins' and the barbaric Goths in 'woolly rustic garb' (Cook and Cook, 9). John Lee Beatty's set reflected the director's intention to root the action in antique Rome by displaying a 'double colonnade painted a dark ash-gray', which half-encircled 'a central platform like the cross section of a little Coliseum' (Disch, 363). In the middle of this platform was 'a sacrificial and bloody opening, sometimes covered with a grill and seething with smoke' that functioned as 'grave, altar, [and] pit' (Cook and Cook, 9). Rich's depiction of this feature stressed its inadequacy to evoke the horror of the play's atrocities: 'The first sight to greet the audience ... is a small, flaming barbecue grill propped up on a slender tripod at center stage ... So why are we greeted by a wimpy barbecue that is less evocative of the barbarous human stew of Shakespeare's ancient Rome than of last weekend's hot-dogs-and-marshmallows cookout in Great Neck?' (C13).

For Rich, this 'wimpy barbecue' epitomised the production's realistic yet tentative representation of the play's violent action, which mitigated the impact of the tragedy's vicious excesses. As Michael Feingold wrote, 'Maggio has neither stylized the gore nor wallowed in it. He steers a middle course, concentrating on the story, keeping the tone stoically low-key, getting through each bloody event without sidestepping it or working it up into a frenzy. It's the most weirdly moderate production of *Titus* I can imagine' (91). One method employed to maintain this 'middle course' was to shroud violent behaviour in a cloak of ceremony. As Maggio told an interviewer, 'The presence of blood per se in the production is handled in a very specific and ritualistic fashion' (quoted in Rothstein, 5). Such a strategy resembled the tactics of Howell, who portrayed violent incidents like the sacrifice of Alarbus with 'a strong sense of ritual' created by handwashing, drums, and the lighting of candles (see p. 52). Yet whereas Howell did not flinch at allowing blood to flow freely during such rituals, Maggio hid the gore and elected to present what Rich dubbed 'a genteel *Titus Andronicus*, which is kind of like doing *The Texas Chain Saw Massacre* without the chain saw or *Sweeney Todd* with an electric razor' (C13).

Howell's ritualisation of violence contributed to her production's generally serious and dignified tone. Likewise, Maggio strove to avoid 'the difficulty of inappropriate laughter, a problem he tried to overcome by ... cutting' approximately 600 lines from the text (Cook and Cook, 9). During the rehearsal process, Maggio expressed concern that his cast might not be able to prevent giggles at inopportune moments, despite his alterations to the script: 'I suspect that it may take us a while to get that kind of derisive laughter under control. But I think we're off to a pretty good start' (quoted in Rothstein, 5). While Deborah Warner played the uncut text and invited the audience to laugh at several macabre moments, Maggio laboured to re-shape the text to avoid the kind of painful comedy that Warner embraced. As Rich observed, Maggio aimed 'to ward off the ridiculousness induced by the plot's nonstop gore' (C13). Such efforts achieved mixed results. While Michael Feingold commented that Jon DeVries played Marcus 'without stumbling over any of the unfortunate laughs' that his role might inspire (91), John Simon wished that

'Maggio's staging could have prevented laughter in certain places, though that is a lot to ask' (64). Another major change to the text instituted by Maggio was to rearrange 1.1 so that the production 'open[ed] with the funeral' of Titus's sons and then 'combine[d] the election business into one scene', an adjustment that Maggio had 'read about ... being done in other productions' (quoted in Rothstein, 5). The only major production before 1989 to institute this rearrangement was Howell's version, which Maggio emulated in structure as well as in tone.

Maggio's cautious gestures in the direction of the play's extremities carried over into the performances of his actors, many of whom exhibited 'tentative uncertainties toward the thrusts of their roles' (Isenberg, 24). The brunt of this criticism fell on Donald Moffat as Titus, whose 'performance, like the production, [wa]s too muted' to achieve 'the bloodcurdling rage that might plunge him credibly into the homicidal' (Rich, C13). Similarly, Pamela Glen as Lavinia came up 'short on both liveliness and vulnerability' (Simon, 64). In a more scornful vein, Frank Rich wrote, 'When Pamela Glen's Lavinia, in the play's most grievous incident, is raped, then loses her tongue and hands, only her diction seems to suffer' (C13).

However, two actors in the Central Park version were generally lauded for rising above the tentative nature of the production and throwing themselves wholeheartedly into their roles (see Figure 10). First, as Tamora, Kate Mulgrew, 'unlike Moffat, enlarged her presence by speaking her lines with precision and intelligence' (Isenberg, 25). Mulgrew was 'Faulknerian, compelling as pleading mother, as anxious seductress, or as ruthless schemer. She swallowed Saturninus with open contempt, resourcefully manipulated Titus' dull masculinity, reveled in sensual ecstasy with Aaron, and even tickled one son's codpiece, pushing the pair gruesomely toward rape and murder' (Cook and Cook, 9). Some critics did consider her Tamora overplayed; as Michael Kuchwara wrote, 'Kate Mulgrew chews the scenery – as well as her sons – as the treacherous Tamora, queen of the Goths' (D3). Yet, most viewers agreed that her portrayal of 'a slinky rather than a fiendish Tamora' (Feingold, 91) was 'irresistible' (Simon, 64).

Second, in the role of Aaron, Keith David gave what Clive Barnes pronounced as 'the best performance' in the production (quoted. in Metz, *Shakespeare's*, 216), although his Moor did not exult in wickedness to the same extent as did his lover Tamora:

10 Kate Mulgrew as Tamora and Keith David as Aaron in Michael Maggio's New York Shakespeare Festival production (1989).

> One can sympathize with Keith David's reluctance to steep himself in villainy as zestfully as Mulgrew, since to do so would be to represent just that stereotype of the black male that bigots since the time of Shakespeare have loved to hate. He does seem to enjoy himself when he's murdering the nurse, but then he is being Machiavellian, which is a higher, even kingly form of villainy. (Disch, 363)

Dorothy and Wayne Cook agreed that David's portrayal of Aaron the Moor was geared toward defusing the play's potentially explosive racial stereotype, which might have proved offensive to a late twentieth-century New York audience:

> David muted the issue of race by so thoroughly individualizing his character. His luxury, lust, and cunning were at once ends in themselves and a means of survival in a hostile and prejudiced society for him and his infant son. Able in combat and noble in appearance, David's Aaron was a malevolent genius, whether staring at the mutilated Lavinia, carrying out his own hellish orders, or disarming and commanding Tamora's sons. Yet he combined the dignity and tenderness of a father with a concluding and triumphant iniquity, as unrepentant savior of his son. (9)

Like Hugh Quarshie in Howell's production (see p. 52), David was 'at his firmest in Aaron's one atypically sentimental scene – his expression of affection for his own newborn child' (Rich, C13). The celebration of blackness lodged in the Moor's loving address to his baby son drew compassion to the character and gave David's portrayal a depth that was rivalled only by Mulgrew's Tamora. The attractiveness of these two prominent villains threatened to tip the play's balance of sympathy toward the Goths rather than the Andronici.

One of the few Romans to receive positive notices was David Purdham, who played Lucius. In Maggio's most significant departure from Howell's example, Titus's eldest son grew into the saviour of his nation at the end of the play. Whereas Howell's version presented 'a maniacal Lucius' who broke his vow to nurture Aaron's child and threatened to become as tyrannical as Saturninus (see p. 112), Maggio depicted Rome as 'a world ironically salvaged by the perseverance of... Lucius' (Cook and Cook, 9). Although Lucius emerged triumphant, the Central Park production as a whole did not. John Simon called Maggio's hesitant effort 'adequate in almost every way; the question is merely whether "adequate" is what you want from such a ranting, atrabilious, heaven-storming drama' (64). Such an assessment reminds us that a truly memorable production of *Titus Andronicus* demands not conventionality and restraint, but a daring and ingenious directorial vision, like the surreal approach adopted by Daniel Mesguich.

CHAPTER II

Peter Stein and Silviu Purcarete

The decade 1989–99 witnessed the resurgence of *Titus* as a political tract, with three major European directors (Peter Stein, Silviu Purcarete, and Gregory Doran) focusing their attention on the ways in which the play can be made to comment on specific contemporary affairs. Their productions (consciously or not) therefore duplicated the approach adopted in 1967 by Douglas Seale, the first director to employ modern dress to draw 'parallels between the violence and wholesale murder of our times and the time of Titus Andronicus' (see p. 28). Seale had set his production in the 1940s and reconceived the war between the Romans and the Goths as the conflict between the Fascists and the Allies during the Second World War. Seale's closely cropped Saturninus resembled Benito Mussolini, surrounded by black-shirted supporters, and Titus appeared as a Prussian military officer, his sons sporting Nazi uniforms and swastikas. The director chose this setting to remind spectators how the horrors of the midtwentieth century had demonstrated that we, today, cannot justifiably view ourselves as any more sophisticated and civilised than the 'coarse' Elizabethans, who drew such pleasure from the play's bloodshed (see p. 38). In the next two chapters, I examine how Stein, Purcarete, and Doran replicated in their productions this Fascist setting, or that of a similarly repressive modern regime, as a means to draw attention to the shockingly contemporary political elements in *Titus*.

Teatro Ateneo, Rome, 1989–90 – Dir. Peter Stein

The last of the four major renditions of *Titus Andronicus* that opened in 1989 was produced in Italian by the Teatro Stabile di Genova, with German director Peter Stein at the helm. This production was Stein's first attempt at Shakespeare since his spectacular version of *As You Like It* (1977), once called 'arguably the most significant Shakespeare production anywhere since Peter Brook's *A Midsummer Night's Dream*' (Patterson, 428). Stein's *Titus* production grew out of the 'Shakespeare Project', a series of seminars with students at the University of Rome's Teatro Ateneo, which featured exercises using the original text of the play. Despite artistic differences with his primary cast members, problems with the theatrical management, and a broken leg sustained during rehearsals, Stein developed these workshop exercises into a full-fledged performance including professional actors and a European tour. He chose *Titus* for this project because of its 'juvenile energy', which he felt made it 'ideally suited for stage apprentices', but he considered the play immature and lacking in 'philosophical depth' and 'world vision' (Goy-Blanquet, 46). He was not confident that Shakespeare had actually written the piece, and when asked about its quality, Stein reportedly exclaimed, 'It's a piece of shit' (quoted in Gulino, 477). Stein's disdain for the play itself may have contributed to the mixed reception accorded his production in Italy and in his native country.

In his depiction of the play's violent horrors, Stein's strategy leaned away from Brook's formalised technique and toward the realistic presentation favoured by Howell. According to John Peter, who saw the production at the Odeon Theatre in Paris, Stein did not shy away from the play's butchery, but portrayed it without excessive gore: 'Amid all the carnage, which is carried out with the utmost sense of cruelty and explicitness, you notice how little actual blood is being shed' (E5). One prominent exception to this lack of bloodshed was the sequence depicting the aftermath of Lavinia's rape and dismemberment. Chiron and Demetrius appeared separately at the beginning of the scene, with blood spattered on their white suits. Lavinia then staggered on stage with her bloody legs wide apart, her head down, and her hair askew covering her face, red stains edging the sleeves of her gown. When Marcus discovered his niece, he pushed her hair aside to reveal blood trickling down the right side of her open mouth. Although Lavinia's face seemed paralysed by the trauma of her sexual assault, her eyes betrayed the intense physical and emotional pain she was suffering.

Certain reviewers seized upon Stein's emphasis on sexual cruelty as an analogue to political brutality, which differentiated the Italian production from Warner's recent version. Michael Coveney wrote that, in Stein's hands, '[t]he play becomes much more a discussion on political and sexual sadism ... than it did in Deborah Warner's very different but comparatively fine 1987 version for the RSC, which treated the play's excesses as a means of testing the human capacity for grief' (Rev. of *Tito*, 35). Goy-Blanquet agreed that the German director used violence in a more politicised fashion than his English counterpart:

> Stein's own reading was radically opposed to Deborah Warner's. If the play is more actable now than a few decades earlier, it is not because its horrors coincide with the contemporary taste, let alone prove too much for our sensitive nerves. They have become so banal, compared with what we commonly see on our TV sets, that they no longer hide the central picture: a major crisis of the state, in a family-based society totally unable to cope with the collapse of the old order. (45)

Whereas Warner focused on the plight of the individual human beings caught up in the vendetta between Titus's family and Tamora's, Stein highlighted the 'crisis of the state' brought about by the threat posed to Rome's 'old order' by the upstart Goths. Stein's portrayal of this ancient conflict in modern dress 'invited a contemplation of the parallels between Renaissance violence and the savagery of our own times, so that the piece worked as a political parable' (Patterson, 434). In contrast to Howell and Maggio, who lodged their conceptions of the play world in Shakespeare's vision of antique Rome, Stein saw the tragedy 'as prophetic rather than historic and [did] everything to underline its twentieth-century relevance' (Billington, Rev. of *Tito*, 37).

Stein stressed the contemporary significance of the play in performance by clothing the actors in costumes, designed by Moidele Bickel, which mixed ancient and modern attire in a style described by one critic as 'Armani-Classico' (Peter, E5). As Michael Billington reported,

> Stein and Bickel ... use costume to imply past centuries while anchoring the play in our own: thus Raf Vallone's Marcus registers he is a tribune of the people by draping a toga over his white linen suit ... Eros Pagni may sport a laurel wreath but he is unequivocally a Fascist general. His triumphant return to Rome is signalled by sounding brass, he is borne on the backs of captive Goths and his four surviving sons have the rounded helmets of Mussolini acolytes. (Rev. of *Tito* 37)

Like Seale, Stein depicted Rome as a totalitarian regime, here defended by Titus's sons decked out in paramilitary uniforms with huge padded shoulders and riot gear. Lucius and his brothers initially came across as brutal thugs who beat Alarbus and the other Goths (shirtless and daubed in red war paint) with nightsticks when they resisted Titus's order to sacrifice his noblest prisoner. The four young Romans dragged Tamora's eldest son toward a trap upstage, then clubbed him down into it as smoke began to rise from the sacrificial flames below. This despotic representation of the Andronici, the play's putative heroes, gave the impression that Rome was indeed a 'giungli di tigri' (translator Agostino Lombardo's rendering of 'wilderness of tigers') in which the native inhabitants were no less savage and repressive than their 'barbaric' enemies.

Bickel's set evoked the same cross between ancient and modern Rome suggested by her costumes. The stage was 'dominated by three mobile, multi-arched, off-white walls with hints of the neo-imperial style of Piacentini' (Billington, Rev. of *Tito*, 37). John Peter also observed this architectural signature, finding the set 'reminiscent of the Caesarist architecture of Mussolini's EUR in Rome' (E5). The EUR (Esposizione Universale Roma), including the building known as the Square Colosseum (a primary location in Taymor's film), was designed for Mussolini by Piacentini during the 1930s. Like the EUR, the walls of Bickel's set were 'constructed of plain slabs of "travertine", reminiscent of much of Italian architecture under fascism' (Couling, 19). The slabs were lined with panels that could be removed to reveal doors for entrances and exits or, in 1.1, a grid-like mausoleum into which the sons of Titus slid the coffins containing the bodies of their brothers slain in battle. To change the size and shape of the acting space, the walls could be drawn in with 'sinister clanking noises' (Gulino, 478). Along with the trap, which was used again for the pit in 2.3, the set featured two additional levels, with most of the action taking place on the main stage, and the upper level 'reserved for power struggles and political action' (Tempera, 29). Downstage, a narrow apron attached to the front of the acting area allowed entrances, particularly processionals, to proceed through the auditorium and up onto the main platform, which further blurred the distinction between the world of the classical characters and that of their contemporary audience.

Several other theatrical elements supported Stein's efforts to blend past and present. The production's lighting designer, Piero Niego, contributed visual effects that heightened the director's 'clean and deadly' conceptual scheme for the production (Gulino, 479). For most scenes, the stage was 'blindingly lit through overhead glass panels, creating an antiseptic world in which the horrific acts of the play appeared cruel and efficient rather than viscerally shocking' (Patterson, 434). However, when the action shifted outside Rome in Act 2, Niego created a forest on the nearly bare stage almost entirely with lighting effects. Billington recorded that the hunting scene (2.2) began 'with the characters ... lining up downstage in shadow while behind them a bright light' blazed; it was 'a typical piece of Stein chiaroscuro' that exactly conjured up 'the world of a Fascist shooting-party' (Rev. of *Tito*, 37).

In the next scene, the platform darkened to a greenish hue, and overhead lights threw a pattern on the stage, which evoked the floor of a sinister woodland grove. This natural location contrasted with the urban sounds, such as 'air-raid sirens, ambulance wails, traffic noises and the sound of bolts being shot and rivets hammered into place' (Billington, Rev. of *Tito*, 37), which were heard as Titus prostrated himself to plead with the tribunes, or when Saturninus raged against the audacity of Titus in 4.4. This 'intrusion of noises from today's road traffic and air raid sirens' into events of the distant past established 'a continuity between the ancient and the modern world' (Tempera, 29). Finally, although the performance used few props, a 'clear allusion to the contemporary Mafia' occurred 'when Titus's hand and his sons' decapitated heads [were] returned to him wrapped in clear plastic bags, a technological torture characteristic of a post-*Godfather* era' (Gulino, 478).

At the end of his production, Stein paid a great deal of attention to a textual matter often glossed over in performance: the potential conflict between the Goth forces, led by Lucius, and the Roman citizens over whom the new emperor plans to rule:

> Stein's gift for animation also brings out the play's political dimension so that the final pile-up of corpses prompts a pitched battle at court between the supporters of the dead Saturninus and the invading Lucius. It is a brilliant touch lending dynamic urgency to Marcus's plea to Rome to knit her broken limbs into one body. (Billington, Rev. of *Tito*, 37)

Lucius entered at the beginning of 5.3 accompanied by four armed Goths in long, dark trench coats, who faced off against the Emperor, his Empress, and four identically armed Roman guards in light-coloured coats. These henchmen maintained a palpable hostility toward one another as Titus took his revenge upon Saturninus and Tamora:

> Sitting on opposite benches, the supporters of the Emperor (in white) and the Goths (in black) snarled at each other throughout the banquet, barely kept in check by their leaders. With the killings, they engaged in a pitched fight that was only broken when Marcus and Lucius, holding hands with Young Lucius, addressed them from the upper stage. (Tempera, 206)

As Marcus pleaded with his auditors, the Goths and Romans below wandered the stage aimlessly, as if thrown into shock by the events they had just witnessed. When Lucius spoke, however, the political chaos at stage level began to resolve itself into order. As Tempera recalls, 'At that point the two factions, made indistinguishable by a trick of light, formed a perfect semi-circle of polite listeners, as if to signify that the Andronici had indeed succeeded in bringing harmony to the city' (206). Yet this harmony came at a cost: the rebirth of Fascism under a new dictator. Horst Zander discerned that 'Lucius' voice at the end turn[ed] into that of a demagogue, whose posture resemble[d] Mussolini' (516n). The crowd hailed their new leader with the title of 'benigno duce di Roma', which undoubtedly linked Lucius to the notorious Il Duce, but it also 'might have been an allusion to the recently growing power of the Neo-fascist party, MSI, in contemporary Italian politics' (Gulino, 478). With such allusions to current controversies, Stein attempted to invest the play's ancient events with an immediate political relevance.

Lombardo's translation of Shakespeare's play, entitled *Tito Andronico*, augmented the contemporary feel of the production by employing language that 'sounded close to modern Italian' and contrasted 'everyday speech with the deliberate intricacies of politicians' syntax'. Stein, who speaks Italian, supervised the translation himself and perpetuated the collaborative nature of the original student seminar by inviting the actors 'to discuss Lombardo's text and offer suggestions, a number of which were kept in the final version' (Goy-Blanquet, 38). Lombardo began with Eugene Waith's Oxford edition of *Titus*, from which Stein had cut 'exactly the same number of lines as Peter Brook had, about one-third of the whole, namely all the passages where he suspected the young Shakespeare of "peacocking"' (Goy-Blanquet, 53n, 38).

Stein's judgement about which lines to cut differed significantly from Brook's, however, especially at the close of the performance, where Stein retained a great deal more of the text that follows Titus's death than did Brook. In the Italian production, after Marcus crowned Lucius with a laurel wreath, the new emperor and his son descended from the upper level to bid farewell to the family patriarch. Titus's body was placed at one end of the banquet table, and Lavinia's at the other, with their feet together in the centre, while both Lucius and his son spoke their tearful laments. With cuts, the production ran for nearly three hours, not including an intermission after the fly scene. Overall, Lombardo was commended for doing 'an extraordinary job in presenting the original text with all its semantic intricacies as well as in its overindulgences, adapting, as much as possible, the Italian language to the flexibility of *Titus*'s blank verse' (Gulino, 480).

As in Maggio's production, two of the most highly praised performers were those who undertook the villains' roles: Paolo Graziosi as Aaron and Maddalena Crippa as Tamora. Graziosi, a white actor, played Aaron in blackface with woolly hair and a short beard, which prompted an Italian reviewer to describe him as a 'Luciferian, irritable figure, all painted in black' (quoted in Gulino, 479) and a British one to call him 'a cynical, soft-spoken, completely ruthless Rastafarian' (Peter, E5). As Aaron spoke of throwing away his 'slavish weeds' during his first soliloquy (2.1.18), he stripped off his ragged overcoat and threw it into the wings, receiving 'a smart jacket, and a gold chain' in return. This change of clothing raised 'echoes of Italy's latest social phenomenon: the north African immigrants, selling anything saleable on the city streets in their hope for a slice of the dolce vita' (Couling, 19).

Aaron's impact as a menacing figure was enhanced by the fact that Chiron and Demetrius were portrayed as accomplished fencers, more than usually mature and capable of deadly violence. In 2.1, Aaron manipulated Tamora's sons with words alone, but in 4.2, when Chiron and Demetrius threatened the Moor's child with their foils, Aaron picked up a curved sword, one of Titus's gifts, and disarmed his dangerous foes easily. He later used the same weapon on the nurse, stabbing her in the stomach. Such intimidating deeds justified the precaution taken by the Goths, who hoisted the captive Moor upside-down by his feet, hanging him by a rope dropped from the flies. In the last scene, during the re-establishment of order that followed the death of Saturninus, Aaron, kneeling, laboured to nurture his child, abandoned by the Goths on the hard ground: 'Hands tied behind his back, he attempted to care for his son, by holding his swaddling clothes between his teeth, with clumsy gestures that were a chilling reminder of Lavinia's helplessness' earlier in the play as she knelt to pick up Titus's hand, wrapped in a scarf, with her mouth (Tempera, 134–5). At the conclusion, the Moor was dragged across the stage to the trap into which Alarbus had been cast, and a revision of the text gave him the final word: 'Stein ends the play on Aaron's speech of unrepentant villainy, at which point Graziosi, buried up to his neck in earth, sticks out his tongue: a symbol both of mutinous defiance and of Aaron's untarnished linguistic power' (Billington, Rev. of *Tito*, 37). For Goy-Blanquet, 'Aaron was the scapegoat of a dubious return to legitimacy ... promising few happy days to the new state' (46).

The Queen of the Goths was 'dazzlingly played' by Maddalena Crippa (Billington, Rev. of *Tito*, 37), whose 'outlandishly provocative' Tamora came across as 'a designer-dressed panther, lithe, highly sexed and utterly unfeeling' (Coveney, Rev. of *Tito*, 35; Peter, E5). Other accounts of Crippa's portrayal of Tamora similarly stressed the animalistic, inhuman quality she brought to the role. Led onstage as a prisoner, Tamora first 'appeared as a monster covered with bags and chains', but after she became empress, 'she changed into a comic-strip "femme fatale" with a long seductive red dress, trimmed with red roses, and red high-heel[ed] shoes' (Gulino, 479). Reconciling her new husband to the Andronici at the end of Act 1,

> She feigns a wary solicitude for Titus and his family while confiding to the audience that she will find a day to massacre them all: she hisses the word 'massacrarli' at us like a rattlesnake. But she also reveals, under her slinky, shot-silk gown, a ferocious sexual animal: tempting her paramour, Aaron, she crawls down an angled plank into the forest on all fours, with bottom arched, like a feral predator in heat. (Billington, Rev. of *Tito*, 37)

Crippa intensified the pitilessness of Tamora by playing up her fascination with violent acts carried out against the chaste Lavinia. As Chiron and Demetrius groped their victim, Tamora 'first retreated into the shadows, then returned to stage centre, irresistibly drawn by the sight of her sons' attack on Lavinia' (Tempera, 145-6). In the last scene, she watched Titus sacrifice his daughter 'with the rapt intensity of a connoisseur of cruelty' (Billington, Rev. of *Tito*, 37).

Stein made additional use of Crippa's talents by doubling Tamora with the 'grotesquely fat, comic Nurse so that the death warrant for the baby came from a distorted parody of his mother' (Tempera, 147). As Revenge, Crippa transformed herself into 'a black-suited widow' with a long veil trailing from her broad, fashionable hat, and her sons, as Rape and Murder, walked on all fours like 'dogs straining upon the leash' (Billington, Rev. of *Tito*, 37). When Saturninus later ordered the brothers to be brought to the banquet to answer for their crimes, Titus stabbed the pie with a knife to designate their whereabouts. Tamora first laughed in disbelief, but seeing that Titus was in earnest, she pitched forward across the table and began retching convulsively. At that point, Titus stabbed her in the back with the same knife. Eventually, Tamora's corpse was dumped on the apron at the front of the stage, which she shared at the final blackout with her lover and bastard child. As Tempera recalled the production's final image, 'At the end, the reconciled Romans and Goths left Tamora's body on stage, sprawled on the proscenium, while Aaron, buried to his neck, kept hurling abuses at the audience, and the black baby lay abandoned, very much alive, in the space between his parents' (29-30). For Horst Zander, the survival of Aaron and Tamora's child meant that 'the evil in this world is not going to die ... but will continue, for instance in [the] son who is present on the stage' (516n).

Standing apart from the evil Goths, as well as from the Fascist Titus and his brutal sons, stood Marcus, played by famous Italian actor Raf Vallone as 'a shrewd, old-fashioned civic dignitary' (Peter, E5). Vallone's star status brought him into conflict with Stein, who envisioned a different acting style and characterisation for Marcus than Vallone was willing to deliver. The actor explained his quarrel with his director's methods: 'I never got on with him ... because his truth was always over the top, never the result of internalizing thoughts and feelings. It was a mode of expression that ran against my professional calling' (quoted in Tempera, 28). This artistic difference led to a clash within the performance, wherein Vallone acted 'in a histrionic style ill suited to the subtleties of Stein's direction' (Patterson, 434). Stein's political reading of the text also called upon Marcus to participate in Titus's slaughter of his enemies at the end of the play, but Vallone balked at this plan because he did not want to risk forfeiting 'the sympathy of his fans' by embodying a vicious character (Goy-Blanquet, 47). Vallone's popularity is evident in an archival video, which records that when he entered aloft for Marcus's first appearance, the audience burst into spontaneous applause. Vallone himself claimed that Stein's conception of Marcus violated the integrity of the character: 'Peter wanted him [...] a lot more violent, to fit within the context of brutality; I did not feel I could do it this way, because Marcus is not violent. The director was intelligent enough to accept my point of view and ... success proved us right' (quoted in Tempera, 157). Vallone's perspective was widely endorsed by members of the Italian press, who extolled his stage presence, even if they disliked the production. D. G. Martini wrote in *Il Giornale*, 'Raf Vallone is the only one who did not suffer from Stein's doubts. He gave Marco Andronico great dignity and nobleness' (quoted in Gulino, 480).

In Vallone's shadow, Eros Pagni as Titus received positive notices, but his performance garnered less attention than one might expect from an actor in a title role. Della Couling spoke of Pagni's Titus as 'a commanding figure, with a deep, reverberating voice', who gradually disintegrated 'into virtual senility, reviving only at the end for his final acts of vengeance' (19). Michael Billington judged him 'very good as the stubborn, lantern-jawed General', but lamented that he lacked 'some of the diabolic wit that ... [Warner's Titus] Brian Cox brought to the later scenes of madness' (Rev. of *Tito*, 37). Although Pagni's Titus wore a chef's cap in the final scene, as Cox did in Warner's production, Pagni's slow, sombre entrance, preceded by Lavinia cradling the fateful pie between her stumps, did not aim to produce the same sort of darkly comic effect as Cox's entry over the banquet table in the RSC version. In fact, one of Stein's few moments of black comedy in his rendition involved Lavinia more directly than it did her father:

Stein took a big risk when he had his Lavinia try to stab herself when her father placed a knife in her mouth with this instruction: 'get some little knife between thy teeth / And just against thy heart make thou a hole' (3.2.16–17). [Lavinia's] vain efforts to perform an impossible task was so funny that the spectators started laughing and then quickly checked themselves when they remembered that laughing about the handicapped is totally inappropriate. (Tempera, 45)

In attempting to portray Titus as a serious, tragic figure, Pagni was impeded by Stein's overall concept for the production, which introduced him as a totalitarian despot. In the same way that Seale's 1967 production caused confusion by presenting the heroic Andronici in the trappings of Nazism (see p. 38), Stein's association of Titus with Mussolini's party hindered Pagni's efforts to earn sympathy from viewers. As Billington pointed out, 'if Titus himself is initially seen as a brutal Fascist, it becomes hard to accept his transition into tragic victim' (Rev. of *Tito*, 37).

Almerica Schiavo, who played Lavinia, faced an obstacle similar to that of Pagni's Titus in that she began the play as an unsympathetic figure. Goy-Blanquet referred to the cast of *Tito Andronico* as 'a pack of unattractive characters, including a Lavinia who was quite as arrogant as the rest of her tribe, undeserving of any sympathy before she got her comeuppance' (45). The attack upon Lavinia by Chiron and Demetrius in 2.3 was so overtly sexual, however, that she eventually became an object of intense pity:

> [T]he brothers mimed explicit acts of anal and vaginal penetration on Lavinia while she went through her pleading lines to Tamora. It was a very powerful scene because Lavinia turned from elegant Roman lady into groveling victim before our very eyes. The slow progress of one rapist's creeping hand up her leg was riveting and even more disturbing than the feigned act of penetration itself[;] the determination of the girl to keep talking ... was more poignant than any attempt at self-defence. (Tempera, 164)

The assault left Lavinia in a nearly catatonic state, from which she did not truly emerge until the fly scene. As Titus insulted upon the fly with a knife (see Figure 11), Lavinia slammed her stump repeatedly on the table as if she too wished to take violent revenge against her enemies. Indeed, once Tamora's sons were hung up by their feet as Aaron was, Lavinia willingly held the

11 Raf Vallone as Marcus, Almerica Schiavo as Lavinia, Eros Pagni as Titus, and Laurence Ales as Young Lucius in Peter Stein's Teatro Ateneo production (1989).

basin to catch their blood. She remained an active participant in the events of the final scene, placing the pie on the table in front of Tamora and later walking slowly across the stage toward her father to receive, without protest, the point of his blade in her stomach. Laid out with Titus on the banquet table, Lavinia appeared to attain a placid peace in death that had eluded her in life.

After opening in Rome, Stein's production toured several Italian cities, including a month-long stay in Genoa, then undertook a trip to Spain and a run in Paris as part of the 1990 Theatre de L'Europe season. Some Italian reviewers responded enthusiastically:

> C. Rubbi pronounced Stein's *Titus* 'worthy to see', and Guido Almansi, who praised Stein's ability in handling Shakespeare's 'faulty play' with mastery, perceptively observed: 'When reading it, *Titus Andronicus* looks exaggeratedly truculent and awkwardly structured. In Stein's hands the play works and intrigues the modern audiences.' (Gulino, 477–8)

Nevertheless, the majority of Italian critics responded to the director's efforts with 'not a little consternation' (Gulino, 477) and gave the production a 'rather cool' reception (Goy-Blanquet, 36). Some resented the presumption of a German director invading Italy to instruct the natives about the violence of their political history: 'Stein was promptly identified [by Franco Quadri] as "a barbarian descended from the North to tell us about another descent of barbarians." His Teutonic vision of eternal Rome made little headway with the Italians ... [b]ecause it came too near home, in Stein's opinion' (Goy-Blanquet, 49). However, German reviewers were no kinder to Stein than his Italian hosts: 'On the whole, the reports of his compatriots were the harshest of the lot, the verdict being that the production was intelligent but strained' (Goy-Blanquet, 49). Stein may have failed to reconcile the tensions between his conception of the play and the expectations of his actors and audiences, but he succeeded in transforming Shakespeare's ancient setting into a modern arena in which contemporary power struggles could play themselves out with an immediate impact upon spectators. As Gulino observed, 'Stein made distant Roman facts from *Titus* look current and real, providing a social mirror where all the crimes and the ambiguous mechanisms of politics in a modern society could be reified and reflected' (478).

National Theatre of Craiova, Romania, 1992–97 – Dir. Silviu Purcarete

The longest-running major production in the stage history of *Titus Andronicus*, directed by Silviu Purcarete, originated at the National Theatre of Craiova, Romania in 1992 and toured extensively, on and off, all over the world for the next five years. International reviewers record performances at the Panasonic Globe Playhouse in Tokyo (1992), the Residenztheater in Munich (1993), the Festival de Theatre des Ameriques in Montreal (1993), the Avignon Festival (1995), and the Parma Theatre Festival (1996). In 1997, the production toured Britain, including stops at the Lyric Hammersmith in London, the Nottingham Playhouse, and the Theatre Royal in Plymouth. Of all the directors who attempted *Titus* in the decade following the RSC's landmark 1987 production, Purcarete most closely resembled Warner in his attitude toward the play's black comedy. In fact, some viewers contended that he 'trusted the power of horror in laughter to an even greater extent than Deborah Warner' (Tempera, 33). While many spectators commended the way that Purcarete's Romanian-language production managed with finesse the 'deliberate, risky and curiously modern borderline in the play between horror and bad-taste laughter' (P. Taylor, Silviu, 4), a few responded with disgust at humour provoked by scenes of physical savagery. The most negative reaction came from Alastair Macaulay in the *Financial Times*, who concluded his review with the remark that 'the effect is invariably absurd. *Titus Andronicus* as comedy? How sick; how unfunny; how dull' (Silviu, 19).

Macaulay, unfortunately, failed to appreciate that absurdity was the whole point of the Romanian production. Emulating his countryman, Eugene Ionesco, Purcarete rendered his *Titus* in the style of the theatre of the absurd, with its mix of broad humour and horrific situations, as well as its focus on characters trapped in hopeless and incomprehensible situations, menaced by sinister forces beyond their control. Whereas Warner's painful comedy existed within a context of psychological plausibility and physical reality, the laughter in Purcarete's production often derived from ridiculous or impossible occurrences within a Rome that resembled Romania under the rule of the Communist party. Moreover, in contrast to Warner's full-text rendition, Purcarete 'ruthlessly cut' the original play to suit his political agenda (Kingston, 37). Commenting on the production's lack of interest in the play's verbal merits, James Christopher tried to imagine the director's intended effect on audiences in his home country: 'It's difficult to gauge what kind of resonance this exhilarating black pantomime might have had in post-Ceauşescu Romania. It is a willful and comic piece of absurdity rather than an act of calculated subversion. Clearly Purcarete's aim was to make the invention as thrilling as the horror. Visual wit is all. What gets lost is the poetry' (10). In its critique of 'the arbitrariness, cruelty and absurdity of tyranny' under Nicolae Ceauşescu (Billington, Silviu, T6), Purcarete's trimmed-down and politicised production followed more closely the example set by Seale's Fascist *Titus* than that of Warner's uncut tragicomic version.

As a metaphor for the absurd environment of a totalitarian state, Purcarete set his *Titus* in what appeared to be a lunatic asylum. Unlike Mesguich, who could afford to construct a toppled library replete with realistic detail, Purcarete was forced by his country's economic situation to suggest a mental hospital on a very low budget: 'the poverty of his theatre (where even nails for scenery are hard to come by) has led him to create a visual style that relies heavily on sound, light, and the frequently ingenious use of cloth. The stage ... is stripped to the firewalls, and in the resultant murky cavern, Purcarete creates ... Shakespeare's clinical Roman nightmare with a few choice brushstrokes' (Remshardt, 263). For example, he relied on curtains as an inexpensive way to vary the size and shape of his various stages, such as that of the Nottingham Playhouse:

> Stefania Cenean's set comprised a series of drapes and screens (usually white) which were hung in a variety of configurations, dropping from the flies with a sudden flurry or raised slowly on a cross beam. On several occasions, all the drapes were removed and the action took place in the empty black box of the Playhouse stage with fly ropes and theatre paraphernalia clearly visible in the wings. There was no attempt, either at its most or its least theatrical, to hide the machinery of the stage itself. (Smith, 111)

Like many practitioners of the theatre of the absurd, Purcarete borrowed the distancing techniques of Brecht's epic theatre as a means to encourage spectators to view events from an intellectual rather than an emotional perspective, and to motivate them to take political action.

Within an abstract setting, Purcarete conjured up the atmosphere of a psychiatric ward primarily through his repeated employment of a hospital trolley. This versatile bed on wheels was used most memorably for Lavinia's initial encounter with her father after her rape and dismemberment. As Marcus lifted a side curtain, the trolley was pushed onto the stage, with Lavinia in a trembling, crumpled heap upon it, her back to the audience. Contemplating his mutilated daughter, Titus worked himself into such a paroxysm of grief 'rant[ing] and roar[ing] about her sufferings ... that he actually sh[ook] her, in her newly maimed condition, right off her hospital bed onto the floor' (Macaulay, Silviu, 19). The dark, absurd humour of this sequence subsequently dissolved into cruelty as Aaron stripped to a loincloth to amputate Titus's hand: '[Titus] lay with his head back on a hospital trolley while Aaron ... sat on top of him, relishing the political and personal subjugation of his victim. But the pose was also the position of lovers and the stage business with a gag and tourniquet seemed both sadistic and pornographic at the same time' (Smith, 112). The link between pain, sexuality, and the hospital bed was renewed after the fly scene, when Saturninus pushed Tamora across the stage on the trolley, wailing in the throes of labour. A few scenes later, the Emperor himself was wheeled onstage lying face down on the bed with an arrow in his backside, which had to be comically extracted by Tamora and her sons before Saturninus could read the message attached to it. Hearing that Lucius had gathered troops to attack Rome, the terrified Emperor scrambled underneath the trolley to bemoan his imminent loss of power.

The rolling bed also figured prominently in the Revenge masque at the beginning of 5.2. The scene began with Titus perched on high in his 'study', the upper half of his body visible above a white drapery spanning the width of the platform. As the disembodied voice of Tamora hailed Titus in the persona of Revenge, three black insects (described variously by reviewers as spiders or flies) crept up the curtain. Only after Titus had humorously swatted away the insects one by one with his book did Tamora, undisguised, make her entrance in the flesh:

> Wheeled on by her sons, she persuaded Titus that she was not Tamora but the goddess, Revenge, [later] mounting him on her hospital trolley. All three of them voiced the rising tones of orgasm while Titus lay passively and knowingly unconvinced beneath her. The spectacle of mother and sons indulging in incestuous climax contrasted with his frigid intelligence. (Smith, 112)

Straddling Titus across the hospital bed, Tamora re-enacted the erotic pose assumed by Aaron earlier in the performance as he cut off Titus's hand, but in this case Titus deceived his seducer with a façade of madness. Purcarete's constant employment of the trolley at the intersection of carnality with pain and/or madness designated Rome as a type of psychiatric facility in which the trapped inmates played out their twisted, psychosexual revenge fantasies upon each other.

In addition to the repeated use of a single prop, the Romanian company depended upon relatively inexpensive sound and lighting effects to call to mind the 'fearful slumber' that comprised the world of *Titus* (3.1.251). As Sue Hall-Smith recalled, Purcarete 'endowed his version with a dream-like/nightmare quality through the use of shadows, hypnotic swirling lights and dissonant sound effects such as howling and roaring' (56n). Silhouettes were created with backlighting on the rear curtain to dramatise the birth of Tamora's son and a flashback in which Lavinia re-lived her assault by Chiron and Demetrius. The lighting design of Vadim Levinschi and Ilie Craciunescu frequently called for the stage to be washed with a garish red that temporarily dyed both the curtains and the characters' white costumes the colour of blood. Like Stein, Purcarete also seized upon Titus's description of Rome as a 'wilderness of tigers' as the basis for his production's soundtrack, which 'consisted of disturbing, howling music intermixed with the predatory growls of tigers' (Smith, 111). A menacing snarl issued from the central trap in which Tamora and Aaron coupled just before Tamora emerged to confront Bassianus and Lavinia in the forest. Such visual and auditory elements led Ralf Erik Remshardt to conclude that, as in the theatre of the absurd, Purcarete's production 'seem[ed] to treat Shakespeare's play mostly as a terrible and nauseating dream of which no sense [could] be made' (264).

This nightmare reminded many viewers of the horrors of life under a totalitarian regime such as the Romanian Communist government. In the same way that Seale's *Titus* associated Saturninus with Mussolini, Purcarete's version of the play linked the emperor of Rome to the dictator Nicolae Ceauşescu, who served as President of Romania from 1974 to 1989. The second half of his term was marked by authoritarian intrusiveness and political repression carried out by the Securitate, the country's brutal secret police force. Claudia Woolgar, who saw the original production in Bucharest, recalled the opening address of the former emperor's eldest son:

> Saturninus appears – standing with his back to the audience, holding a burning torch, and waving to an unseen crowd, lit red. It is Ceauşescu on his balcony ... Suddenly, white sheets unfurl, trapping the huge stage of the National Theatre into an enclosed box, and the lights shift. The white becomes a murky gray, the gray a blood red, the red a devilish orange ... In this world of impending doom, a mountain of bones is visually projected onto the side sheets and Shakespeare's bloodiest play speaks clearly of all who died under Ceauşescu's regime. (171)

Ceauşescu and his wife Elena were deposed in 1989 by a military coup, and after a brief trial, both were executed by firing squad.

According to Tempera, Purcarete maintained that 'parallels with the Romanian uprising of 1989 and its bloody aftermath were not as relevant in his mind as most critics suspected' (32), and indeed, the production's set and costumes did very little to locate the action in any specific time or place. However, most spectators found the performance 'profoundly contemporary' (Bate, Rev. of *Titus*, 18) and agreed with Billington that it was 'impossible to divorce the production from Ceauşescu's Romania' (Silviu, T6).

The opening curtain rose to reveal 'the screaming, distorted face of an unspecified dictator', perhaps the dead emperor, 'projected onto a white sheet backdrop' (Woolgar, 171). Two large television screens on an audio-visual cart displayed 'the jabbering heads of competing demagogues' (P. Taylor, Silviu, 4): Saturninus and Bassianus, making their pleas for the people's voice in speeches that echoed like the hollow words of 'despotic politicians' (Smith, 111). In the 1993 Montreal performance, Purcarete also staged 'the savage triumphal parading of the captive Tamora and her sons into Rome by towing a couple of TV sets across the stage, with the garishly coloured extreme close-up faces of the captives grimacing out at the audience' (Conlogue, Silviu, C8). Later, a victorious Titus, holding a microphone, delivered his return tribute to Rome as if speaking at 'a press conference' (Christopher, 10). Such references to manipulated news coverage of political events harkened back to the final days of Ceauşescu's regime, when state-controlled media outlets reported that anti-government demonstrations calling for the President's ousting were actually spontaneous outpourings of support for him.

The broadcast of the candidates' speeches was watched by Young Lucius, who entered the stage before the opening curtain and sat with his back to the audience. When Saturninus and Bassianus concluded their appeals, the boy stood up to exit, and the TV monitors were wheeled off the stage. By inserting Young Lucius into the opening scene as an observer (a representative of the innocent Romanian populace) and making use of his presence in other sequences that do not feature him in Shakespeare's play, Purcarete followed Jane Howell, whose BBC-TV version made extensive use of the reactions of Titus's grandson to underline the effects of violence on the younger generation (see pp. 49–50). In this respect, Purcarete's production helped to hand down to succeeding stage and cinematic versions of the play Howell's strategy of augmenting the role of Young Lucius as a method for shaping the audience's response to the tragedy.

However, Purcarete did not emulate Howell's graphic depiction of the play's violence. Some brutal events, such as Titus's slaying of Mutius, were relegated to off-stage action, or, like Aaron's murder of the nurse, were performed on a stage so darkened as to render the act invisible. As Titus slit the throats of Chiron and Demetrius, the actors' bodies were positioned in such a way that spectators could not see the knife come into contact with the victims' flesh:

> When Titus finally executes [Tamora's sons], the business is handled by l[a]ying them on the ground with their feet pointing toward the audience. As he cuts their throats, the little red-stockinged legs quiver like those of cattle in an abattoir. The throat-cutting itself, always an awkward business, is no problem here because the men's heads are concealed from view by their enormous bellies. (Conlogue, C8)

Instead of employing explicit bloodshed as the means to establish the horrific nature of revenge, Purcarete substituted an 'atmosphere of fear and uncertainty' (Woolgar, 171) characteristic of life in a totalitarian state as a by-product of the characters' desire to enact retribution upon their enemies.

Purcarete's primary method for creating this paranoid atmosphere was to make the ever-present curtains surrounding and subdividing the stage into a sinister dramatic representation of an arbitrary, repressive state authority that might, at any moment, seize and swallow up the characters. During the forest scene, Lavinia and Bassianus entered the stage for a lovers' tryst and began undressing themselves. When Chiron and Demetrius attacked Bassianus, a curtain fell between Lavinia and her husband, and she was left alone on the floor downstage centre. As she rose and fearfully approached the curtain, it suddenly grasped her from behind, stopping her mouth and binding her about the waist, as if with unseen hands (see Figure 12). After Tamora confronted her captive, the malevolent force shoved Lavinia forward onto her stomach and slowly dragged her under the drapery by the legs as she pleaded in vain for mercy. Since Lavinia wore, during this assault, 'a simple peasant dress and headscarf', which was common attire in Romania, this costume allowed her rape 'to be constructed as a metaphor for the degradation of the Romanian people' (Hall-Smith, 47n). However, the sinister force operated on behalf of Titus's family as well as against it. In 5.2, when Titus called to his relatives to seize Chiron and Demetrius, the curtains grasped Tamora's sons about the face and shoved them forward onto the ground to be pulled underneath to their doom, as Lavinia was. The political neutrality of this evil presence suggested that, in the totalitarian state depicted in this production, citizens of any faction might be

12 Ozana Oancea as Lavinia in Silviu Purcarete's National Theatre of Craiova, Romania production (1992–97).

silently abducted at any moment. As Woolgar reminded Western viewers, accustomed to thinking themselves safe in their own homes, such a danger existed as a daily threat in Ceauşescu's Romania: 'In a land where no one trusted anyone, because one's own mother could be a Securitate informer, the presence of an invisible enemy was a familiar one' (171).

After Titus took his well-sharpened knife to the throats of his captives, the lights went to blackout, and the audience heard a familiar cry. Since the start of the production, at moments of intense sorrow, 'an anonymous figure clad in gold' had crossed the stage, howling lamentingly (Phillips, 26). As the opening curtain rose, this figure in gold was seated cross-legged in a spotlight in the middle of the stage behind a burning candle, and his first scream triggered the candidates' speeches on the TV monitors. Such shrieking punctuated the entirety of Act 1, particularly while the figure in gold traversed the platform after Titus had murdered Mutius, and similar crossings preceded Titus's address to the tribunes in 3.1 and Tamora's trip across the stage in labour in Act 4. Just before the interval, placed between Shakespeare's 3.1 and 3.2, the howling figure in gold accompanied Young Lucius as he called out a farewell to his exiled father. In Purcarete's absurd version of Rome, this 'unknown chorus figure ... made no sense in terms of the story of the play, but ... offered a powerful emblem of the emotional anguish caused by bereavement, internment and physical pain' (Smith, 111).

Purcarete's association of the play's violence with the political brutality of the Ceauşescu government came to a climax in 5.3, which began with a spotlight on Lavinia:

> When the lights went up on the banquet scene, she was sitting cross-legged, facing the audience, with the basin in front of her ... Suddenly, Titus covered her head with a large napkin hiding a knife, then cut her throat with a gesture so swift that the audience realized what had happened only when he showed them the weapon while Lavinia started bending – in a very controlled, graceful movement – in to the basin where she quietly bled to death. (Tempera, 167)

No one at the banquet appeared to notice Lavinia's slow demise as Titus, 'sporting a chef's hat as big as a sombrero', removed the covers of two entrée dishes 'to reveal the heads of Chiron and Demetrius. With the delicacy of a triple-rosetted *chef de cuisine*,

Titus slice[d] off some ear', tasted it himself, and fed it to Tamora (Bate, Rev. of *Titus*, 18). The humour provoked by Titus's oversized chef's hat (as in Warner's production) continued through Tamora's forced cannibalism and the ironic staging of the final scene's triple murder:

> The culinary deliberation and delicacy of touch suggested the ear was a dainty titbit rather than a lump of human flesh. Tamora sat with it in her open mouth, paralysed by the sight of her sons' severed heads on the table in front of her. The feast froze before Titus stabbed the fleeing Empress, Saturninus stabbed Titus and Lucius stabbed Saturninus as the characters circled in a merry-go-round of bloodshed. At such points, the production relished the dark and extreme comedy of Shakespeare's play. (Smith, 112)

The comic irony of this sequence was enhanced by a shift in the production's soundtrack:

> The multiple killings then [took] place not in chaos and uproar but, with elegant timing, to the E flat major Larghetto of Mozart's last piano concerto. The production ha[d] been punctuated throughout by unearthly howls and dissonant, metallic strings. Mozart [brought] it to a close on an aesthetic harmonisation, but with no illusions of political restoration. (Bate, Rev. of *Titus*, 18)

As Hall-Smith added, 'This final fusion of aesthetic beauty with the physical horror of the action became a metaphor for the fall of the Ceauşescu regime' (47).

The collapse of Saturninus's rule promised no positive political restoration in Purcarete's rendition because Lucius was not presented as the saviour of Rome that some previous directors had made him. Instead, Purcarete linked the new emperor to Ion Iliescu, a leader of the 1989 revolution who was chosen the following year as Romania's first post-Communist president. Iliescu was elected democratically, but he also became the target of allegations of voter fraud and manipulation of the electorate through state-controlled media. After Lucius stabbed Saturninus and fled the stage, his image appeared, holding a torch, on one of two TV monitors pulled slowly across the stage, while Aemilius, on the other screen, called for Titus's son to become the next emperor. Subsequently, a huge portrait of Lucius was projected onto the back curtain, recalling both the screaming face of the dictator that was visible there at the beginning of the performance and the emergence of Romania's current president: 'while Shakespeare put a strong, *just* emperor on the throne, Purcarete filled the stage with a tyrant's face – not distorted this time, but sinister in its normality. And the actor whose face this is slips silently down a trap door into a smoky, red underworld. Who is he? How did Iliescu win the election?' (Woolgar, 171, italics original). Purcarete reinforced the anxiety incited by the accession of Lucius by rearranging the text so that the performance concluded with a speech from Marcus, who clearly opposed his nephew's rise to power. Stephen J. Phillips recorded the version of this ending staged at Plymouth:

> As the curtain began to fall, Marcus appealed directly to the audience, concluding with three of the anonymous Roman Lord's lines (5.3.84–86): 'Tell us what Sinon hath bewitched our ears, / Or who hath brought the fatal engine in / That gives our Troy, our Rome, the civil wound.' When the curtain cut him off in mid-speech, he bent down to the stage floor to shout his words at us. There was a guttural snarl, and the houselights snapped up. Marcus was trapped behind the proscenium arch in the wilderness of tigers that his nephew had joined. (27)

By suggesting that Rome under Lucius would be no less cruel and unforgiving than Rome under Saturninus, Purcarete implied that the Romanian people could expect no more benevolent government from the democratically-elected Iliescu than from the Communist Ceauşescu.

The final scene of Purcarete's production, like the conclusion of Lambermont's version, did not include Aaron, who appeared on stage for the last time in 5.1. Played by Ilie Gheorghe, Aaron initially wore only 'a red loin cloth covered by a long and bushy parody of pubic hair ... with stylized dark green makeup on his face and a red skullcap' (Phillips, 26). The Moor's pubic ponytail 'was a simulacrum of the long black hair of his beloved Tamora' (Coveney, Silviu, 57), with whom he mated in the forest, his animalistic grunts mingling with the growls of tigers on the soundtrack. Later, his capture by Lucius and the Goths was portrayed as if he were a wild beast caught in a snare. At the beginning of Act 5, the Goth army, represented by seven masked and black-robed figures carrying tall spears and moving as a cluster with very short, quick steps, discovered Aaron speaking to his son from behind a curtain. Lifting the curtain with their spears, they trapped the Moor in a net that raised him above the soldiers' heads, from which position he begged for the life of his child and bragged of his outrageous crimes. At the end of the scene, the Goths penetrated the net from all sides with their weapons, leaving them in place like a ball of yarn pierced by several knitting needles.

This image reappeared unexpectedly in the lobby of the host theatre as spectators exited the auditorium: 'Here Shakespeare's unrepentant Aaron, though lashed to a collar of spears, is still unsubdued. He lurches menacingly toward the crowd like a giant spider, hissing and growling, his face twisted with pure malevolence' (Remshardt, 264). In Plymouth, Phillips noted the immediate and unsettling effect of this bold choice:

> If we traditionally retreat behind a bourgeois aesthetics and appropriate Shakespeare and Mozart to prettify our existence rather than confront it, we were denied this option as we made our way to the foyer. Aaron was there, 'fastened in the earth', as Lucius commands in the text [5.3.182], but still gloating over his achievements. It was a shock ... Evil does not melt away after a worthy evening spent admiring high culture, and Shakespeare's tragedy was not presented as a transcendent work of art that leaves our bloody world behind. (27)

German reviewers responded negatively to the avant-garde quality of this display, but Remshardt rightly pointed out that, under a totalitarian government, directors must employ audacious strategies for constructing meaning and making an impact upon viewers:

> Western political theatre has long outgrown such tactics, one thinks ... But in this moment of aesthetic dissonance lies encapsulated the difference between a theatre audience weaned on the luxuries of relative freedom and a theatre bred under the wary gaze of capricious authority. In Romania, theatre cannot afford to be merely a clever diversion; it is, as the director remarks, 'a kind of social exorcism'. (264)

Through his version of *Titus*, Purcarete called up the evil spirits of his country's past (the political tyrants, like Ceauşescu, who had persecuted his people), and attempted to dispel them with an absurd mixture of dark comedy and horrific violence.

This combination of humour and menace was typified by Tamora's 'very short, very fat, balding' sons' (Bate, Rev. of *Titus*,

19), whose 'gross physicality and bizarre blue eye-shadow made them figures of fun as well as horror':

> Demetrius (Valer Dellakeza) and Chiron (Tudorel Filimon) were malevolent twins – a cross between Tweedledum and Tweedledee and something from *The Adams Family* [sic]. In white shirts, black baggy shorts with braces and long red socks and carrying little tomahawks, they traversed the stage looking for the innocent Lavinia, snapping as much at each other as [at] their declared prey ... They were a curious mixture of childlike naivety and grotesque cruelty. (Smith, 112)

The small axes wielded by Chiron and Demetrius, given to them by Aaron in 2.1, functioned as the sons' weapons of choice, much like the spikes brandished by Tamora's boys in Mesguich's production. Chiron and Demetrius taunted Lavinia with their axes in silhouette prior to the start of 2.4, but brilliant frontlighting dispelled the shadows and Lavinia tumbled forward onto her mangled arms. Here, Purcarete had put actress 'Ozana Oancea into a gown with extra-long sleeves, tie[d] them off', and 'bathe[d] the lower portion of each sleeve in red dye' (Conlogue, Silviu, C8). Throughout Marcus's speech of discovery, Lavinia dragged herself away from her uncle, slowly and painfully propelling her trembling body across the stage floor with her stumps.

When Marcus brought the mutilated Lavinia back to Titus on the trolley in the next scene, their encounter served as an ironic echo of their initial meeting in the play:

> Purcarete built the entire father–daughter relationship to culminate in this moment. When Lavinia first entered in Act I, her reunion with Titus was that of two lovers, with the father fondling and playfully biting her rear ... As she lay quivering with shock on a hospital bed, again Stefan Iordache kissed her mouth and then quickly spanked her, in a mirthless repetition of the same routine. (Tempera, 183)

Iordache's performance puzzled English-language reviewers, who preferred to see Titus acted in a naturalistic mode. Jeremy Kingston described the appearance of Iordache's Titus as 'grizzled' and his manner as 'grumpy, grunting with mad laughter', which caused his interpretation to come across as 'lavish with externals but impoverished within' (37). While Billington praised Iordache's Titus as 'wonderfully volatile' (Silviu, T6), Macaulay lamented the way in which the actor switched 'from bass register to tenor and back again, from fortissimo to piano (and back again) – for no expressive reason, just to make an impression' (Silviu, 19). Billington suggested that Purcarete was 'more concerned with scoring directorial points than with character and situation' (Silviu, T6); but more likely, the Romanian director encouraged an acting style appropriate to the theatre of the absurd rather than to traditional British Shakespeare productions. Although Macaulay condemned Purcarete's version as 'flashy, cheap-minded, crudely sensationalist, [and] atrociously acted' (Silviu, 19), the ingenuity and longevity of the production call for a more balanced overall assessment. Purcarete's rendition may have been 'a series of magnificent theatrical moments rather than a sustained or coherent dramatic story' (Smith, 111), but it also created 'a visually striking and emotionally unified world' (Billington, Silviu, T6).

In contrast to the relatively optimistic performances staged by Lambermont and Maggio, the highly politicised productions directed by Stein and Purcarete did not offer Rome the future prospect of a benevolent government. While the North American productions implied that Lucius would rule stoutly and justly, the Italian and Romanian versions suggested that Titus's eldest son would reign no less despotically than his predecessor. As we shall see, in Gregory Doran's equally political production, the director attempted to have it both ways: to invest Lucius with the repressive values of his father's generation, but also to imply that his accession could lead to a positive reconciliation of the warring factions within his country.

CHAPTER III

Gregory Doran

Market Theatre of Johannesburg, South Africa, 1995 – Dir. Gregory Doran

One of Britain's most celebrated Shakespearean actors, Antony Sher, was born in South Africa but left home at the age of 18 to pursue his career in the United Kingdom. During the 1980s, Sher conspicuously supported the UN's cultural boycott of his homeland, but with the lifting of sanctions in the early 1990s, he and his partner and collaborator, director Gregory Doran, under the auspices of the National Theatre Studio, agreed to conduct a workshop exchange with the Market Theatre of Johannesburg which eventually grew into a multi-ethnic and multinational production of *Titus Andronicus*. Sher and Doran chose *Titus* for this project because of 'the relentless reflection it holds up to the cycles of violence and revenge that shook South Africa for the lifetime of every adult in their audience' (Kustow, 10). In *Woza Shakespeare!*, their jointly authored production diary of the experience, Doran wrote, 'I think it's a play about our capacity for cruelty, and our capacity for survival; about the way violence breeds violence; about the search for justice in a brutal universe. It's about a world I recognise around me, particularly here in Africa' (Sher and Doran, 25). The play's exploration of 'race and bigotry', as well as 'its anatomy of the consequences of colonial conquest' (Gevisser, 83), made it particularly appropriate for a nation just emerging from many years of subjugation of its indigenous people. Apartheid, an oppressive political system, served for Sher and Doran the same function that Fascism and Communism had performed for Seale, Stein, and Purcarete: it represented a modern political equivalent of Rome ruled by the tyrant Saturninus.

Unlike Purcarete, however, Sher and Doran chose to set their 1995 production explicitly in Sher's homeland, within the very recent past. One year before, in the country's first open ballot, the African National Congress had swept peacefully into power under Nelson Mandela despite widespread fears of violent retribution. In his diary, Doran commented on the resemblance of this potentially divisive event to the hot rivalry between Saturninus and Bassianus for the empery in Act 1 of *Titus*: 'It is fascinating to be doing a play in which a fiercely contested election threatens to topple the state into chaos, here in South Africa. The first anniversary of the country's historic elections will take place during the run' (Sher and Doran, 112). The production opened at the Market Theatre at the end of March, 1995 and ran for eight tumultuous weeks with Sher in the title role, culminating in a televised filming by the South African Broadcasting Corporation. In July, the company travelled to England for five days of performances at the West Yorkshire Playhouse in Leeds and a similar stay at the RNT's Cottesloe the following week. British audiences generally appreciated the way in which the production's novel setting transformed the play's far-fetched excesses into dreadful yet believable events. As Benedict Nightingale observed, 'What makes [*Titus*] preposterous is precisely what made it suitable for presentation in a South Africa still licking its wounds. It is a crazy piece for a crazy place' (31).

Some critics, like Nick Curtis, did complain that Doran's relocation of the action to a modern apartheid state was 'politically naive': 'there is no clear analogy between Titus's Rome and South Africa, and Doran's production clumsily depicts the in-fighting of a corrupt white elite while marginalising or demonising the black, [and] the coloured ... supporting characters' (Gregory, 44). To be fair, Doran did not insist upon Rome as a 'wholesale allegory' for South Africa (Wainwright, 11), but Curtis's remark does highlight the racial divisions within South African society that the director exploited in his reconception of the play's Romans, Goths, and Moors. With some exceptions, Rome's ruling family and the Andronici were portrayed as Afrikaners (white descendants of the early Dutch and European settlers, also known as Boers); the Goths appeared as coloured (mixed-race) subjects; and Aaron took shape as a South African black native. Tamora, Queen of the Goths, was played by a white actress, Dorothy Ann Gould, because, had she been coloured like the rest of her people, her illegitimate child with Aaron would not betray her cuckolding of Saturninus.

Doran also cast a coloured actor, Ivan D. Lucas, in the double role of Bassianus and the Clown. Both Lucas and white actor Gys de Villiers as Saturninus were shaved bald, prompting Curtis to call them 'the colonialist skinhead sons of the dead emperor squabbling over Rome's laurel crown' (Gregory, 44). Near the beginning of the play, Saturninus, wearing a yellow suit and black armband, took the laurel crown off his dead father's head and was about to place it on his own when Bassianus, dressed in a black leather jacket and grey turtleneck sweater, intervened. The two brothers jointly held the crown as they spoke their opening speeches, but Marcus, sporting a red sash to indicate his status as a tribune, placed his hand on the crown to announce Titus as a candidate for the empery, whereupon Saturninus and Bassianus both let go of the laurel wreath.

The subsequent return of Rome's conquering army established the general and his soldiers as Afrikaners through their distinctive accents, a choice justified by Doran's perception of a resemblance between the play's portrayal of the Andronici and the Boer frame of mind:

> Titus's family are of old Roman stock, with a self-righteous belief in their own importance. Like the Afrikaner nation, they are God-fearing and pure-bred. Shakespeare even gives Titus the surname 'Pius'. Roman piety meant unswerving loyalty to Family, Church and State. Such piety is quintessential to the old Afrikaner mentality. (Sher and Doran, 48)

With bleached hair and beard, Sher's Titus immediately struck many reviewers as 'a dead-ringer for Eugene Terre Blanche' (Gevisser, 83), the founder of the Afrikaner Weerstandsbeweging (AWB), a neo-Nazi white supremacist group that opposed the end of apartheid and supported an independent Boer republic within South Africa. According to Richard Wilcocks, Sher spoke 'in an appropriately harsh Afrikaner accent, rather like that of the repulsive Eugene Terre Blanche when he deigns to speak English' (33).

A former policeman, Terre Blanche held ties to the military through his father, who served as an officer in the South African Defence Force (SADF). Sher reinforced this connection at the beginning of the play by donning the regimentals of the SADF and endowing all aspects of his movement and behaviour with a military bearing. The battle-weary general wore a Sam Browne belt over his camouflage uniform, decorated with campaign medals: 'His sturdy, upright frame bulging beneath army fatigues, the bristling white whiskers defiantly jutting out, the beret set in an uncompromising line above his cold, commanding eyes, all sp[oke] of a man born to be obeyed and untroubled by any thoughts of conscience' (Tinker, 46). The great city to which the conquering hero returned was 'reduced to the shell of a grim, grey building with old tyres, bicycle wheels and other urban debris piled at its sides' (Nightingale, 31). Titus's Rome was, in this production, 'strangely reminiscent of South Africa's black townships. He st[ood] proudly in the back of an army jeep, pulled along by the cowering Goths' (Tinker, 46). This image of a victorious general drawn along by his vanquished foes reminded British reviewers of a role played by Sher three years previously, the conqueror Tamburlaine, who famously rode in a chariot pulled by his defeated enemies. Sher himself, however, relished this moment as an emotional homecoming. After a long, self-imposed absence from the South African stage, his first speech as a professional actor in his native land, spoken from the military vehicle, allowed him to 're-salute his country with his tears' (1.1.75). Later in the performance, Titus honked the horn of the same army jeep to wake Saturninus and Tamora to hunt the panther and the hart.

Titus's sons, particularly his eldest, were portrayed in the same strict military tradition. Martin Le Maitre, also wearing an SADF uniform, played Lucius as 'a hard-line man of war, reactionary, racist, his father's son' (Sher and Doran, 174). In the opening scene, he moved with martial precision, always stamping his foot before carrying out one of his general's commands. His imposing physical presence also enhanced Titus's initial authority when it was challenged by Saturninus: 'Much taller than Titus, [Lucius] was a beefy soldier very much aware of his father's rank. His attempt at participating in grown-up conversation in Act I – "Proud [Saturnine, interrupter of the good / That noble minded Titus means to thee!" (1.1.208–9) –] was cut short when Titus barked an order and his son stood to attention and fell back' (Tempera, 216).

After the mutilated Lavinia was revealed to her father, Lucius fell to his knees and watched as Titus offered to cut off his own hands, 'For hands to do Rome service is but vain' (3.1.80). As Sher spoke this line, he tore off his medals and threw them on the stage floor, symbolically disavowing his long years of military service to the state. At the end of the scene, however, Lucius crouched to pick up Titus's decorations, vowing, in his exile, to requite his family's wrongs upon the Rome that had disdained his father's service.

As Lucius's sister, Jennifer Woodburne embodied Lavinia as a paragon of Afrikaner womanhood. Blonde and 'dressed in virginal white' (Bate, Rev. of *Titus*, 18), led on stage for the first time by her uncle Marcus, she reminded Lynda Murdin of 'a young Grace Kelly'. South African reviewer Digbi Ricci wrote that, after eloping with Bassianus, 'Lavinia, in wedding-gown and short white gloves, has a Voortrekker-maiden quality' (81). The Voortrekkers, an Afrikaans language youth group, was founded in 1931 as an alternative to the Boy Scouts, which was perceived as too British by some Afrikaners. The organisation, which later included girls, placed more emphasis on Boer citizenship and Christianity than did its British counterpart, and it therefore appealed to the pious nationalism of the Afrikaner elite. As a 'Voortrekker maiden', Lavinia's racial purity was thrown into relief, not only by her coloured fiancé Bassianus, but also by the mixed-race sons of Tamora, who conspired to spoil her chastity. Jane Edwardes, viewing the production in Johannesburg, later recalled the sharp contrast 'between Jennifer Woodburne's white, mincing Lavinia and Oscar Petersen and Charlton George as the sharp-dressing, fast-talking "Cape-Coloureds", Chiron and Demetrius, who rape her' (Gregory).

Yoked together as they dragged Titus's jeep on stage, the Goth brothers were originally blindfolded and wearing loincloths, but with their mother's rise to power, they changed into garish purple and red tailored suits with two-toned shoes. South African critics, such as Garalt MacLiam, described them as Tamora's 'rapacious sons, *skollies* with finely tuned street-smarts' (2, italics original). In the words of Martin Orkin, 'skollies' are 'sub-income Cape teenage delinquents' (277) who roam the flats on the outskirts of Cape Town looking for trouble. During a panel discussion at the National with members of the Market Theatre company, Doran revealed that he drew upon the culture of the Cape Flats to characterise the Goth princes, particularly the custom among gang members to carry flick-knives in imitation of

American movies. These switchblade knives, like the spikes in Mesguich's production and the tomahawks in Purcarete's, served as Chiron and Demetrius's favourite weapons throughout the Market Theatre performance.

In the same panel discussion, Doran justified his decision to cast a white actress as Tamora by clarifying his own complex perception of the racial difference between the Goths and the Romans. Whereas the Andronici were portrayed as high-born whites (pure-bred Afrikaners), the Goths encompassed any other racial mix or category, including underprivileged whites. Dorothy Ann Gould as the Queen of the Goths therefore spoke with a 'raw, guttural, poor-white accent' (Sher and Doran, 124) to reinforce the family relationship between herself and her coloured sons. A captive in guerrilla fatigues and shorts, her skin covered with tattoos, and her dark hair flowing wildly, Gould endowed Tamora with a fierce sensuality (see Figure 13). As MacLiam wrote, 'In a sexually charged performance, Gould lends her queen a barbaric ferocity that causes one to shrink into one's seat and hold the deep conviction that when this woman swears an oath of vengeance against Titus ... it is one she will carry out' (2). Doran recorded in his diary how Gould used a prop, Alarbus's dog tags, to communicate the force of this vendetta:

> During the workshop someone brought in a picture of a line of squatting prisoners in Vietnam, each with an identity tag round his neck. We used this in Act I. All the Goths are given tags. After the execution, Lucius carelessly chucks Alarbus's identity tag at his weeping mother's feet. Dotty's [*sic*] decided that Tamora keeps her dead son's tag with her, wearing it round her neck, to give her strength to pursue her sworn vengeance on the Andronici. (124)

Later in the opening act, as Tamora promised Saturninus that she would find a day to massacre Titus and his sons – 'To whom I suèd for my dear son's life' (1.1.453) – Tamora fingered Alarbus's dog tags around her neck as a memento of her painful loss.

Tamora's lover Aaron was the only major character in Doran's production played by a black African actor, Sello Maake ka Ncube, whose angry defiance represented 'the rage of the shackled black masses ... [H]e created an intensely powerful presence on stage; in his swaggering body and lilting voice there was sexuality and cold rage; one felt how he felt brutalised and fetishised' (Gevisser, 83, 84). In an interview, Doran insisted that, in the historical context of

13 Dorothy Ann Gould as Tamora in Gregory Doran's Market Theatre production (1995).

apartheid, Aaron inevitably became a more complex and intriguing character: 'the danger with the Moor is that he ... can seem a stereotypical stage villain, whose malignity is motiveless. But in South Africa, as soon as he comes onto the stage, you feel the weight of oppression and subjugation on his shoulders, and his desire to get out of that' (quoted in Parry, 10–11). South African critic Christopher Thurman agreed that, in the Market Theatre version, Aaron was 'no longer an irredeemably malevolent villain like Iago or Edmund, but an angry man seeking reparation for the oppression of his race, a sympathetic figure in the mould of a post-Holocaust Shylock. He [was] cruel and conniving because he ha[d] abandoned any hope of being treated fairly himself' (32). Indeed, when the Goths were raised to prominence by Tamora's marriage to the Emperor, Aaron alone retained the same costume (leather vest, tattered pants, and red tennis shoes) that he wore as a prisoner. Despite his vow to abandon 'slavish weeds and servile thoughts' (2.1.18), Aaron appeared on the morning of the hunt as a vassal serving coffee from a thermos to Titus and his sons.

As in many productions, the Moor earned considerable sympathy for his display of fatherly protectiveness in 4.2, but in a South African context, Aaron was perceived to be defending his son's race as emphatically as he safeguarded the child's life. The scene began with an inserted segment during which Tamora appeared in a window above, lying on her back with her head hanging down, screaming in labour pains, attended by her nurse (Daphne Hlomuka), the only black African woman in the ensemble. By casting a black actress in this role, Doran was

> presumably alluding to the South African phenomenon of the 'maid', or domestic worker. To any politically aware South African, her few lines would have had significant connotations. When she hailed 'gentle Aaron' (4.2.55) she was sincere; when she described Tamora's 'joyless, dismal, black, and sorrowful issue' (4.2.66), she was sympathetic rather than insulting; but her description of 'the babe as loathsome as a toad' (4.2.67) indicted her for being brainwashed into the ideology of the oppressor. (Thurman, 32)

In rehearsal, Doran exhorted Aaron to respond indignantly to the self-hatred implicit in the Nurse's racial slurs:

> 'Zounds, ye whore!' he cries. 'Is black so base a hue?' I encourage Sello to honour that thought ... It's a moment when perhaps for the first time Aaron dares publicly to claim his rights as a human being, and a black man ... And suddenly we're blasted with his anger. A lifetime of the humiliations of apartheid, decades of his people's struggle, centuries of his race's oppression, howl up through Sello now as he delivers the line. (Sher and Doran, 161)

Clutching his precious child, Aaron fought off the advances of Tamora's knife-wielding sons with furious kicks until they abandoned their intent to kill their brother. Having won compassion from spectators for his parental bravery, Aaron immediately complicated an audience's response to his racial pride by slaughtering the black nurse, turning 'a friendly hug ... into a stab' as he ripped 'his scimitar-shaped panga up her spine' (Sher and Doran, 161). As Thurman observed, 'Despite such validations of Aaron's thoughts and actions, his maliciously expedient murder of the nurse thoroughly contradicted them' (32).

Aaron recaptured some of the sympathy he gained and then lost in 4.2 at the start of the next act, partly through a textual rearrangement. The scene began with the Moor holding his son, speaking the speech beginning 'Peace, tawny slave' (5.1.27–36) which is reported second-hand by the Goth soldier who apprehends him in Shakespeare's play. At the end of the speech, Aaron was attacked by two Goths, whom he fought off until one of them seized and threatened his baby, which constrained him to give himself up. Again, Doran highlighted Aaron's fatherly instincts as a means to humanise his villain, but the character's race served the same purpose even more powerfully later in the scene. After Aaron's capture, Lucius appeared with the rest of the Goth army, and Titus's eldest son had clearly, in the interim, gone native. Instead of his SADF uniform, Lucius wore the guerrilla fatigues of the Goths and crouched with his comrades, later engaging in an aboriginal war dance around the suited and bowler-hatted Aemilius. Doran recalled how, in rehearsal, when the soldiers turned Aaron over to Lucius, the general ordered the execution of both child and father:

> Somebody works out how to tie a non-slip noose and puts it over Sello's head. Suddenly the central image of the scene comes into focus. It's shocking. 'It's just like those old photos of blacks being hanged in the Deep South,' says Martin [Le Maitre]. He's right. Necklacing is a system of execution used by blacks on blacks, but this is a lynch mob. And it gets more like the Ku-Klux-Klan, when Lucius instructs the Goths to hang Aaron's baby in front of its father's face. (Sher and Doran, 174)

Since the threatened violence was interracial, Doran pictured it within an American, rather than a South African context, which would have suggested a necklacing (the black-on-black practice of placing a tyre filled with gasoline around the chest and arms of a victim and setting it on fire). However, the theatrical setting itself did evoke the township executions of the 1980s and 1990s; the stage was 'littered with old tyres and petrol cans, suggestive of ritual killings by "burning necklaces"' (Coveney, Gregory, 11). Presented as a sufferer from racially-tinged brutality, Aaron appeared 'less an incorrigible black villain than a man driven to blood and revenge by an amoral society' (Billington, Gregory, T21).

In addition to Aaron and the Nurse, Doran cast a black actor, Paulus Kuoape, as the 'Boy', who performed some of the actions of Young Lucius but spoke none of his lines. This choice was dictated by Doran's desire to find a place for the talented but non-English-speaking actor in the company, and it further required a rethinking of Titus's extended family: the followers who assist him in the arrow scene (4.3) and with the apprehension of Chiron and Demetrius. The black 'Boy' clearly would not work as the beloved grandson of a racist Afrikaner general, so Doran reconceived him and the other relatives as 'an underclass of drop-outs, runaways and homeless tramps', who functioned 'as a little tin-pot army which Titus gather[ed] around him, replacing the rather anonymous family group' Shakespeare created (Sher and Doran, 125). This 'ragged-arse army of skinny street kids, the kind they tell you not to talk to on dangerous Jo'burg street corners' (Kustow, 10), first appeared following the interval between 3.1 and 3.2, in a setting variously described as a squatters' camp or a rubbish dump, buzzing with insects. After Marcus killed one of these flies and Titus berated him, the action moved without a break into 4.1, where Lavinia located the Boy, 'whose school satchel improbably turned out to contain a copy of Ovid's *Metamorphoses*' (Tempera, 24). The entry of Titus and his followers for the arrow scene parodied the general's earlier triumphant return to Rome: he came on stage 'to the same music in a shopping trolley pushed by the ragamuffin remnant of his broken family' (Bate, Rev. of *Titus*, 18). Standing in this shopping cart, in the same military posture that he had displayed at the back of the jeep at the beginning of the play, Titus presented a lunatic caricature of the military giant who had commanded his uniformed soldiers so forcefully in the opening scene.

The garbage dump setting of the second half of the production gave rise to a prop motif that permeated the performance: the use of black garbage bags in connection with dead bodies or dismembered body parts. At Titus's initial return to Rome, the corpses of two of his sons killed in battle were encased not in coffins but in black plastic bags, which were carefully laid to rest on the ground. During the forest scene, the pit into which the body of

Bassianus was thrown was filled with bulging black trash bags, which served as padding when Martius and Quintus fell from the upper level down the length of some camouflage netting to the stage floor. When Titus offered his hand in exchange for the lives of his two sons, Aaron grabbed 'a piece of black plastic from the rubbish heap around the stage and [laid] it out to perform the amputation. After three terrible chops of the panga, Titus pull[ed] his mutilated arm away from a pre-wrapped hand ... and wrap[ped] his stump in the plastic' (Sher and Doran, 149). The hand was later returned to Titus, along with the severed heads of his sons, in a single black dustbin liner, which Lavinia kissed lovingly. She did not, however, bear the hand off stage in her mouth, since Marcus covered all three body parts with his coat and carried them away himself. Finally, as Doran noted in his diary, he elected to swaddle Tamora's newborn child in the same black plastic: 'We'll be using a doll in performance, concealed in a black bin bag – after all the Nurse is bringing the baby to Aaron to dispose of it' (Sher and Doran, 150). In Doran's South African version of Rome, this repeated use of bin bags to contain bodies and body parts designated human flesh as a disposable commodity, no different from the other rubbish littering the stage.

Such disregard for the human body coincided with the play's fascination with excessive violence, which, according to Doran's programme note, did not appear at all out of place in Sher's home country:

> It is undoubtedly an extremely violent play, but approaching *Titus* in a society like South Africa, which has suffered decades of atrocious violence, we noticed a strange reversal occur: the acts of brutality, rather than appearing gratuitous or extreme, seemed only too familiar, and our attention turned instead to how people deal with that violence, to the impact of grief, and to man's capacity for survival.

With one prominent exception, Doran staged the tragedy's violent acts in the tradition of Howell with 'gritty realism' (Dessen, 'Improving', 6), but 'without ever resorting to stagey bloodletting' (Tinker, 46). The anomalous instance of stylised violence encompassed the rape of Lavinia and its aftermath. The groundwork for this assault was laid in a wordless sequence that followed the end of Act 1, when Saturninus heaved a rock through a window to initiate a celebration of his marriage to Tamora, which devolved into a riot, complete with wholesale looting by the newly risen Goths. A mannequin wearing a fancy blue dress was lowered from a window aloft, and Tamora snatched the gown, turned her back to the audience, partially disrobed, and put on the dress, leaving the mannequin naked. Since, as Bate noticed, this bridal gown was 'effectively ... stolen from Lavinia, the mannequin [became] an image of her', which Doran employed symbolically to depict the attack on Titus's daughter later in the play (Rev. of *Titus*, 18).

Menaced by Chiron and Demetrius in the forest, Lavinia miscalculated the effect of her appeal to Tamora for mercy, based on Titus's generosity in letting her live. Tamora, grasping Alarbus's dog tags on a chain around her neck, recalled her own vain efforts to plead for the life of her eldest son and instructed her remaining offspring to satisfy their lust on Lavinia. At the end of the sequence, as a tinkling, music-box waltz began to play, Lavinia slipped into a zombie-like passivity, and Demetrius danced his victim off stage to rape her. During rehearsals, Jennifer Woodburne suggested that, at the beginning of 2.4, Lavinia had 'retreated into her own mind to shut out the horror of her attack' (Sher and Doran, 127). Thus, Doran had her enter as if she were locked in her own little world:

> Lavinia waltzes back in, all muddied and mutilated, dancing to a tune in her head ... While she dances, the two boys ... taunt her by raping the mannequin that has been abandoned at the end of the looting scene ... The boys lick and fondle the dummy's breasts, and simulate violent penetration, using a knife; all while Lavinia distractedly dances around them. Demetrius pulls off the dummy's hands and waves them at her obscenely. Then they run away laughing, leaving their victim in the forest. (Sher and Doran, 128)

While Lavinia waltzed partnerless in the foreground, 'her lipstick [was] smeared (by a silent female figure) into a scar and flesh-coloured mitts (adequately suggesting a post-mutilated condition) [were] placed onto her hands' (Macaulay, Gregory, 15). Sher recorded that Doran elected to display the application of these devices for representing Lavinia's maimed condition so that spectators would not 'waste time wondering how it's done' (Sher and Doran, 143). During this sequence alone, the presentation of violence in the Market Theatre production resembled the stylised techniques employed by Peter Brook.

Lavinia's traumatic experience, instead of prompting her to desire revenge, ultimately caused her to resist participation in Titus's vendetta against Tamora's family. After apprehending Chiron and Demetrius, Titus seized Lavinia and drew her unwillingly within inches of his captives' faces as he recounted their crimes against her. Picking up one of the fallen flick-knives, Titus also located a discarded basin in the dump; but, as he explained to Lavinia her role in the execution of her attackers, she desperately shook her head: no. Undeterred, a crazed Titus forced her to sit on the ground and hold the basin while he cut the throats of Tamora's sons, kneeling with their backs to the audience. Lavinia appeared devastated by her role in these proceedings, and as Titus carried off the basin of blood, she screamed and fled the stage. In the subsequent banquet scene, the damaging effect of Titus's pressure on Lavinia led unexpectedly to her death at his hand. Doran wrote, 'Lavinia has been curled up in a corner of the dump, pining like a sick dog ... Her relationship with her father has ruptured badly. She is horrified that he has turned into the same kind of torturer as her attackers. He is weary of her crippled whimpering presence' (Sher and Doran, 177). As Titus served his pie, Marcus (unaware of the contents) held out his plate for a slice, and Titus, determined to implement his plot, was prepared to oblige him. To protect her uncle, Lavinia leaped forward shrieking, snatched the pie between her stumps, and hauled it onto the floor. Doran chronicled the way in which Titus both pacified his daughter and prevented her from disrupting his scheme by engaging in an impromptu mercy killing:

> As he rocks her backwards and forwards, he slowly waltzes her round. I get [musical director] Dumi [Dhlamini] to reprise the tinkling waltz tune we heard when Lavinia 'gave up her spirit'. A tune we now refer to as the rape waltz. Titus suffocates her in his embrace and she slips quietly to the floor. It is all over almost before anyone has noticed. Some of the company worry *why* Titus kills his own daughter. Tony's solution is simple. 'She's a sick dog,' he says. 'She needs to be put down.' (Sher and Doran, 177)

The reprise of the 'rape waltz' as Titus 'put down' Lavinia complicated Titus's putative act of mercy by associating it with the brutal violation Lavinia had already endured. In this re-enactment of Lavinia's trauma, perpetrated by her own father, the stylised violence of the rape scene was transformed into a realistic suffocation that overcame her resistance to his plot once and for all.

South Africans are no strangers to real-life violence, and according to members of the Market Theatre cast such as Charlton George (Chiron), they often use 'humour to deal with the horror' (quoted in Armitstead, T8). Doran's production, like Warner's, did invite audience laughter, but only in a limited number of isolated scenes, and it was not always able to suppress unwanted sniggering at inappropriate moments, for 'there were some loud laughs in the audience at the most unexpected times' (de Beers). One segment in which Sher successfully courted amusement was the fly scene, in which Titus clearly made his 'hand' puns for the benefit of Lavinia, who reacted with giggles. Titus's outraged response to the murder of the fly, as well as his change of heart at the comparison between the fly and Aaron, raised hearty laughter from spectators. A less successful instance of intentional humour involved the location of the Emperor's angry tirade against Titus at the beginning of 4.4: 'Saturninus' initial reaction to the arrows was played on a darkened stage with the only light on his face; when the lights came up, he was sitting on a toilet next to a closed door so that the remainder of the scene was linked to this gag' (Dessen, 'Improving', 6). As the Emperor sat, 'literally caught with his trousers down ... clutching the arrows and voicing his frustration' (Bate, Rev. of *Titus*, 18), Tamora stood outside the stall and tried to calm Saturninus, who repeatedly inhaled hits from a canister of gas, presumably nitrous oxide. Reviewers almost uniformly disparaged this sequence as 'crass' and '[s]illy' (Curtis, Gregory, 44; Spencer, 17).

Some critics also derided the Market Theatre production for its presentation of Tamora disguised as Revenge. While Doran's intention seems to have been to clothe the Empress as an African tribal matriarch, South African reviewer Diane de Beers claimed that Tamora's costume 'read like South Sea Voodoo rather than anything from this continent'. In a skirt of leather straps and bracelets made of long, hanging blades of grass, Tamora appeared handless, and her outfit was dominated by a mask of a wild boar which she wore on the back of her head. When she hailed Titus above in the window of his study, she turned downstage so that the boar's mask faced Titus and her own features were visible to the audience. For Rape and Murder, Doran took his cue 'from Titus's reference to Chiron and Demetrius as "a pair of [cursèd] hell-hounds'" (5.2.144) and dressed them up as their African equivalent, 'hyenas' (Sher and Doran, 148). After trapping Tamora's sons, Titus tore off their animal masks and conveyed them to a couple of his conspirators, who wore them in the banquet scene, 'baying and jigging just as Chiron and Demetrius had done when they raped Lavinia' (Bate, Rev. of *Titus*, 18). Since her sons seemed to be present before her eyes, Tamora did not at first believe Titus when he announced that they were baked in the pie that she had just consumed; but when the counterfeit hyenas took off their masks, she rose and vomited, howling in revulsion.

Losing all control, Tamora rushed at Titus and attempted to strangle him, initiating a series of murders, most by unusual means. In their scuffle, Titus forced Tamora's face into the pie and suffocated her in the remains of her own sons. Saturninus then leapt forward, grabbing the knife used to cut the pastry, and stabbed Titus in the back. To calm himself after this ordeal, Saturninus took a quick fix from his canister of nitrous oxide, but Lucius seized him from behind and held the gas mask in place until the Emperor perished from an apparent heart attack brought on by this overdose. For a few moments, none of the survivors seemed to know what to do, but Lucius eventually moved the action forward by commanding his uncle to 'shed obsequious tears' (5.3.151) over the dead body of Titus.

At this point, the post-apartheid context of the production and the bleak ending of the play came into conflict, producing a contradiction that the Market Theatre version was not fully able to resolve. Since Doran wanted his production to harmonise with the spirit of reconciliation that had recently swept South Africa, he elected to cut and rearrange the text to allow the performance to conclude on a hopeful note. At the same time, his depiction of the new Emperor as a dyed-in-the-wool Afrikaner like his father ran against the grain of such optimism. After Lucius bid farewell to Titus, 'Aaron was brought on to give his defiance, receive his sentence, and be taken off along with Tamora's body' (Dessen, 'Improving', 7). Therefore, according to Thurman, 'Aaron remained at the end of the play as he was at the beginning: chained and oppressed by the white Afrikaner Nationalist, represented in a new generation by Lucius' (33). In contrast to Nelson Mandela, whose election ushered in a period of relatively peaceful transition of political power, Lucius was portrayed as 'a chip off the old military block – he has returned wearing the medals which his father cast off in disgust when Rome wrongly condemned two other sons to death. He hardly seems likely to call free elections' (Bate, Rev. of *Titus*, 18). As Tamora's body was carried out, Lucius spoke his final lines in the original text, denying her in death the pity that she had refused to others.

To avoid concluding with this merciless proclamation, Doran gave the production's final words to Marcus, shifting one of his earlier speeches to the end of the performance: 'O, let me teach you how to knit again / This scattered corn into one mutual sheaf, / These broken limbs again into one body' (5.3.69–71). Commenting on the local application of this speech, Doran wrote, 'After such appalling tragedy on both sides, this healing must be the prevailing priority ... These words hold such resonance in South Africa, where the new political orthodoxy is reconciliation. But in order for this unifying idea to be meaningful, justice must be done, and be seen to be done' (Sher and Doran, 179). Jeffrey Wainwright called this 'epilogue of hope that the torment might cease and the body politic be healed' an 'inspired alteration', and one that 'most directly refers the play to South Africa's modern history' (11). Following Marcus's petition for unity, the entire cast returned for a celebratory curtain call, complete with dancing and musical instruments in the hands of the actors. Thus a production that began with a funeral procession for a dead political leader and 'a cry of lamentation' like those that 'echoed across the townships throughout the 1980s' (Bate, Rev. of *Titus*, 18) ended with a joyous song of hope for a reborn nation. What remained unclear was how 'Rome's' new ruler, who began the play as a racist and a reactionary, might learn to knit the broken limbs of his country into a whole and sound body.

Doran's liberties with the text provoked little backlash in the press compared to his decision to have his actors speak in various South African accents. During early rehearsals, the director ran up against an assumption among his cast that Shakespeare had to be performed in a received pronunciation that made the verse sound 'bland and featureless' (quoted in Armitstead, T8). As Sher noted in his diary,

> Although we stress that we want to find a South African way of playing Shakespeare, practically every actor does his or her speech in an assumed English accent ... I'm on the edge of my seat, fascinated and tense – because, of course, that's *me* on the

stage. I've spent a lifetime burying my South Africanness, in the belief that good acting, proper acting and certainly Shakespearean acting, has to be English. As soon as Greg encourages the actors to try again, using their own accent, their own energy, their own *centre*, they transform. Suddenly they become the actors who amazed audiences around the world ... with their rawness, their passion. (Sher and Doran, 45, italics original)

Indeed, when the production came to England, British reviewers tended to praise the 'freshness and commitment' (Bate, Rev. of *Titus*, 18) that the Market Theatre cast, inexperienced with Shakespeare, brought to their delivery of the verse. One critic wrote, 'The South African accent slows down the speaking but refurbishes the cruder passages with a new emphatic vigour' (Coveney, Gregory, 11). Sher himself, recovering the cadences of his youth, was praised in London's *Sunday Times* for making his pronunciation a vehicle for the characterisation of the play's tragic hero: 'Sher squeezes volumes out of Afrikaans nasality and twang, leaning into long vowels like a sailor hauling against a gale, drawing from his accent a desolate poetry in Titus's bereavement ... The accent helps him convey a religious sense of rectitude, the muscular force of a career soldier, and a yearning bewilderment that you see on some Afrikaner faces here, after the collapse of all they held dear' (Kustow, 10).

Back in South Africa, however, the production's use of indigenous accents incited a firestorm of criticism, stemming in part from the country's own troubled self-image and its complex postcolonial relationship to its British cultural heritage. Several reviewers complained that the accents were both inaccurate and inconsistent; as de Beers lamented, 'Never have South Africans tried so hard to sound like South Africans – and alas, failed so dismally.' Other critics, like Mark Gevisser, observed that all of the attention paid to accents interfered with the actors' performances; he regretted that Sher's Titus, among others, often seemed 'constrained by the need to get the pronunciation right' (84). Responding to the prevalence of flattened vowels and rolled rrrr's spoken by many of the characters, Doran's harshest critic, Digbi Ricci, declared that the production was 'hobbled, nay, mangled, by the use of offensively exaggerated South Effrican accents' (82). Ricci's own joke at the expense of South African pronunciation hints at a type of cultural self-loathing that was expressed more overtly in a letter sent to Sher by a local woman, who apologised for not attending the production because she 'could not abide the excruciating experience of the ugly accents of southern Africa abusing some of the most beautiful language ever written' (quoted in Sher and Doran, 226).

This admission typified the clash between many white South Africans' preconceptions about the performance of Shakespeare and the attitude governing the Market Theatre production itself. While Doran saw the speaking of the play's verse as a means to address his South African spectators 'in accents and images pertinent and accessible to that audience' (quoted in Wilcocks, 33), many of his viewers expected to hear not their own Afrikaans accent, but the eloquent and poetic lyricism of renowned 'British' Shakespearean actors, including Sher himself. Although Ricci claimed, 'Nobody is demanding the crystalline voices of a Vanessa Redgrave or a John Gielgud from a local cast' (82), his intense disappointment with the production reveals a nostalgic expectation that the Market Theatre actors would at least strive to reproduce the magniloquence of a bygone era. As Michael Kustow observed,

> There is a great knot of post-colonial cultural reflexes in all this. After years of cultural isolation, it is not surprising that South African whites should want to make up for what they have been deprived of: well-spoken English versions of the Bard, presented as if he were grand opera. But Sher and his colleagues have tried for something more dangerous, more urgent ... Quite simply, they have sidestepped all the 19th-century wrappings in which an older idea of Britishness embalmed Shakespeare. (10)

In certain ways, the risk that Sher and Doran took by frustrating the expectations of their South African audience did not pay off; attendance was low, and Sher wrote to a local paper to chastise his countrymen for their failure to support the production. In an editorial entitled, 'You made us Philistines', Jeremy Brooks responded that Sher himself was partially responsible for this apathy as a result of his participation in a cultural boycott that had cut South Africa off from access to, and appreciation for, high art: 'Come off it, Mr Sher. The answer is this: South Africans, white and black, no longer give a fig for what is happening to our arts and theatre. And blame for this should be laid squarely at your door.'

While Brooks's accusation may have been true for certain

white South Africans, black citizens probably had more practical reasons for their reluctance to attend the show. According to Sello Maake ka Ncube, black people were afraid to come to the Market Theatre because of its location in a high-crime area; those who did see the show not only had no objection to the South African accents, but they also displayed an 'amazing and positive' reaction to the production ('Discussion'). Kustow recounted a personal anecdote about a black spectator's response to the Moor's defence of his child: '"I am of age to keep my own," he cries [4.2.104–5], clutching his baby son to his chest. Next to me, a young black man in a business suit yells approval of Aaron's affirmation. No cultural obstacles for this spectator, who has just realised Shakespeare understood black pride' (14). Similarly, Doran described a particular evening's performance attended by an all-black audience comprised of members of the Anglican Church Society of Soweto:

> In fact they identify with the way Sello plays Aaron to such an extent that they cheer him right the way through the plot to rape Lavinia. It is not until he hacks off Titus's hand that they suddenly turn against him. When Aaron turns to the audience and says defiantly: 'Let fools do good, and fair men call for grace / Aaron will have his soul black like his face' [3.1.203–4] – the Anglican Church society jeer and boo him. Then, in the second half when the Nurse brings Aaron's black child to be killed, the audience rally to his side once again. Aaron defies the order to murder his child just because of his colour ... The reaction Michael Kustow witnessed at this point is now amplified throughout the whole house: 'Yebo!' the audience shriek out, 'Yebo!' yelling their approval and their solidarity. (212–13)

Far from rejecting the production's political stance, or resenting Sher's role in the cultural boycott, those black South African viewers who witnessed the Market Theatre performance appear to have responded enthusiastically to its examination of racial identity and the violence stemming from interracial conflict.

Perhaps more thoroughly than any of the other productions examined in this chapter, Doran's Market Theatre version of *Titus Andronicus* incorporated aspects of his most prominent predecessors' approaches to performing the tragedy. Like Jane Howell, Doran staged most of the play's violent acts realistically, but he represented the rape and mutilation of Lavinia in a stylised fashion, *à la* Peter Brook. In the manner of Deborah Warner's

RSC version, the Market Theatre production sought to bring out the play's dark comedy, but only in isolated segments of the play (and not always successfully). Above all, Doran aimed for a political rendition of *Titus* in the new tradition inaugurated by Douglas Seale and continued by Peter Stein and Silviu Purcarete. To the extent that Doran and Sher set in motion a lively discussion about art, violence, and race relations in contemporary South Africa, their production was a significant achievement. Four years later, Julie Taymor's film version of the play, based on her New York stage production, went two steps further by incorporating even more comprehensively all four lines of descent in the play's stage history and by extending its political application to nations all over the world.

CHAPTER IV

Julie Taymor: 1994 and 1999

Julie Taymor first directed *Titus Andronicus* with Theatre for a New Audience at St Clement's Church in New York City from 3 to 27 March 1994, a staging that cemented her reputation as a leading Shakespearean director. During an interview included on the DVD version of the film *Titus* (1999), Taymor recalled that she was offered the opportunity to direct the play based upon her previous experience in creating stylised theatrical depictions of violence; yet, she quickly realised that such an approach would not do justice to *Titus Andronicus*:

> [T]here are so many acts ... of violence that, if you totally stylise it, with the red streamers ... you can distance yourself in order to look at the action, but it doesn't get you on a gut level ... So I immediately ... wanted to deal with the violence on two levels, and to unsettle the audience by never knowing on what level [they] would experience something, [so] that [they didn't] become numb by the elegant beauty of the stylisation, and [they didn't] become numb from the visceral reality, which is what we do on television.

Taymor's reference to 'red streamers' showed her awareness of the Asian techniques employed by Peter Brook several decades before. Although she appreciated the distancing effect that Brook's formalisation of violence created, she rejected the exclusive use of such a strategy because, in her mind, it fails to strike the audience 'on a gut level'. Therefore, she combined stylisation with the 'visceral reality' used on television by Jane Howell, as a means to keep spectators off balance and continuously sensitive to the shocking brutality of the play's events.

On stage, Taymor followed Brook's lead in her decisions to cut the text heavily and to stylise her production, especially in the aftermath of Lavinia's rape and mutilation, as well as in her

'Penny Arcade Nightmares': carnivalesque interludes depicted as plays-within-the-play by means of a smaller proscenium stage on which abstract sideshow versions of the story's events were replayed. However, Taymor also represented, with a graphic realism akin to Howell's, violent actions such as the amputation of Titus's hand and the execution of Tamora's sons, the latter of which Brook relegated to off-stage action (see p. 58). Moreover, Taymor's staging emulated Howell's script in its rearrangement of the play's major opening events, along with its concluding suggestion that Lucius had broken his promise to raise Aaron's baby. When Taymor directed *Titus* on film, she based her screenplay on the script of her stage production, but she further reduced the number of lines and enhanced her most distinctive staging choice derived from Howell: the decision to employ the son of Lucius as an observer of Rome's cruelty. At the end of the film, Young Lucius ultimately matures into an active opponent of violent revenge.

Taymor's stage production and film also incorporated aspects of the other two lines of descent in the performance history of *Titus Andronicus*. Like Deborah Warner, Taymor took full advantage of the text's opportunities for black comedy, but her blending of ancient and modern Rome, chiefly her incorporation of Fascist elements within classical settings, placed both versions of the tragedy squarely in the political tradition inaugurated by Douglas Seale. For Taymor, Shakespeare's play on stage became a vehicle for commenting on the exploitation of violence as a form of entertainment in the contemporary world. The film *Titus* then adapted Taymor's stage version to fit the director's new outlook at the turn of the millennium, a historical moment that combined continuing bloodshed with glimmers of hope for the future.

Although Taymor's film was praised for being 'faithful to the letter and spirit of *Titus Andronicus*' (Nochimson, 48), she did cut approximately 'an hour and a half' from the running time of the full text (Burt, 100), slightly more than she had eliminated from her stage production. In her programme at Theatre for a New Audience, she acknowledged 'her debt to Peter Brook's version of the text' (Lennox, 35), a debt most evident in her film's severe reduction of the action that takes place after the death of Titus. Elsewhere, Taymor restored many of the riskier lines that Brook had cut, but she did omit the two sequences in the play featuring the Clown (4.3.77–110 and 4.4.39–48), as well as the whole of 2.2, in which Titus wakes Saturninus and Tamora to hunt the panther. There, as she did in other parts of the film, Taymor translated Shakespeare's poetry into the visual language of cinema by showing the hunt in progress without any dialogue.

Taymor further demonstrated her gift for 'finding visual equivalents for the dramatist's figurative verse' (Bate, Introduction, 10) by shooting on locations that reduced the need for dialogue by serving as metaphors for the characters' emotional states. For instance, the scene of Titus pleading for the lives of his condemned sons took place at the intersection of two stone highways upon which Titus prostrated himself in the dust. This setting underlined for viewers that Titus had arrived at 'a crossroads in his life' (Taymor, *Illustrated*, 179) with regard to his relationship to his family and to Rome. Similarly, Taymor located the discovery of the ravished Lavinia (2.4) in 'a swamp, like a burnt-out forest' that became an emblem for her 'ravaged' state (quoted in Noh, 14). Moving from a theatrical staging to film, Taymor relied more heavily on visual landscapes than on dialogue to convey the psychological torment of Titus and his progeny.

In her stage production, Taymor alternated between a stylised and a realistic presentation of violent acts by contrasting the 'poetic metamorphosis' sustained by the mutilated Lavinia with the graphically brutal chopping off of Titus's hand in the next scene (Blumenthal et al., 184). After Lavinia's assault, she stood 'mortified and quivering, unable to move ... She wore black gloves, the fingers of which were mere twigs, a grotesque reminder of her lost limbs'; and yet, in the following scene, 'Aaron cut off Titus' hand with a jackknife, with all the gruesome bloodiness and pain in full audience view' (Lanier, 467). In the tradition of Howell's naturalistic presentation of violence, the blood from Titus's wound 'kept seeping through the rag that bound the stump' (Lennox, 36), but in the formalised mode favoured by Brook, Lavinia's similar loss of limbs was 'poetic' and aestheticised, relying on the audience's suspension of disbelief for its effect. Lavinia stood perched upon a truncated column, a type of pedestal, wearing her 'torn, soiled, many-layered crinolines, with the severed tongue represented by a red vertical line drawn at the center of the mouth' (Lennox, 35). The height of the pedestal initially provided a practical reason for Marcus's verbally extensive delay before taking Lavinia down in an attempt to comfort her, but the space that separated Marcus from his niece was ultimately metaphorical rather than physical, for at the end of the scene, Marcus was able to help Lavinia down from the column and into his arms.

However, when Taymor filmed this sequence, she adapted the stylisation of the scene to the more realistic medium of cinema. The scene began in the swamp with Chiron and Demetrius jeering at the maimed Lavinia, standing in her sullied petticoats on top of a gnarled tree stump. As Marcus emerged from the forest, he spied Lavinia from a distance and spoke the first half of his speech (cut to a total of 15 lines) as he strode toward her, so the space that separated them was truly physical rather than metaphorical. In an interview, Taymor revealed that she substituted a tree stump for the stage production's pedestal owing to the higher standard of realism ostensibly required by film, but she employed the overall image 'in a theatrical way' by retaining the replacement of Lavinia's hands with twigs. Yet instead of lashing the twigs to black gloves, which would necessitate suspension of disbelief, Taymor used cinematic special effects to offer 'heightened reality' (quoted in Johnson-Haddad, 35): the genuine appearance of twigs as hands, but without the blood that would issue from real wounds. Employing blue-screen gloves and computer-generated twigs, Taymor aimed to create a 'surreal and poetic' effect that avoided 'falling into the trap of utter realism', which might detract from the audience's identification with Lavinia's emotional torment by focusing too much attention on the 'grotesque and horrific' image of her dismembered body (Blumenthal et al., 236). Taymor concurrently intensified the representation of the young woman's missing tongue in the film by offering a more realistic version of the injury than the red vertical line used on stage. As Lavinia turned to face her uncle, she opened her mouth in a silent howl, spewing forth streams of crimson blood. To moderate the realism of this sickening sight, however, Taymor stylised the presentation, as well as Marcus's horrified facial reaction, by slowing down the speed of the film, rendering the moment as part of a waking nightmare, almost too terrible to be true.

Taymor sustained this bad-dream quality throughout the tragedy in the theatre and on the screen by interpolations she dubbed 'Penny Arcade Nightmares' (PANs), which she devised 'to portray the inner landscapes of the mind ... in a dreamlike, surreal, and mythic manner' (Blumenthal et al., 186). Whereas Mesguich set his production in an entirely surreal world, Taymor selectively employed surrealism to help juxtapose Brook's stylisation of violence with Howell's realistic approach. In the open performance space at St Clement's Church, designer Derek McLane constructed a proscenium 'framed in gold, with a sumptuous red-velvet curtain' (Barbour, 6) that offered 'connotations of formality, opulence, and high art' (R. Gross, 551). At five points during the production, miniature versions of this frame, featuring 'tattered red velvet curtains' (Blumenthal et al., 186) were brought on stage 'to stir associations with vaudeville, melodrama, and other low-brow spectacles' (McCandless, 494). To the accompaniment of 'Elliot Goldenthal's score, which played against the purity, elegance, and beauty of the imagery with a demonic, carnivalesque twist' (Blumenthal et al., 186), two 'weird clowns – a blubbery henchman and a trench-coated spook – present[ed] these attractions with the air of sideshow barkers' (Blumenthal, 9). Depicting the violated bodies of Alarbus, Lavinia, her brothers, and Titus himself, these 'tableaux vivants ... were further abstracted by their being positioned behind a traslucent layer of plastic that was scarred with scratches and spattered and smudged with black ink, like a rotting old photograph' (Blumenthal et al., 186). As David McCandless noted, these 'peep shows' defamiliarised 'the use of violence as entertainment by showcasing bodily degradation as sleazy diversion, inviting, only to confound, a sadistic, voyeuristic gaze primed for titillating spectacle' (494). In an early version of her film's screenplay, Taymor retained 'the red revenge curtain to inaugurate' each PAN, but she eventually abandoned this feature 'because it was too theatrical' (quoted in De Luca and Lindroth, 30). Instead, she incorporated the same basic PAN images within the large frame of the cinema screen, but in doing so, she both rearranged their order and eliminated their function as direct critiques of violence as low-brow sensationalist entertainment.

On stage, Taymor placed her first PAN at the end of Act 1, 'a point where seeming tranquillity between the enemies, Titus and Tamora, had been established' (Blumenthal et al., 187). The red revenge curtains of a smaller proscenium parted to disclose the torso of Alarbus, gasping his final breaths, surrounded by the limbs lopped from his body during the human sacrifice conducted off-stage by Titus's sons. Although Tamora did not witness this brutal act, the first PAN allowed the audience to perceive the image of the dismembered Alarbus as it appeared in his mother's fevered imagination. On screen, Taymor employed special visual and audio effects within the PAN to suggest that, despite the apparent truce between Titus and Tamora, their mutual resentment, smouldering beneath the surface, was about to burst into flame. In the film's screenplay, Taymor's stage directions describe how the initial PAN re-enacted, in jumbled order, the events surrounding the sacrifice of Alarbus:

> TAMORA and TITUS remain in the Piazza face to face and frozen. A surreal sequence of images overtakes the screen between the two profiles. The background Piazza becomes an inferno. Through the flames the torso and limbs of a classical Roman marble sculpture fly towards the camera. On the chest of the sculpture a bloody line magically appears that is a replica of the line TITUS cut into the chest of ALARBUS, TAMORA'S ELDEST SON. The music is replaced by the sound of human breathing. Suddenly the chest of the statue is visibly breathing, rapidly, faster and faster for just five seconds and then stops. (64)

In this nightmarish vision, the limbs of Alarbus are already lopped before Titus marks him to die. Earlier, as Titus had cleaned his ritual blade, Taymor had offered successive shots of Titus and Tamora through the flames that flared up as Alarbus's entrails were fed into the sacrificing fire. This blaze, which Taymor called, in her DVD commentary, 'the fire of vengeance', reappeared during the first PAN as flames engulfing Titus and Tamora in an inferno of violent retribution.

Taymor's second PAN, which occurred at the end of 2.3 in her staging of the play, represented the assault on Lavinia by the rapacious sons of Tamora. To the sound of 'carny music gone mad', the curtain opened to reveal Lavinia 'stripped to her torn petticoat atop a truncated column'. Her head was crowned with 'the head of a doe', and her hands were 'gloved with the doe's hooves' (Blumenthal et al., 187). Below her, Chiron and Demetrius, 'manipulating life-sized tiger cut-outs', executed 'stylized predatory lunges' at their victim (McCandless, 495). Of course, Taymor derived some these visuals from the text (Chiron and Demetrius as cubs of 'that ravenous tiger, Tamora' [5.3.194] and Lavinia as the 'dainty doe' they pluck to ground [2.2.226]), but here and elsewhere, she also drew images from modern films such as *The Seven-Year Itch* (1955). In *Playing with Fire* (Blumenthal et al., 188), Taymor's caption for a photo of **PAN** #2 reads, *'The original concept included the effect of wind blowing up her petticoat, causing her to use her doe arms to keep the skirts down. The famous image of Marilyn Monroe holding her dress down over the subway grate seemed an apt modern iconic parallel to add to this scene of humiliation and rape.'* As a part of her critique of violence as entertainment, Taymor transformed the image of Monroe coquettishly displaying her body into the cheap, titillating spectacle of a woman struggling in vain to defend her chastity against a violent attack.

When Taymor filmed **PAN** #2 for the film *Titus*, she elected to move it to the opening scene of Act 4: 'All of a sudden it hit me during the editing that the right place for that **PAN** was in the flashback, as Lavinia is writing in the sand with the stick. I love it there because when a woman has to tesify at a rape trial she is re-experiencing the rape' (quoted in De Luca and Lindroth, 30). Through this relocation, Taymor changed the sequence from a stylised, yet objective representation of the incident as it was happening to an equally stylised yet subjective flashback to Lavinia's traumatic experience. Marcus's injunction to Lavinia to take his staff in her mouth symbolically re-enacted her recent sexual violation, which propelled her into an imaginative re-experience of the rape itself. As Kim Solga observed,

> [Lavinia] looks long and hard at the staff's crown (shaped to be ... a wooden penis) and rejects it ... after almost but not quite taking it in her mouth. Pressing the staff instead into the crook of her neck like a violin, she roars into action accompanied by a hard-core metal track; the effect is an extraordinary audio/visual dissonance, the edgy music seeming to fly from Lavinia's manic bow. (70)

Since the 'hard-core metal track' that played during this **PAN** duplicated the music underscoring the film's previous scene (a wordless segment that depicted Chiron and Demetrius cavorting in their dungeon playroom), the soundtrack of the flashback alone conjured up the riotous behaviour of the two brothers. In addition, Lavinia's 'ferocious writing in the sand' was 'intercut with a bombardment of surreal images of her rape and dismemberment' (Taymor, *Illustrated*, 117). The director superimposed the growling faces of Chiron and Demetrius over clips of real tigers leaping at Lavinia from either side. As in the stage version,

Lavinia, the doe-woman, stood atop a truncated pedestal and strove to hold down her billowing petticoat, but on screen Taymor used computer graphics to layer in a tinted black-and-white forest background, dry leaves blowing in the wind, and rapidly changing close-ups of Lavinia's horrified face. In such ways, the film's version of this PAN dramatised Lavinia's subjective experience, not of the rape itself, but of the trauma of reliving it through the revelation of her assailants' identities.

The third PAN in Taymor's stage production (which corresponds to the second PAN in *Titus*), occurred near the beginning of Act 3, when 'the curtain unfurl[ed] to reveal the grotesque figure of a lamb-man, a creature with the head and arms of a man and the body of a lamb, upside down and seemingly floating within the frame' (McCandless, 495). *Playing with Fire*'s caption for a photo of this freak-show spectacle explains that '*Titus is visited by a vision of Mutius ... the son he has wrongly murdered. Half boy/half sacrificial lamb, this image occurs when Titus is pleading for the life of his two innocent but condemned sons*' (Blumenthal et al., 188). The placement of this vision in the scene where Titus begs unsuccessfully for the lives of Martius and Quintus implies that their deaths came as a form of cosmic reprimand for Titus's slaughter of his youngest son. Mutius had been sacrificed to appease Titus's misguided sense of Roman honour, and the sin of the father was now being visited upon his sons.

When this PAN appeared on screen, Taymor retained its location but added several new elements that altered its identification of Titus's crime and punishment. After Titus threw himself facedown in the dusty road to plead for his sons, he saw a vision of an angel: a red-headed young girl dressed in black playing a trumpet, who flew across the frame and revealed a sacrificial lamb on an altar down the road. Then, as a blade approached the lamb's body, its head transformed into the face of Mutius. In this expansion of PAN #3, Taymor represented Titus's sacrifice of his son as a revision of 'the story of Abraham and Isaac' (*Illustrated*, 184). By placing Mutius the lamb-man on an altar and by heralding this image with the appearance of an Angel, the director evoked the climactic moment when the Angel stayed the hand of Abraham before he could carry out God's directive. 'Abraham was ready to kill his son because of the law of God,' Taymor said in an interview. 'That is exactly what Titus did' (quoted in De Luca and Lindroth, 30). However, Taymor further complicated this sequence by conflating the sacrifice of Mutius with that of Tamora's son earlier in the opening scene. In her DVD commentary, Taymor pointed out that the blade that approached the body of the lamb was 'the sacrificial sword that we saw cut the chest of Alarbus'. The addition of this sword, used in the religious rite that put Alarbus to death, therefore located Titus's sin not in his excessive devotion to honour, but in his 'cruel, irreligious piety' (1.1.130) that originally sanctioned human sacrifice. Taymor's cinematic rendition of this PAN thus portrayed the deaths of all three of Titus's sons as a form of divine retribution for Titus's initial failure to stay his hand in the sacrifice of Alarbus.

In the Theatre for a New Audience production, the fourth PAN differed from the previous three by breaking the established convention of stylised imagery. Taymor staged the return of Titus's hand, along with his sons' heads, as a type of sideshow attraction hosted by a messenger in the guise of a carnival barker. This messenger wheeled out the gold proscenium frame with its red curtain and seated Titus and his family in front of it as audience members. When the curtain was opened, these viewers were 'assaulted by the sight of the two heads floating in yellowish liquid in glass specimen jars and the amputated hand draped over a mound of black velvet'. Unlike earlier PANs, whose stylised presentation had marked them as abstract versions of an event or a character's state of mind, this 'still life' PAN was 'actually happening' and thereby signalled the point at which bad dreams had become indistinguishable from real life (Blumenthal et al., 187). As McCandless notes, this spectacle did not 'simply frame violence – or its gruesome effects – as entertainment; it use[d] an image of violence-as-entertainment to violate Titus. The freakish nightmares, previously confined to an abstract commentary space, bec[a]me reality' (500). The cinematic version of this sequence, however, did not appear to be a PAN at all. The Clown, like the strongman Zampano in Fellini's *La Strada* (1954), arrived on a motorcycle with a sideshow wagon attached to it. When he lifted the door of the wagon to reveal the heads and hand, the resulting framed still life could not be linked back to the previous cinematic PANs because they were not framed by a curtained proscenium, as they had been in the stage version. On film, Taymor's PANs had been signalled by surreal, digitised special effects, which this sideshow segment lacked. Instead, the only subtle link to the previous PAN was the Clown's assistant, the counterpart of Zampano's wife Gelsomina, played by the same young red-haired actress who had portrayed the Angel in the Mutius PAN. Therefore, on the screen, this sequence, free of dreamlike qualities, did not mark the point at which nightmare had become reality.

Rather, this blurring of the nightmarish and the real was postponed until PAN #5, which was performed in essentially the same way in both productions, the primary difference being the continued appearance of the proscenium frame in the stage version. At St Clement's, as Titus soaked in a bathtub writing vengeful decrees in his own blood, a loud knocking disturbed his contemplation, and the gold frame and curtain entered Titus's space to the distant strains of carnival music. Taymor wrote that she 'wanted the audience to believe that what appears as the curtain opens is a figment of Titus's tortured mind' (Blumenthal et al., 187). On screen, the gold frame was replaced by the surreal special effects that had indicated all but one of the PANs earlier in the film. In a distorted voice-over, Tamora called to Titus, followed by a cut to an extreme close-up on the eyes of Revenge. In both productions, this vision seemed, at first, to be a figment of Titus's diseased imagination. Shortly, as Taymor recorded, the stage production's proscenium curtains opened to reveal Tamora and her sons in their allegorical disguises:

> Seated in front of a whirling wheel of Boschian demons sits the goddess Revenge. Her crown of daggers reminds us of the Statue of Liberty, while the black blindfold suggests Blind Justice. Where hands should be she wears two coned gauntlets. Her pendulous breasts form her shield and a plastic tube is attached to one of her nipples, feeding smoke into the mouth of Murder, who sports a tiger head as a hat. Above her right shoulder perches Rape, dressed only in a girl's training bra and panties and his head enveloped in the outstretched wings of an owl ... While framed, the controlled nightmare appears as if it is from Titus's point of view, but once the masqueraders step out of the frame, the vision becomes reality. (Blumenthal et al., 187)

In the film *Titus*, shots of Revenge, Murder, and Rape matching the preceding description were intercut with Titus rising from the bathtub and addressing his 'imaginary' visitors from an open window. After Titus vowed to descend and speak to Revenge, the film's special effects were abandoned, and spectators were offered the equivalent of the masqueraders stepping out of the frame on stage: a shot of Tamora and her sons standing in Titus's backyard in 'real' disguises, enjoying the success of their ruse. Taymor's screenplay confirmed that this final cinematic PAN took on the function of PAN #4 on stage: 'By the last of these surreal sequences the line between illusion and substance becomes blurred. The nightmare takes over the plot and madness becomes clarity, preparing us for the worst when the most unimaginable will actually occur' (185).

The 'most unimaginable' events in the play take place in its final scene, which Taymor presented, at St Clement's, as if the PAN frame had expanded to include the entire stage. The theatre's main curtain was closed for the first time, and the golden proscenium was illuminated with footlights. This 'reframing of the main stage' served to 'heighten the audience's awareness that the play's bloody climax [was] merely a conventionalized *representation*' of violence offered for spectators' consumption (R. Gross, 552, italics original). The Clown then reprised 'his weird madcap dance that heralded the spectacle of his mobile sideshow', which linked the upcoming spectacle to his 'earlier unveiling of decapitated heads and severed hand' (McCandless, 500). Within this smaller gold frame was a simple window whose white chiffon curtains were blown open by a gentle breeze to reveal two pies cooling on the sill. As McCandless detected, Taymor fortified the metatheatrical effect of these framing stages 'by converting some of the dinner guests into conspicuously dispassionate witnesses of the grisly multiple murders':

> After Titus kills Lavinia, the guest/witnesses slowly raise their drinking glasses in an eerily synchronized, robotic toast, a gesture they repeat after Lucius's shooting of Saturninus ends the hugger-mugger succession of killings. Explicitly identified as consumers, these soulless figures exhibit an automatic, culturally conditioned, vacant aesthetic appreciation for violent spectacle. (500)

On the screen, Taymor replaced these dinner guests with a crowd of spectators at the Colosseum, who viewed the aftermath of Titus's bloody banquet silently and offered no signs of approval of the violence they had witnessed. The only remnant of the stage production's framing of the final scene as a PAN was the 'red velvet curtain' through which Titus entered to serve his gruesome meal (Taymor, *Illustrated*, 163). Compared to her staging,

Taymor's film relied less heavily on Brook's stylised imagery to carry its critique of violence as entertainment.

As Taymor moved from stage to screen, she also modified many of the elements she borrowed from Howell's realistic BBC-TV rendition. Although Pascale Aebischer reports that 'Taymor, in a telephone interview, acknowledged seeing Howell's video but denied being consciously influenced by it' ('Women', 142n), Howell's fingerprints were all over both of Taymor's *Titus* productions, especially in their depictions of the killing of Chiron and Demetrius. In Howell's version, the executions took place 'in an abattoir [smokehouse] where the two gagged and squealing figures hang upside down alongside slabs of meat. When their throats are cut, a large quantity of blood gushes down to be collected by Lavinia' (see p. 51). Suspending actors by their legs alone for an extended period can be dangerous, so on stage, Taymor turned Tamora's sons 'upside down, strapped to metal slabs that rise out of truncated classical columns, paralleling the image of Lavinia's rape. As Titus cuts their throats, Lavinia catches their blood in a basin' (Blumenthal et al., 190). For much of the stage version of this scene, the metal slabs atop the columns were tilted to support the bulk of the actors' weight, but when Taymor acquired the freedom, in her film version, to start and stop shooting to relieve her actors, she altered her arrangement of the sequence to resemble Howell's staging more carefully. Her screenplay's stage directions read: 'CHIRON and DEMETRIUS, bound and naked, hang upside down suspended from meat hooks. Upon seeing TITUS and LAVINIA, the BOYS whimper through their gagged mouths' (161). On stage, the metal slabs atop columns primarily connected the boys' execution to Lavinia's rape and mutilation, but in the film, the direct suspension of Chiron and Demetrius upside down from meat hooks in the kitchen of Titus's house linked this sequence back to the earlier amputation of Titus's hand in the same room. As Taymor revealed in her DVD commentary, 'I was going to shoot this in a smokehouse, but we couldn't have another location, and there's something, just, so right about returning to this kitchen, and the pots and pans, and the salamis, and the cheeses hanging next to the boys.' In her desired location, Taymor would have imitated Howell's version of this segment even more faithfully, by having Titus dispatch his gagged and squealing victims while they hung in an abattoir like sides of beef.

For most of the film, Taymor refrained from vivid depictions of bloodshed, but she filmed the murder of Chiron and Demetrius in a graphic and lifelike manner. As Titus slashed the thoats of Tamora's sons, Lavinia, without visible reluctance, held out her basin to catch the gushing crimson streams. This explicit butchering seemed all the more horrific because the violence earlier in the film had been presented either in a stylised fashion (the aftermath of the assault on Lavinia), or in a realistic way without specific focus on bodily wounds (i.e. the stabbing deaths of Mutius and Bassianus). Even Aaron's removal of Titus's hand, portrayed in a gruesome and messy fashion in Taymor's staging, occurred in a bloodless manner in her film: '[T]here is the distinct and audible thump of the blade cutting through Titus's bone. The camera, however, does not display the blood and gore that presumably accompanies the severing and the "thump". Rather, it turns first to a close-up of Titus's face responding to the pain and then to a close-up of the young Lucius's face registering anguish as he peeks through the kitchen door' (Lindroth, 111). This concentration, not on the ghastly sight of Titus's bleeding stump, but on the anguish he shares with his grandson, implied that 'the human *reaction* to violence is of more consequence than the violence itself' (Bate, Introduction, 12, italics original).

In this scene and throughout her film, Taymor employed Young Lucius, as Howell did, to channel viewers' responses to the play's events. Both directors featured Titus's grandson as an observer in many scenes in which he does not appear in Shakespeare's play, and both expanded his role to include actions that directly affected the meaning of their productions. For instance, Taymor and Howell both began their performances with prologues involving Young Lucius that portrayed him as an anachronism within the classical world. Howell's version opened with the image of a skull juxtaposed with the face of the boy 'wearing distinctive (eighteenth-century rather than Roman or Elizabethan) eyeglasses' (see p. 49), which underlined his initial function as a watcher of deadly incidents. Likewise, both Taymor's stage production and her film began by establishing Young Lucius as an observer from an even greater chronological distance by characterising him as a contemporary child. When the curtain rose at St Clement's,

> a boy wearing a T-shirt, jeans and sneakers (and a paper-bag mask over his head) plays war at a kitchen table. As air-raid sirens blare,

he bashes soldiers together, douses them with ketchup and mustard and then, increasingly frantic, hides under the table. That game over, he moves to the side of the stage to observe the next battle entertainment: the play of *Titus Andronicus*. (Blumenthal, 8)

Taymor's film opened with essentially the same scene of juvenile war-play on a modern kitchen table, but as the boy's aggression escalated, an explosion shook the room and a figure wearing First World War goggles (the Clown) scooped up the crying child and carried him down a flight of stairs, through a pair of doors, and into the Roman Colosseum, raising the boy aloft to the cheers of an unseen crowd. Within the ancient world, the modern boy, paralleling his counterpart in Howell's production, assumed the part of Young Lucius by welcoming his grandfather back to Rome and assisting him in the performance of his religious rites. Taymor's script for both productions, like Michael Maggio's, copied Howell's decision to rearrange 1.1 so that Titus's homecoming and sacrifice of Alarbus preceded the squabbling of Saturninus and Bassianus. This choice allowed Taymor to proceed without a break from her prologue introducing the impressionable Young Lucius to her first employment of the boy as a witness to his family's violent deeds.

On stage, Taymor did not use Young Lucius again until his first appearance in the playtext at the beginning of 3.2; however, on film, she emulated Howell by planting the boy as an observer in several early scenes, including the sequences featuring the rivalry between the Emperor's two sons and the abduction of Lavinia from Saturninus. In Shakespeare's play, Lucius and Young Lucius do not appear on stage together until 5.3, but Taymor's film united them very early, partly to help audiences perceive the family bond between the modern boy of the prologue and his Roman sire. As Titus and his entourage arrived at the Capitol, Young Lucius ran to his father, who picked him up in an embrace and carried him partway up the steps. After the boy watched Titus murder Mutius, Lucius returned to pick up the dead body, and his son bolted across the square to join his father as they exited the scene. Taymor also included Young Lucius as one of the spectators of the 'still life' PAN of 3.1 and its aftermath, including the farewell between Titus and his banished son. Once Titus parted from his son, Lucius hugged his own child, then kissed him twice on the forehead as Lucius spoke his final speech before heading into exile. In such ways, Taymor played up the affectionate paternal relationship between Lucius and Young Lucius as the only healthy father-son bond within the family of the Andronici.

Immediately thereafter, Taymor interpolated into her film a wordless sequence in which Young Lucius visited the shop of a woodcarver, filled with the dismembered limbs of wooden saints and madonnas. This inserted segment marked a transition between the boy's role as an observer to his function as a participant in the action. At the woodcarver's shop, Young Lucius purchased a pair of wooden hands, which he brought home to give to his disfigured aunt. On a practical level, these prosthetics saved Taymor the expense of bluescreening out Lavinia's hands in later scenes, but they also offered the director an opportunity to show 'the development of the child from innocence through knowledge to compassion' (quoted in Johnson-Haddad, 35). While Young Lucius may previously have sympathised with the suffering of those around him, this scene evinced for the first time his capacity to take action to ease that pain. As Taymor remarked in her DVD commentary, the boy 'becomes a player' by 'trying to find a solution for his aunt's lost hands'. For Lisa S. Starks, this considerate gift demonstrated that, instead of 'becoming the revenging warrior of the next generation', Young Lucius had developed into a 'healer, transformer, and nurturer' (136) of Rome's innocent victims of violence.

However, Taymor's cinematic presentation of the subsequent fly scene suggested that the boy had not yet completely rejected the thirst for revenge that had plagued the rest of his family. Like Brook, Taymor reassigned the killing of the fly from Marcus to Young Lucius (see p. 26), along with the lines defending the murder because of the fly's resemblance 'to the Empress' Moor' (3.2.67). Berated by Titus for his thoughtless act of slaughter, the boy fabricated an excuse that played to his family's 'hatred for the blackamoor', which showed that he had absorbed from them their racial animosity, 'as children will' (DVD commentary). For the rest of the film until the final scene, Young Lucius collaborated in Titus's plans for revenge against Aaron and Tamora, but without ever engaging in or witnessing violent actions. After Lavinia revealed the names of her attackers, the boy vowed to carry Titus's message to Chiron and Demetrius with his 'dagger in their bosoms' (4.1.117), and in the following scene, he delivered

Titus's bundle as promised. He also accompanied Titus, 'pulling a red "radio flyer" wagon filled with tools and weapons' (Taymor, *Screenplay*, 128), as the Andronici gathered to shoot their arrows to the Gods. At the final banquet, Young Lucius, like his counterpart in Howell's production, helped his grandfather to serve the cannibalistic pie, but unlike Howell's boy, who participated in the capture of Chiron and Demetrius and witnessed their grisly deaths, Taymor's Young Lucius, absent from those scenes, appeared to have no knowledge of the pie's contents.

In Taymor's film, Young Lucius did not fully reject violent revenge until he witnessed the carnage that followed Titus's revelation of the pie's filling. Once Tamora shoved away her plate in revulsion, Titus stabbed her through the neck with a carving knife. Enraged, Saturninus threw Titus on the tabletop, grabbed a candelabra (biting out one of the candles), and plunged a sharp spike into Titus's chest. Here, Taymor inserted a reaction shot of the boy rushing forward with concern for his dying grandfather. Lucius then seized Saturninus and dragged him on his back the full length of the table, knocking tableware to the floor, while Young Lucius ran parallel to his father along the opposite side. When Saturninus landed again in his chair, Lucius grabbed a serving spoon and plunged it down Saturninus's throat. Taymor conceived of this mayhem as a variation on the film's prologue, so that 'what was a kitchen table in the beginning where the child innocently plays and stabs at his food with his forks and his knives' became the banquet table where 'candelabras kill' and spoons became deadly weapons (DVD Commentary). As Lucius spits on the choking Emperor, Taymor used the Time-Slice system to stop the action while simultaneously allowing the camera to pivot around the table to show the boy responding with alarm and disbelief at his father's vicious assault, which concluded with Lucius firing his revolver into Saturninus's head. Young Lucius, now a witness to genuine violence that echoed his mealtime aggression, became fully aware of the gruesome cost of the cycle of revenge.

Taymor's employment of Young Lucius at the very end of her stage production strongly resembled Howell's use of the boy in the cynical conclusion of her BBC broadcast, but both of these versions differed significantly from the role taken by Young Lucius in the more optimistic ending offered by Taymor's film. Howell concluded her production by implying that Lucius would prove no less ruthless an emperor than his predecessor, based on his broken promise to Aaron to raise up the Moor's son. When Marcus, standing aloft with his nephew, spoke the line 'Behold the child' (5.3.118), the tribune displayed a small coffin containing the dead body of the baby, then Marcus and Lucius raised their hands together in triumph. Young Lucius showed 'surprise at his father's becoming emperor' and moved 'back to the coffin' which had been handed below. During the play's final speech, the camera focused on Young Lucius 'staring at the coffin' (see p. 112) with tears in his eyes; then viewers saw 'his face upturned with an expression of sadness and confusion' (Maher, 146). By using the boy as a filter for the audience's response to the accession of his father, Howell clearly intended her spectators both to recoil from Lucius's treachery and to adopt a pessimistic view of Rome's prospects for healing old wounds.

In her Theatre for a New Audience production, Taymor not only borrowed the same prop used by Howell to indicate the new Emperor's broken vow, but also used Young Lucius in a similar way to guide the response of viewers to the execution of Aaron's child:

> [T]he boy focused his gaze upon a small black coffin, representing Aaron's doomed son. As the lights faded, he placed his hand on the coffin in a gesture of compassion for the innocent child ... a gesture that reached across boundaries of race and nation and measured the distance the boy had travelled since the opening scene. Mingled sounds of shrieking birds and crying babies reminded the boy (and the audience for which he was surrogate) of the persistence of violence and of the pain its innocent victims continue to suffer. (Lanier, 469)

As a surrogate for the audience, Young Lucius modelled an empathetic reaction to the violent deaths of blameless sufferers 'distinct from that of the jaded, robotic connoisseurs' (McCandless, 509), the dispassionate dinner guests who had lifted their glasses to toast Lavinia's murder with aesthetic approval. However, when Taymor began rehearsing the film version of this final sequence, she encountered resistance from Angus Macfadyen, the actor who would be playing Lucius in the film. On her DVD commentary, Taymor recalled, 'In my original script, the baby was brought out in the end in a coffin ... Angus rightly said that this man would never kill Aaron's child. He may do horrible things, but if he made that pledge ... he will keep his word. So then I came up with the idea of bringing the baby out in a cage, which, in many ways, is even worse.' As a man of integrity, who had often demonstrated fatherly affection for his own son, Macfadyen's Lucius refused to break his vow to raise up the Moor's child, but Taymor still saw Lucius as being capable of doing 'horrible things', such as keeping the baby in a cage like an animal or a prisoner. In Taymor's film, it fell to Lucius's son to demonstrate the compassionate treatment of Aaron's offspring that might break the cycle of vengeful cruelty.

At the sound of the gunshot that killed Saturninus, the banquet was transported back to the Colosseum. The Romans and Goths walked away from the table, except for Young Lucius, who turned to watch his father depart and eventually ascend a podium. Facing a microphone, Lucius directed the crowd's attention to the imprisoned infant by pointing to the Clown, who held Aaron's baby aloft in a small cage in the same way that he had lifted Young Lucius near the start of the film. The repetition of this gesture linked the innocent child to Lucius's son and thereby prepared the audience for the boy's most pivotal act of intervention, his decision to release the offspring of his family's tormentor. Having learned compassion from his traumatic experience, Young Lucius removed Aaron's son from the cage and carried him, in an endlessly long and slow march, through an arch of the Colosseum and into the dawn of a new day. By freeing the child of his enemy, and thereby casting off the Andronici's obsession with violent retribution, the Young Lucius of Taymor's film offered spectators some hope that, even though the new Emperor Lucius might favour the pitiless punishment of wrongdoers, his son and successor would, in the future, rule with humanity and forgiveness.

This hopeful conclusion prompted more negative commentary from critics and reviewers than any other aspect of Taymor's film. Some viewers condemned it as 'schlocky' (Burt, 94) or 'sentimental' (E. Walker, 204), while others found it 'inauthentic' (Fedderson and Richardson, 76) and 'not believable', because Taymor had failed to convince an audience that Young Lucius had 'learned enough to craft a new beginning' (Coursen, 135). A few writers also complained that the upbeat interpolation seemed 'untrue to Shakespeare's text' (Bate, Introduction, 12); as Thomas Cartelli observed, 'Whereas the Young Lucius of the play text demonstrably promises to do everything in his power to *emulate* the fallen Titus, the Young Lucius of the film ... promises to *differentiate* himself from the patriarchal mold of his grandfather and father alike' (177, italics original). Contrasting the final moments of Taymor's two productions, McCandless called the conclusion to the film 'a wish-fulfillment fantasy, a dénouement uncomfortably comparable to a Hollywood Happy Ending' (510). On the other hand, Lisa Starks argued that the film's final scene was 'by no means a conventional Hollywood happy ending' because it was too 'ambiguous to provide neat closure' (136). This ambiguity was represented by the imminent dawn into which Young Lucius carried the child of Aaron and Tamora, which, according to Taymor, suggested only the possibility of redemption because it was just a 'slice of the sun coming up. It's not a full sunrise' (quoted in Lindroth, 114). During her DVD interview, Taymor admitted to worrying that the last segment of the film was 'going to be sentimental', but she added, 'I didn't want to tell the story if I didn't have that one sliver of hope.'

While Taymor felt the need to interpolate a hopeful ending based on the promise of the next generation, Deborah Warner's uncut RSC production, which featured a more 'positive and trustworthy' Lucius, managed to fashion a similarly optimistic ending out of the original text by focusing on 'the Andronici as [a] family' who reunited in shared grief for the dead Titus (see pp. 112, 116). Overall, Taymor's work, especially her film, resembled Warner's view of the play more closely in its 'purposeful evocation of ... laughter for striking effects' (see p. 119). By embracing the play's painful comedy rather than attempting to skirt it, Taymor distinguished her efforts from those of Peter Brook, who cut every line that threatened to provoke uncomfortable laughs. As Taymor suggested, 'He didn't get the humor, Brook, he kind of missed that. It's in the script, and I think it's what makes it almost "theater of the absurd"' (quoted in Eby). Taymor did not, however, like Silviu Purcarete, set the entire play in a hopeless and absurd universe. Rather, she emulated Warner's example by fostering the tragedy's 'black comic undertone' (Barbour, 6) within a psychologically plausible and comprehensible world.

The amputation of Titus's hand provided Taymor with several opportunities for dark comedy. When Aaron first proposed the exchange of a hand for the lives of Titus's condemned sons, Marcus and Lucius simultaneously asserted their own fitness to make the sacrifice. While the two men raced off with comical eagerness to fetch an axe, Titus deceived them both by leading Aaron to the kitchen in a tracking shot underscored by the up-tempo jazz rhythm of strings and muted trumpets. As Titus shooed away the cook, Aaron tested out slicing tools, humorously rejecting a pair of poultry scissors in favour of a meat cleaver. Before Aaron brought the knife down on Titus's exposed wrist, the music suddenly ceased, and the Moor, with a quizzical look, seemed to ask Titus for the go-ahead to proceed. The horror of the actual chopping off of Titus's hand was intensified by the levity of the action that preceded it, as well as by the casual way in which Aaron treated the dismembered appendage afterwards. The Moor slipped the hand into an ordinary zip-lock bag, which he later hung from the rear-view mirror of his car like a graduation tassel, a symbol of his outrageously evil accomplishment in defrauding the Andronici.

In her film's version of 3.2, Taymor located the scene's humour in an exchange between Titus and his grandson, to whom she assigned the killing of the fly. As Titus berated Young Lucius for bringing grief to the fly's father, who would surely 'buzz lamenting doings in the air' (3.2.62), Titus lowered his voice into a kind of baby talk appropriate for the scolding of a much smaller child, then tenderly kissed the dead insect. When Young Lucius replied that he had killed the fly for its resemblance to Aaron, Titus's face brightened, and he intoned 'O, O, O!' (3.2.68) in a way that expressed comical understanding, agreement, and finally congratulation of his grandson for his brave deed. Then Titus borrowed Young Lucius's knife, and with the point of the blade, he pecked repeatedly at the insect on the table, provoking his whole family to laughter. Even Lavinia giggled, covering her mouth politely with her wooden prosthetic hand. Titus, chuckling at his own antics, pulled his smiling grandson onto his lap and observed wryly that, between them, his family members still had the power to kill a fly that resembled their enemy.

Anthony Hopkins, in the title role, did not truly begin to rival Warner's Titus, Brian Cox, in 'tragicomic absurdity' until the film reached Act 5 (see p. 70). Hopkins's notoriety with viewers as Hannibal 'The Cannibal' Lecter from *The Silence of the Lambs* (1991) added an additional layer of intertextual humour to the sequence during which Titus butchered the sons of Tamora as the main ingredients for the pie to be fed to their mother. After informing Chiron and Demetrius that Tamora would be enticed to 'swallow her own increase' (5.2.191), Hopkins took a sharp intake of breath through his tongue and teeth strongly reminiscent of Lecter's signature slurping sound as he famously recalled one of his cannibalistic feasts. For many film-goers, this allusion provided a comic flashback to Hopkins's earlier role during one of the film's most harrowing segments. As Aebischer wrote, 'If the audience of Taymor's film is even more delighted at the execution of the rapists than was that of the RSC *Titus Andronicus* starring Brian Cox, then that is because they bring to the film their knowledge of Lecter and the enjoyably perverse pleasure afforded by his sophisticated culinary revenges' ('Vampires', 129).

After Titus's kinsmen took down the dead bodies, Taymor cut immediately to an image adapted from the moment in her New York production when the entire stage became a PAN at the beginning of 5.3. On screen, instead of making the smaller proscenium just one visual element of the *mise-en-scène*, Taymor filled the frame with a close-up on the windowsill holding the two steaming meat pies. Mary Lindroth testified that this transition achieved a startling and humorous effect: 'The juxtaposition of the disturbing death scene with the "homey" and appealing kitchen scene encourage[d] audiences to laugh at death and violence ... It should be repellant that such an act could incite laughter, and yet ... [a]t both the screenings I attended, audiences laughed out loud' (113). Part of the darkly comic effect of this sequence derived from the contrast between the macabre deaths that preceded it and the merry music on the accompanying soundtrack: 'a lilting popular song called "Vivere" (Live!) that flourished on the radio in Fascist Italy the week before Mussolini was killed' (Nochimson, 49).

This song bridged the cut from the pies cooling in the kitchen window to the dining room, where the Emperor and Empress arrived for their meal. Like Brian Cox, Hopkins as Titus 'entered dressed as a cook (in white with a chef's hat)', but instead of walking '*over* the banquet table' with the pie as Cox did (see p. 70, italics original), Hopkins raced around the table towing the pie on a metal cart, doling out huge slices with a satisfying 'plop' as each serving hit the plate. The chef looked on intently as Tamora (Jessica Lange) took her first bite, and Hopkins chortled and licked his lips as he encouraged the Empress to savour her portion. As the dramatic irony of the scene become nearly unbearable, with several seconds' worth of close shots of various diners ingesting mouthfuls of pie, Lavinia finally appeared in the doorway to bring this comical, yet horrifying segment to a close. At such moments, Taymor's film strongly resembled Warner's RSC production in their shared exploitation of opportunities for black humour.

Where Taymor and Warner parted ways was in their attitude toward the specific political and historical contexts of their productions. In the estimation of Stanley Wells, Warner aimed to examine a universal theme, 'the personal and the social consequences of violence', separate from any individual modern examples of violent strife (see p. 75). Therefore, Warner's design for her production featured some 'classical Roman overtones' but 'evoked no specific period' (see p. 63). Taymor, however, made a strong and consistent attempt to connect her stage version and film to particular instances of contemporary bloodshed, social discord, and political repression, which placed her efforts directly in the line of descent originated by Douglas Seale. Like Peter Stein, Taymor mixed the ancient and the modern, with several aspects of set design, costumes, and music that evoked specific recent eras: the Fascist 1930s, the Cold War 1950s, and the present-day 1990s, still plagued by racial discord, juvenile delinquency, domestic violence, and ethnic cleansing. Nevertheless, in her film, Taymor altered her stage production's bleak ending to express a brighter outlook for the world at the dawn of a new millennium.

In both her New York production and her film, Taymor underlined the immediate relevance of the violence in *Titus Andronicus* by inventing a hybrid epoch for the play that 'juxtaposed elements of ancient barbaric ritual with familiar, contemporary attitude and style' (Blumenthal et al., 229). She justified this intermingling of various eras by appealing to the mixed costume design, suggested by the Peacham drawing, that prevailed on the Renaissance stage: 'In productions in Shakespeare's day, they wore Elizabethan clothes and togas. Shakespeare was blending times and so am I, playing with reference points so you get a feeling about the twentieth century – this imagery of totalitarianism' ('Bloody', 128). Taymor's comparison of repressive modern governments to the totalitarianism of Rome through postmodern anachronism in design seems appropriate to *Titus Andronicus* in particular because the play itself is a type of 'early modern pastiche' that collapses all of Roman history, 'making Troy, the Tarquins, Caesar and the Goths all simultaneously available to the story' (Rutter, 'Looking', 14).

At St Clement's, Taymor's setting fused several styles in a 'compendium of Western culture from classical to punk' (Blumenthal, 8). Scenic designer Derek McLane's set consisted of 'ancient Roman columns that were black-and-white xeroxed photo blow-ups on stretched translucent plastic that could track in and out of the space. The back wall was occupied by a plastic cyc[lorama] that was distressed and scarred with black ink.' The stage also featured two versatile set pieces, 'a Victorian, Roman-style bathtub that tripled as the public bath where the soldiers purified themselves, the pit in the forest, and Titus's bath', as well as 'a 1950s chrome, red-topped kitchen table that served not only as what it literally was but also as a sacrificial altar and the final banquet table'. In the production's prologue, Young Lucius played at war on this table until the sounds of 'screaming sirens' and exploding bombs became unbearable, and he covered his ears and crawled 'under the table to hide' (Blumenthal et al., 192). In the 1950s context created by the red and chrome kitchen furniture, the boy's posture recalled images of Cold War children shielding themselves under their desks during an atomic bomb attack drill.

In her film, Taymor retained the red and chrome table for the opening sequence, but she replaced her plastic-coated Roman columns with on-location shooting at authentic historical sites: 'Instead of re-creating Rome, 400 A.D., the locations of the film would include the ruins of Hadrian's villa, the baths of Caracalla, the Colosseum, and so on, as they are today, with all their corroded beauty, centuries of graffiti, and ghastly, ghostly history' (Blumenthal et al., 229). The Colosseum, which hosted the scenes that framed the film, supplanted the small gold proscenium on the stage as the metatheatrical space where Taymor's critique of violence would be located. By substituting this 'theater-within-a-film' for the stage production's 'theater-within-a-theater' (McCandless, 500), Taymor found a cinematic equivalent for her penny arcade to represent 'the archetypal theater of cruelty, where violence as entertainment reached its apex' (Blumenthal et al., 230). At the Colosseum, Taymor also established the blending of time so crucial to her vision: 'There, ancient armor and weapons, motorcycles, tractors, tanks, and horse-drawn chariots, are comfortably jumbled together like the toys on the boy's kitchen table' (Blumenthal et al., 236). The ancient and modern vehicles, and the soldiers who drove them, were all caked with blue mud from their recent battles, which unified the chronologically disparate elements of the scene.

Another significant location in Taymor's film, the Esposizione Universale Roma, also served to combine the ancient and the modern, as well as to associate Shakespeare's Rome with the totalitarian government of twentieth-century Italy. For the initial clash between Saturninus and Bassianus, production designer Dante Ferretti 'suggested E.U.R., Mussolini's government centre, whose principal building is referred to as the "square Colosseum" because of its myriad arches. Built by Italy's Fascist leader to recreate the glory of the ancient Roman empire, this surreal and almost futuristic architecture and setting perfectly embodied the concept for the film' (Blumenthal et al., 229). This massive edifice loomed behind Young Lucius as he read a newspaper account of the death of the Emperor, marked by nine long black banners unfurled simultaneously from the arches along the top floor of the building. Young Lucius then joined the procession carrying Saturninus toward the Capitol in a 1930s black convertible that Taymor described as 'Mussolini's car' because it came from the Fascist period (quoted in Eby). As in Peter Stein's production, the architecture and accoutrements of Taymor's setting evoked 'the analogy between ancient Rome and Fascist Italy, particularly Benito Mussolini's Rome' (Hall-Smith, 55).

Titus also suggested Fascism through the portrayal of Saturninus (Alan Cumming), whose distinctive hairstyle resembled 'the androgynous "New Romantic" pop stars of the 1980s and Adolf Hitler in equal measure' (Barker, 89). Taymor emphasised this connection by dressing Saturninus for his first scene in Nazi colours: all black leather, except for the red lapels on his long coat. By contrast, the Emperor's sons in Taymor's stage production 'recalled the Kennedy-Nixon debates. Saturninus exuded sleaze in an ill-fitting brown suit, while Bassianus showed sophistication in a dark, well-tailored one' (Lennox, 35). Overall, Taymor used costumes in her New York version of the play less to create overt Fascist images than to 'express personalities of people'. Titus was 'garbed as a series of archetypes: a Roman centurion, a dapper general in an Eisenhower jacket, a kindly grandfather in grey cardigan and plaid shirt, a madman in a bathrobe and a pastry chef' (Lanier, 467). As for the women, Tamora 'could have come out of Visconti's film *The Damned*, which is set in the 1930s, while Lavinia ... was dressed like Grace Kelly' (Blumenthal et al., 192). Lavinia's costume, by recalling the high fashion of Princess Grace, represented a 1950s notion of wholesomeness and purity, while Tamora's dresses subtly reminded spectators of the Nazi decadence portrayed in Visconti's film.

Elliot Goldenthal's soundtrack for both the staging and the film also reflected Taymor's 'esthetic of temporal melange' (Nochimson, 49). Douglas Lanier wrote that 'Goldenthal's score for the film *Titus* provide[d] a good example of his musical idiom, which [was] characterised by dense textures, minimalist patterning, expressive use of dissonance and Stravinsky-like rhythms and allusions to disparate musical genres whose clash mirror[ed] the postmodern collision of styles in Taymor's visual design' (461). For the arrival of the Roman army at the Colosseum, Goldenthal used 'Korean musical instruments' (Nochimson, 49) that swelled into 'a full male chorus and sweeping symphonic grandness'. A 'boogie-cool jazz amalgam' (Taymor, *Illustrated*, 182) underscored the clash between supporters of the Emperor's two sons, as well as the raucous wedding party for Saturninus and Tamora. The humiliation of various characters was accompanied by 'a Bach-like pity theme', and the PANs sometimes featured 'circus ditties' (Nochimson, 49). Critics generally praised Goldenthal for the way in which his musical score echoed the collision of eras and styles essential to Taymor's visual design.

One final visual element associated with both productions that amalgamated the past and the present was the image of the Capitoline Wolf, the legendary beast that suckled Romulus and Remus, the founders of Rome. A poster for the Theatre for a New Audience production designed by Taymor herself took the form of a scratched photograph featuring a side view of a dog, with its head turned toward the viewer, wearing three sets of human breasts strapped to its body. On the ground beneath the animal lay a single naked newborn baby, gazing up at the prosthetic teats (see Figure 14). No reviewer noted any employment of this modern version of the she-wolf image in the stage production itself, but the film *Titus* made extensive use of a similar lupine icon. In the Senate chamber, Saturninus sat on an oversized throne beneath 'a huge, metal wolf, which snarls through the

14 Publicity poster for Julie Taymor's Theatre for a New Audience production (1994).

clench of its ineffectual muzzle' (Coursen, 138). The same she-wolf graced the handlebars of the soldiers' motorcycles, the hood of Saturninus's car, and the fountain spouts at the royal wedding celebration (see Figure 15). As Young Lucius entered the wood-carver's shop, he wore 'a high school jacket with the image of the Roman she-wolf embroidered on the back' (Bowman, 59). By placing this mythological image on modern vehicles and cloth-

15 Wolf heads on the handlebars of motorcycles and the hood of Saturninus's car in Julie Taymor's film *Titus* (1999). Produced by Julie Taymor and Conchita Airoldi.

ing, the director enhanced her presentation of Rome as a place where the past and the present exist side by side.

Taymor's deliberately anachronistic design assisted in her efforts to make Shakespeare's play about ancient Rome comment on several contemporary political issues. For example, by introducing Aaron the Moor as an outsider, alienated from both the Romans and the Goths, who despise him for his colour, Taymor brought the issue of race to the forefront of her film. Aaron first appeared at the very end of the triumphal procession filing into the Colosseum, chained by the neck to a cart containing the spoils of the war and set apart by being 'the only prisoner forced to walk'. As the Goths ascended to prominence, the Moor remained 'very isolated, wandering around Saturninus' coronation celebration without speaking to anyone, only to leave and walk the parapets alone, scheming' (Crawford, 117). Taymor counteracted Aaron's isolation from society by allowing him to deliver all of his asides and soliloquies directly to the camera, which forged a bond of understanding, if not of sympathy, with the audience. In Taymor's mind, Aaron was not born '[n]ihilistic, atheistic, cold and calculating', but became so as a result of racist prejudice (*Illustrated*, 178). In Aaron's nihilism, Taymor found 'an extraordinary contemporary image' of the type of disaffected black man living 'in any ghetto' who 'doesn't give a damn about the consequences of his violence, doesn't give a damn about the future' (quoted in McCandless, 493–4). Of course, Aaron eventually began to care about the future with the birth of his son, at which point he emerged as 'a loving father, ready to sacrifice himself for the life of his child' (Taymor, *Illustrated*, 178). As in Gregory Doran's South African production, the scene in which Aaron traded his confession for the life of his baby boy was performed 'as a modern-day lynching' (Crawford, 117), with Aaron mounting a ladder and placing the noose around his own neck. Given a reprieve by Lucius for a later, more lingering punishment, the Moor was carried into the Colosseum, his arms tied to a tree branch, 'clad only in a loincloth ... held aloft as if to be crucified' (Vaughan, 75). By likening Aaron to Christ on the cross, Taymor suggested that this black man was about to die a scapegoat for the sins of a society, not unlike our own, that had made him into the evil monster that he was.

In both versions of her production, Taymor also implied that social forces, embodied in modern entertainment media, were enticing young males to engage in violence as a pastime, in fantasy as well as in the real world. Specifically, Chiron and Demetrius, in the film, represented 'a distinctly contemporary threat of generational difference: with their glamorous, leather-clad, rock-star androgyny, attention-deficit disorders, [and their] penchant for video games, drugs, booze, and kinky sex' (McCandless, 493). Indeed, Taymor directly connected the brothers' 'addiction to violent video games' (Aebischer, 'Women', 145) to their attack upon Lavinia. In her screenplay, Taymor began the scene following Lavinia's off-camera assault with a stage direction indicating that Chiron and Demetrius taunted their victim 'in a frenetic state of fear, agitation and exhilaration' (89). Taymor subsequently repeated the adjectives 'frenetic' and 'agitated' to describe the boys' behaviour in their dungeon during a wordless sequence that followed the fly scene. While Chiron danced madly around the room, heavy metal music blaring through his headphones, Demetrius stood thrusting his hips into a video game featuring a female motorcycle rider. Seen from the rear, Demetrius appeared to be, as Taymor phrased it, 'mercilessly fucking the machine' (114) in a re-enactment of his rape of Lavinia, to the accompaniment of the same rock music that would later underscore Lavinia's own flashback PAN. Since video game violence was often blamed for the shootings at Columbine High School near Littleton, Colorado (which occurred in the same year that *Titus* was released), Pascale Aebischer accused Taymor of 'seeking to associate [Tamora's sons] with the high-school killings that shocked the United States in the late 1990s' ('Women', 145). However, Taymor herself contended on her DVD commentary that she had used Shakespeare's play to criticise violence in digital media 'way before Littleton ... back in 1994 when I directed the play off-Broadway'. On stage, she depicted Tamora's sons 'battering their brains out' with video games 'so they wouldn't have enough time to think about what they had done'. Touched with guilt over their actions, Chiron and Demetrius sought distraction in the same violent fantasy world that contributed to their willingness to engage in genuine violence in the first place. By depicting this brutal cycle, Taymor's film presented 'a contemporary critique of violence-as-entertainment, a critique that emerges in the depiction of Chiron and Demetrius as video-game junkies whose visual mastery of virtual beings is too easily transposed to real bodies' (Lehmann, 274).

Along with Tamora's boys, Lucius's son was also depicted as an impressionable victim of violence in the media. During the prologue to Taymor's stage production, the soundtrack that punctuated Young Lucius's table-top battle started with 'the comic sounds of TV violence – the Three Stooges, Popeye, Kung Fu movies, and such', but the noise gradually mutated into 'the real sounds of actual violence – a man beating a screaming woman, gunfire, ambulance sirens, bombs dropping, WAR'. Young Lucius began his fun 'innocently playing with his food and toys', but hearing the sounds of TV mayhem, he became 'ferociously violent' (Blumenthal et al., 192), perhaps eventually capable of the same type of brutality perpetrated by Chiron and Demetrius. Indeed, according to Lanier, as the scene progressed, Young Lucius grew, like the sons of Tamora, 'increasingly frenetic' as a result of his exposure to 'contemporary media violence' (469). However, by developing empathy for actual human victims of violence, Young Lucius ultimately differentiated himself from Chiron and Demetrius and matured into the type of young man who would not act out violent fantasies in real life.

The play's most emblematic of victim of violence, Lavinia, meets her death in a manner that Taymor associated with atrocities against women still performed in modern times. During the film's version of the banquet scene, as Lavinia entered, dressed like a bride in white with a black veil, Titus quizzed the Emperor about the actions of 'rash Virginius' (5.3.36). Lavinia did not break eye contact with her father until Saturninus validated the centurion's slaying of his daughter, at which point Lavinia lifted her veil, turned around, and willingly leaned back into the embrace of Titus, who grasped her chin and 'intimately, lovingly' snapped her neck (Taymor, DVD commentary). Some critics objected to the portrayal of this murder 'not as something reprehensible that the victim might resist' but as a necessary act to release both Lavinia and Titus from their shame at her loss of chastity; however, Taymor revealed in an interview that 'she never considered resistance to be an option' (Aebischer, 'Women', 144). Rather, she wanted to depict the way in which women today still submit passively to bride burnings and honour killings committed against them by their families: 'People say, "My God, Titus killed his daughter." Absolutely, he killed his daughter and they're doing it today in Bosnia and in many Muslim countries' (quoted in De Luca and Lindroth, 30). This reference to Bosnia reminds us that the sacrifice of Lavinia must be viewed in relation to the circumstances surrounding Taymor's filming of the opening and closing sequences on location in the Colosseum at Pula, Croatia a mere two months before a renewal of the Balkans conflict. As Aebischer noted, 'This proximity to actual conflicts in which rapes were perpetrated on a large scale as a method of warfare and nation-building, resulting in "honour killings" of Muslim rape-victims by their male relatives, put the Shakespearean rape in a modern context within which it had to be perceived as a personal, sexual crime *and* as a political act and expression of power' ('Women', 142, italics original).

Taymor's film concluded back on location in the Balkans with the aftermath of Lucius's assassination of Saturninus: 'With the reverberating blast of gunshot, the camera zooms out from the table to reveal the entire scene, minus the walls, set at the center of the Colosseum. This time, the bleachers are filled with spectators, watching. They are silent. They are us' (Blumenthal et al., 242). These silent spectators, as substitutes for 'us' in attendance at the archetypal theatre of cruelty, the Colosseum, implicated the viewer in the consumption of violence as entertainment. This critique of media exploitation of violence carried over from Taymor's stage production, which the director justified with reference to the 'racism, ethnic cleansing, and genocide [that] have almost ceased to shock by being so commonplace and seemingly inevitable':

> Our entertainment industry thrives on the graphic details of murders, rapes, and villainy, yet it is so rare to find a film or play that not only reflects the dark events but also turns them inside out, probing and challenging our fundamental beliefs on morality and justice. For *Titus* is not a neat or safe play, where goodness triumphs over evil, but one in which, through relentless horror, the undeniable poetry of human tragedy emerges in full force. (Blumenthal et al., 183)

In 1994, Taymor did not see *Titus* as a play in which 'goodness triumphs over evil', and therefore she concluded its 'relentless horror' with the image of Young Lucius mourning over Aaron's dead son. Five years later, however, as the year 2000 approached, Taymor felt obliged to mark the beginning of a new epoch with a more optimistic conclusion. She ended her account of the film in *Playing with Fire* by remarking, '*Titus* will premiere as the millennium comes to an end. May the child finally exit the Colosseum as the new millennium rolls in' (Blumenthal et al., 243). In this particular sense, Taymor's film was a genuine product of its historical moment.

CHAPTER V

Yukio Ninagawa, Bill Alexander, Gale Edwards, Richard Rose, and Lucy Bailey

During the decade following the release of Julie Taymor's film, at least one major stage production of *Titus Andronicus* represented each of the four lines of descent in the play's performance history. Yukio Ninagawa's Japanese production exhibited the influence of Peter Brook's stylised technique, while both Bill Alexander, for the RSC, and Gale Edwards, for the Shakespeare Theatre of Washington, DC, followed the realistic example set by Jane Howell. Richard Rose's Stratford, Ontario production, set in Fascist Italy, emulated the political approach established by Douglas Seale, and Lucy Bailey's production at Shakespeare's Globe Theatre resembled the darkly comic vision of Deborah Warner. Three of these five directors (Ninagawa, Edwards, and Rose) also took inspiration from Taymor's film, as evidenced by their focus, at the end of their productions, on the relationship between Young Lucius and Aaron's baby.

Ninagawa Company, Saitama, Japan, 2004, 2006 – Dir. Yukio Ninagawa

In 1995, Yoshiko Kawachi speculated about the lack of interest in producing *Titus Andronicus* in Japan, concluding that the play's barbarous violence, cannibalism, and doubtful authorship had rendered the play unpalatable to his nation's performers and audiences. Yet he also predicted, 'In the not too distant future I expect that a Japanese dramatic company will perform an epoch-making *Titus Andronicus* fusing Shakespearean text and Japanese dramaturgy' (493). Less than ten years later, Kawachi's prophecy came true in Yukio Ninagawa's staging, which originated in 2004 at the Sai-no-Kuni Saitama Arts Space as the thirteenth entry in Ninagawa's project to produce all of Shakespeare's plays. It was revived at the same location in May 2006, then proceeded to Stratford-upon-Avon the following month to become 'the first Japanese-speaking Shakespearean production to be performed in the Royal Shakespeare Theatre' (Kawai, 281) as part of Stratford's Complete Works Festival. This memorable production, which combined Asian and Western stage elements, closed at Plymouth's Theatre Royal at the end of June 2006.

One of Ninagawa's formative theatrical experiences was attending 'Peter Brook's *A Midsummer Night's Dream* (1970), which he saw performed in Tokyo in 1973, a year before he began to direct Shakespeare' (Kawai, 276). As many reviewers observed, in *Titus Andronicus*, Ninagawa borrowed from Brook's *Dream* both its metatheatrical, non-representational staging and its white box set; but he also drew on Brook's 1955 *Titus* for a stylised presentation of violence, particularly the use of red wool threads to represent blood (which, after all, derives from Ninagawa's own Asian theatrical tradition). Unlike Brook, however, Ninagawa prioritised faithfulness to Shakespeare's text; and the Japanese translation that he employed, although it did not equal Deborah Warner's uncut text, still preserved more lines than Brook's edited version, especially at the end of the tragedy. Ninagawa also seized some of the play's opportunities for dark humour, but far fewer than did Warner. Julie Taymor's influence on Ninagawa was most evident in his pervasive exploitation of the image of the Capitoline Wolf, as well as his use of Young Lucius to offer a concluding assessment of the play's violent events.

The production began in a metatheatrical mode, with performers and crew members openly preparing for the start of the show both in the lobby and on stage:

> dangerous-looking Japanese warriors, clad in white costumes that hybridize Roman motifs with the shapes and weapons associated with the samurai period, [we]re already warming up in the foyer well before the advertised starting time. In the auditorium itself ... actors and stagehands gathered informally about the stage among mobile rails of costumes and, disconcertingly, racks of prop severed heads, well after the audience ha[d] taken their seats. (Dobson, '2006', 303)

Some reviewers commented on 'the *Verfremdungseffekt* of actors warming up onstage' (Billing, 203), but Ninagawa himself claimed, in an interview included on the Japanese DVD release of the performance, that he did not intend 'to adopt Brechtian technique'. Rather, he hoped to foreground the intercultural nature of the production:

> Asian actors feel a sort of embarrassment to play European characters, because we know we physically do not look like Englishmen or Romans no matter how hard we try. So, it is my intention to display that discomfort in order to remove it, by consciously approaching the border between cultures, not by denying it with a sense of inferiority and obsequiousness.

Eschewing a futile attempt to deny cultural difference, Ninagawa metatheatrically highlighted 'the border between cultures' by displaying his actors' assumption of their roles, as signified by the donning of costumes that were themselves a hybrid of Roman and samurai garments.

At the RST, Ninagawa's actors conducted most of their warm-ups on designer Tsukasa Nagagoshi's all-white set, which prompted Kate Bassett to call the production 'Japan's answer to Peter Brook's legendary white-box staging of *A Midsummer Night's Dream*' (Yukio, 12). A geometric grid of markings projected onto the walls during the pre-show added to the metatheatrical effect by drawing attention to the constructedness of the setting:

> Huge white flats dominated the RSC's main stage, but we seemed to be looking at the back of the flats, since one could see the lightly stenciled numbers and letters that would help the stage-hands put the flats in the correct positions. Upstage loomed a two-level structure with arches/windows on the top level, almost as if we were looking at a non-curved section of the Colosseum. (Gilbert, 37)

Later in the play, Ninagawa frequently used the five arches aloft at the rear of the stage to allow certain characters to dominate others on the main level below. For example, when Saturninus chose Tamora as his empress, she appeared aloft with him alongside Aaron and her sons, looking down on Titus. These positions were reversed in 5.2 as Titus, perched in a single open archway above, pretending to be mad, gained an advantage over the deceived Tamora as Revenge beneath him. Several of the production's massed entrances, such as the return of the Roman soldiers and their prisoners, or the parallel procession of Martius and Quintus being led to their execution, proceeded through the house and up a staircase at the front of the stage. No effort was made to render this stark and immaculate setting as a verisimilar representation of ancient Rome.

As the actors milled about, the disembodied voice of the company stage manager began to give instructions in Japanese over the theatre's public address system that were simultaneously translated into English on surtitle boards (large monitors placed on either side of the proscenium arch), which later featured Shakespeare's text as the actors spoke their dialogue in Japanese. At the stage manager's request, 'a huge white statue on a plinth started moving downstage, quietly motorized; the statue showed a standing wolf, teeth visible, and underneath the wolf Romulus and Remus, the legendary founders of Rome, being suckled by the wolf' (Gilbert, 37). This massive replica of the Capitoline Wolf commanded Ninagawa's stage for most of the play's scenes, in the same way that the head of the harnessed she-wolf loomed over the Senate chamber in Julie Taymor's film. Positioned primarily in a side view, but occasionally rotated 90 degrees so that either the wolf's head or its tail faced the audience, the statue indicated changes of location on Ninagawa's non-representational platform. As a symbol of Rome, the fierce sculpture branded the Romans as 'a race weaned on animal savagery' (Brantley, 7).

At the end of the pre-show, the playing area was flooded with illumination: 'Suddenly the lights changed, almost as if a thunderbolt of bright white light had struck the stage; the grid of letters and numbers disappeared, and everything – the flats, arches, the wolf (now center) – was super-white' (Gilbert, 37). The disappearance of the grid on the walls suggested to viewers that the set, formerly a theatrical construction, was now to be transformed by their imaginations into a vision of Shakespeare's Rome. The dead Emperor's sons, in voluminous white Asian robes belted at the waist, sported enormous buckles in the shape of wolf heads, echoing the image of the statue on stage. Whereas Taymor, in her film, placed the head of the she-wolf on Roman attire and vehicles as a means to blend ancient and modern Rome, Ninagawa's costume designer Lily Komine incorporated a similar decorative motif on her garments as a method for combining ancient Japanese and ancient Roman cultural elements in a single outfit.

One section of the performance that did not feature the wolf statue was the series of scenes in the forest during Act 2, where Ninagawa relied upon a mixture of lighting effects and artificial plants to create a woodland setting. During a blackout, 'a forest of approximately fifty huge white plastic lilies [wa]s brought onstage. As the onstage lights snap[ped] back on, this field of ethereal flowers and the white walls of the set (now lit through leaf-patterned gobos) [we]re revealed as a dense canopy of leaves.' Then, for Aaron's soliloquy at the start of 2.3, 'a vast white tree [wa]s added (flown centre stage), behind which the audience [wa]s called upon to imagine a pit' (Billing, 206). Ninagawa apparently sensed the same awkwardness that many producers have long discovered in the fall of Titus's sons into the bloody hole (see p. 11), and he therefore staged the sequence with the action only partly visible to spectators. Quintus stood in plain sight to one side of the tree to speak to his fallen brother; but when Martius accidentally pulled Quintus into the pit, his descent was blocked by the trunk of the tree. Ninagawa did not use a trap to represent the text's below-stage level, but relied instead upon the imagination of his audience to envision the realm of the pit beneath the surface of the platform.

On the brilliantly lit white stage, Komine's costumes provided most of the colour and texture in the *mise-en-scène*. In the opening act, the Roman army was dressed in 'broken-down, post-modern-Japanese interpretations of Kabuki Samurai outfits and Classical military attire' with 'helmets and face-guards that [we]re an eclectic evocation of Japanese warriors, ancient Greek hoplites and Roman gladiators' (Billing, 205). Beneath their armour, some of the soldiers wore brown, fur-like undergarments that linked their ferocity to that of the snarling wolf. The Goth prisoners, by contrast, were dressed in more vibrant colours: Chiron, Demetrius, and Alarbus were stripped to the waist and sported long skirts in blue, green, and dark red respectively. Tamora, at first, appeared in a shapeless black robe with a hood that covered her face, but her elevation to empress was reflected in her family's adoption of 'the white of imperial Rome'. Returning from offstage, Tamora (Rei Asami) was dressed in a 'long white sheath with a big-collared white robe over it' while her sons wore 'white robes over their colored skirts'. For hunting, she changed into 'tight-fitting black trousers, black shirt, black stiletto-heeled boots, all topped with a long white coat trimmed with leopard fur'. In this way, Tamora adopted 'the white of Rome' and its bestial savagery, but kept 'her "native" black underneath' (Gilbert, 41).

The only member of the Goth party to disdain the white garments of Rome was Tamora's Moorish lover: 'Only Aaron [made] no concession whatsoever to Rome's icy whiteness, keeping his red-leather skirts and open red tunic (that barely cover[ed Shun] Oguri's slender and multiple-tattooed torso) throughout the performance as a testament to his position as the play's greatest outsider' (Billing, 205). Aaron's alienation was based on his race, but Oguri's only distinguishing racial marker was his blond hair, which set him apart from the rest of the dark-featured Japanese cast. Since his skin colour was only slightly darker than that of his fellow actors, the audience was called upon to imagine that his blond hair signified his blackness. Such a convention may have worked in Asia, but the imaginative leap became more difficult for race-conscious Western spectators in Act 4, when the Nurse brought in Aaron's son, represented by 'a plastic baby that seem[ed] far blacker than either Oguri or Asami' (Billing, 211n). In England, the literal blackness of the newborn child seemed incongruous to viewers who had laboured thus far to envision Aaron's darker skin colour in their mind's eye without visual assistance.

The suspension of disbelief was less arduous in 5.2, when Tamora entered wearing a long white robe and a thickly feathered black wig. She then opened the robe to reveal a similarly feathered black dress, which gave her the appearance of a bird of prey. The Empress made no attempt to disguise her face, but instead assumed the false identity of Revenge by taking 'her voice an octave up and well-nigh sing[ing] to Titus in a wheedling manner reminiscent of Peking opera' (Dobson, '2006', 304). Her sons accompanied her in identical white robes over coloured scarves, skirts, and tall geta-style platform shoes, with elaborate Asian headpieces in animal shapes. Demetrius wore the head of a bat, while Chiron, with several cobras rising from his scalp, resembled a Gorgon. When Titus descended to speak to his visitors, Rape and Murder stood on their platform shoes and held their garments up backwards, all the way to their foreheads, so that the animal headdresses appeared to gaze at Titus over the tops of the robes with the eyes of monstrously tall beasts. The animal imagery of this scene and others convinced reviewer Nicholas de Jongh that the key to Ninagawa's concept for the production was 'Shakespeare's evocation of Rome as "a wilderness of tigers"' (Yukio, 34).

Like Jeannette Lambermont at Stratford, Ontario, Ninagawa adapted Brook's formalised approach by incorporating various Asian stage elements 'derived from the great Japanese theatre styles of Noh, Bunraku and Kabuki' (Carnegy, 59). Yet while the Canadian company merely appropriated the trappings of Asian theatre to dress up a method-based performance, Ninagawa's troupe employed the acting style appropriate to traditional Japanese theatre, which struck many Western reviewers as overdone and artificial. One wrote, 'Some of the heightened and stylised acting ... [came] across as almost risibly melodramatic, even pseudo-operatic with much sforzando roaring' (Bassett, Yukio, 12), and another agreed that '[e]ach expression, movement or gesture on stage [was] over-emphasized ... almost like watching opera' (Holt, Yukio). This operatic technique required a demanding commitment of energy, which sometimes lent 'a thrilling intensity' to the performances (Spencer, Yukio, 31), but it also risked a narrowing of the actors' emotional range. As Christian M. Billing complained, 'most scenes [we]re played in fifth gear, creating a constant and intense assault on the spectator's senses' so that, in moments of heightened passion, there was 'nowhere for Ninagawa's actors to go' (208). Overall, the production relied for its impact not on 'a close emotional engagement' with the characters, but on the exhibition of 'grand and ruthless stage images' (Dobson, '2006', 304).

These gorgeous images, combined with the play's violent acts, prompted one reviewer to recall 'a famous German critic's summation of classical Japanese theatre': 'Chrysanthemums and butchery' (Carnegy, 59). Indeed, Ninagawa warned an interviewer that the production would be 'so beautiful' that it would 'be painful to look at it'. Since there was 'not a single drop of blood shed' on the stage (quoted in Secher, 9), this cruel beauty was conveyed primarily by a formalised technique already familiar to those conversant with the play's stage history: 'Yukio Ninagawa brings a Japanese staging so stylised that it keeps turning the horror into visual poetry. In particular, it takes up and multiplies the most famous device of Peter Brook's 1955 staging, whereby red streamers trailed from the mouth and arms of Lavinia ... where her tongue and hands had formerly been' (Macaulay, 'Yukio', 14). In the Japanese production, every act of bloodshed enacted on stage or off used 'Kabuki-derived strands of red wool' (Billing, 205) to represent blood on the clothing and bodies of nearly all the main characters in the play. In the opinion of Paul Taylor, this stylised depiction of carnage should have had 'a cushioning effect', but instead, it unexpectedly 'concentrate[d] and heighten[ed] the horror' (Yukio, 20).

The red wool threads appeared prominently in the opening scene of the production, as Titus's returning army sported 'filaments attached haphazardly to parts of their costumes, evoking the random splatterings of battle blood'. These crimson strands also clung to the garments of the Goth prisoners, as well as to the corpses of Titus's sons (constructed out of 'bubble-wrap shaped and held by clear plastic tape'), which were borne onstage by Roman soldiers in two plexiglass coffins. After the sacrifice of Alarbus, his lopped limbs, represented by a plastic mannequin head and hand with dangling threads, were returned to Titus, who tossed them carelessly in the direction of his Goth captives. These dismembered body parts and the red wool streaming from them were patently artificial, and yet they were 'not only deeply disturbing in their suggestion of blood, but also in their evocation of limbs that ha[d] been violently ripped from their sockets, pulling with them an assortment of veins, muscles and sinews' (Billing, 205).

However, the most harrowing instances of stylised bloodshed occurred in the forest scenes. Chiron and Demetrius murdered Bassianus by stabbing him in the shoulder and side, and when they withdrew their daggers, they pulled handfuls of red strands from the folds of his costume to denote his gushing wounds. The subsequent attack on Lavinia was not dramatised, but it was suggested by a graphic formalised depiction of its outcome. To the sound of howling wolves, the lights went up part way on the field of white lilies, and Lavinia, her hair dishevelled, entered from the rear of the stage, her hands obscured by numerous red threads that hung from her wrists to the floor. A few strands also trailed from the corners of her mouth and adhered to her torn white gown (see Figure 16). As she collapsed centre stage, Tamora's sons followed behind her, apparently crying; but it soon became clear from their 'sickening laughter' that they were actually 'mocking Lavinia's disability in a cruel parody of her movements'. Moreover,

> Demetrius and Chiron's naked bodies [we]re decked out in Lavinia's blood: small streamers of red wool [we]re attached to their torsos ... but the greatest impact [came] from their genitals – which [we]re entirely obscured by long flowing strands of wool: the vaginal ... blood of their violated victim showing not on the woman herself, but on the anatomy of her assailants as a graphic reminder of the sexual nature of their crime. (Billing, 206)

Lavinia repeatedly raised her 'bleeding' stumps toward the sky as Tamora's sons reviled her, and when they fled the stage, Lavinia attempted to hide her shame amid the giant lilies.

After Marcus discovered Lavinia and brought her to Titus, Aaron arrived with his bogus offer from the Emperor to pardon Martius and Quintus. The slicing off of Titus's hand was then performed with no pretence at realism. While Aaron drew a long curved sword, Titus turned his back to the audience and offered his arm to him. Aaron grasped the general's left hand and drew it behind Titus's body out of sight, then he brought the blade down with a sweeping circular blow. The impact of the wound was

16   Hitomi Manaka as Lavinia in Yukio Ninagawa's production for the Ninagawa Company (2006). Photo by Ellie Kurttz.

conveyed by the reactions of Titus and Lavinia, who both roared in pain and collapsed to the stage floor. When Titus rose at the re-entry of Marcus and Lucius, his wrist bore the same streaming threads that Lavinia wore, and he held in his grasp an artificial version of his amputated hand, with long red strands trailing from it. These same threads adhered to the hand and the heads of Martius and Quintus when the Messenger returned them to Titus. Lavinia subsequently tried to comfort her father by kissing him, which left threads dangling from his mouth as well. At the height of Titus's onrushing madness, 'clutching a red-streamer-bedecked plastic amputated hand, with further streamers trailing from his maimed wrist, he loll[ed] backward against the statue of the wolf, uttering a terrible mirthless rasping laughter' (Dobson, '2006', 304). Titus's placement against the wolf sculpture at the nadir of his grief suggested that the ferocious savagery inherent to Rome had rebounded against the Andronici and was ultimately responsible for the violence done to them.

Later, to take revenge for these violent outrages, Titus signalled to the fly space, and two red ropes dropped down, which were used by his relatives to secure Tamora's captured sons with their arms bound behind their backs. Lavinia approached her attackers and beat them furiously with her stumps until she exhausted herself. She also willingly held the basin as Titus approached the boys and placed his dagger against their throats. At that point, one of the attendants pushed the victim's head forward and simultaneously pulled a hank of red wool out of his coloured scarf, allowing some of the threads to trail into Lavinia's basin to represent collected blood. This murder sequence, like many of the production's violent moments, was ironically accompanied by 'gorgeous chunks of slow movements from Handel' (Macaulay, 'Yukio', 14) and punctuated by the howling of wolves. Titus tenderly embraced his daughter, and her crazed eyes betrayed her pleasure at being able to assist in this retribution against her tormentors.

Titus and Lavinia entered together during the banquet scene, with Lavinia dressed as a bride, all in white. Once Saturninus endorsed the actions of Virginius, Titus walked the width of the stage and raised Lavinia's veil, kissing her and embracing her from behind. As Handel began to play, Titus grasped his daughter's windpipe and slowly stangled her, causing crimson threads to stream from her mouth. The other banqueters leapt to their feet, except Tamora, who remained calmly seated and continued to eat her meal. During the confusion, the cart carrying the two pies was pushed centre stage, and the faces of Chiron and Demetrius became grotesquely visible to the audience within the pies, which dripped strands of red wool. At the revelation of the pies' ingredients, Tamora finally rose in alarm, and all the banqueters groaned loudly and held their stomachs. Seizing a carving knife, Titus stabbed Tamora in the back, then whirled her around to display the threads streaming from the bodice of her white gown. Tamora ultimately collapsed on the plinth of the wolf sculpture; and at the end of the scene, when all the other dead bodies were carried ceremoniously off stage, her corpse was left behind 'adorning the statue of the she-wolf' (Billing, 210), a testament to the bestial ferocity she had shown toward the Andronici. According to Patricia Lennox, the production's formalised violence and larger-than-life acting style paradoxically generated a believable version of the carnage in the play's final scene: 'The bloody frenzy of the ending was over quickly, and because the entire performance had been a bold opera, for once the chain-reaction deaths did not seem absurd' (108).

Despite Ninagawa's debt to Brook's staging, the Japanese director diverged from his predecessor in that he 'always professed his faithfulness to the text. Throughout his career, his aim was not to reinterpret or to adapt Shakespeare's play but to bring it in close rapport with the modern world and make it easier for his audiences ... to understand' (Kawai, 272). For *Titus Andronicus*, Ninagawa called upon Kazuo Matsuoka to produce 'a close, literal and very full' modern Japanese translation of the play (Dobson, '2006', 304), which ran 'three-and-a-half hours with one ... twenty-minute interval' after the fly scene (Billing, 208). In an interview, Ninagawa claimed that he had staged the play 'without changing one word of Shakespeare's text' (quoted in Secher, 9), but Billing reported that Marcus's speech upon discovering the maimed Lavinia was 'heavily cut' (207). Given the immense cultural differences between Elizabethan England and contemporary Japan, Matsuoka's translation, even without its cuts, clearly could not avoid 'changing' the words of the play, but Ninagawa's intention to remain faithful to the text, nearly in its entirety, more closely resembled Deborah Warner's approach than Peter Brook's.

On the other hand, Ninagawa did not rival Warner in taking

advantage of the play's many opportunities for painful humour. Although one reviewer described the production as both 'bleak and darkly funny in places' (Mock, 19), the comedy was mostly confined to slapstick elements in the staging of 3.2. The fly scene appeared to take place well after the conclusion of the previous scene, for while Titus, Marcus, and Lavinia were still carrying the two heads and hand that they bore off stage in 3.1, Lavinia's hair and gown had been cleaned up considerably. The ends of her sleeves were still dyed red, but she retained none of the wool threads that signified flowing blood. Rather, these strands continued to dangle from the heads and hand that Titus's family placed upon the table and to which they bowed reverently. This solemn mood later broke as Titus picked up his hand, used it to illustrate his puns on his handless condition, then passed it casually to Marcus to hold. At the end of the speech in which he castigated Marcus for killing the fly, Titus smacked his brother on the head with a silver tray; but the biggest laugh came when a wide-eyed Titus quickly forgave Marcus for his violent act because of the fly's resemblance to Aaron. Aside from this sequence, Ninagawa declined to seek humour in the increasing derangement of Titus, as both Warner and Taymor had done. For the banquet scene, Titus entered 'sporting a tall white toque (à la Warner/Cox and Taymor/Hopkins)' (Billing, 209), and the guests laughed at his appearance; but since nearly all of them were also wearing white, his costume did not seem particularly humorous or out of place. Nor did Kotaro Yoshida, as Titus, display any of the manic comic energy that Cox and Hopkins had brought to their performances of Titus's final revenge. Thinking, perhaps, of these earlier embodiments of the title role, Charles Spencer wrote of Ninagawa's production, 'What's largely missing here is the play's bracing black comedy – a truly great *Titus Andronicus* makes you laugh as well as shudder' (Yukio, 94).

Ninagawa did catch something of the play's mixture of emotions in the 'memorably ambiguous' final moments of his production (Bassett, Yukio, 12), which some commentators compared to the conclusion of Taymor's film because of its focus on Young Lucius nurturing Aaron's child. Earlier in the production, Ninagawa had employed Young Lucius exactly as the text suggests, retaining all of his lines, with no special focus on the boy until after his father had spoken the play's final speech and the surviving characters began to leave the stage. As the Goth carrying Aaron's baby was about to exit, Young Lucius 'plucked him by the sleeve, took the baby out of his arms, and returned to kneel, downstage, facing the audience ... Then with the baby on his lap, Lucius threw back his head and let out scream after scream: a story of raw pain wordlessly filled the theatre as the lights went down on two small bodies' (Rutter, Shakespeare, 219n). Billing disparaged this ending as 'very noticeably derivative of the use of Young Lucius at the conclusion of Julie Taymor's 1999 film' (210). However, while reviewers of Taymor's film agreed that her closing images gave it an optimistic conclusion, Ninagawa's critics disagreed over how to interpret his production's final moments. Lennox heard 'Young Lucius's howls of anguish' and understood them as part of a 'bleak end' (108), yet Paul Taylor saw the same closing sequence as 'a moment of ambiguous hope' and a 'cause for optimism' because Young Lucius, despite all the carnage he had witnessed, had not been 'desensitised by atrocity' (Yukio, 20). Billing surmised that spectators were being 'asked simultaneously to thank the gods for youth, which has it in it [to] forgive the guilty and heal the wrongs of the past, whilst they [we]re also prompted to wonder, given the extreme, conscience-scarring trauma to which this particular boy ha[d] been subjected, whether it w[ould] ever be capable of doing so' (210).

Based on Ninagawa's own comments, Taylor's optimistic interpretation of Young Lucius's inarticulate cries seems closest to the director's conscious ambition. During his DVD interview, Ninagawa proclaimed, 'I intend to evoke emotion and hope for breaking the chain of vengeance.' Just as Taymor had offered Young Lucius as a future ruler striving to exit the theatre of cruelty, Ninagawa concluded his production by portraying Titus's grandson as an empathetic young man willing to bring the cycle of revenge to an end. In a different forum, Ninagawa admitted that the play's brutality can be offensive to contemporary audiences, but he added, 'life is full of such desperate situations: murder, atrocity, revenge. When I recognised the connections between the play and what is happening in the world today, I knew I had to find some hope in this story' (quoted in Secher, 9). Ninagawa's vague reference to 'what is happening in the world today' sets his directorial practice apart from Taymor's specific and political approach to the play. Whereas Taymor intentionally evoked images related to particular modern atrocities – the Holocaust, Kosovo, and the Columbine massacre – Ninagawa's nonrepresentational and stylised production more generally reflected what the director called 'today's turbulent world, a world beset with endless war in one place or another' (quoted in Curtin). Although Ninagawa employed elements derived from Taymor's film, he generally eschewed her political and historical specificity in favour of Brook's unlocalised and formalised representation of the play world.

Royal Shakespeare Company, Stratford-upon-Avon, 2003 – Dir. Bill Alexander

Deborah Warner's 1987 version of *Titus Andronicus* for the RSC was so successful that it took sixteen years for the company to work up the courage to mount another production of the play. Director Bill Alexander, whose staging at the Royal Shakespeare Theatre ran from 12 September to 7 November 2003, spoke openly about his struggle to emerge from Warner's shadow:

> I'm carefully reading the Arden edition of *Titus*, which ... has plenty of references to past productions. One in particular is mentioned on nearly every page: Deborah Warner's 1987 production ... I saw it myself in the Swan and it was, indeed, wonderful ... However, no director likes to be constantly told how brilliant another director's previous production was. Time to stop reading ... in case I come across more ideas I can't use because they were used by Warner. (14)

Although Alexander could exclude performance choices made by Warner, he could not avoid having his efforts compared unfavourably to hers by a critic such as Michael Dobson, who wrote, 'I suffer from the great disadvantage ... of having seen Deborah Warner's Swan production in 1987, which still ranks as one of the best productions of Shakespeare ... I've ever seen, and which is likely to go on overshadowing all other attempts on this difficult play for some time to come. Alexander's, sadly, achieved nothing like the same effect' ('2003', 284). Other reviewers, such as John Gross, observed that Alexander was striving for a different effect than Warner's darkly comic rendition and concluded that he had attained modest success on his own terms:

> Alexander opts for a more sombre approach than his most famous predecessors, Peter Brook and Deborah Warner, and it pays divi-

dends. There is humour in the play anyway, inescapably – the sadistic humour of the rapists and killers, the appalled laughter which is sometimes a victim's last line of defence. Alexander doesn't neglect this aspect, but he concentrates on what lies at the heart of the play – grief, anger, outrage, a struggle to articulate the unspeakable. (5)

While Alexander did not 'neglect' the play's humour completely, he also did not commit to it wholeheartedly, which distinguished his production from Warner's. Alexander's 'sombre approach' also differed from Brook's stylisation of violence by presenting the play's atrocities in an unspectacular and realistic manner, more in keeping with the example set by Jane Howell.

Whereas Warner appeared untroubled by the text's tendency to provoke uncomfortable laughter, Alexander and his cast seemed threatened by the comic potential of the play. Speaking of the quick series of murders in the final scene, Alexander admitted, 'We are having to work hard to avoid the "bad laugh" – the audience finding the violence funny instead of shocking' (14). As a result of this anxiety, the director may have overcompensated, creating what Michael Billington called 'a dark, dignified production in which crude sensationalism and mocking laughter are kept at bay' (Bill, 26). According to Paul Taylor, Alexander's staging merely 'offer[ed] escape valves – permitting irreverence at some moments so as to forestall it at others'. For instance, Alexander began the banquet scene by having Titus enter looking like Sweeney Todd in 'a suspiciously blood-soaked apron' (Bill, 16). Further along, 'laughter came from the audience when Titus answered the Emperor's call for his [stepsons] by pointing to the meat pie' (Armion, 57). Such levity, in Taylor's estimation, was incorporated as a means to deter nervous giggling during the rapid-fire killings at the climax of the scene, where the director feared the 'bad laughs' that might compromise the play's tragic effect. The 'overwhelming seriousness' (Segal, 27) of the majority of the performance, however, left Billington 'guiltily hunger[ing] for a little more playful malevolence' (Bill, 26).

Unlike Warner, Alexander cut many lines throughout the play, especially in the opening and closing scenes, and he relocated other speeches to cover the gaps. The production omitted the killing and burial of Mutius entirely (see Epilogue) and drastically reduced the dialogue occurring after the death of Titus. In order to preserve suspense, the script did not include several asides in which characters foreshadow their actions, such as Aaron's promise to return the heads of Martius and Quintus (3.1.201) or Titus's private admission that he has seen through the disguises of Tamora and her sons (5.2.142–4). Young Lucius did not appear in the fly scene, so the lines he speaks there (and the ones spoken to him at the end of 3.2) were missing, and the character made his first appearance as 3.2 blended into 4.1 as a single scene.

This reduction in Young Lucius's role distanced the RSC production from the current trend, initiated by Howell and extended by Taymor, of emphasising the effect of violence on the younger generation. Alexander further differentiated his version of the play from Taymor's film by downplaying the political and historical potentials of the play in the design of his setting and costumes. Ruari Murchison's stark set featured no scenery at all, but 'was dominated by a rough brick rear wall, and a stage paved with a large trefoil design, in which some of the bricks were already broken, allowing the sand (into which Lavinia would eventually scrawl the names of her attackers) to show through' (G. Walker, 60). The stage offered no upper level, which made 'the action of Act 1 more fluid and efficient' by eliminating the need for actors to mount and descend from the gallery, but it also removed 'the symbolism of the upper stage as a divine, superior location' (Armion, 55) used so successfully by Ninagawa three years later. Alexander did occasionally employ a lower level: Aaron buried his gold in a small trap at the beginning of 2.3, and a large knot-shaped space in the wooden floor stage right could be lowered to create the pit into which Martius and Quintus fell, then later raised to house the sandy plain on which Lavinia wrote. As Titus returned to Rome, 'a giant pagan face-mask symbolising the Andronicus family vault' was flown in behind a scrim (G. Walker, 60), which then parted in the middle to represent the opening of the tomb. Instead of being laid to rest below stage level, the two coffins holding the remains of Titus's sons were carried out through the scrim's opening and 'hoisted into the air as part of a burial ritual' (Walton, 68). Since this 'wooden stage, common to all the main-house productions of the 2003 season' lacked 'historical specificity' (Hall-Smith, 51; Billington, Bill, 26), it did not link the issues raised in the play's performance to any particular time or place.

Along with its unfurnished set, the production's costumes

(uncredited) did very little to locate the action in ancient Rome or anywhere else. As Katherine Duncan-Jones observed, 'Explicit signals of "Romanness" [we]re also avoided, with a conspicuous lack of togas, sandals or classical architecture' (19). In a small concession to classical design, the play began on a dark, 'empty stage wreathed in smoke, onto which the rival factions rushed with their distinctive banners and sashes' (Jackson, 184–5). These orange and blue sashes hinted at antique Rome and differentiated the followers of Saturninus and Bassianus, but neither colour coding nor costume elements were applied to distinguish the Romans from the Goths: 'A procession of people clad in dark, drab, nondescript robes herald[ed] the return of Titus, his captives manacled and chained together. Titus, too, [wa]s clad in black, with a laurel wreath around his head' (Pulford, 10). Both the victors and their prisoners wore 'modern tracksuit bottoms' beneath their robes (P. Taylor, Bill, 16), which tended to blur the distinctions between the two nations without anchoring the design to a specific era. Owing to their lack of both aesthetic appeal and historical specificity, Michael Coveney referred to Alexander's costumes as 'the worst in living memory' (Bill, 55).

The RSC production succeeded to a greater degree in its handling of the play's violence in a realistic, but not especially graphic, manner, which may have been dictated by Alexander's preoccupation with avoiding unwelcome laughs. As David Bradley, who assumed the title role, disclosed, 'Bill has made the decision "less is best" with this production. If you use too much blood you evoke laughter of the worst kind, so he uses very little on stage. However, there are one or two violent moments on stage and the theatre is warning that it is not suitable for under 14-year-olds' (quoted in Holt, 'Filch'). Like the disclaimer posted at the 1988 revival of Warner's production (see p. 121), this warning did not prevent some squeamish spectators from engaging in an experience that proved overwhelming. Benedict Nightingale reported, 'A woman near me tottered out when Eve Myles's crazily twitching Lavinia weaved about with a sack containing her father's hand dangling from her teeth; but ... the horrors weren't unduly emphatic' (Bill, 19; see Figure 17). Indeed, Alexander chose not to display the severed body parts of the Andronici – the Messenger returned Titus's hand and his sons' heads in separate bags – and blood appeared more often on clothing than on the actors' bodies. One prominent exception to the absence of explicit violence was the 'highly realistic' amputation of Titus's hand:

> Aaron slowly [cut] off the hand of Titus who crie[d] out in agony as blood drip[ped] on the stage. Paradoxically, other gory episodes such as the final banquet [we]re performed with a minimum amount of stage blood, suggesting that the production refuse[d] to indulge in gory realism and gratuitous violence, limiting the role of the blood scenes to their diegetic function. (Armion, 56)

Although several reviewers recalled audience members fainting or refusing to return to their seats after the intermission following 3.1, most commentators agreed with Kate Bassett that Alexander had 'avoid[ed] reducing this tragedy to shock-horror melodrama' (Bill, 8).

Another key to understanding the treatment of bloodshed in

17 Eve Myles as Lavinia in Bill Alexander's Royal Shakespeare Company production (2003).

the RSC production may be found in Bradley's remark, 'The play takes violence to the extreme and the relationship of Titus to his daughter was crucial to me. It is only when she is mutilated that he starts to communicate with her and it helped me find the humanity in the character' (quoted in McMullen). Bradley linked the production's portrayal of violence to Titus's rapport with Lavinia, as if the emotional trauma of her mutilation was a necessary condition for the fulfilment of their father–daughter bond. Both Lavinia and Titus found their humanity over the course of the performance, as the bodily injuries they sustained gave them empathy for the suffering of others and brought them closer together. Initially, Lavinia was depicted as a 'tiresome minx' (Duncan-Jones, 19), especially in the forest scenes, where her sarcastic speeches in response to discovering Tamora with Aaron in a compromising position made her appear smug and self-righteous. One critic wrote of Lavinia that 'her delight in mocking Tamora made one a little less sympathetic to her, and although she paid a terrible price, [one] almost felt that she had contributed to her own fate' (Pulford, 10). Lavinia's re-entry following her off-stage attack constituted another instance of realistic and gruesome bodily harm. To the accompaniment of '[g]hostly music' (Walton, 70), a 'fissure opened in the back wall of the set, and at first only light and smoke issued from it. Then Lavinia appeared, followed by her assailants. Her face was bloody and swollen, and her movements were spasmodic' (Jackson, 185). She 'came stumbling onstage, moaning, convulsing, arms hanging loosely, her sleeves bunched at the ends, covered in blood. She was crying, blood issuing from her mouth, a searing gash across her cheek, where the knife ha[d] severed her tongue' (Pulford, 10–11). Chris Towner noted that Lavinia's 'shuffling, blood-spattered entrance shocked into absolute silence an audience hitherto inclined to the occasional giggle', but he also suggested that 'her post-trauma twitching might have been stayed before it became such an irritating distraction'. Along the same lines, Duncan-Jones found the young woman's metamorphosis 'spectacularly distressing, though her cries and yelps conflict[ed] with a text which suggests that she is wholly mute' (19). For the rest of her life, Lavinia's 'harrowing repertoire of groans and whimpers' were 'her only means of communicating her dreadful distress' (Spencer, Bill, 22).

Titus's emotional transformation became evident in the following scene, when he was forced to confront the spectacle of his mutilated child. At the beginning of the play, he appeared psychologically exhausted, unable to return the hug Lavinia gave him at their reunion. When Marcus led the maimed Lavinia on stage in 3.1, Titus at first remained 'a cold, stiff-upper-lip type, strangely detached, keeping his distance from his daughter, turning away as he [saw] her severed limbs and torn out tongue' (Pulford, 10). Alexander postponed physical contact between Titus and Lavinia until after Titus had delivered the three long speeches of 'sorrow, loss and incomprehension', which heightened the effect of the family members' eventual embrace:

> Here, it seemed, was a man ... for whom family honour meant so much that he could only respond to the needs of a raped and mutilated daughter through public utterance, speaking of love rather than showing it. Thus, when he finally dragged his ... unwilling feet across the stage and held Lavinia in his arms, the effect was all the more powerful ... for having be[en] delayed so long. (Walker, 59, 60)

In a nod to realism, Titus wrapped his arm in a tourniquet before submitting his limb to Aaron's knife, and at the moment when he sacrificed his hand in a vain attempt to save his sons, 'Lavinia r[an] straight to him. David Bradley then br[ought] Titus powerfully alive, his passion and hatred contrasting greatly with his former aloofness' (Pulford, 10). Alexander's study of Bate's Arden edition, however, later worked against his employment of violence to reconnect Titus with his daughter. Although most editions of the play indicate with a stage direction that *'Lavinia kisses Titus'* (3.1.248) after the Messenger brings back her father's hand and her brothers' heads, Alexander followed Bate, the first editor to suggest different recipients of the 'comfortless' kiss to which Marcus refers (3.1.249). As Jackson recalled, 'Lavinia kissed the bags containing the heads of Martius and Quintus' in a 'surprising gesture of affection and piety' (185).

Toward the end of the production, Alexander depended upon sound effects, rather than blood, to convey the force of violent actions. Having captured Tamora's sons in 5.2, the relatives of Titus forced them to their knees, and Lavinia stood in front of them with her basin, one after the other, blocking the audience's view of their execution. However, as Titus slit their throats, 'the slice of the knife [wa]s amplified throughout the auditorium'

(Walton, 70). Similarly, 5.3 began with Lavinia hooded, dressed all in white, already looking like a ghost. After serving slices of pie to Tamora and Saturninus, Titus approached and unhooded Lavinia, kissed her, and performed his final act of slaughter in a manner that many reviewers found particularly striking. Angie Pulford wrote, 'The most horrifying moment for me was in the banquet scene ... when Titus kills Lavinia. As he cups her chin and breaks her neck there is a distinct crack. It made the audience gasp, and sent a shiver down my spine' (11). Dobson agreed that 'the killing of Lavinia ... was as shocking as ever – the cracking sound effect as Titus unceremoniously ... snapped her neck was perhaps this production's highlight' ('2003', 285). So startling was this 'sickening crunch' (Jackson 186) that Saturninus, seated at the table, tipped over backwards in surprise. During this sequence, Titus and Lavinia 'stare[d] deep[ly] into one another's eyes ... carrying a strong emotional bond to their graves' (Walton, 70–1).

The shocking intensity of Lavinia's death overwhelmed the potentially comic effect of Saturninus's pratfall. Elsewhere in the production, however, the Emperor was depicted as a childish tyrant, worthy of ridicule. As Pulford wrote, 'John Lloyd Fillingham as Saturninus portrayed the Emperor as weak, mincing, petulant, often truculent – his changeable nature besotted and influenced by the strong Tamora, who had him right under her thumb' (10). Tamora's power over her husband was most evident in 4.4, where the knife in Titus's letter, as well as the news of Lucius's approach, sent Saturninus trembling to his knees, and Tamora was forced to comfort him like a mother calming a terrified child. Maureen Beattie played the queen of the Goths as a 'feisty Glaswegian' (Duncan-Jones, 19), which 'gave her Tamora a touch of exoticism' (Jackson, 185), but Alexander did not pursue a connection between the Goths and the Scots by having Tamora's sons share her accent. As Revenge, Tamora simply donned a black cloak, which made her look 'like the cowled Scottish widow in the property ad' (Billington, Bill 26). Yet while Tamora ruled the Emperor, she was in turn driven by Joe Dixon's 'jovially devilish' Aaron (Parsons, 147), who brought a 'powerful physical presence to the role that underscored his capacity to dominate Tamora and her sons through rhetoric alone' (Walker, 60). So strong was the Moor's sensual hold over his mistress that, 'whenever thinking of her "lovely Aaron" Tamora place[d] her hand between her legs, and both Chiron and Demetrius seem[ed] magnetized by his potent masculinity' (Walton, 70).

In contrast to Dixon's Aaron, David Bradley's Titus did not strike a physically imposing figure; he made 'no pretence to be a mighty Titus but [wa]s a frail old man from the beginning' (Parkes). Those reviewers who praised Bradley's efforts enjoyed the sardonic quality he brought to the role: 'His is a commanding performance from the first: severe, ascetic, his long bony face combining with the long, thin nose that stretches to his chin to suggest an age-old hawk or wizened, watchful eagle. And when he despairs, it's the despair of a man who has seen it all: grim, bleak, mocking, self-mocking' (Nightingale, Bill, 19). One of the high points of his portrayal was his laugh at the nadir of Titus's misery, which Charles Spencer called 'a deadly cackle at the meaningless horror of human nature that sends shivers coursing down the listener's spine' (Bill, 22). Some commentators, however, thought Bradley to be 'essentially miscast, failing to convince fully either as a warrior or a patriarch' (Duncan-Jones, 19). Paul Taylor concurred that Bradley's 'distinctly unmilitary bearing' put one 'more in mind of a dodgy archbishop or a shady eminence grise than a punch-drunk old bull of a warrior' (Bill, 16). What some spectators read as 'excellent low-key irony' in Bradley's performance (Billington, Bill, 26) others saw as 'cadaverous neutrality' that contributed to a 'dull production' (Coveney, Bill, 55). Like Michael Maggio's equally realistic yet understated Central Park version fourteen years earlier, Alexander's *Titus* – epitomised by Bradley's 'restrained' performance (Bassett, Bill, 8) – did not commit to a full-tilt, visceral representation of the play's physical and emotional horrors, and as a result, 'the production d[id]n't quite work' (Duncan-Jones, 19).

Shakespeare Theatre Company, Washington, DC, 2007 – Dir. Gale Edwards

In the androcentric world of Shakespearean performance, *Titus Andronicus* has never been popular among directors. Therefore, since the late twentieth century, when major theatre companies decided to stage the play, they often turned to female directors, who were more willing than their male counterparts to brave the play's challenges, perhaps because their opportunities to produce Shakespeare's tragedies were otherwise severely limited. Assistant director Buzz Goodbody took over Trevor Nunn's production of *Titus* when it transferred to the Aldwych in 1973, and since that time, Jane Howell, Deborah Warner, Jeannette Lambermont, Julie Taymor, and Lucy Bailey (Shakespeare's Globe, 2006) have all had their chances to direct major productions. Most recently, Australian Gale Edwards, whose feminist version of *The Taming of the Shrew* for the RSC in 1995 sparked heated controversy, directed the play for the Shakespeare Theatre Company as part of the Shakespeare in Washington Festival (2007). One of the ways in which this staging stood out from its predecessors was in its portrayal of Lavinia, not as a helpless victim, but as a strong young woman who resisted her victimisation and took an active role in punishing the perpetrators of the crimes against her.

Actor Colleen Delany, who played Lavinia, confided that Edwards wanted the character to have 'a fierceness and strong will of her own' (quoted in Horwitz, C5), which Delany succeeded in conveying to the audience. She bravely defended Bassianus from Chiron and Demetrius's attack, and although her rape and mutilation 'slowed her down ... it did not seem to change her character', which remained 'as tough as old boots', particularly in her 'remarkable' attempt to prevent the amputation of Titus's hand (Williams, Gale, 12). According to Edwards, Lavinia's ordeal transforms her into an avenger as single-minded as her deranged father: 'Lavinia ... desperately tr[ies] to communicate who did it to her so that revenge can be achieved. All she wants is revenge' (*Windows*). As William Proctor Williams noticed, Lavinia jumped at the chance to become directly involved in her family's retribution against her assailants:

> [H]er absolute glee at the killing of Chiron and Demetrius ... created a Lavinia quite different from the ... injured creature of Laura Fraser in Taymor's film ... [A]s all those on stage exited with the bodies ... she advanced front and center, outside the closing curtains, and with a spot on her lifted both her bandaged stumps above her head in a classic gesture of triumph. (Gale, 12)

Delany reported that Edwards intended Lavinia to be perceived as 'a pure and noble character at the beginning', but to be 'corrupted and crushed by choosing' vengeance as her raison d'être (quoted in Horwitz, C5). Once Lavinia had achieved her revenge, the director believed, she no longer had a reason for living, and she willingly 'offer[ed] herself up for death' at her father's hand (*Windows*). This ultimate submissiveness conflicted, to some degree, with the otherwise strong and fiercely defiant nature that Lavinia had displayed up to that point in the play.

As Williams points out above, Edwards's depiction of a generally resilient Lavinia differed sharply from the presentation of the character in Taymor's film. However, in other respects, Edwards was heavily influenced by Taymor, especially in her rejection of Brook's stylised approach to the play's violence: 'We stage all the violence as Shakespeare requests; if he says their throats are slit on stage, we slit their throats ... It's not the confetti version, where people open their mouths and confetti falls out, or streamers ... There is blood, but it's kept to a minimum' (*Windows*). Edwards declined to follow Brook's lead in relegating the slitting of the throats of Tamora's sons to off-stage action, and her refusal to allow streamers to fall out of Lavinia's mouth constituted a dismissal of formalised violence in favour of a realistic, but judicious, use of stage blood. Peter Marks confirmed that, with one main exception, the bloodshed in the Shakespeare Theatre production did not seem excessive: 'Only occasionally d[id] the vengeance wreaked on one character or another become stomach-churning, as when Lavinia, her tongue freshly cut out, open[ed] her mouth to wail and blood gushe[d] forth' (C5). Such a description reminds one of the corresponding moment in Taymor's film, when Lavinia, perched on a tree stump, answered her uncle's question, 'Why dost not speak to me?' (2.4.21) by spewing forth a mouthful of blood. While Taymor, possessing the option to use special effects, slowed down this sequence to give it a nightmarish quality, Edwards, limited to the resources of the stage, elected to treat the segment with utter realism, in the manner of Howell.

Despite Edwards's claim that she 'tried to honour the text', she did transpose sections of the play freely and cut 'probably 800 lines' of the original script (*Windows*). As in Alexander's production, 3.2 and 4.1 were combined into one scene, but in Edwards's case, both were 'heavily cut ... with Lavinia and Young Lucius exiting just before the fly killing ... and not re-entering until the boy ran in with his books pursued by Lavinia' (Williams, Gale, 12). With omissions, the play ran for approximately two hours and fifteen minutes (*Windows*), excluding an interval after 3.1. In a puzzling alteration, Edwards reassigned the Messenger's return of Titus's hand and his sons' heads, as well as the sympathetic seven-line speech accompanying it, to Aaron, which not only changed the effect of the speech entirely, but also made 'nonsense' of Aaron's later claim (uncut) that he had watched the delivery of Titus's hand 'through the crevice of a wall' (5.1.114) and laughed heartily at it (Williams, Gale, 14). In her most prominent transposition, Edwards followed Howell and Taymor by reversing the order of the political wrangling between the dead Emperor's sons and the return of the Roman army in Act 1, so that the performance began 'not where it opens in the usual text but with Titus' triumphal entry' (Williams, Gale, 12).

The historically eclectic design of Taymor's film also appears to have influenced the setting and costumes of Edwards's 'retro-futurist staging', which featured 'ebony flooring polished to a mirror finish, the better to reflect villainy [and] gauzy sable curtains with voluminous folds for cloaking deceit' (Mondello). Set designer Peter England's abstract, overwhelmingly black stage reflected colour only in Act 2, 'when complemented by Mark McCullough's lighting design ... particularly the shimmering forest images that shifted from shades of blue to violet, to green, and to red, the reflections of their fragile branches in the polished ebony floor multiply[ed] their density and a sense of danger' (Montouri, 128). These branches were represented by vertical sticks planted on large rolling trucks, which could be shifted into various formations, including the path through which the maimed Lavinia made her entrance. Edwards herself admitted that the forest set looked 'slightly Asian', but she added, 'We're not setting it in Japan, we're setting it in an abstract world' (*Set Slideshow*).

Costume designer Murrell Horton called the period for the production's clothing 'Kabuki Greek' with a 'modern flavor': an anachronistic mixture of classical, Asian, and contemporary fashion elements (*Costume Slideshow*). Williams referred to this diverse combination as 'the typical mix of ancient and modern we have grown used to in the last decade or so. Titus is usually in antique military gear, as are his sons, though his dress becomes more ragged and miscellaneous as the play progresses; the other Romans are in business suits, though ... the Goths seem to prefer chain mail from the head to the waist and baggy trousers' (1). Around the house, Titus wore a 'kimono coat', and Lavinia's outfit in the hunting scene was shaped by images that Horton drew from Japanese fashion magazines. Whereas Taymor's setting and costumes evoked specific and recognizable eras in Roman and American history, the eclectic design of Edwards' production created 'it's own world' (*Costume Slideshow*): a timeless universe whose Asian elements belied Edwards's disavowal of stylisation in favour of realism.

Two symbolic features of the set provoked diverse interpretations among Washington viewers, who tend to interpret local productions in the context of the US government. First, projected on the back wall of the stage, a 'set of staring eyes ... greeted the audience as they entered the theatre', which Williams initially took as a warning that 'the Patriot Act is watching you' (Gale, 1). Likewise, Peter Marks originally saw 'the wary visage of Big Brother', but later gestures made by Saturninus and Bassianus designated the eyes as those of 'the great Roman emperor who has just died' (C5). Second, Titus and his sons returned to Rome upon a rough, charred wooden path running diagonally across the stage. They 'followed the audible drumbeat along this "path", which was ... formed by the coffins of the twenty-one sons who had died in battle, now literally supporting their father and his country's cause' (Montouri, 127; see Figure 18). From this action, Williams took the general point that 'a war leader walks over the coffins of the war dead' (1), but Deborah Montouri understood it as an allusion to Bush administration policies: 'In cold contrast to the current practice of concealing the American soldiers' coffins returning from Afghanistan and Iraq, this public honouring of the war's casualties served as a reminder that great nations are often built upon the sacrifices of their soldiers' (127).

Although Edwards generally did not follow Taymor in employing her design elements for political ends, she did borrow 'extensively from Julie Taymor's campy film version of the play', particularly her outlandish clothing for Tamora and her sons: 'Like Taymor's, Edwards's Goth princes [were] transformed into the modern-day goths ... of underground pop culture, decked out in black leather and metal. Their lewd behavior here extended to making a homemade porn video featuring themselves and a prostitute gamboling on a sofa shaped like a huge pair of lips' (Montouri, 127). The vulgar actions of Chiron and Demetrius in Edwards's production recalled the orgy scene of Taymor's movie, during which Tamora's sons frolicked nude around a pool with various female attendants. Taymor's glitzy costumes for the

18 Christopher Scheeren as Quintus, Danny Binstock as Mutius, Chris Genebach as Lucius, David Murgittroyd as Martius, and Sam Tsoutsouvas as Titus in the Shakespeare Theatre Company's 2007 production of Shakespeare's *Titus Andronicus*, directed by Gale Edwards.

Empress, particularly her gold lamé gown for the wedding reception, found an echo in the outrageous garments of Edwards's Tamora: 'Her dress when she enters at 1.1.303 ... is of a dazzling tastelessness which has to be seen to be really appreciated. She runs through a range of more or less deafening costumes ... and finally almost paralyzes the senses in the dress she uses in her disguise as Revenge in 5.2' (Williams, Gale, 1, 12). As Montouri recorded, 'a sequined Tamora ... appeared under a twirling disco ball, flashing exaggerated red talons and sporting blood red horns. Her sons' transparent disguises were yet another variation on a theme by Taymor. Murder resembled a ghostly, smirking tiger, Rape, a ballerina in drag, complete with rouged nipples and a flesh-colored tutu split at the crotch, the dark clothing beneath suggesting pubic hair' (127). Adapting the costumes of Rape and Murder from Taymor's final PAN, Edwards camped up her version of the Revenge masque even more thoroughly by transforming Tamora from the Statue of Liberty into a disco queen.

This Shakespeare Theatre production, like the BBC version and Taymor's film, concluded with a focus on Young Lucius in relation to Aaron's baby, but Edwards's version presented an even less optimistic outlook than Howell's 'stark, unrelenting' ending (see p. 112). Observing how the new Emperor brutally punishes both Aaron and Tamora, Edwards deduced that 'Lucius, our hero, is not going to be heroic at all. He's going to continue the circle of violence and revenge, and to ... say, show no pity, show no forgiveness ... a terrifying thought' (*Windows*). To underline Rome's bleak prospects, Edwards finished the play by showing the effect of Lucius's vindictiveness on his impressionable son. As 'the old emperor's eyes, once again looming over the scene, dripped blood' (Montouri, 127), Edwards appended a final sequence which she intended as a direct response to the movie's optimistic conclusion:

> [I]f you've seen the Julie Taymor film, the boy in the film picks up the baby and walks off into the sunset ... In this production, the little boy picks up the baby, he sits in front of us cross-legged on the floor ... and the last image of the show is him pulling a dagger out of his pocket and raising it above his head. And after the blackout, we presume, he kills the child. (*Windows*)

Williams noted that this particularly grim finale seemed to be Edwards's overt attempt to place her production in contrast to those of her predecessors: 'It was certainly a departure from Taymor's reading of the play and much more terrible than Howell's reading, since her Young Lucius [wa]s shocked by the baby being killed whereas Edwards' Young Lucius was going to do the killing himself' (Gale, 14). On the whole, Edwards's performance choices, especially her serious and lifelike dramatisation of violence, consigned her production to the realistic line of descent; but her most obvious borrowings from Howell's BBC version (her rearrangement of the opening scene and her concluding spotlight on Young Lucius with the baby) appear to have reached her through the intermediary example of Julie Taymor's film.

Stratford, Ontario Shakespeare Festival, 2000
– Dir. Richard Rose

One year after the release of Taymor's *Titus*, the Stratford, Ontario Shakespeare Festival presented director Richard Rose's production of the play at the Tom Patterson Theatre, where it ran from 27 June to 30 September 2000. The Festival apparently hoped to capitalise on the revival of interest in the tragedy sparked by the film, but the production's proximity to Taymor's work in both time and design made the derivative nature of Rose's efforts clear to many audience members, and the stage version suffered by comparison. In the political tradition launched by Douglas Seale and continued by Taymor, Rose set the production in Fascist Italy and intended to use that setting to comment on political strife in various contemporary states. Rose also emulated Taymor by employing both realistic and stylised touches in his depiction of the play's violent acts. Although Rose, like Taymor, appreciated the absurd quality of the play's black humour, his actors did not fully succeed in conveying that dark comedy to spectators. At the end of his production, Rose (anticipating Gale Edwards' staging seven years later) also adapted Howell's and Taymor's focus on Young Lucius to imply a continuation of the cycle of revenge.

One reviewer wrote of the Stratford performance that, like 'the Taymor film, this production [wa]s set in fascist Italy. But it ha[d] none of the movie's deliciously decadent excesses.' In other words, designer Charlotte Dean created costumes from the same period that Taymor had chosen but eschewed Taymor's camp aesthetic in favour of 'crisply militaristic uniforms and formal-wear' (T. Brown, E3). Rome's senators were 'dressed formally in grey or black cutaways, grey vests and gloves, and striped cravats', and Titus 'was attired in a major general's grey uniform'. Saturninus's 'gold encrusted white military coat, white jodhpurs, black riding boots, and squat, black fez recalled the dress of Il Duce himself' (Watermeier, 31), while his followers were outfitted as Mussolini's 'black-shirted thugs' (Liston, 86). At first, the Goths also sported martial apparel, but their queen changed into civilian-style clothing once she became Empress of Rome: 'Tamora initially appeared in a dark-colored, double-breasted, military-style coat. Extravagant wine-colored fox fur at the cuffs and collar of the coat and a fox fur beret of the same hue hinted at her "Gothic" savagery.' In this modern European context, 'Aaron's costume, a sort of traditional "Moorish" outfit – long damask coat, striped silk waist sash, billowy pants – seemed ... exotically out of time and place' (Watermeier, 31).

Set designer Teresa Przybylski, taking her cue from the recent death of the Emperor, fashioned a stage with a 'funeral look' (T. Brown, E3) that 'hint[ed] at the rise of fascism' (K. Taylor, R6). To the strains of the *Dies Irae* of the Verdi *Requiem*, the lights came up on 'a raised black platform running the length of the Patterson Theatre's long, narrow, rectangular [thrust] stage. A bier draped with a metallic grey mantle dominated the downstage end of this platform. A silver, laurel leaf chaplet, the symbol of the late Emperor of Rome, rested on top of the coffin' (Watermeier, 31). Seated upon benches flanking the sides of the stage were the supporters of Saturninus and Bassianus, who responded noisily to the speeches of Marcus and Titus delivered into old-fashioned standing microphones, which resembled the microphone employed for the same purpose in Taymor's film. The vault of the Andronici was represented by a trap at centre stage, into which two bodies on stretchers were lowered, but this moment was the only instance of the use of an alternative level in the entire performance. Since the action was played almost entirely on the thrust portion of the platform, Rose altered the text elsewhere (such as in the Revenge masque of 5.2) to allow all of the characters to remain permanently at stage level. For variety in blocking in the second half of the play, Rose brought on a long rectangular black table, which allowed Lucius, and later Aaron, to stand upon it to address the Goths from a higher plane. This table also hosted the Andronicus family dinner in 4.1 and the banquet at the end of the play.

However, the most highly praised staging element of the Stratford production was the 'effectively evocative' lighting design of Graeme S. Thompson (Ouzounian, D1). As the corpses of Titus's sons were buried, 'Lights shining through transparent panels in the floor eerily evoked the entombed, mummy-wrapped remains of ancestral Andronici' (Watermeier, 31). At the end of this rite, the lights faded, and the bodies appeared to lie at rest, but the corpses were illuminated again in 3.1 as Titus, standing in a spotlight alone at centre stage, sank into prostration at the thought of the twenty-two sons for whose deaths he never wept. In the forest scenes of Act 2, the pit was located on the same spot as the tomb of the Andronici, but Rose elected not to employ a fall into the trap. Instead, he called upon Thompson to create a dark circular area in the middle of the stage surrounded by overhead lighting, so that when Martius walked into the pit, he appeared to be swallowed up by a black hole in the ground (when, in reality, he remained at stage level). Quintus was eventually pulled into the same dark space, and ropes were cast into the blackness to pull both brothers out of the pit and into the light. In this way, the framing of Titus's sons for the murder of the Emperor's brother was 'staged symbolically' (Liston, 86), without any attempt to present a realistic tumble into the 'fell devouring receptacle' (2.3.235).

Rose's willingness to stage some scenes in a non-representational fashion carried over into his presentation of the play's carnage, which emulated Taymor's film by alternating between lifelike and stylised depictions of violence. The only sequence in the production that featured visible bloodshed was the entrance of Lavinia at the beginning of 2.4: 'A painful deformity of her open mouth and a trickle of blood there gave credence to the cutting out of her tongue, and the stumps of her arms, covered with cloth, were realistic' (Liston, 86). No gore accompanied the multiple murders at the final banquet, but all of them were performed in a naturalistic manner. In the middle of a farewell embrace, Titus 'swiftly, surprisingly, dispassionately' broke Lavinia's neck (without any accompanying sound effect); he then 'killed Tamora with a single, quick, deadly thrust of a knife' (Watermeier, 32). Seeing Titus assassinate the Empress, Saturninus shot him: 'Though guns had been present from the beginning, this was the first use of one. Lucius then choked Saturninus while all others on stage, with drawn pistols, neutralized both factions. When Aemilius declared Lucius Emperor, all signified their acceptance of the proclamation by putting their pistols away' (Liston, 86). Just as Taymor had postponed the use of modern weapons until the end of the banquet, Rose also delayed the use of his characters' guns until the bloodless mayhem of his production's final scene.

At other points, Rose turned to his lighting designer to help represent violence in a more stylised way. William T. Liston suggested that this 'symbolically realistic' approach may have been dictated by the 'openness of the thrust stage' at the Patterson Theatre, which 'meant that ... Titus' chopping off of his hand could not really be concealed from the audience; turning his back, for instance, did not hide his hand from many eyes. Titus extended his arm toward the front, and as Aaron struck the lopping blow the lights went out, but not soon enough to obscure the fact that the blade did not touch Titus' (86, see Figure 19). Rose repeated this technique at the end of 5.2, when Titus's attendants captured Tamora's sons and placed them, bound and gagged, on their backs on top of the long table, with their heads hanging off the side facing the audience. As Titus cut their throats, a 'sudden blackout with a deafening burst of sound' signified their ghastly deaths (Ouzounian, D1). Kate Taylor found this 'compromise' between realism and formalism in the depiction of violence unsatisfying: 'Rose's approach prove[d] neither naturalistic enough ... nor stylish enough ... to build much heartfelt horror. Rose manage[d] the bloodshed of *Titus* rather than confronting it' (R6). In contrast to Taymor, who offered both horrifyingly realistic and stylised, yet grotesquely beautiful, atrocities, Rose's blackouts and trickles of blood did not achieve the visceral effect that many viewers seem to expect from *Titus Andronicus*.

Another instance of violence in Rose's production, the slaying of Mutius by his father, was handled in an unusual and arresting

19 James Blendick as Titus and Xuan Fraser as Aaron in Richard Rose's Stratford, Ontario production (2000).

way. When Mutius blocked Titus's path to retrieve Lavinia for the Emperor, Titus lost his temper and struck Mutius with a riding crop until he dropped to his knees; then he grabbed Mutius and slammed his head, twice, into the floor, 'crushing his skull' (Watermeier, 32). After this outburst, Titus walked away as if he had simply disciplined his wayward child, without realising that he had killed him 'almost by accident' (Liston, 85). It was not until Lucius returned to the stage to reprove his father for his rash deed that Titus recognised that he had slain his son. This decision to represent the death of Mutius as an unintentional act altered the production's initial portrayal of Titus, showing him to be ruled not so much by a callous devotion to patriarchal order as by his own violent disposition.

As Titus, James Blendick set the tone for a rather sombre production. Robert Cushman wrote of the actor's performance, 'He speaks in the round and resonant Old Stratfordian style ... and with a matter-of-fact authority distinctively his own. What he lacks is the terrible, logical insanity brought to the role by Brian Cox on stage or Anthony Hopkins on screen' (B6). Both Warner and Taymor boasted a lead actor capable of bringing off the dark comedy, as well as the tragic demise, of Titus, but most reviewers found Rose's version of the play to be weighted too heavily toward tragedy. Tony Brown asserted that *Titus Andronicus*

> should be played for fun and entertainment, not deep meaning and dark artistry. This was clearly understood by ... Julie Taymor, whose recent film version of *Titus* was brilliant both for its depiction of the gory stuff and for its light, almost frivolous touch. Nothing is light or frivolous about the Stratford production, which is led by James Blendick, who takes Titus' every line most seriously. (E3)

Blendick's ponderous delivery conflicted with Rose's belief (which he shared with Taymor) that the play resembles the theatre of the absurd: 'Some people say the play is too horrible and too gruesome ... [or] that certain events in the play are laughable, and my feeling is, that's the point ... The characters have entered situations that are so absurd ... that people will laugh at some terrible, horrible things' (62). In practice, Blendick earned 'a grim laugh here and there' (K. Taylor, R6), particularly in the fly scene, but at the end of the play, spectators found the action more silly than absurd: 'The audience erupted in laughter when Titus entered in 5.3 wearing a contemporary white chef's jacket and toque ... When Titus announced the contents of the pies, members of the assembled dinner party gagged or rushed from the table to vomit off-stage, and, again, the audience broke into laughter' (Watermeier, 31). Following Warner and Taymor, Rose clothed Titus *'like a cook'* (5.3.25, sd), but his staging of the final banquet did not help Blendick to portray the 'terrible, logical insanity' that Cox and Hopkins found in Titus's absurd behaviour.

Rose also concluded his production with an image that recalled previous versions of the play that had concentrated on Young Lucius's relationship to Aaron's infant. In the opening scene, Titus's grandson, dressed as a Hitler Youth, stood beside his Aunt Lavinia and 'looked on all th[e] action, as he did through much of the play, in the traditions of Jane Howell's BBC production and Julie Taymor's recent film *Titus*' (Liston, 85). Like these two directors, Rose employed Young Lucius to observe his elders' brutality and demonstrate what he had learned through his actions in the play's final moments. At the end of the Stratford production, Lucius spoke his lines denying pity to Tamora, and spat upon her body. As the other characters left the stage, Young Lucius approached the baby abandoned on the banquet table and picked up a knife. Phillip Psutka, who played Young Lucius, remembered that Rose instructed him to hold the knife over the baby, but not to threaten it directly. In comparison to Gale Edwards's later version of this business, Rose's staging was more ambiguous: Young Lucius might kill the child of the damned Moor, or he might not. In any case, Rose intended to emphasise the potential effect of witnessing violence on members of the next generation; as he told an interviewer, 'There are children in this play: Shakespeare put them there because they are the future. This is not going to stop. Once the lines have been crossed, the cycle of revenge doesn't stop' (quoted in Prosser, 6).

In other published remarks, Rose revealed that, like Taymor, he was constantly thinking about how his production might comment on international politics, especially the persistence of eye-for-an-eye retribution all over the globe. In the weeks leading up to the performance, he pinned 'newspaper reports of contemporary murder and mayhem' to the wall of the production's rehearsal room, and he once admitted, 'If I hadn't had to make my decisions six months ago ... I might have set the production in Sierra Leone' (quoted in Prosser, 6). Although Rose stuck to his original choice to locate the production in Fascist Italy, this setting was still designed to underline the relevance of the play's treatment of violence to contemporary hostilities throughout the world: 'We've had wars of late in Kosovo, Bosnia, Rwanda, but ... [b]ecause we're not as worried about being attacked by nuclear missiles, we have a chance to look at the essence of those wars. They're very clan-oriented, very much family against family, which [is what] this play is about' (quoted in McMahon, A5). By emphasising the 'clan-oriented' nature of the play's violence, and by comparing it to the bloodshed currently raging in some of the same specific locations, like the Balkans, singled out by Taymor, Rose evidenced both the political bent of his production and the extent to which it drew upon the example set by the film *Titus*.

Shakespeare's Globe Theatre, London, 2006
– Dir. Lucy Bailey

Lucy Bailey's production of *Titus Andronicus* ran at the Globe Theatre from 20 May to 13 August 2006, which overlapped with the Ninagawa Company's run in Stratford-upon-Avon and prompted numerous comparisons between the two vastly dissimilar stage versions. Ben Brantley's joint review contrasted their approaches to the play's violence, noting that 'while the Ninagawa Company borrows from the pristine style of vintage Peter Brook', Bailey's Globe production 'is awash in stage blood and simulacra of severed heads and hands' (7). Michael Dobson added that, 'Though Bailey's *Titus* lacks the spectacular grandeur and eerie cruel beauty of Ninagawa's, it has a much more developed sense of the black humour that is never far away from Elizabethan and Jacobean revenge tragedy' ('2006', 308). By choosing a naturalistic, rather than a stylised, method to portray bodily mutilation, and by exploiting enthusiastically the text's opportunities for dark comedy, Bailey became the only director of a major production in the two decades following Deborah Warner's triumph to attempt to follow in her footsteps. However, Bailey did not emulate Warner's use of an uncut script, nor did she rearrange 1.1 or exploit the figure of Young Lucius. With its unspecified era and location, Bailey's version, like Warner's, eschewed any effort to make a sustained political statement. Yet whereas Warner used blood 'sparingly', preferring to coat her maimed victims in 'clay or mud' (see p. 64), Bailey let the gore flow freely, to the point that 'audience members were dropping like flies at the sheer shock-horror of it all' (Spencer, Yukio, 31). This combination of graphic bloodshed and black humour justified Brantley's reference to the Globe's offering as 'Bailey's Grand Guignol staging of *Titus*' (7).

Until 1962, the Grand Guignol offered explicitly horrific entertainments, and their success was judged by the number of patrons who passed out at the revolting spectacle. Before the Globe production of *Titus*, several earlier performances, including the RSC versions directed by Brook, Nunn, and Warner, had also proudly induced many viewers to lose consciousness (Tempera, 45). Indeed, as Douglas Hodge, Bailey's Titus, recalled, 'Olivier used to count the fainters in his diary ... It was a sign of how well he was doing' (29). Yet while Olivier elicited this visceral reaction in a stylised production, Hodge and his fellows imitated the Grand Guignol by relying upon the shock value of gruesomely realistic special effects. According to Wendy Attwell, Bailey believed that she needed 'real blood' to make an impression on contemporary audiences:

> And bloody it is indeed: Lavinia displaying the ragged-flesh of her wrist stumps and dribbling red streaks; blood-soaked heads in sacks, loose hands flying about ... There can be no doubt that the graphicness of these scenes and the media warnings about them has attracted a congregation composed of curious thrill-seekers; of those who would not usually be interested in such a play as *Titus* but who have come for the blood and are enjoying the splattering.

Bailey's production often played to these 'thrill-seekers', the stereotyped groundlings of the Globe Theatre, whose tastes reputedly run toward irreverent humour and spectacles of violence.

Bailey frequently involved the groundlings in the mayhem, either by allowing the action to spill off the main platform down the two ramps attached to the forestage and into the yard, or by blocking entrances so that the actors proceeded through the crowd up the ramps and onto the stage. Her aim was to make the theatrical experience 'interactive': 'The joy of the Globe is that it is in the round, and you can do a semi-promenade production. We are attempting a kind of 'whole theatre' – the company will come at the audience from all directions; we want them to feel that they are part of this madness' (quoted in Lee, 'Ritualistic', 16; 'Culture', 15). The 'semi-promenade' element of the staging arose from the fact that groundlings were warned in advance 'to be prepared to move at a moment's notice':

> Time and again throughout the production, costumed 'extras' cleared pathways among the standing spectators for processions of actors, most notably during Titus's victorious entrance in 1.1 ... Two moveable towers, recalling both the mobile carts on which productions of the medieval religious drama allegedly took place and the vehicles used for Roman triumphal processions, were in nearly constant use from the play's outset, when Saturninus and Bassianus each used one to campaign for election as Rome's next emperor. (Preussner, 117–18)

The rolling towers replaced the gallery above the stage as the location for actions that occur aloft in the text, such as Titus's appearance in his study in 5.2 and the speeches of Marcus and Lucius to the astonished Romans at the end of the play. While the trap on the main platform was used to stand for the tomb of the Andronici, the forest pit was represented by a large camouflage net unfurled outward into the yard, whose deployment 'caused considerable scrambling about for the [g]roundlings trying to keep out of the way of the production' (Williams, Lucy, 65). These staging choices disoriented yet excited many of the audience members in the yard, but 'those with the expensive gallery seats could experience these effects only vicariously. As sometimes happens at the Globe, the production seemed designed for two separate and unequal audiences, with the five-pound standing spectators holding the more valuable tickets' (Preussner, 119).

Bailey's use of towers for 'above' spaces was dictated by the production's set design, which swaddled the entire stage, including the upper gallery behind the platform, in black fabric:

> Designer William Dudley created quite a stir by swathing the arena's *frons scenae* and pillars in black cloth and by stretching an open-weave [velarium], containing a central hole or oculus ... across the open space at the top of the theatre. These features ... were meant to contribute to an overall atmosphere of the theatre as an 'Elizabethan gladiatorial space', according to Bailey's program notes ... though the black swathing did preclude action on the upper or 'balcony' level of the stage. (Preussner, 122)

The Globe's stage doors and discovery space remained permanently open, which made these 'cavernous exits seem to lead to the mouth of hell' (Billington, Lucy, 36). Bailey explained that she darkened and enclosed the open-air theatre to reconceive the Globe as a type of Colosseum:

> My instinct was to create a black claustrophobic space, which is why I wanted the velarium ... I was also struck by the raw physicality of the play; the confrontation of man and man ... led me to understand the theatre space as an arena, a bloodbath in the literal sense ... [S]o William Dudley and I developed the idea of a temple of death ... where the most terrible things are done to the point of satiation; the arena filled with blood. (quoted in Lee, 'Culture', 14)

William Proctor Williams argued that Dudley's design did not fully achieve Bailey's aims:

> The velarium ... on bright sunny days made the yard feel more like a continental sidewalk café than a temple of death, and at night produced no effect at all ... If one sat in the upper gallery, the awning was just a few inches above head height, and this very close damping of the line of sight ... isolat[ed] ... the audience member from what was going on below, making the performance a theatrical event in which one was prevented from participating. (Lucy, 65)

While some gallery viewers felt curiously removed from the performance, the groundlings stood in the yard 'where, in the corresponding part of the Colosseum, the gladiators would have wielded their weapons'; consequently, the groundlings 'had the sense not so much of watching a spectacle at the Colosseum as of participating in one' (Shore, 6).

The groundlings were initially forced to relocate themselves for the triumphant return of Titus, carried through the yard on a litter by eight Goth prisoners. To accompany this procession, composer Django Bates provided thunderous drumbeats and ear-piercing trumpets, while elsewhere in the performance he featured 'an assortment of obscure folk instruments' (Preussner, 122), including long, wooden horns (Swedish näverlurs) that sounded 'sometimes like the authentic trumpetings of ancient battle horns, sometimes more like the last strangulated brayings of a heifer dying of anthrax' (Hart, 23). Bates wrote that he chose for these horns a conflicting harmonic series that 'resulted in a floating harmony that hovered uneasily between many keys' and 'ensured that satisfying musical resolutions were impossible' (19). The discomfort produced by this dissonant music was exacerbated by an eerie sound of 'scraping metal' (Hart, 23) that emanated from backstage whenever the characters performed acts of violence.

For their victorious homecoming, the Andronici donned a chronologically varied mix of plumed classical headgear, 'modern skateboard knee and elbow pads artfully cut and styled to suggest Roman armour', and 'baseball boots with the toecaps cut off' to represent sandals (Dobson, '2006', 308). Other Roman males 'were mainly dressed in tunics' with 'black lycra bicycling shorts underneath'. The Goths wore 'a good deal of fur' (Williams, Lucy, 65) and 'cat-like warpaint on their faces' that made them resemble 'recently caged tigers' (Dobson, '2006', 308). Dudley, who also designed the costumes, gave the captives 'natty dreadlock style wigs' (Loveridge) and 'heathery-hued checked robes' (Collins, 49) that designated the Goths as a Celtic tribe. After Saturninus freed his prisoners, Chiron and Demetrius 'exchanged their Gothic/Celtic garb for short purple and white tunics', but 'Tamora continued to wear her original tartan dress over her recently-acquired Roman gown of solid purple' (Preussner, 152). Bailey associated Tamora's treasured Celtic heritage with her fanatical dedication to revenge: 'It is a fanaticism we have seen in Ireland, a tribal loyalty that can murder innocents' (quoted in Lee, 'Culture', 15). This reference to Irish troubles might have provided a basis for localised political comment, but the production demonstrated an 'eccentric attempt to get away from strictures of time and place' (Morley, 29) in both setting and costumes (as evidenced by the traditional Elizabethan dress worn by the Roman Nurse and Clown) which reflected Bailey's ageless message that 'revenge leads to more and more disastrous suffering' (quoted in Lee, 'Culture', 15).

This suffering was most graphically and realistically portrayed in the forest scenes of Act 2. Chiron and Demetrius captured Bassianus and Lavinia by throwing nets over them, stabbing Bassianus repeatedly. Lavinia was still wearing this mesh covering when she entered after the assault to be taunted sadistically by her attackers, who pulled the netting away as they left the stage, revealing Lavinia twitching and trembling, her costume covered with blood. Rosie Millard observed the intense impact that this harrowing sight had on spectators:

> The mutilated Lavinia, delicately played by Laura Rees, provides the most stomach-churning scene of all. Minus hands, tongue and virginity, she appears on stage, shuddering in shock, dreadfully mute, for what seems like an age, before she slowly turns her head and lets flow a long stream of black blood from her mouth. At this point, at least three people in the audience fainted. In the interval, a steward told me that 15 people had been carried out. (50)

This 'chillingly vivid and real' depiction of Lavinia's desecration (Curtis, Lucy, 17) was enhanced by the reaction of her uncle Marcus, who tore strips from Lavinia's dress to bind her stumps and wiped her bloody mouth with his scarf as he spoke his long discovery speech in its entirety. The deadly serious tone of this explicitly gruesome segment contrasted with the violent scenes in the rest of the performance, which were played with an air of comic irreverence.

Deborah Warner's production of *Titus* 'encouraged laughter' as early as the opening scene, which 'made possible a wide range of effects or reactions later in the play' (see pp. 68, 70). Likewise, Bailey's stage version initially portrayed Aemilius as a comic drunkard and reassigned to him the lines spoken by the Captain (1.1.64–9) announcing Titus's return. He also spoke directly to the amused groundlings, 'throwing some drink over them as he gestured' (Williams, Lucy, 72). Later in the scene (1.1.220–2), the same tipsy figure spoke for the Romans to promise their acceptance of Titus's choice for emperor. Bailey's decision to promote humour at the start of the performance gave viewers permission to laugh at the darkly comic moments in subsequent scenes, but it also had the effect of branding Aemilius as a burlesque figure, which coloured the audience's reaction to other, more serious actions. For example, Aemilius (like Taymor's Clown) fulfilled the role of the piteous Messenger returning to the Andronici the hand of Titus and the heads of his sons, but spectators, conditioned to receive Aemilius as a comedic figure, laughed heartily at lines that the director did not seem to intend as a funny speech.

Bailey's production succeeded more fully in the embodiment of Aaron as a menacing, yet comic character. By retaining the Moor's asides, the Globe version allowed actor Shaun Parkes to establish a conspiratorial relationship with the audience during his soliloquy at the beginning of Act 2, and spectators shared his glee at the results of his plotting until the final scene. His pretended discovery of the hidden gold in 2.3 and his Vice-like aside to the audience, promising the return of the heads of Martius and Quintus (3.1.201–4), evoked considerable laughter. His funniest moment was his revelation to Tamora's sons that he had 'done' their mother (4.2.76). This line has often provoked laughs, even in the most serious productions, but the Globe's archival video of Bailey's rendition recorded sustained hilarity followed by applause. This comic tone abruptly turned dark when Aaron took off the Nurse's glasses and tossed them on the floor. As she searched blindly for them on all fours, Aaron circled behind her, hiked up her skirts, and stabbed her between the legs, laughing maniacally. This horrific murder was both 'suggestive of anal rape' and 'tempered with comedy' (Preussner, 120; Attwell). Aaron recovered sympathy through his self-sacrifice for his child in Act 5, and viewers laughed uproariously as he was dragged off through the yard, repenting any 'good deed' he might ever have done (5.3.188).

Aaron also participated in the graphic yet comic amputation of Titus's hand, the point in the performance at which Titus also became a humorous character. The Moor entered holding a log block and a small hand axe with which to carry out Saturninus's putative offer of exchange. In response, Douglas Hodge as Titus looked heavenward and, 'with dripping sarcasm, cri[ed], "Oh, gracious Emperor!" [3.1.157]' (Nathan, 42). The Andronici's quarrel over whose hand was to be sacrificed degenerated into a 'parody of a child's playtime game, in which hands are furiously and repetitively piled on top of each other, the winner's being on top' (Collins, 50). Titus soon fooled his son and brother into leaving the stage, and just as they re-entered, Aaron delivered three quick chops of the axe to Titus's wrist. The Moor held up the severed hand and squeezed blood from it, while Titus leaped to his feet, grasping his bloody stump in such a way that the audience sniggered at his pain. Later, after the hand was returned, Hodge 'brilliantly capture[d] the play's black comedy ... when, faced with yet another unspeakable calamity, Titus erupt[ed] not into howls or tears, but into wild, nihilistic laughter' (Spencer, Lucy, 26).

Hodge continued to elicit amused responses from spectators in the usually humorous sections of the fly scene, but the arrow scene (4.3) also unexpectedly became a comic segment:

> [W]hen the Andronici entered to shoot their arrows at the gods, they did so from a concealed position underneath the stage ... Titus then climbed onto the main stage ... and, on the lines, 'I'll dive into the burning lake below / And pull [Justice] out of Acheron by the heels' [4.3.44–5], dived forward into the arms of his (literal) supporters who had remained below him in the yard. (Preussner, 118)

As the Andronici loaded their bowstrings, the audience chuckled at 'the black humour of Titus struggling to shoot an arrow with only one hand' (Edwardes, Lucy, 130), which eventually reduced him to attempting to use his foot to pull back the string. After his relatives loosed their arrows, a 'surprised squawk and flurry of falling feathers' (Collins, 50) prompted Titus to ask, 'Publius, what hast thou done?' (4.3.68). Although many reviewers found the 'painfully visceral humour' of this scene 'diabolically and winningly funny' (Shore, 6; P. Taylor, Lucy, 9), others condemned the interpolated comedy as 'ill-judged slapstick' (Hart, 23).

Bailey also exploited the comic opportunities in Tamora's disguised visit to Titus's house with her sons in 5.2. The Empress entered wearing her purple gown with a cape attached to her wrists and neck, while Chiron and Demetrius personified 'Rape and Murder in ankle-length dresses and red platform shoes' (Hart, 23). Holding rattles in their hands, the boys and their mother turned their backs to the audience and put on red, classically styled theatrical masks to hide their identities from Titus (see Figure 20). Tamora (Geraldine Alexander) held her arms straight out and bent at the elbows, which allowed Titus to make the audience laugh by imitating her awkward stance as he expressed his mock astonishment at Revenge's likeness to the Empress. As Tamora and her sons took off their masks to discuss Titus's request to detain Rape and Murder, Titus peered around a stage pillar, and the Goths, turning back to Titus, comically held their masks toward him to resume their disguise. Once Tamora exited, Titus ordered his relatives to capture the princes, whom they hung upside down by the ankles. Hodge then played his threatening speech to the captive Goths for comedy, earning hearty laughs for his description of the cannibalistic pie. He conveyed the 'spirit of dangerous jocularity' that Billington found

20 Tamora (Geraldine Alexander) as Revenge, accompanied by Chiron (Richard Riddell) and Demetrius (Sam Alexander) in Lucy Bailey's production at Shakespeare's Globe Theatre (2006).

characteristic of Warner's production (see p. 67) by showing how Titus could not resist toying with Chiron and Demetrius, 'making several false passes at them' with his knife 'before he finally cut their throats' (Williams, Lucy, 72). Lavinia, kneeling, caught the blood in a basin, and prior to leaving the stage, she used her stumps to toss Titus an apple, which he popped into the gaping mouth of Demetrius.

Lavinia also played a crucial role in the 'wacky black farce' of the Globe production's final scene (Bassett, Lucy, 11). She arrived at the banquet with her father, carrying between her stumps the pie, which she tossed heavily upon the table. Hodge, 'wearing a huge chef's hat, brandishing a large knife and grinning maniacally' (Foster, 17), recalled Warner's Titus both in appearance and in the manic humour of his physicality. Messily serving portions of pie, Titus 'conspicuously licked his fingers' after serving a slice to Tamora, 'much to the audience's delight' (Preussner, 120). When the time came to offer Lucius a portion, Titus 'accidentally' knocked the plate into his son's lap and apologised with a hapless shrug. Lavinia, who had been, since the interval following 3.1, 'wrapped from head to foot in a bandage-like costume ... as if already part-mummified' (Dobson, '2006', 308), sat on her father's lap 'like a floppy ventriloquist's dummy' as Titus questioned the Emperor about Virginius (Spencer, Lucy, 26). Receiving the approval he sought, Titus killed Lavinia 'with a dreadful tenderness, suffocating her, Othello-like, rather than violating her ruined body any further' (Dobson. '2006', 309).

The series of murders that followed Lavinia's sacrifice proceeded realistically, but without any of the copious bloodshed that had characterised violent acts throughout the rest of the performance. When Titus revealed to Tamora the ingredients of the pie, she stood up and laughed incredulously; but when the look on Titus's face convinced her of his sincerity, she began to cough and choke. Titus then leaped upon the table, shoved Tamora's face into the pie, and stabbed her in the neck. In response, Saturninus picked a knife up off the table and called to Titus, who held his arms out toward the Emperor as if inviting the thrusts that Saturninus delivered to Titus's stomach. The play's final murder recalled the killing of Lavinia in several earlier productions in that, when Lucius twisted the Emperor's head to break his neck, 'the sound of cracking bones rang out from the stage with the clarity of a pistol shot' (Shore, 6). On the archival video, audience members let out a collective gasp at the sound of the Emperor's neck breaking, followed by nervous laughter. Once order was finally restored to Rome, a few actors tapped their 'dead' fellows on the shoulder, and the deceased characters sprang up to join the rest of the cast in a jig, which included several groundlings invited onto the stage.

The Globe company's three-hour performance earned thunderous applause, along with positive critical notices. Charles Spencer called it 'a shatteringly powerful and inventive production' (Lucy, 26), and Paul Taylor added that it was 'the best production' he had seen at the Globe in its ten years of existence (Lucy, 9). However, some reviewers complained that, in its pursuit of Grand Guignol shock and black humour, the production missed the 'psychological subtlety' and 'tragic dimension' of the play (de Jongh, Lucy, 38; Basset, Lucy, 11) that Warner had captured so well. Other viewers, like Williams, quarrelled with the production's suitability for its theatrical space, wondering why so much trouble was taken to transform an outdoor Elizabethan theatre into the equivalent of an enclosed black box: 'In short, there was absolutely no reason why this production should be, or need be, performed at the Globe' (Lucy, 65). Although Bailey's rendition did not use Shakespeare's Globe to investigate Elizabethan staging practices, the production did exploit the intense actor–audience relationship that the reconstructed theatre was also built to explore. Seven years before Bailey's production, Mariangela Tempera had written, 'Perhaps, it will be up to the new Globe, with its policy of audience participation, to re-establish the conditions that made the grotesque horrors of [*Titus Andronicus*] so pleasurable for the Elizabethans' (50). The popular success of Bailey's efforts, at least among the thrill-seeking groundlings, demonstrated the foresight of this speculation.

EPILOGUE

Looking toward the future

In the preceding pages, I have used the name 'Shakespeare' as a convenient shorthand for the creative force behind the text of *Titus Andronicus*; however, contemporary critical developments suggest that the term is, in fact, somewhat misleading. Post-Restoration editors, reacting to the play's violent horrors and stylistic shortcomings tended to deny the existence of Shakespeare's hand in the tragedy entirely. However, twentieth-century editors, while acknowledging the arguments against Shakespeare's authorship, generally contended that he was responsible for the whole work. Towards the end of the century, scholarly editions of the play (such as Eugene Waith's Oxford [1984], Alan Hughes's New Cambridge [1994], and Jonathan Bate's Arden 3 [1995]) began to account for some of the play's inadequacies by positing various strata of alterations. In particular, they argued that inconsistencies between Act 1 and the rest of the play resulted from a late, and somewhat clumsy, Shakespearean revision of his own original draft.

Centuries of debate over the play's authorship culminated in the publication of Brian Vickers's *Shakespeare, Co-Author* (2002), which sought to establish a new scholarly consensus about Shakespeare's collaboration with George Peele in the tragedy's composition. Vickers summarises his work, and the efforts of like-minded colleagues, as follows:

> Peele was no doubt a useful co-author for Shakespeare, with his longer theatrical experience and greater knowledge of the classical world, but his style was distinctively different. Over the last eighty years, scholars have applied, by my count, twenty-one separate tests to the play, each of which has confirmed the presence of a co-author. This long scholarly tradition identif[ies] at least Act I as Peele's work, often adding three other scenes (2.1, 2.2, 4.1) ... Surely this quantity of independent tests, mutually

confirming each other, will now be enough to gain Peele recognition as co-author of 'The Most Lamentable Tragedy of *Titus Andronicus*'. (243)

One specific feature of the playtext that has been linked repeatedly to its collaborative creation is the death and burial of Titus's youngest son Mutius. Following Vickers's demonstration that Act 1, which includes all of the Mutius material, belongs to Peele, not Shakespeare, critic Brian Boyd advocated the complete removal of the troublesome Mutius passages from the text as expendable interpolations inconsistent with Shakespeare's plan for the tragedy as a whole. Such a suggestion raises the issue of Shakespeare's assumed priority in the collaborative composition of *Titus*, which affects not only the editorial choices made in scholarly editions, but also the staging decisions made in theatrical productions based on such editions. To explore this issue, I will concentrate on the productions of three recent directors (Gregory Doran, Julie Taymor, and Bill Alexander) who made strong performance choices regarding Mutius, all influenced to some degree by claims about the composition of the play in editions or other criticism that they consulted. These directors' stage treatments of Mutius offer a basis for predicting what the future may hold for the performance of *Titus Andronicus* in a world that accepts Peele as its co-author.

To appreciate the staging difficulties presented by Act 1 of *Titus*, one must be aware of the textual discontinuities connected to the slaying and interment of Mutius. After Bassianus and Titus's sons steal Lavinia away from Saturninus, Mutius intercedes between his father and his departing siblings, calling, 'Brothers, help to convey her hence away, / And with my sword I'll keep this door safe' (1.1.287–8). Titus turns to the Emperor and cries, 'Follow, my lord, and I'll soon bring her back' (1.1.289), but in the early texts, Saturninus does not follow; rather, he apparently leaves the stage with his Goth prisoners, since a subsequent stage direction requires him to enter aloft with Tamora, her sons, and Aaron. Titus then confronts Mutius, kills him, and berates Lucius for joining with Mutius and his brothers in disgracing their father: 'Nor thou, nor he, are any sons of mine; / My sons would never so dishonour me' (1.1.294–5). After Lucius refuses to restore Lavinia to Saturninus, the Emperor re-enters above and declares, 'No, Titus, no, the emperor needs her not' (1.1.299).

Here Saturninus replies belatedly to Titus's entreaty 'Follow, my lord, and I'll soon bring her back', and the murder of Mutius comes as a curious interruption in the exchange between Titus and the Emperor. Waith's note on this passage cites approvingly Gary Taylor's suggestion that 'these lines presenting the death of Mutius may be additions to a first draft of the scene' (*Titus*, 96n), and Bate concurs in a note on Saturninus's rejoinder that 'the belatedness of the reply is also accounted for if the killing of Mutius is an insertion not in the first draft' (*Titus*, 147n). In this imagined original version of the scene, Mutius does not die, and Saturninus's reply to Titus immediately follows the general's promise to fetch Lavinia.

Later in Act 1, after Saturninus exits to wed Tamora, Titus remains on stage to contemplate in solitude his exclusion from the nuptials: 'I am not bid to wait upon this bride. / Titus, when wert thou wont to walk alone, / Dishonoured thus and challengèd of wrongs?' (1.1.338–40). Puzzlingly, Titus displays no agitation at all over his murder of Mutius, but he agonises over the comparatively minor slight of not being invited to the Emperor's wedding. Over the next fifty lines, Titus debates with his brother Marcus and his remaining sons the propriety of burying Mutius with his ancestors. Near the end of this section, Titus finally capitulates to his family's entreaties and allows the burial, at which point Marcus delivers lines that transition awkwardly back to the subject of Saturninus's marriage: 'My lord, to step out of these dreary dumps, / How comes it that the subtle queen of Goths / Is of a sudden thus advanced in Rome?' (1.1.391–3). Waith annotates this entire section with the remark that it may have been 'added after the rest of the scene was written ... Marcus' comment on Titus' "dreary dumps" (l. 391), which seems inappropriate here, would be natural following l. 340, as would his question about Tamora' (*Titus*, 99n). Bate agrees that the two passages initially appeared together: 'In the original draft, [338–40] and [391–8] would have fitted together well, with Titus alone and then joined solely by Marcus, his remaining Sons returning with Bassianus and Lavinia at [398]SD' (*Titus*, 150n). Hughes adds, 'The abrupt non-sequitur here is awkward and supports [Dover] Wilson's suggestion that [ll. 341–90] and Mutius's death are revisions' (68n). Again, the three editors posit an original draft in which Titus was upset only about his social ostracism, not his killing of his own son, because the latter event did not occur. Furthermore, Waith implies that Marcus's allusion to Titus's melancholy mood was no gross understatement in the first version, since it referred merely to Titus's hurt feelings over having been snubbed, not his distress over the burial of Mutius against his will.

The received text of *Titus* also appears to contradict itself when referring to the total number of Titus's deceased sons. In his opening speech, Titus reminds the Romans that 'of five-and-twenty valiant sons, / Half of the number that King Priam had' (1.1.79–80), only the four who have returned from war with him remain alive. Shortly after, he alludes to having 'buried one-and-twenty valiant sons, / Knighted in field, slain manfully in arms / In right and service of their noble country' (1.1.195–7). Titus suffers no sorrow over the honourable loss of his progeny on the battlefield, but in Act 3, when his sons Martius and Quintus are condemned to die for their putative role in the murder of Bassianus, Titus exhibits intense grief:

> For two-and-twenty sons I never wept,
> Because they died in honour's lofty bed.
> For these two, tribunes, in the dust I write
> My heart's deep languor and my soul's sad tears.
> (3.1.10–13)

Waith accounts for the discrepancy between the number of sons for whom Titus 'never wept' in Act 1 as opposed to Act 3 as follows:

> If Mutius is added to the 'one-and-twenty' sons Titus says he has buried (1.1.195), this total is correct, but he would hardly refer to the son he killed as having 'died in honour's lofty bed' ... Shakespeare may originally have planned to show only three sons in Rome. In this case he simply failed to alter 'two-and-twenty' here, as he had done at 1.1.195, when he added a fourth son to the number accompanying Titus to Rome. (*Titus*, 130n)

Bate's note on this passage reads, 'Mutius is now numbered among the sons who died honourably: perhaps Titus has forgiven him, perhaps Shakespeare has muddled his numbers, or perhaps the killing of Mutius was added after this scene was drafted' (*Titus*, 191n). In both cases, Waith and Bate account for these textual irregularities with reference to an original draft in which Mutius was neither killed nor buried, and perhaps did not appear at all. However, in these editors' view, the alterations to this early version of the play, though clumsily managed, were performed by Shakespeare himself.

Using Waith's edition as his base text (Williams, 'Hamlet's', 197), director Gregory Doran formulated his own script for his 1995 South African production of *Titus*, with Antony Sher in the title role. In their production diary, Doran recounts their mutual decision to eliminate Mutius from the performance:

> We reached a crucial decision. We'll be cutting the death of Mutius. Within minutes of his first entrance, Titus kills one of his sons for disobeying him. It's a tricky one. How do you find any journey for Titus to go, if he's barking mad to start with? From a close study of the text, it seems that the death of Mutius might have been an afterthought, a late rewrite. It interrupts a conversation, and Marcus is given the clumsiest segue imaginable in an attempt to get back to the plot: 'My lord, to step out of these dreary dumps ...' Mutius is for the chop. (111)

Sher and Doran, perceiving an actor's difficulty in finding a coherent development in the character of Titus if he is insane from the beginning, seek authority for an adjustment to the script in 'a close study of the text' that appears to derive, at least in part, from Waith's editorial apparatus. They accept the argument that the death of Mutius was a late addition to the original draft because it coincides with their desire to portray a gradual movement in Titus from sanity to madness. As Sher later admitted, 'Now that we've cut [Titus's] hysteria in Scene 1, killing his own son, I think I can map out an interesting journey for him – from rock-solid pillar of the community to bewildered outcast to wounded animal to psychotic avenger' (117). Of course, it might also be argued that Titus takes a different kind of psychological journey through the play: from a general who, in the service of honour, can witness the deaths of twenty-one sons without crying (and even kill one himself), to a father who learns to suffer deeply and empathetically when his children are harmed. Such a reading of Titus's developmental path does not require the elimination of Mutius from the script of a performance.

In the same year as Doran's production, Jonathan Bate published his Arden 3 edition of *Titus*, which 'inspired' Julie Taymor as she prepared to direct her cinematic version of the play (quoted in Johnson-Haddad, 35). In response to the difficulties surrounding the death of Mutius outlined by Bate (104–7), Taymor elected to retain most of the 'revised' passages but to employ other performance choices designed to counteract the implausible aspects of Titus's rash act. For example, whereas Doran believed that Titus must be 'barking mad' to kill his son for disobeying him, Taymor reasoned that the murder was explicable as a facet of Rome's patriarchal society: 'The reason I kept this in ancient Rome, blended with contemporary elements, is because such an action was legal. If a child disobeyed you in ancient Rome, they could be killed. We would have a very hard time with this in a totally modern setting. So there are actions here that we have to accept as part of a culture or a period' (quoted in De Luca and Lindroth, 30). Doran, committed to a contemporary South African setting, felt obligated to eliminate a deed that, in such a context, made his protagonist appear insane, but Taymor, deriving her eclectic setting from anachronistic features in the text, incorporated aspects of classical Rome alongside modern elements in order to justify the legality, and therefore the sanity, of Titus's actions.

Although Taymor considered Titus well within Roman law to kill his disobedient son, she also believed that he would come to regret having done so. Therefore, she interpolated her film's second PAN, which appeared 'to emanate from Titus's own guilty conscience' (Cartelli, 167). As Taymor explained in her screenplay,

> The image of Mutius, Titus' youngest son whom he himself rashly and wrongly murdered in the first act, appears in the form of a sacrificial lamb ... Again, this is to remind us of the inner torment and guilt that has never left Titus. Though the narrative never brings up the event of Mutius' death once it is done, there can be no doubt that it haunts Titus and underlies his pleas for mercy. (184)

Although Taymor admits that, in the playtext, the killing of Mutius occurs suddenly and is quickly forgotten, she simultaneously claims that 'there can be no doubt' that the murder of Mutius 'haunts Titus' and shapes his later behaviour. Here Taymor imposes her own moral view of the killing on Titus, assuming that, despite Titus's confidence in the legality of Mutius's murder, Titus would come repent his rash action. In the absence of any dialogue to express this 'inner torment and guilt', Taymor inserted a wordless segment in which Titus's remorse was expressed with symbolic visual imagery intended to offset the text's omission of verbal sentiments of regret. As in Doran's case, Taymor's encounter with editorial arguments pertaining to the textual legitimacy of the Mutius material prompted her to make performance choices that addressed these controversies, but Taymor's strategy was to compensate for the text's inadequacies in performance rather than simply to eliminate them.

Bate's Arden edition, like Hughes's edition the previous year (10–13) and Waith's a decade earlier (*Titus*, 11–20), raised the possibility of Shakespeare's collaboration with Peele only to dismiss it (*Titus*, 79–83). Vickers, in the course of his subsequent argument for Peele's hand in the play, castigated all three editors for their 'partisan' and 'perfunctory' treatment of the co-authorship question (210), detailing the ways in which they ignored, overvalued, or distorted the evidence unearthed by previous scholars. In a review of Vickers's book, a chastened Bate offered a retraction of his former stance against co-authorship:

> Ten years ago, I completed a new Arden edition of *Titus Andronicus* ... I so wanted to praise the play ... that I uncritically accepted the arguments for solo authorship put forward both by usually trustworthy scholars and seemingly persuasive stylometricians brandishing computer printouts and big-number statistics. The profound methodological flaws of the latter have now been exposed and new research ... has been published which provides compelling evidence that the first act of the play was actually written by George Peele. Next time I edit *Titus* I will follow Vickers's example and credit it to 'William Shakespeare with George Peele'. (Rev. of *Shakespeare*, 3–4)

Bate's vow to credit the play to both Shakespeare and Peele in a new edition raises the issue of the effect that such an attribution might have on the editing of the text itself. No major new edition of *Titus* has appeared since the publication of Vickers's book, but one may speculate about one of the questions that will arise in such a volume based on recent critical and performative treatments of Mutius during the post-Vickers era.

In 2003, Bill Alexander's RSC production of *Titus*, like Doran's version, cut the character of Mutius entirely, but for different reasons. Although Alexander records that he consulted Bate's Arden text closely (14), he ultimately disregarded that edition's single-author stance and accepted the arguments put forward by Vickers in 2002 in favour of collaboration:

> Alexander ... suspected that the first act was the work of George Peele, not Shakespeare, a view supported by his reading of Brian Vickers, *Shakespeare, Co-Author* ... Confident that Act I was by Peele, Alexander felt that he would not alter the shape of Shakespeare's design if he radically edited the exposition of the work. Consequently he re-shaped the whole of Act I to make it possible for Saturninus and Tamora to remain on-stage throughout, following their initial entrance. He dispensed with the 'above' and 'below' of the Folio text and, most radically, cut Mutius and the plea for his honourable burial. In total approximately one hundred lines were omitted (largely from Act I) but Alexander was emphatic about remaining faithful in the remainder of the play to the language of the Folio text. (Hall-Smith, 50–1)

As a direct result of his reading of Vickers, Alexander felt justified in treating the text of Act 1, written by Peele, differently from of the rest of the play, written by Shakespeare. While he believed that he must remain faithful to Shakespeare's language and design, he regarded Peele's contribution as less sacred material that could be radically reshaped or reduced. In an interview, Alexander defended his removal of Mutius's death with reference to Shakespeare's co-author: 'I think Peele only put it in to create the scene where the other brothers plead for his burial in order to give time for the actor playing Tamora to change into the regal dress of an Empress, and this made the whole sequence an episode too long. Anyway, I don't think it is necessary for her to change' (quoted in Armion, 56). Since, in Alexander's opinion, this concern for a practical yet unnecessary staging matter could be laid at the feet of the dramatically inferior Peele, he did not hesitate to eradicate Mutius from his production.

One year after Alexander's RSC *Titus*, Brian Boyd published 'Mutius: An Obstacle Removed in *Titus Andronicus*', which argued forcefully that the death and burial of Titus's youngest son were inserted by Peele at a late stage in his composition of Act 1, entirely without Shakespeare's knowledge as he wrote his share of the play. Boyd shared with Alexander the assumption that Shakespeare was responsible for the design of the play: '[S]ince the structure of the whole play appears to be beyond the design skills of any other dramatist of the late 1580s or early 1590s, it must have been ... Shakespeare who drew up the author's plot of the play, from which Peele worked in writing the scenes he had been assigned' (198). According to Boyd, since the two playwrights worked independently on their own sections of the play, certain prominent discontinuities arose between the two segments as a result of Peele's unauthorised interpolation of the Mutius material: 'I propose that the author's plot that Shakespeare drew up for the start of the play never included the killing of Mutius, that his own conception of Titus is quite at odds with his hero's killing a son casually and without regret, and that he composed his own part of the play unaware that Peele had added this incident' (198).

To support this claim, Boyd pointed to the discrepancy that arises in 3.1 when Titus refers to the 'two-and-twenty sons' for whose death he did not mourn:

> [T]he whole point of the Mutius sections ... is that Titus feels his and his family's honour has been utterly besmirched by Mutius ... We would therefore expect Titus to think only twenty-one sons had died honourable deaths. But if Shakespeare never intended a Mutius to appear at all, if he composed his part of the play unaware that Mutius's death had been added, the lines make perfect sense as they stand. (204)

In contrast to late twentieth-century editors who blamed Shakespeare for sloppy revision of his own work, Boyd exculpated Shakespeare by holding Peele solely responsible for the irregularity created by his unsanctioned change of plan. Boyd speculated that Peele added the death of Mutius, followed by his uncle and brothers' plea for his burial, as a parallel to the sacrifice of Alarbus, which is also accompanied by a family member, Tamora, pleading for Titus to relent (207). However, in Boyd's view, this extra episode blemished the structural integrity of Shakespeare's design: '[A]n event as significant as the hero killing his own child in the opening scene of the play would surely – *unless* it were a last-minute insert – have later repercussions' (204). Since Shakespeare's portion of the play makes no mention of Mutius, Boyd presumes that Shakespeare's plot 'surely' could not have been so inexpertly constructed as to include the protagonist's murder of his own son as an isolated and extraneous event. Peele, acting without Shakespeare's consent, must be held accountable for this artistic blunder.

Therefore, Boyd called for the character Mutius, an obstacle to the production of a consistent and aesthetically sound printed version of *Titus*, to be 'purge[d] ... from the text': 'Even if the killing of Mutius was accepted into the play in Elizabethan performance ... there seems ample justification for critics to treat the play as it appears to have been designed and written by Shakespeare, *without* the killing of Mutius, since such a version of *Titus Andronicus* offers coherence in place of the contradictions of the *textus receptus*' (199, 208, italics original). Echoing Alexander, Boyd asserted that Mutius, an alien to Shakespeare's design, does not belong in the text, and only Shakespeare's textual intentions matter. By my assessment, however, a species of bardolatry undergirds this argument and renders its conclusion suspect. No author's plot from *Titus* has survived, and even if it did exist, we have no reason to assume that Shakespeare alone composed it, aside from the presumption that, if it was well constructed, Shakespeare must have been wholly responsible for it. Moreover, even if it could be shown that Peele deviated from Shakespeare's original design, there is no inherent justification, in a collaborative text, for the privileging of one co-author's intentions over the other's. Even Bate's imagined edition credited to 'William Shakespeare with George Peele' preserves a hierarchical approach to the authorship question that raises the possibility that the next editor of a major scholarly edition of *Titus* will choose to follow Boyd's advice and banish Mutius from the text.

If future editors accept Peele as Shakespeare's co-author, they may also, like Boyd, treat the scenes he contributed to *Titus* as second-rate work, subject to extensive emendation to make them accord with the artistically superior sections of the play composed by Shakespeare. Some performances based on such editions would then be more likely to deviate from the received text by making changes to 1.1, 2.1, 2.2, and 4.1, such as the wholesale elimination of Mutius. This alteration, as we have seen, would produce a drastically different characterisation of Titus, who would no longer be, at the beginning of the play, so devoted to the Roman conception of family honour that he would kill his own son to defend it. Other productions might, like Taymor's film, retain Mutius, but they might also, I suspect, be under increased pressure to use extra-textual performance choices to render the murder plausible and consistent in order to justify its inclusion. On the positive side, the co-authorship studies of Vickers and Boyd, along with future editions influenced by such scholars' work, may encourage directors to reconsider radically their assumptions about the text of *Titus Andronicus* and how it can be staged. Such a re-examination may then intersect with the existing stylised, realistic, darkly comic, and political lines of descent to produce new stage and screen interpretations which grapple with the play's peculiarities in novel and surprising ways.

APPENDIX

A. Significant twentieth- and twenty-first century productions of Titus Andronicus

1923	Robert Atkins	Old Vic
1931	Nugent Monck	Norwich
1955	Peter Brook	Stratford-upon-Avon
1956	Hal Todd	Oregon Shakespearian Festival
1956	Frederick Rolf	New York
1967	Douglas Seale	Baltimore, Maryland
1967	Gerald Freedman	New York Shakespeare Festival
1967	James Sandoe	Colorado Shakespeare Festival
1972	Trevor Nunn	Stratford-upon-Avon
1974	Laird Williamson	Oregon Shakespearian Festival
1977	Paul Barry	New Jersey Shakespeare Festival
1978	Brian Bedford	Stratford, Ontario
1978	Adrian Noble	Bristol Old Vic
1981	John Barton	Stratford-upon-Avon
1985	Jane Howell	BBC Television
1986	Pat Patton	Oregon Shakespearian Festival
1987	Deborah Warner	Stratford-upon-Avon
1988	Mark Rucker	Santa Cruz, California
1989	Jeannette Lambermont	Stratford, Ontario
1989	Daniel Mesguich	Theatre de l'Athénée, Paris
1989	Michael Maggio	New York Shakespeare Festival
1989–90	Peter Stein	Teatro Ateneo, Rome
1992–97	Silviu Purcarete	National Theatre of Craiova, Romania
1994	Julie Taymor	Theatre for a New Audience, New York
1995	Gregory Doran	Market Theatre of Johannesburg, South Africa
1999	Julie Taymor (Film)	20th Century Fox
2000	Richard Rose	Stratford, Ontario
2003	Bill Alexander	Stratford-upon-Avon

2004–06	Yukio Ninagawa	Ninagawa Company, Saitama, Japan
2006	Lucy Bailey	Shakespeare's Globe Theatre
2007	Gale Edwards	Shakespeare Theatre Company, Washington, DC

B. Major actors and production staff in recent productions discussed

Stratford-upon-Avon, 16 August 1955

Director: Peter Brook   Set Design: Morris Kestelman
Costume Design: Doris Zinkeison

Titus	Laurence Olivier	*Saturninus*	Frank Thring
Tamora	Maxine Audley	*Lucius*	Michael Denison
Lavinia	Vivien Leigh	*Marcus*	Alan Webb
		Aaron	Anthony Quayle

New York, 2 August 1967

Director: Gerald Freedman   Set Designer: Ming Cho Lee
Costumes and Masks: Theoni V. Aldredge

Titus	Jack Hollander	*Saturninus*	Robert Stattel
Tamora	Olympia Dukakis	*Lucius*	Jonathan Reynolds
Lavinia	Erin Martin	*Marcus*	Clayton Corbin
Aaron	Moses Gunn	*Narrator*	Charles Durning
		Demetrius	Raul Julia

Stratford-upon-Avon, 12 October 1972

Director: Trevor Nunn   Designer: Christopher Morley

Titus	Colin Blakely	*Saturninus*	John Wood
Tamora	Margaret Tyzack	*Lucius*	Ian Hogg
Lavinia	Janet Suzman	*Marcus*	Mark Dignam
Aaron	Calvin Lockhart	*Bassianus*	Tim Pigott-Smith

Ashland, Oregon, 22 June 1974

Director: Laird Williamson   Stage Designer: Richard L. Hay
Costume Designer: Robert Morgan

Titus	Denis Arndt	*Saturninus*	Richard Riehle
Tamora	Mona Lee Fultz	*Lucius*	Michael Hall
Lavinia	Christine Healy	*Marcus*	A. Bryan Humphrey
Aaron	Ernie Stewart	*Demetrius*	Eric Booth

Stratford, Ontario, 26 August 1978

Director: Brian Bedford   Designer: Desmond Heeley

Titus	William Hutt	*Saturninus*	Frank Maraden
Tamora	Jennifer Phipps	*Lucius*	Rod Beattie
Lavinia	Domini Blythe	*Marcus*	Max Helpmann
		Aaron	Alan Scarfe

BBC Television, 1985

Director: Jane Howell   Set Designer: Tony Burroughs
Costume Designer: Colin Lavers

Titus	Trevor Peacock	*Saturninus*	Brian Protheroe
Tamora	Eileen Atkins	*Lucius*	Gavin Richards
Lavinia	Anna Calder-Marshall	*Marcus*	Edward Hardwicke
Aaron	Hugh Quarshie	*Demetrius*	Neil McCaul

Ashland, Oregon, 18 June 1986

Director: Pat Patton   Set Designer: William Bloodgood
Costume Designer: Jeannie Davidson

Titus	Henry Woronicz	*Saturninus*	Ivars Mikelson
Tamora	Joan Stuart-Morris	*Lucius*	Douglas Markkanen
Lavinia	Nancy Carlin	*Marcus*	Larry Paulsen
		Aaron	Peter Temple

Stratford-upon-Avon, 28 April 1987

Director: Deborah Warner   Designer: Isabella Bywater

Titus	Brian Cox	*Saturninus*	Jim Hooper
Tamora	Estelle Kohler	*Lucius*	Derek Hutchinson
Lavinia	Sonia Ritter	*Marcus*	Donald Sumpter
Aaron	Peter Polycarpou	*Demetrius*	Piers Ibbotson
Bassianus/ Clown	Mike Dowling	*Chiron*	Richard McCabe

Santa Cruz, California, 5 August 1988

Director: Mark Rucker   Set Designer: Joe Ragey

Titus	J. Kenneth Campbell	*Saturninus*	Brian Torrington
Tamora	Molly Mayock	*Lucius*	Ed Gueble
Lavinia	Elizabeth Atkeson	*Marcus*	Brad Myers
Aaron	Bruce A. Young	*Demetrius*	David A. Baker

Stratford, Ontario Shakespeare Festival, 29 May 1989

Director: Jeannette Lambermont   Designer: Patrick Clark

Titus	Nicholas Pennell	*Saturninus*	Keith Dinicol
Tamora	Goldie Semple	*Lucius*	Eric Coates
Lavinia	Lucy Peacock	*Marcus*	James Blendick
Aaron	Hubert Baron Kelly	*Demetrius*	Juan Chioran
Bassianus	Geordie Johnson	*Chiron*	Andrew Jackson

Theatre de l'Athénée, Paris, 17 October 1989

Director: Daniel Mesguich   Set Designer: Louis Bercut
Costume Designer: Laurence Forbin

Titus	Christian Blanc	*Saturninus*	Serge Maggiani
Tamora	Andrea Schiffer	*Lucius*	Xavier Briere
Lavinia	Catherine Rougelin	*Marcus*	Michel Baumann
Aaron	Abossolo M'Bo	*Demetrius*	Jean-Damien Barbin
Bassianus	Herve Furic	*Chiron*	Frederic Cuif

New York Shakespeare Festival, 20 August 1989

Director: Michael Maggio   Set Designer: John Lee Beatty
Costume Designer: Lewis D. Rampino

Titus	Donald Moffat	Saturninus	Don R. McManus
Tamora	Kate Mulgrew	Lucius	David Purdham
Lavinia	Pamela Glen	Marcus	Jon DeVries
Aaron	Keith David	Demetrius	Don Harvey
Bassianus	Robert Curtis-Brown	Chiron	Bill Camp

Teatro Ateneo, Rome, 21 November 1989

Director: Peter Stein   Designer: Moidele Bickel

Titus	Eros Pagni	Saturninus	Roberto Mantovani
Tamora	Maddalena Crippa	Lucius	Luca Zingaretti
Lavinia	Almerica Schiavo	Marcus	Raf Vallone
Aaron	Paolo Graziosi	Demetrius	Graziano Piazza
Bassianus	Pietro Bartolini	Chiron	Armando De Ceccon

National Theatre of Craiova, Romania, 1992

Director: Silviu Purcarete   Designer: Stefania Cenean

Titus	Stefan Iordache	Saturninus	Valeriu Dogaru
Tamora	Mirela Coiaba	Lucius	Valentin Mihali
Lavinia	Ozana Oancea	Marcus	Tudor Gheorghe
Aaron	Ilie Gheorghe	Demetrius	Valer Dellakeza
Bassianus	Marian Negrescu	Chiron	Tudorel Filimon

Theatre for a New Audience, New York, 3 March 1994

Director: Julie Taymor   Set Designer: Derek McLane
Costume Designer: Constance Hoffman

Titus	Robert Stattel	Saturninus	Ned Eisenberg
Tamora	Melinda Mullins	Lucius	Curzon Dobell
Lavinia	Miriam Healy-Louie	Marcus	Michael Rudko
Aaron	Harry Lennix	Demetrius	Sebastian Roche
Bassianus	Steven Skybell	Chiron	Jean Loup Wolfman

Market Theatre of Johannesburg, South Africa, 29 March 1995

Director: Gregory Doran   Set Designer: Nadya Cohen
Costume Designer: Sue Steele

Titus	Antony Sher	*Saturninus*	Gys de Villiers
Tamora	Dorothy Ann Gould	*Lucius*	Martin Le Maitre
Lavinia	Jennifer Woodburne	*Marcus*	Dale Cutts
Aaron	Sello Maake ka-Ncube	*Demetrius*	Charlton George
Bassianus/ Clown	Ivan D. Lucas	*Chiron*	Oscar Petersen

20th Century Fox, 25 December 1999

Director: Julie Taymor   Set Designer: Carlo Gervasi
Costume Designer: Milena Canonero

Titus	Anthony Hopkins	*Saturninus*	Alan Cumming
Tamora	Jessica Lange	*Lucius*	Angus Macfadyen
Lavinia	Laura Fraser	*Marcus*	Colm Feore
Aaron	Harry Lennix	*Demetrius*	Matthew Rhys
Bassianus	James Frain	*Chiron*	Jonathan Rhys Meyers

Stratford, Ontario Shakespeare Festival, 8 June 2000

Director: Richard Rose   Set Designer: Teresa Przybylski
Costume Designer: Charlotte Dean

Titus	James Blendick	*Saturninus*	Scott Wentworth
Tamora	Diane D'Aquila	*Lucius*	Evan Buliung
Lavinia	Marion Day	*Marcus*	Peter Hutt
Aaron	Xuan Fraser	*Demetrius*	Aaron Franks
Bassianus	Timothy Askew	*Chiron*	Paul Dunn

Stratford-upon-Avon, 12 September 2003

Director: Bill Alexander   Set Designer: Ruari Murchison

Titus	David Bradley	*Saturninus*	John Lloyd Fillingham
Tamora	Maureen Beattie	*Lucius*	Bradley Freegard
Lavinia	Eve Myles	*Marcus*	Ian Gelder
Aaron	Joe Dixon	*Demetrius*	Martin Hutson
Bassianus	Fergus O'Donnell	*Chiron*	Daniel Brocklebank

Ninagawa Company, Saitama, Japan, 21 April 2006

Director: Yukio Ninagawa   Set Designer: Tsukasa Nakagoshi
Costume Designer: Lily Komine

Titus	Kotaro Yoshida	*Saturninus*	Shingo Tsurumi
Tamora	Rei Asami	*Lucius*	Takashi Hirota
Lavinia	Hitomi Manaka	*Marcus*	Haruhiko Jo
Aaron	Shun Oguri	*Demetrius*	Hiro Okawa
Bassianus	Eiji Yokota	*Chiron*	Yutaka Suzuki

Shakespeare's Globe Theatre, 20 May 2006

Director: Lucy Bailey   Designer: William Dudley

Titus	Douglas Hodge	*Saturninus*	Patrick Moy
Tamora	Geraldine Alexander	*Lucius*	David Sturzaker
Lavinia	Laura Rees	*Marcus*	Richard O'Callaghan
Aaron	Shaun Parkes	*Demetrius*	Sam Alexander
Bassianus/ Caius	Simon Wilson	*Chiron*	Richard Riddell

Shakespeare Theatre Company, Washington, DC, 3 April 2007

Director: Gale Edwards   Set Designer: Peter England
Costume Designer: Murell Horton

Titus	Sam Tsoutsouvas	*Saturninus*	Alex Podulke
Tamora	Valerie Leonard	*Lucius*	Chris Genebach
Lavinia	Colleen Delany	*Marcus*	William Langan
Aaron	Peter Macon	*Demetrius*	Ryan Farley
Bassianus	Michael Brusasco	*Chiron*	David L. Townsend

BIBLIOGRAPHY

Aebischer, Pascale. 'Vampires, Cannibals and Victim-Revengers: Watching Shakespearean Tragedy Through Horror Film', *Shakespeare Jahrbuch* 143 (2007): 119–31.

——. 'Women Filming Rape in Shakespeare's *Titus Andronicus*: Jane Howell and Julie Taymor', *Études anglaises* 55 (2002): 136–47.

Alexander, Bill. 'Off with their hands', *Guardian* 22 September 2003: 14.

Armion, Clifford. '"Rome Is But a Wilderness of Tigers": The Staging of *Titus Andronicus*: An Exchange with Bill Alexander', *Cahiers elisabethains* 65 (2004): 55–7.

Attwell, Wendy. Rev. of *Titus Andronicus*. Dir. Lucy Bailey. The Shakespeare Revue. Web. 20 June 2006.

Baal, Georges. '*Titus Andronicus* directed by Daniel Mesguich: The Other Stage Beyond Misery', *Theatre Research International* 16 (1991): 109–28.

Bailey, Lucy, dir. *Titus Andronicus*. Shakespeare's Globe Theatre. Archival video. Shakespeare's Globe Education Centre, 2006.

Barbour, David. 'Carnival of Horror', *TCI: Theatre Crafts International* 28.5 (1994): 6.

Barker, Roberta. *Early Modern Tragedy, Gender, and Performance, 1984–2000*. Houndmills: Palgrave Macmillan, 2007.

Bassett, Kate. Rev. of *Titus Andronicus*. Dir. Bill Alexander. *Independent on Sunday* 28 September 2003: Features 8.

——. Rev. of *Titus Andronicus*. Dir. Lucy Bailey. *Independent on Sunday*, 4 June 2006: 11.

——. Rev. of *Titus Andronicus*. Dir. Yukio Ninagawa. *Independent on Sunday*, 25 June 2006, Features: 12.

Bate, Jonathan. Introduction. Titus: *The Illustrated Screenplay*. By Julie Taymor. New York: Newmarket, 2000. 8–13.

——. Rev. of *Shakespeare, Co-Author: A Historical Study of Five Collaborative Plays*. By Brian Vickers. *Times Literary Supplement*, 18 April 2003: 3–4.

——. Rev. of *Titus Andronicus*. Dir. Gregory Doran. Rev. of *Titus Andronicus*. Dir. Silviu Purcarete. *Times Literary Supplement*, 28 July 1995: 18–19.

——, ed. *Titus Andronicus*. Arden Shakespeare. 3rd edn, London: Routledge, 1995.

Bates, Django. 'Unsettling Sounds', Programme. Shakespeare's Globe Theatre. *Titus Andronicus*, 2006. 19.

Beauman, Sally. *The Royal Shakespeare Company: A History of Ten Decades*. Oxford: Oxford University Press, 1982.
Billing, Christian M. Rev. of *Titus Andronicus*. Dir. Yukio Ninagawa. *Shakespeare* (BSA) 3 (2007): 203–12.
Billington, Michael. Rev. of *Tito Andronico*. Dir. Peter Stein. *Guardian*, 28 November 1989: 37.
——. Rev. of *Titus Andronicus*. Dir. Bill Alexander. *Guardian*, 24 September 2003: 26.
——. Rev. of *Titus Andronicus*. Dir. Lucy Bailey. *Guardian*, 1 June 2006: 36.
——. Rev. of *Titus Andronicus*. Dir. Silviu Purcarete. *Guardian*, 22 May 1997, Features: T6.
Blumenthal, Eileen. Rev. of *Titus Andronicus*. Dir. Julie Taymor. *American Theatre* 11.6 (1994): 8–9.
——, Julie Taymor, and Antonio Monda. *Julie Taymor: Playing with Fire: Theater, Opera, Film*. 3rd edn, New York: Abrams, 2007.
Bowman, James. Rev. of *Titus*. Dir. Julie Taymor. *American Spectator* 33.2 (2000): 58–9.
Boyd, Brian. 'Mutius: An Obstacle Removed in *Titus Andronicus*', *Review of English Studies* 55 (2004): 196–209.
Brantley, Ben. Rev. of *Titus Andronicus*. Dir. Yukio Ninagawa and Dir. Lucy Bailey. *New York Times* 8 July 2006, late edn.: 7.
Brook, Peter. *The Empty Space*. New York: Atheneum, 1969.
——. 'Search for a Hunger', *Encore* (July–August 1961): 16–17.
Brooks, Jeremy. 'You made us Philistines', National Theatre Archive. *Sunday Times* (Johannesburg), 30 April 1995.
Broude, Ronald. 'Roman and Goth in *Titus Andronicus*', *Shakespeare Studies* 6 (1970): 27–34.
Brown, Ivor. *Shakespeare Memorial Theatre 1954–56: A Photographic Record*. London: Reinhardt, 1956.
Brown, Tony. Rev. of *Titus Andronicus*. Dir. Richard Rose. *Cleveland Plain Dealer*, 29 June 2000: E3.
Bulman, James C., ed. *Shakespeare, Theory, and Performance*. London: Routledge, 1996.
Burt, Richard. 'Shakespeare and the Holocaust: Julie Taymor's *Titus* Is Beautiful, or ShakesploiMeets (the) Camp', *Colby Quarterly* 37 (2001): 78–106.
Carlson, Marvin. 'Daniel Mesguich and Intertextual Shakespeare', *Foreign Shakespeare: Contemporary Performance*. Ed. Dennis Kennedy. Cambridge: Cambridge University Press, 1993: 213–31.
Carnegy, Patrick. Rev. of *Titus Andronicus*. Dir. Yukio Ninagawa. *Spectator* (London), 1 July 2006: 59–60.
Cartelli, Thomas. 'Taymor's *Titus* in Time and Space: Surrogation and Interpolation', *Renaissance Drama* 34 (2005): 163–84.

Christopher, James. Rev. of *Titus Andronicus*. Dir. Silviu Purcarete. *Observer* (London), 25 May 1997, Review: 10.
Collins, Eleanor. Rev. of *Titus Andronicus*. Dir. Lucy Bailey. *Cahiers elisabethains* 70 (2006): 49–51.
Conlogue, Ray. Rev. of *Titus Andronicus*. Dir. Jeannette Lambermont. *Globe and Mail* (Toronto), 31 May 1989: A13
Cook, Dorothy, and Wayne Cook. Rev. of *Titus Andronicus*. Dir. Michael Maggio. *Shakespeare Bulletin* 8.1 (1990): 9.
Cook, Judith. *Shakespeare's Players*. London: Harrap, 1983.
Costume Slideshow. Shakespeare Theatre Company. Videoclip. Web. 7 July 2009.
Couling, Della. Rev. of *Tito Andronico*. Dir. Peter Stein. *Independent* (London), 5 December 1989: 19.
Coursen, H. R. *Shakespeare in Space: Recent Shakespeare Productions on Screen*. New York: Lang, 2002.
Coveney, Michael. Rev. of *Tito Andronico*. Dir. Peter Stein. *Observer*, 20 May 1990: 35.
———. Rev. of *Titus Andronicus*. Dir. Bill Alexander. *Daily Mail*, 26 September 2003: 55.
———. Rev. of *Titus Andronicus*. Dir. Gregory Doran. *Observer*, 16 July 1995, Review: 11.
———. Rev. of *Titus Andronicus*. Dir. Silviu Purcarete. *Observer* (London), 6 June 1993: 57.
Crawford, Kevin. 'A "black, black, black man": Aaron's Represented Blackness on Stage and Screen', *Journal X* 7 (2002–3): 101–28.
Crosse, Gordon. *Fifty Years of Shakespearean Playgoing*. London: Mowbray, 1941.
Curtin, Sean. Rev. of *Titus Andronicus*. Dir. Yukio Ninagawa. *The Japan Society*. Web. 13 May 2009.
Curtis, Nick. Rev. of *Titus Andronicus*. Dir. Gregory Doran. *Evening Standard* (London), 19 July 1995: 44.
———. Rev. of *Titus Andronicus*. Dir. Lucy Bailey. *Evening Standard* (London), 5 June 2006: 17.
Cushman, Robert. Rev. of *Titus Andronicus*. Dir. Richard Rose. *National Post* (Toronto), 29 June 2000: B6.
de Beers, Diane. Rev. of *Titus Andronicus*. Dir. Gregory Doran. National Theatre Archive. *PTA News* (Pretoria), 31 March 1995.
de Jongh, Nicholas. Rev. of *Titus Andronicus*. Dir. Lucy Bailey. *Evening Standard* (London), 31 May 2006: 38.
———. Rev. of *Titus Andronicus*. Dir. Yukio Ninagawa. *Evening Standard* (London), 22 June 2006: 34.
De Luca, Maria, and Mary Lindroth. 'Mayhem, Madness, Method: An Interview with Julie Taymor', *Cineaste* 25.3 (2000): 28–31.
Dessen, Alan C. *Elizabethan Stage Conventions and Modern*

Interpreters. Cambridge: Cambridge University Press, 1984.

———. 'Improving the Script: Staging Shakespeare and Others in 1995', *Shakespeare Bulletin* 14.1 (1996): 5-8.

Disch, Thomas M. Rev. of *Titus Andronicus*. Dir. Michael Maggio. *Nation*, 2 October 1989: 362-4.

'Discussion: The *Titus Andronicus* Company', Royal National Theatre. Audio recording. 21 July 1995.

Dobson, Michael. 'Shakespeare Performances in England, 2003', *Shakespeare Survey* 57 (2004): 258-89.

———. 'Shakespeare Performances in England, 2006', *Shakespeare Survey* 60 (2007): 284-319.

Doran, Gregory. 'Director's Note', Programme. *Titus Andronicus*. Royal National Theatre. 1995.

Duncan-Jones, Katherine. Rev. of *Titus Andronicus*. Dir. Bill Alexander. *Times Literary Supplement*, 3 October 2003: 19.

Eby, Douglas. 'Julie Taymor on Making *Titus*', Web. 5 August 2009.

Edwardes, Jane. Rev. of *Titus Andronicus*. Dir. Gregory Doran. National Theatre Archive. *Time Out* (London) 19 July 1995.

———. Rev. of *Titus Andronicus*. Dir. Lucy Bailey. *Time Out* (London) 7 June 2006: 130.

Farjeon, Herbert. *The Shakespearean Scene: Dramatic Criticisms*. London: Hutchinson, [1949].

Fayard, Nicole. 'Daniel Mesguich's Shakespearean Play: Performing the Shakespeare Myth', *Theatre Journal* 59 (2007): 39-55.

Fedderson, Kim, and J. M. Richardson. '*Titus*: Shakespeare in Pieces', *Shakespeare and Renaissance Association of West Virginia: Selected Papers* 25 (2002): 70-80.

Feingold, Michael. Rev. of *Titus Andronicus*. Dir. Michael Maggio. *Village Voice* 29 August 1989: 89, 91.

Foster, Julia. Rev. of *Titus Andronicus*. Dir. Lucy Bailey. *A Groat's Worth of Wit*. 18.2 (2007): 17.

Freedman, Gerald. Introduction. *Titus Andronicus*. London: Folio Society, 1970: 3-5.

Gevisser, Mark. Rev. of *Titus Andronicus*. Dir. Gregory Doran. *Shakespeare in Southern Africa* 8 (1995): 83-4.

Gilbert, Miriam. 'Hearing with Eyes: Watching Shakespeare', *Shakespeare Bulletin* 25.4 (2007): 35-45.

Gross, John. Rev. of *Titus Andronicus*. Dir. Bill Alexander. *Sunday Telegraph* (London), 28 September 2003, Review: 5.

Gross, Robert. Rev. of *Titus Andronicus*. Dir. Julie Taymor. *Theatre Journal* 46 (1994): 551-2.

Gulino, Fabiola. 'Peter Stein's *Titus* at the Teatro Genova, 1990', *Titus Andronicus: Critical Essays*. Ed. Philip C. Kolin. New York: Garland, 1995: 476-81.

Gussow, Mel. Rev. of *Titus Andronicus*. Dir. Jeannette Lambermont. *New York Times*, 12 June 1989, late ed.: 13.

Hall-Smith, Sue. 'Recent stage, film and critical interpretations', *Titus Andronicus*. Ed. Alan Hughes. New Cambridge Shakespeare. Updated edn, Cambridge: Cambridge University Press, 2006: 45–60.

Hart, Christopher. Rev. of *Titus Andronicus*. Dir. Lucy Bailey. *Sunday Times* (London), 4 June 2006: 23.

Hayman, Edward. Rev. of *Titus Andronicus*. Dir. Jeannette Lambermont. *Detroit News*, 31 May 1989: 3D.

Hodge, Douglas. Interview with Jasper Rees. *Daily Telegraph* (London), 14 June 2006, Features: 29.

Holt, Sandy. 'Filch transfuses farce into the bloodbath', Shakespeare Centre Library. *Stratford Herald*, 18 September 2003.

———. Rev. of Titus Andronicus. Dir. Yukio Ninagawa. Shakespeare Centre Library. *Stratford Herald*, 22 June 2006.

Horwitz, Jane. 'Warehouse May Seek New Arts Space', *Washington Post*, 2 May 2007: C5.

Hosley, Richard. 'The Gallery over the Stage in the Public Playhouse of Shakespeare's Time', *Shakespeare Quarterly* 8 (1957): 15–31.

Hughes, Alan, ed. *Titus Andronicus*. New Cambridge Shakespeare. Cambridge: Cambridge University Press, 1994.

Hulse, S. Clark. 'Wresting the Alphabet: Oratory and Action in "Titus Andronicus"', *Criticism* 21 (1979): 106–18.

Isenberg, Seymour. Rev. of *Titus Andronicus*. Dir. Michael Maggio. *Stages* 4.5 (1989): 24–5.

Johnson-Haddad, Miranda. 'A Time for *Titus*: An Interview with Julie Taymor', *Shakespeare Bulletin* 18.4 (2000): 34–6.

Jones, Edward Trostle. *Following Directions: A Study of Peter Brook*. New York: Lang, 1985.

Kawachi, Yoshiko. '*Titus Andronicus* in Japan', Titus Andronicus: *Critical Essays*. Ed. Philip C. Kolin. New York: Garland, 1995. 487–94.

Kawai, Shoichiro. 'Ninagawa Yukio', *The Routledge Companion to Directors' Shakespeare*. Ed. John Russell Brown. London: Routledge, 2008: 469–83.

Kennedy, Dennis. 'Performing Inferiority: Shakespeare's Lesser Plays in the Twentieth Century', *Shakespeare and the Twentieth Century*. Ed. Jonathan Bate, Jill L. Levenson, and Dieter Mehl. Newark: University of Delaware Press, 1998: 60–74.

Kramer, Joseph E. '*Titus Andronicus:* The "Fly-Killing" Incident', *Shakespeare Studies* 5 (1969): 9–19.

Kuchwara, Michael. Rev. of *Titus Andronicus*. Dir. Michael Maggio. *Philadelphia Inquirer*, 22 Aug. 1989: D3.

Kustow, Michael. Rev. of *Titus Andronicus*. Dir. Gregory Doran. *Sunday Times* (London), 9 April 1995: 10, 14.

[Lambermont, Jeannette]. 'A Brief Background Discussion for *Titus Andronicus*' [Document included with promptbook at Stratford, Ontario Theatre Archive].

——. Promptbook. *Titus Andronicus*. Stratford Shakespeare Festival. 1989.

Lanier, Douglas. 'Julie Taymor', *The Routledge Companion to Directors' Shakespeare*. Ed. John Russell Brown. London: Routledge, 2008: 457–73.

Lee, Libbi. 'A Culture of Revenge', Interview with Lucy Bailey. Programme. Shakespeare's Globe Theatre. *Titus Andronicus*. 2006: 14–15.

——. 'A Ritualistic Space', Programme. Shakespeare's Globe Theatre. *Titus Andronicus*. 2006. 16–17.

Leggatt, Alexander. 'Playing Titus', Unpublished paper. 'Rethinking *Titus Andronicus*', Shakespeare Association of America Seminar. Seattle, WA. 10 April 1987.

Lehmann, Courtney. 'Crouching Tiger, Hidden Agenda: How Shakespeare and the Renaissance Are Taking the Rage Out of Feminism', *Shakespeare Quarterly* 53 (2002): 260–79.

Lindroth, Mary. '"Some Device of Further Misery": Taymor's *Titus* Brings Shakespeare to Film Audiences with a Twist', *Literature/Film Quarterly* 29 (2001): 107–15.

Liston, William T. Rev. of *Titus Andronicus*. Dir. Richard Rose. *Cahiers elisabethains* 59 (2001): 85–7.

Loveridge, Lizzie. Rev. of *Titus Andronicus*. Dir. Lucy Bailey. Globe Education Centre. www.curtainup.com. 5 June 2006.

Macaulay, Alastair. Rev. of *Titus Andronicus*. Dir. Gregory Doran. *Financial Times*, 15 July 1995, Arts: 15.

——. Rev. of *Titus Andronicus*. Dir. Silviu Purcarete. *Financial Times*, 23 May 1997, Arts: 19.

——. Rev. of *Titus Andronicus*. Dir. Yukio Ninagawa. *Financial Times*, 23 June 2006, Arts: 14.

MacLiam, Garalt. Rev. of *Titus Andronicus*. Dir. Gregory Doran. *Star* (Johannesburg), 31 March 1995, Tonight: 2.

Maher, Mary Z. 'Production Design in the BBC's *Titus Andronicus*', *Shakespeare on Television: An Anthology of Essays and Reviews*. Ed. J. C. Bulman and H. R. Coursen. Hanover: University Press of New England, 1988: 144–50.

Marks, Peter. Rev. of *Titus Andronicus*. Dir. Gale Edwards. *Washington Post*, 11 April 2007: C5.

Marshall, Herbert, and Mildred Stock. *Ira Aldridge: The Negro Tragedian*. New York: Macmillan, 1958.

Mazer, Cary M. 'Historicizing Alan Dessen: Scholarship, Stagecraft, and the "Shakespeare Revolution"'. *Shakespeare, Theory, and Performance*. Ed. James C. Bulman. London: Routledge, 1996: 149–67.

McCandless, David. 'A Tale of Two *Titus*es: Julie Taymor's Vision on Stage and Screen', *Shakespeare Quarterly* 53 (2002): 487–511.

McGee, C. E. 'Shakespeare in Canada: The Stratford Season, 1989', *Shakespeare Quarterly* 41 (1990): 114–20.

——. 'The Stratford (Ontario) Festival 1989: A Canadian's Overview', *Shakespeare Bulletin* 7.6 (1989): 12–14.

McMahon, Michael. '*Titus*: "A play for all time"'. *Ottowa Citizen*, 9 January 2000: A5.

McMullen, Marion. 'Potter Villain Is Out for Blood', Shakespeare Centre Library. *Coventry Evening Telegraph*, 12 September 2003.

Metz, G. Harold. 'The Early Staging of *Titus Andronicus*', *Shakespeare Studies* 14 (1981): 99–109.

——. *Shakespeare's Earliest Tragedy: Studies in* Titus Andronicus. Madison, NJ: Fairleigh Dickinson University Press, 1996.

——. 'Stage History of *Titus Andronicus*', *Shakespeare Quarterly* 28 (1977): 154–69.

Millard, Rosie. Rev. of *Titus Andronicus*. Dir. Lucy Bailey. *New Statesman*, 12 June 2006: 50.

Miola, Robert S. *Shakespeare's Rome*. Cambridge: Cambridge University Press, 1983.

Mock, Roberta. Rev. of *Titus Andronicus*. Dir. Yukio Ninagawa. *Western European Stages* 19.1 (2007): 15–20.

Mondello, Bob. Rev. of *Titus Andronicus*. Dir. Gale Edwards. Washington City Paper, 12 April 2007. Web. 7 July 2009.

Montouri, Deborah. Rev. of *Titus Andronicus*. Dir. Gale Edwards. *Shakespeare Bulletin* 25.4 (2007): 121–31.

Morley, Sheridan. Rev. of *Titus Andronicus*. Dir. Lucy Bailey. *Daily Express* (London), 31 May 2006: 29.

Murdin, Lynda. Rev. of *Titus Andronicus*. Dir. Gregory Doran. National Theatre Archive. *Yorkshire Post*, 14 July 1995.

Ouzounian, Richard. Rev. of *Titus Andronicus*. Dir. Richard Rose. *Toronto Star*, 28 June 2000: D1.

Nathan, John. Rev. of *Titus Andronicus*. Dir. Lucy Bailey. *Jewish Chronicle*, 9 June 2006: 42.

Nightingale, Benedict. Rev. of *Titus Andronicus*. Dir. Bill Alexander. *Times* (London), 25 September 2003, Features: 19.

——. Rev. of *Titus Andronicus*. Dir. Gregory Doran. *The Times* (London), 14 July 1995: 31.

Ninagawa, Yukio, dir. *Titus Andronicus. Sai no Kuni Shakespeare – Yukio Ninagawa x William Shakespeare V DVD Box*. DVD. 2008.

Nochimson, Martha. Rev. of *Titus*. Special Edition DVD. *Cineaste* 26.2 (2001): 48–50.

Noh, David. 'Re-imagining *Titus*', Interview with Julie Taymor. *Film Journal International* 103.2 (2000): 12, 14, 16.

Palmer, D. J. 'The Unspeakable in Pursuit of the Uneatable: Language and Action in *Titus Andronicus*', *Critical Quarterly* 14 (1972): 320–39.

Parkes, Diane. Rev. of *Titus Andronicus*. Dir. Bill Alexander. Shakespeare Centre Library. *Birmingham Evening Mail*, 29 September 2003.

Parsons, Gordon. Rev. of *Titus Andronicus*. Dir. Bill Alexander. Shakespeare Centre Library. *Morning Star*, 9 Oct. 2003.

Paster, Gail Kern. *The Idea of the City in the Age of Shakespeare*. Athens, Georgia: University of Georgia Press, 1985.

Patterson, Michael. 'Peter Stein', *The Routledge Companion to Directors' Shakespeare*. Ed. John Russell Brown. London: Routledge, 2008: 425–40.

Pechter, Edward, ed. *Textual and Theatrical Shakespeare: Questions of Evidence*. Iowa City: University of Iowa Press, 1996.

Peter, John. Rev. of *Tito Andronico*. Dir. Peter Stein. *Sunday Times* (London), 13 May 1990: E5.

Potter, Christopher. Rev. of *Titus Andronicus*. Dir. Jeannette Lambermont. Stratford, Ontario Theatre Archive. *Ann Arbor News*, 20 June 1989.

Preussner, Arnold. Rev. of *Titus Andronicus*. Dir. Lucy Bailey. *Shakespeare Bulletin* 24.4 (2006): 115–23.

Price, H. T. 'The Authorship of "Titus Andronicus"'. *Journal of English and Germanic Philology* 42 (1943): 55–81.

Prosser, David. 'Andronicus Now: From Honour to the Heart of Darkness', *Fanfares* (Summer 2000): 6.

Proudfoot, G. R. 'Peter Brook and Shakespeare', *Themes in Drama* 2 (1980): 162–3.

Psutka, Phillip. Personal interview, 24 July 2009.

Pulford, Angie. Rev. of *Titus Andronicus*. Dir. Bill Alexander. *Groat's Worth of Wit* 14.4 (2003): 10–11.

Ravenscroft, Edward. *Titus Andronicus, or The Rape of Lavinia*. 1687. London: Cornmarket, 1969.

Rawson, Christopher. Rev. of *Titus Andronicus*. Dir. Jeannette Lambermont. *Pittsburgh Post-Gazette*, 24 June 1989: 18.

Reese, Jack E. 'The Formalization of Horror in *Titus Andronicus*', *Shakespeare Quarterly* 21 (1970): 77–84.

Remshardt, Ralf Erik. Rev. of *Titus Andronicus*. Dir. Silviu Purcarete. *Theatre Journal* 46 (1994): 262–7.

Ricci, Digbi. Rev. of *Titus Andronicus*. Dir. Gregory Doran.

Shakespeare in Southern Africa 8 (1995): 81–2.
Rich, Frank. Rev. of *Titus Andronicus*. Dir. Michael Maggio. *New York Times*, 21 August 1989, late ed.: C13.
Rose, Richard. Interview with Mike Beitz. 'Exploring honour in *Titus Andronicus*', *Beacon Herald* (Stratford, Ont.). Festival edn 2000: 62.
Rothstein, Mervyn. 'Retooling Shakespeare's "B-Movie Thriller"'. *New York Times*, 13 August 1989, sec. 2: 5.
Rutter, Carol Chillington. 'Looking Like a Child—or—*Titus*: The Comedy', *Shakespeare Survey* 56 (2003): 1–26.
——. *Shakespeare and Child's Play: Performing Lost Boys on Stage and Screen*. London: Routledge, 2007.
Scuro, Daniel. '*Titus Andronicus:* A Crimson-Flushed Stage!' *The Ohio State University Theatre Collection Bulletin* 17 (1970): 40–8.
Secher, Benjamin. 'Death, mutilation—and not a drop of blood', *Daily Telegraph* (London), 10 June 2006, Art: 9.
Segal, Victoria. Rev. of *Titus Andronicus*. Dir. Bill Alexander. *Sunday Times* (London), 28 September 2003, Features: 27.
Set Slideshow. Shakespeare Theatre Company. Videoclip. Web. 7 July 2009.
Sher, Antony, and Gregory Doran. *Woza Shakespeare!:* Titus Andronicus *in South Africa*. London: Methuen, 1996.
Shore, Robert. Rev. of *Titus Andronicus*. Dir. Lucy Bailey. *Around the Globe: The Magazine of Shakespeare's Globe* (Autumn 2006): 5–7.
Sidnell, Michael J. Rev. of *Titus Andronicus*. Dir. Jeannette Lambermont. *Journal of Canadian Studies* 24.4 (1989–90): 148–60.
Simon, John. Rev. of *Titus Andronicus*. Dir. Michael Maggio. *New York*, 4 September 1989: 62, 64.
Smith, Peter J. Rev. of *Titus Andronicus*. Dir. Silviu Purcarete. *Cahiers elisabethains* 52 (1997): 111–13.
Sommers, Alan. '"Wilderness of Tigers": Structure and Symbolism in *Titus Andronicus*', *Essays in Criticism* 10 (1960): 275–89.
Spencer, Charles. Rev. of *Titus Andronicus*. Dir. Bill Alexander. *Daily Telegraph* (London), 25 September 2003: 22.
——. Rev. of *Titus Andronicus*. Dir. Lucy Bailey. *Daily Telegraph*, 1 June 2006, Features: 26.
——. Rev. of *Titus Andronicus*. Dir. Yukio Ninagawa. *Daily Telegraph* (London), 23 June 2006, Features: 31.
Stamm, Rudolf. 'The Alphabet of Speechless Complaint: A Study of the Mangled Daughter in Shakespeare's *Titus Andronicus*', *The Triple Bond: Plays Mainly Shakespearean in Performance*. Ed. Joseph G. Price. University Park: Pennsylvania State University Press, 1975: 255–73.

Starks, Lisa S. 'Cinema of Cruelty: Powers of Horror in Julie Taymor's *Titus*', *The Reel Shakespeare: Alternative Cinema and Theory*. Ed. Lisa S. Starks and Courtney Lehmann. Madison, NJ: Fairleigh Dickinson University Press, 2002: 121–42.
Sterling, Wallace. Rev. of *Titus Andronicus*. Dir. Jeannette Lambermont. *Shakespeare Bulletin* 7.6 (1989): 18–19.
Taylor, Kate. Rev. of *Titus Andronicus*. Dir. Richard Rose. *Globe and Mail* (Toronto), 29 June 2000: R6.
Taylor, Paul. Rev. of *Titus Andronicus*. Dir. Bill Alexander. *Independent* (London), 29 September 2003, Features: 16.
——. Rev. of *Titus Andronicus*. Dir. Lucy Bailey. *Independent* (London), 31 May 2006: 9.
——. Rev. of *Titus Andronicus*. Dir. Silviu Purcarete. *Independent* (London), 24 May 1997, sec. 2: 4.
——. Rev. of *Titus Andronicus*. Dir. Yukio Ninagawa. *Independent* (London), 22 June 2006, Features: 20.
Taymor, Julie. *Titus: The Illustrated Screenplay*. New York: Newmarket, 2000.
——. '*Titus*: Bloody Arcades', Interview with John Wrathall. *Film / Literature / Heritage: A Sight and Sound Reader*. Ed. Ginette Vincendeau. London: British Film Institute, 2001: 125–9.
——, dir. *Titus*. DVD. Twentieth Century Fox, 2000.
Tempera, Mariangela. *Feasting with Centaurs:* Titus Andronicus *from Stage to Text*. Bologna: CLUEB, 1999.
Thurman, Christopher. 'Sher and Doran's *Titus Andronicus* (1995): Importing Shakespeare, Exporting South Africa', *Shakespeare in Southern Africa* 18 (2006): 29–36.
Tinker, Jack. Rev. of *Titus Andronicus*. Dir. Gregory Doran. *Daily Mail* (London), 14 July 1995: 46.
Towner, Chris. Rev. of *Titus Andronicus*. Dir. Bill Alexander. Shakespeare Centre Library. *Stratford Herald*, 25 September 2003.
Trewin, J. C. *Peter Brook: A Biography*. London: Macdonald, 1971.
Tricomi, Albert H. 'The Aesthetics of Mutilation in "Titus Andronicus."' *Shakespeare Survey* 27 (1974): 11–19.
——, 'The Mutilated Garden in *Titus Andronicus*', *Shakespeare Studies* 9 (1976): 89–105.
Trigano, Shmuel. 'How French Society Views the Jews', Institute for Global Jewish Affairs. No. 51. 15 Dec. 2009. Jerusalem Center for Public Affairs. Web. 28 December 2010.
Tynan, Kenneth. *Curtains: Selections From the Drama Criticism and Related Writings*. New York: Atheneum, 1961.
Ungerer, Gustav. 'An Unrecorded Elizabethan Performance of *Titus Andronicus*', *Shakespeare Survey* 14 (1961): 102–9.

Vickers, Brian. *Shakespeare, Co-Author: A Historical Study of Five Collaborative Plays*. Oxford: Oxford University Press, 2002.
Waith, Eugene M. 'The Metamorphosis of Violence in *Titus Andronicus*', *Shakespeare Survey* 10 (1957): 39–49.
——, ed. *Titus Andronicus*. Oxford Shakespeare. Oxford: Clarendon, 1984.
Walker, Elsie. '"Now is a time to storm": Julie Taymor's *Titus* (2000)', *Literature/Film Quarterly* 30 (2002): 194–207.
Walker, Greg. Rev. of *Titus Andronicus*. Dir. Bill Alexander. *Cahiers elisabethains* 65 (2004): 58–61.
Watermeier, Daniel J. Rev. of *Titus Andronicus*. Dir. Richard Rose. *Shakespeare Bulletin* 19.2 (2001): 31–2.
Walton, Nick. Rev. of *Titus Andronicus*. Dir. Bill Alexander. *Shakespeare Bulletin* 21.4 (2003): 67–71.
West, Grace Starry. 'Going By the Book: Classical Allusions in *Titus Andronicus*', *Studies in Philology* 79 (1982): 62–71.
Westwood, Doris. *These Players: A Diary of the 'Old Vic'*. London: Heath, 1926.
Wikander, Matthew H. 'The Spitted Infant: Scenic Emblems and Exclusionist Politics in Restoration Adaptations of Shakespeare', *Shakespeare Quarterly* 37 (1986): 342–3.
Wilbern, David. 'Rape and Revenge in *Titus Andronicus*', *English Literary Renaissance* 8 (1978): 159–82.
Williams, William Proctor. 'Hamlet's Pockets: Problems with Stage Directions', *Inside Shakespeare: Essays on the Blackfriars Stage*. Ed. Paul Menzer. Selinsgrove: Susquehanna University Press, 2006: 192–9.
——. Rev. of *Titus Andronicus*. Dir. Gale Edwards. *Shakespeare Newsletter* 57 (2007): 1, 12, 14.
——. Rev. of *Titus Andronicus*. Dir. Lucy Bailey. *Shakespeare Newsletter* 56 (2006): 65–6, 72.
'Windows on Shakespeare – Titus', 19 April 2007. Shakespeare Theatre Company. Podcast. Web. 27 July 2010.
Woolgar, Claudia. Rev. of *Titus Andronicus*. Dir. Silviu Purcarete. *The World and I* 8.2 (1993): 166–71.
Worthen, William B. *Shakespeare and the Authority of Performance*. Cambridge: Cambridge University Press, 1997.
Zander, Horst. '"Seeking the Soul with a Dagger": *Titus Andronicus* in Germany', *Titus Andronicus: Critical Essays*. Ed. Philip C. Kolin. New York: Garland, 1995: 495–518.

INDEX

Page numbers in italics refer to illustrations.

Aebischer, Pascale 208, 217, 225, 227
African National Congress 178
Afrikaner Weerstandsbeweging (AWB) 179
Airoldi, Conchita *223*
A Knack to Know an Honest Man 87
Aldridge, Ira 9, 14, 47
Aldwych Theatre (London) 116, 251
Ales, Laurence *162*
Alexander, Bill 128, 229, 242–6, *246*, 248–50, 252, 275, 280–1, 283
Alexander, Geraldine 270, *271*
Alexander, Sam *271*
Almansi, Guido 162
Anglican Church Society of Soweto 195
Arndt, Denis 33–4
Asami, Rei 233–4
Ashley, Audrey 54, 105
Atienza, Edward 19
Atkeson, Elizabeth 46, 102
Atkins, Eileen 51, 53
Atkins, Robert 15–16
Attwell, Wendy 264
Avignon Festival 163
Audley, Maxine 24

Baal, Georges 141–2
Bach, [Johann Sebastian] 221
Bailey, Lucy 128, 229, 251, 263–70, *271*, 273
Baker, David 49
Bale, Doug 55, 106
Bannister, N. H. 13
Barbican Theatre 62
  The Pit 62–3, *65*, *69*, 73–4, 76, 101, 121
Barnes, Clive 148
Barry, Paul 36–7, 59, 61, 107, 114, 117
Barton, John 56, 59, 77, 80, 82–3, 102
Barton, Todd 35
Bassett, Kate 231, 246
Bate, Jonathan 188, 248, 274, 276–80, 283
Bates, Django 266
Beattie, Maureen 249
Beatty, John Lee 146
Beauman, Sally 18–19, 25
Beckerman, Bernard 36
Beckett, [Samuel] 143
Bedford, Brian 53–6, 58–61, 76, 98, 100, 104–6, 119–20, 122
Bercut, Louis 137–8
Berkowitz, Gerald M. 80
Berry, Ralph 54, 98, 105–6
Bickel, Moidele 153–4

Billing, Christian M. 235, 239, 241
Billington, Michael 40, 42–3, 49, 66–8, 75, 78, 153, 155, 160–1, 175–6, 243, 270
Binstock, Danny 255
Blakely, Colin 40, 42–3, *44*, 120
Blanc, Christian 145
Blanche, Eugene Terre 179
Blendick, James *260*, 261–2
Blezard, William 19
Blumenthal, [Eileen]
  Playing with Fire 202, 204, 227
Blythe, Domini 54, 100–1
Booth, Eric 33–4
Bosch, [Hieronymus] 206
Boyd, Brian 275, 281–3
  'Mutius: An Obstacle Removed in *Titus Andronicus*' 281
Boy Scouts 181
Bradley, David 245, 247–8, 250
Brantley, Ben 263–4
Brecht, [Bertolt] 144, 165, 231
British Broadcasting Company (BBC) 49, 61, 127–8, 168, 212, 256, 262
  'The Shakespeare Plays' 49
Brook, Peter 3, 6, 15, 17–20, *21*, *23*, 25–9, 31–2, 35–7, 40, 42, 55–62, 76, 82, 92, 97–100, 104, 106, 119–22, 127–9, 131, 134, 136–7, 139–40, 142–3, 145, 152, 157, 188, 195, 197–9, 201, 208, 211, 215, 229–31, 235, 239, 242–3, 252, 263–4
  A Midsummer Night's Dream production 18, 152, 230–1
  The Empty Space 17
Brooks, Jeremy 194

Brown, Ivor 25
Brown, Tony 261
Browne, Roscoe 17
Bulman, James C. 125
Bungalow Players (Denver) 16
Bunraku 134, 136, 235
Bush, [George W.] 254
Bywater, Isabella 62

Calder-Marshall, Anna 52–3, 100
Campbell, J. Kenneth 46–7
Capitoline Wolf 221–2, *223*, 230, 232–3, 238
Carlin, Nancy 34, 100–1
Carlson, Marvin 137–8, 144
Carriere, Berthold 132
Cartelli, Thomas 214
Cats 59
Ceauşescu, Elena 167
Ceauşescu, Nicolae 164, 167–8, 171–4
Cedrone, Lou 38
Cenean, Stefania 165
Center Stage (Baltimore) 28, 37, 127
Charpentier, Gabriel 105
Chastain, Sheffield 49
Chioran, Juan *133*
Christopher, James 164
Clark, Patrick 132
Clark, Wilfred 24
Coliseum 146
  see also Colosseum
Colorado Shakespeare Festival 59, 61–2, 71, 79, 81
Colosseum 154, 207, 210, 214, 219, 221, 224, 227–8, 231, 266
  see also Coliseum
Columbine High School (Littleton, Colorado) 225, 242

Cook, Dorothy and Wayne 149
Corbin, Clayton 32
Couling, Della 160
Cournot, Michel 145
Coveney, Michael 102, 153, 245
Coward, Noel 118
Cox, Brian 68–9, *69*, 70–2, 77, 79–80, 85, *86*, 91, 99, 101–2, 112, 115, 119, 122, 160, 216–17, 240, 261–2
Craciunescu, Ilie 167
Crippa, Maddalena 157–9
Cross, [Gustav] 107
Crosse, Gordon 15–16
Cumming, Alan 220
Curtis, Nick 178
Cushman, Robert 261

David, Keith 148–9, *149*, 150
David, Richard 18–20, 22, 27, 97–9, 120, 122
Davies-Prowles, Paul 49
Dean, Charlotte 257
de Beers, Diane 190, 193
de Jongh, Nicholas 235
Delany, Colleen 251
Dellakeza, Valer 175
Denison, Michael 23, 98
Dessen, Alan C. 125–30
de Villiers, Gys 179
DeVine, Lawrence 54
DeVries, Jon 147
Dewhurst, Colleen 16
Dhlamini, Dumi 189
Dignam, Mark 116
Dixon, Joe 249–50
Dobson, Michael 242, 249, 263
Doran, Gregory 129, 151, 176–9, 182, *183*, 184–96, 224, 275, 278–80
Dowling, Mike 67

Downes, John 9
Dudley, William 265–7
Dukakis, Olympia 32, 99
Duncan-Jones, Katherine 245, 247
Durang, Charles
History of the Philadelphia Stage 13
Durning, Charles 30

Earl of Sussex's Men 7
Edmondson, James 71, 79
Edwardes, Jane 181
Edwards, Gale 128, 229, 250–5, *255*, 256–7, 262
Embassy Theatre (London) 16
England, Peter 253
Esposizione Universale Roma (EUR) 154, 220
Evans, G. B. 110

Farjeon, Herbert 15–16
Fascism 38, 120, 122, 127, 151, 153–6, 159, 161, 164, 177, 198, 217–18, 220, 229, 257–8, 263
Faulkner, [William] 148
Fayard, Nicole 144
Feingold, Michael 147
Fellini, Federico 41–2, 205
Satyricon 41
Strada, La 205–6
Ferretti, Dante 220
Festival de Theatre des Ameriques (Montreal) 163, 168
Filimon, Tudorel 175
Fillingham, John Lloyd 249
Findlater, Richard 22, 57
Finney, Albert 68
Fraser, Laura 251
Fraser, Xuan *260*
Freedman, Gerald 28–31, 33,

37, 40, 55, 59, 61, 76, 99, 119–21, 131
Freimuth, William 28, 118
Friar Bacon and Friar Bungay 16

Gallagher, Noel 54
Gardner, R. H. 38
Genebach, Chris *255*
George, Charlton 181, 190
Gevisser, Mark 193
Gheorghe, Ilie 173
Gielgud, John 194
Glen, Pamela 148
Goldenthal, Elliot 201, 221
Goodbody, Buzz 251
Gould, Dorothy Ann 178, 182, *183*
Goy-Blanquet, Dominique 139–40, 153, 158, 161
Grand Guignol 16, 28–9, 120, 264, 272
Graziosi, Paolo 157–8
Gross, John 242
Gulino, Fabiola 163
Gunn, Moses 9, 32
Gussow, Mel 53, 68, 70, 72, 134

Hall-Smith, Sue 166, 172
Hampton, Wilborn 37
Handel, [George Frideric] 238
Hardwicke, Edward 52–3
Harron, Mary 64, 67
Harvey, Brett *48*
Hay, Richard 34
Hayes, George 9, 15, 47
Henslowe, Philip 7
Hewison, Robert 63
Hitler, [Adolph] 220, 262
Hlomuka, Daphne 184
Hobson, Harold 22, 41–2
Hodge, Douglas 264, 269, 271

Hogg, Ian 111, 116
Hollander, Jack 32
Hopkins, Anthony 216–17, 240, 261–2
Horton, Murrell 253
Hosley, Richard 88
Howell, Jane 49–53, 55–6, 60, 76, 83–4, 88–9, 91, 100, 102–3, 106, 112–13, 115–17, 120–1, 127–9, 131, 146–8, 150, 152–3, 168–9, 187, 195, 197–9, 201, 208–10, 212–13, 229, 243–4, 251–3, 256–7, 262
Hughes, Alan 274, 276, 280
Hugo, François-Victor 142
Hulse, S. Clark 59
Hutchinson, Derek 71, 112
Hutt, William 53–4, 61

Ibbotson, Piers 64, *86*
Iliescu, Ion 172–3
Ionesco, Eugene 164
Iordache, Stefan 175
Irving Theatre (London) 16

Jackson, Andrew *133*
Johnston, J. L. 23
Jones, Edward Trostle 26
Jones, Stephen *48*
Jonson, Ben
  Bartholomew Fair 7–8
Judaism 140

Kabuki 132, 233, 235–6, 253
Kafka, [Franz] 143
ka Ncube, Sello Maake 182, 184–5, 195
Kawachi, Yoshiko 229
Kelly, Grace 181, 221
Kelly, Hubert Baron 135–6
Kennedy, Dennis 144
Kennedy, [John F.] 220

Kerr, Walter 31
Kick Theatre (London) 62
Kingston, Jeremy 40–1, 175
Kohler, Estelle 67, 72–3, 85, *86*, 98
Komine, Lily 232–3
Kraft, Barry 59
Kuchwara, Michael 148
Ku-Klux-Klan 185
Kuner, Mildred C. 31–2
Kuoape, Paulus 186
Kurttz, Ellie *237*
Kustow, Michael 194–5
Kyd, Thomas
   The Spanish Tragedy 4, 7–8, 10, 22, 59, 62, 85, 122

Lambermont, Jeannette 128, 131–2, *133*, 134–6, 145–6, 173, 176, 235, 251
Lange, Jessica 217
Lanier, Douglas 221, 226
Leggatt, Alexander 79, 91, 103
Leigh, Vivien 18, 20, *21*, *23*, 24, 40
Le Maitre, Martin 180, 185
Lennox, Patricia 239, 241
Levin, Bernard 57
Levinschi, Vadim 167
Lévi-Strauss, [Claude] 139
Lindroth, Mary 217
Liston, William T. 259
Lombardo, Agostino 154, 156–7
   Tito Andronico 156, 161
Lucas, Ivan D. 179
Lyric Hammersmith (London) 163

McAfee, Annalena 72
Macaulay, Alastair 164, 175–6
McCabe, Richard 64, *86*
McCandless, David 201, 205, 207, 215
McCullough, Mark 253
MacFadyen, Angus 213–14
McLane, Derek 201, 219
MacLiam, Garalt 181–2
Maddermarket Theatre (Norwich) 16
Maggio, Michael 128, 131, 146–8, *149*, 150, 153, 157, 176, 210, 250
Maher, Mary 50–1, 84
Mallet Gina 55
Manaka, Hitomi *237*
Mandela, Nelson 178, 191
Market Theatre (Johannesburg) 129, 177–8, 181–3, *183*, 188, 190–1, 193–6
Marks, Peter 252, 254
Marlowe, Christopher 62, 135
   Doctor Faustus 4
   Tamburlaine 4, 8, 74, 180
   The Jew of Malta 4, 92
Martini, D. G. 160
Matsuoka, Kazuo 239
Maxwell, J. C. 5, 63, 77, 107
Maycock, Molly 46, 98
Mazer, Cary M. 126–7
Memorial Theatre (Stratford) 26
Meres, Francis 8
Mesguich, Daniel 128, 131, 136–40, 142–6, 150, 164, 175, 182, 201
Miles, Kevin *21*
Millard, Rosie 268
Miola, Robert 46
Moffat, Donald 148
Monck, Nugent
   Norwich Players 16
Monk, Wendy 43
Monroe, Marilyn 203
Montague, Lee *21*

Montouri, Deborah 254–5
More, Robert 134
Morley, Christopher 44
Mozart, [Wolfgang Amadeus] 172, 174
Mulgrew, Kate 148–9, *149*, 150
Murchison, Ruari 244
Murdin, Lynda 181
Murgittroyd, David *255*
Mussolini, Benito 38, 112, 151, 153–4, 156, 161, 167, 217, 220, 257
Myers, Brad 46, 59, 119
Myles, Eve 245, *246*

Nagagoshi, Tsukasa 231
National Theatre (London) 181
  Cottesloe Theatre 178
  National Theatre Studio 177
National Theatre of Craiova, Romania 163, 167, *170*
  see also Theatre National de Craiova, Romania
New Jersey Shakespeare Festival 36, 82, 107, 114
New York Shakespeare Festival 28, 61, 128, 131, 146, *149*
  Delacorte Theatre 29, 146
Niego, Piero 155
Nightingale, Benedict 41, 178, 245
Ninagawa, Yukio 128, 229–33, 235, *237*, 239–42, 244, 263
  Ninagawa Company (Saitama, Japan) 229, *237*, 263
Nixon, [Richard M.] 220
Noh 133, 235
Nottingham Playhouse 163, 165
Novick, Julius 54, 101

Nunn, Trevor 39–42, *44*, 53, 55–60, 76, 101, 107, 111, 114–17, 120–2, 251, 264

Oancea, Ozana *170*, 175
Odeon Theatre (Paris) 152
Oguri, Shun 234
Old Vic Theatre (London) 15–16, 32, 98, 118, 121
Olivier, Laurence 3, 6, 15, 18, 20–2, *23*, 24, 27–8, 40, 42, 60–1, 71, 79–80, 100, 119, 122, 134–5, 145, 264
Oman, Timothy W. 37
Oregon Shakespeare Festival 33, 59, 61, 70, 82–3, 90, 94, 97, 100–1, 104, 116
Orkin, Martin 181
Osborne, Charles 68
Ovid 6, 60, 122, 186
  Metamorphoses 122, 186

Pagni, Eros 153, 160–1, *162*
Panasonic Globe Playhouse (Tokyo) 163
Parkes, Shaun 268
Parma Theatre Festival 163
Patriot Act 254
Patton, Pat 34–5, 37, 56–60, 67, 76–7, 83, 91, 97–9, 101, 104, 106
Paulsen, Larry 35, 59
Peacham, Henry 7–8, *8*, 9–10, 46, 93, 218
Peacock, Lucy 134
Peacock, Trevor 52–3, 113, 117
Pechter, Edward 125
Peele, George 127, 274–5, 280–3
Peking opera 234
Pennell, Nicholas 132, *133*, 134

Penny Arcade Nightmares
    (PANs) 198, 200–7, 210,
    217, 221, 225, 255, 279
Peter, John 152, 154
Petersen, Oscar 181
Petrie, Hay 15
Phillips, Stephen J. 173–4
Piacentini, [Marcello] 154
Pigott-Smith, Tim 116
Poel, William 15
Portman, Jamie 54
Potter, Christopher 135
Pratt, Desmond 23
Price, H. T. 5
Protheroe, Brian 53
Proudfoot, G. R. 25–6
Przybylski, Teresa 258
Psutka, Phillip 262
Pulford, Angie 249
Purcarete, Silviu 129, 151,
    163–9, *170*, 171–8, 182,
    196, 215
Purdham, David 150

Quadri, Franco 163
Quarshie, Hugh 9, 52–3, 117,
    150
Quayle, Anthony 9, 18, 22–4,
    27, 47, 119
Quin, James 9, 13, 47

Ran 132
Ratcliffe, Michael 68–9
Ravenscroft, Edward
    *Titus Andronicus, or The
    Rape of Lavinia* 9–14,
    17, 19, 25, 63, 76, 81,
    99, 103, 116, 121
Rawson, Christopher 132
Redgrave, Vanessa 194
Rees, Laura 268
Regent's Park (London) 45
Remshardt, Ralf Erik 167, 174

Residenztheater (Munich) 163
Ricci, Digbi 181, 193–4
Rich, Frank 146–8
Richards, Gavin 112
Riddell, Richard *271*
Ridley, M. R. 61, 107
Ritter, Sonia 64, *65*, 66, 72–3,
    101
Riverside Shakespeare
    Company (New York) 37
Rose, Richard 129, 229,
    257–60, *260*, 261–3
Royal Shakespeare Company
    (RSC) 4, 39, *44*, 56, 61–2,
    65, *69*, 77, *86*, 126–8, 131,
    134, 139, 153, 160, 163,
    196, 215, 217–18, 229,
    231, 242, 244–5, *246*, 247,
    251, 264, 280–1
    Complete Works Festival
    128, 230
    Royal Shakespeare Theatre
    230
    Swan Theatre 62–3, 67, 73,
    75–6, 80, 84–5, 89, 98,
    101, 109, 116, 242
Rubbi, C. 162
Rucker, Mark 44, *48*, 53, 55–6,
    58, 76, 83, 102, 119–21

Sai-no-Kuni Saitama Arts
    Space 230
Sandoe, James 62, 79, 81, 104
St Clement's Church (New
    York) 197, 201, 206–7,
    209, 219
Scheeren, Christopher *255*
Schiavo, Almerica 161, *162*
Scuro, Daniel 26, 57, 98
Seale, Douglas 28, 37, 53, 55,
    76, 120–2, 127–8, 151,
    154, 161, 164, 167, 177,
    196, 198, 218, 229, 257

Securitate 167, 171
Semple, Goldie *133*, 136
Seneca 57
Shakespeare in Washington Festival 251
Shakespeare Santa Cruz 44–5, *48*, 49, 52, 59, 61, 84, 87, 98, 102, 119
Shakespeare's Globe Theatre (London) 128, 229, 251, 263–6, 269, *271*, 271–3
Shakespeare Theatre Company (Washington, DC) 128, 229, 250–2, *255*, 256
Shakespeare Theatre Workshop (New York) 17
Shakespeare, William
　3 Henry VI 5
　All's Well That Ends Well 3
　A Midsummer Night's Dream 18
　As You Like It 152
　Coriolanus 101
　Hamlet 4–5, 7, 66, 72, 110, 114, 134
　　'The Mousetrap' 134
　Henry IV, Part 1 118
　Henry V 88
　Julius Caesar 4
　King Lear 3–4, 24, 33, 35, 40, 72, 79–81, 115, 184
　Macbeth 17, 22, 80, 100, 111, 114
　Measure for Measure 3, 35
　Much Ado About Nothing 16
　Othello 47, 80, 184, 272
　Richard III 47, 73, 114, 143
　Romeo and Juliet 4, 104, 106, 109
　The Comedy of Errors 134
　The Merchant of Venice 184
　The Taming of the Shrew 251

The Tempest 7, 85
The Two Gentlemen of Verona 56
Timon of Athens 80
Sher, Antony 177–81, 187–90, 192–4, 196, 278
　Woza Shakespeare! 177
Shulman, Milton 22, 24
Simon, John 147, 150
Simon, Neil 59
Siskind, Jacob 54
Sisson, Rosemary Anne 23–4, 120
Solga, Kim 203
Somerset, C. A. 14
Sommers, Alan 90
Source Theatre Company (Washington, DC) 28, 118
South African Broadcasting Corporation 178
South African Defence Force (SADF) 179–80, 185
Spencer, Charles 63, 72, 240, 250, 272
Spenser, [Edmund] 6
　The Faerie Queene 93
Starks, Lisa S. 211, 215
Statue of Liberty 206, 255
Stein, Peter 129, 151–62, *162*, 163, 167, 176–7, 196, 218, 220
　As You Like It production 152
Sterling, Wallace 136
Stewart, Ernie 33–4, 116
Stewart, Patrick 77–81, 91, 102
Stratford Festival Canada 53, 104
　see also Stratford, Ontario Shakespeare Festival
Stratford, Ontario Shakespeare Festival 100–1, 128–9, 131–2, *133*,

134, 136, 229, 235, 257–8, 260, 261
Tom Patterson Theatre 257–9
see also Stratford Festival Canada
Stravinsky, [Igor] 221
Stuart-Morris, Joan 98
Styan, J. L. 125–6
The Shakespeare Revolution 125
Sullivan, Dan 32
Sumpter, Donald 64, *65*, 66, 72, 116
Suzman, Janet 40, 43, *44*
Sweeney Todd 102, 147, 243

Tate, Nahum
King Lear 3
Taylor, Gary 276
Taylor, Kate 260
Taylor, Paul 236, 241, 243, 250, 272
Taymor, Julie 129, 196–221, *222*, *223*, 224–30, 232, 240–2, 244, 251–63, 275, 278–80
Titus (film) 129, 197–221, *223*, 224–9, 232, 241–2, 244, 251–4, 256–9, 261–3, 278–9, 283
Teatro Ateneo (Rome) 129, 151–2, *162*
Teatro Stabile di Genova 151
Tempera, Mariangela 144, 156, 159, 168, 273
The Adams Family [sic] 175
The Duchess of Malfi 5
The Godfather 155
The Revenger's Tragedy 4–5
The Seven-Year Itch 202
The Silence of the Lambs 216

The Texas Chain Saw Massacre 147
The Tragedy of Hoffman 4
Theatre de l'Athénée 128, 136
Theatre de L'Europe 162
Theatre for a New Audience (New York) 129, 197–8, 205, 213, 221, *222*
Theatre National de Craiova, Romania 129
see also National Theatre of Craiova, Romania
Théâtre National de Lille 145
Theatre Royal (Plymouth) 163, 173–4, 230
Thébaud, Marion 145
Thompson, Graeme S. 258–9
Thurman, Christopher 183, 185, 191
Tocci, Margaret M. 28
Todd, Hal 33
Torrington, Bryan 46
Towner, Chris 247
Trewin, J. C. 17–18, 20–2, 42, 98, 104, 106, 119
Tricomi, Albert 90
Trinity College Dramatic Society (University of Toronto) 79, 91, 103
Tsoutsouvas, Sam *255*
Tynan, Kenneth 20, 22, 24–6, 79, 118

Vallone, Raf 153, 159–60, *162*
Verdi, [Giuseppe]
Requiem (Dies Irae) 258
Vickers, Brian 274–5, 280–1, 283
Shakespeare, Co-Author 274, 280–1
Visconti, [Luchino]
The Damned 221
'Vivere' 217

Voortrekkers 181

Wainwright, Jeffrey 192
Waith, Eugene 5, 7–8, 13, 107,
　156, 274, 276–8, 280
Walker, Alex 24
Walter, Wilfrid 15
Wardle, Irving 41–3, 76
Warhol, Andy 41
Warner, Deborah 4, 62–4, *65*,
　67, *69*, 73–6, 80–1, 83–4,
　86, 99, 104, 112, 116–17,
　119–22, 126–9, 131,
　134–6, 139, 147, 153, 160,
　163–4, 172, 190, 195, 198,
　215–16, 218, 229–30,
　239–40, 242–3, 245, 251,
　261–4, 268, 271–2
Waugh, Evelyn 26–7, 120
Webb, Alan *23*
Wells, Stanley 50, 53, 64,
　67–8, 70, 75–6, 99, 122,
　218
Westwood, Doris 15
West Yorkshire Playhouse
　(Leeds) 178

Wilcocks, Richard 179
Williams, William Proctor
　251–4, 266, 272
Williamson, Laird 33–5, 37,
　60, 90, 94, 101, 104, 106,
　116, 119
Wilson, [John] Dover 276
Wood, John 41–2, 111, 115–16
Wood, Sarah Eily 43
Woodburne, Jennifer 181, 188
Woolgar, Claudia 167, 171
Woronicz, Henry 35–6, 99
Worsley, T. C. 24
Worthen, William B.
　Shakespeare and the
　　Authority of Performance
　　125
Woudhuysen, H. R. 64, 67,
　75

Yoshida, Kotaro 240
Young, B. A. 41–2, 44
Young, Bruce 9, 47–8, *48*

Zander, Horst 156, 159
Zaraffa, The Slave King 1

Lightning Source UK Ltd.
Milton Keynes UK
UKHW010847110619
344185UK00006B/799/P